STIGMA AND GROUP INEQUALITY

Social Psychological Perspectives

THE CLAREMONT SYMPOSIUM ON APPLIED SOCIAL PSYCHOLOGY

This series of volumes highlights important new developments on the leading edge of applied social psychology. Each volume focuses on one area in which social psychological knowledge is being applied to the resolution of social problems. Within that area, a distinguished group of authorities present chapters summarizing recent theoretical views and empirical findings, including the results of their own research and applied activities. An introductory chapter frames the material, pointing out common themes and varied areas of practical applications. Thus, each volume brings trenchant new social psychological ideas, research results, and fruitful applications bearing on an area of current social interest. The volumes will be of value not only to practitioners and researchers, but also to students and lay people interested in this vital and expanding area of psychology.

Series books published by Lawrence Erlbaum Associates:

- *Reducing Prejudice and Discrimination*, edited by Stuart Oskamp (2000).
- *Mass Media and Drug Prevention: Classic and Contemporary Theories and Research*, edited by William D. Crano and Michael Burgoon (2002).
- *Evaluating Social Programs and Problems: Visions for the New Millennium*, edited by Stewart I. Donaldson and Michael Scriven (2003).
- *Processes of Community Change and Social Action*, edited by Allen M. Omoto (2005).
- *Applications of Nonverbal Communication*, edited by Ronald E. Riggio and Robert S. Feldman (2005).
- *Stigma and Group Inequality: Social Psychological Perspectives*, edited by Shana Levin and Colette van Laar (2006).

STIGMA AND GROUP INEQUALITY

Social Psychological Perspectives

Edited by

Shana Levin
Claremont McKenna College

Colette van Laar
Leiden University

The Claremont Symposium on Applied Social Psychology

LEA LAWRENCE ERLBAUM ASSOCIATES, PUBLISHERS
2006 Mahwah, New Jersey London

Lawrence Erlbaum Associates, Inc., Publishers
10 Industrial Avenue
Mahwah, New Jersey 07430
www.erlbaum.com

Cover design by Kathryn Houghtaling Lacey

Library of Congress Cataloging-in-Publication Data

Claremont Symposium on Applied Social Psychology (2004)
Stigma and group inequality : social psychological perspectives / [edited by] Shana Levin, Colette van Laar.
p. cm.
Proceedings of a symposium held in the spring of 2004 in Clarement, California.
Includes bibliographical references and index.
ISBN 0-8058-4415-5 (cloth : alk. paper)
ISBN 0-8058-4416-3 (pbk. : alk. paper)
1. Stigma (Social psychology)—Congresses. 2. Self-perception—Congresses.
3. Social role—Congresses. I. Levin, Shana, 1968– II. Van Laar, Colette. III. Title.

HM1131.C58 2004
305'.01—dc22 2005051235
CIP

Books published by Lawrence Erlbaum Associates are printed on acid-free paper, and their bindings are chosen for strength and durability.

Printed in the United States of America
10 9 8 7 6 5 4 3 2 1

Contents

Preface

"Ask yourself what would happen to your own personality if you heard it said over and over again that you were lazy, a simple child of nature, expected to steal, and had inferior blood. Suppose this opinion were forced on you by the majority of your fellow citizens. And suppose nothing that could do would change this opinion—because you happen to have black skin" (p. 142), pioneering social psychologist Gordon Allport challenged his readers in 1954 to consider. Today, 50 years later, people still suffer from stigma based on many different group memberships: African Americans and Latinos are negatively stereotyped in the intellectual domain, women are negatively stereotyped in the math domain, and those who are mentally ill suffer from more global devaluation.

This book is a culmination of the efforts of a working group on stigma and group inequality. Our work on this topic began informally in 2002 and grew into the idea to organize more formal discussions and panel presentations at the 2003 Annual Meeting of the International Society of Political Psychology. Building on the success of these presentations, we organized the Twenty-First Annual Claremont Symposium on Applied Social Psychology on the topic of stigma and group inequality. We held this one-day conference in the spring of 2004 in Claremont, California. All of the chapters in this volume were presented at the conference and discussed the next day at our final working group meeting.

In each of the chapters, the authors provide a snapshot of the latest theoretical and empirical work on social psychological approaches to stigma and group inequality. Social psychology has a long tradition of research on stereotyping, prejudice, and discrimination. For a large part of its history, this research focused on the views and responses of members of dominant groups to members of minority groups. In the past 15 years, however, a new line of research has emerged that focuses on the perspective of stereotyped or stigmatized groups. Many of the authors in this book were key pioneers in this field of research. Together with more recent work, this research has led to a variety of theoretical and methodological innovations in the study of stigma and has moved the field to a new depth of understanding of these processes. As a result, we have obtained much better knowledge of how stigma affects the stigmatized individual, his or her interaction partners, the stigmatized and nonstigmatized groups to which they belong, and relations between the groups.

This wealth of groundbreaking theoretical and empirical work is captured in this book. As such, the volume is an important addition to earlier scientific work on stigma and prejudice. The chapters of the book are written by experts in clear language that is accessible to a wide audience of teachers, administrators, managers, parents, community leaders, and concerned citizens who are trying to understand and improve the plight of stigmatized individuals in schools, at work, at home, in the community, and in society at large. With the cutting-edge research presented in each chapter, the book is also a valuable resource for undergraduate and graduate students and scholars in the fields of social psychology, organizational psychology, educational psychology, sociology, social work, anthropology, communications, public policy, and political science.

The volume is organized around three major sections: responses to stigma, stigma in the social context, and stigma and the social basis of the self. The initial chapter by Colette van Laar and Shana Levin presents the overall structure of the volume and highlights three main themes covered in the chapters: the effects of stigma and the processes that account for these effects, the variables that moderate the effects of stigma on outcomes, and the lessons that can be learned from this work to mitigate the negative effects of stigma at the individual, interpersonal, and structural or institutional levels.

The first section of the volume discusses the tradeoffs that stigmatized individuals must contend with as they weigh the benefits derived from a particular response to stigma against the costs associated with it. The chapters in Part I focus particularly on the potential costs associated with confronting and not confronting discrimination. Carol Miller begins by providing an overview of a stress and coping perspective on reactions to stigma that has three major components: appraisals of stigma-related stressors, coping responses to these stressors, and the roles that identification to the self, to other people, and by other people that prejudice has occurred play in both appraisal and coping processes. The next two chapters address the ways in which confronting stigmatization can affect how group members are likely to be perceived and received by members of the dominant group. First, Cheryl Kaiser begins by reviewing theory and research on interpersonal responses to discrimination claimants, arguing that the stigmatized are reluctant to report discrimination because discrimination claimants often incur social rejection. She then proceeds to describe a dominant ideology threat model of reactions to discrimination claimants, explaining that this interpersonal rejection occurs because discrimination claims threaten meritocracy beliefs. In the next chapter, Nichole Shelton, Jennifer Richeson, Jessica Salvatore, and Diana Hill extend the work introduced by Kaiser to consider the intrapersonal costs of not confronting perpetrators of prejudice. The authors summarize two studies that they conducted concerning the affective and cognitive consequences of not challenging prejudice, concluding that individuals should confront prejudice when they are firmly committed to challenging discrimination and they think they should confront in a particular situation—otherwise they will suffer serious intrapersonal costs of not confronting prejudice. Next, Diane Quinn discusses the unique situation of individuals who have stigmatized identities that may be concealed from others, such as those who have a history of an eating disorder or mental illness. In addition to selecting an optimal coping strategy when their stigmatized identity is revealed to others, these individuals must also contend with difficulties deciding when and to whom to reveal the nature of their stigma in the first place. In the final chapter of this section, Janet Swim and Margaret Thomas suggest that in selecting the best coping response for a given situation, members of stigmatized groups will choose the strategy that helps them reach their core social goals—among them the need to belong, the need for self-enhancement, the need for understanding, the need to trust others, and the need to be in control.

Part II of the volume discusses the ways in which environments can threaten one's intellectual performance, sense of belonging, and self-concept. In the first chapter of this section, Michael Inzlicht and Catherine Good argue that situational cues such as the ratio of men to women in a testing room can have substantial effects on women's performance and engagement in the testing domain. The authors propose various environmental modifications that may reduce the threat associated with these situational cues. In the next chapter, Rodolfo Mendoza-Denton, Elizabeth Page-Gould, and Janina Pietrzak discuss the ways in which these environments can interact with personal characteristics, leading some individuals to perceive ethnic discrimination more readily and to react to it more intensely and negatively. For these individuals, the authors argue that having friends from other ethnic groups is especially beneficial for social and academic outcomes. However, Linda Tropp cautions in the next chapter that we must keep in mind that in threatening environments that foster perceptions of prejudice and discrimination, contact with members of other ethnic groups may generally be a less effective means for promoting positive intergroup outcomes among members of minority status groups. Brenda Major concludes this section with a synthesis of new theoretical perspectives on stigma that have challenged traditional views, noting that there is considerable variability in responses to stigma across different stigmatized groups, across individuals within stigmatized groups, and even within the same individual across situations.

In Part III of the volume, the authors argue that the experience of possessing a stigmatized identity is shaped by social interactions with others in the stigmatized ingroup as well as members of other outgroups. Tracy McLaughlin-Volpe begins by considering the positive consequences for members of stigmatized minority groups of forming social relationships with members of the majority outgroup. Specifically, she argues that when one develops a close relationship with members of an outgroup, that outgroup will, to some degree, become a part of a person's self-concept. Furthermore, this inclusion of the majority outgroup in the self will facilitate the adjustment of minority group members in institutions dominated by majority group members. However, Stacey Sinclair and Jeff Huntsinger demonstrate in the next chapter that when members of stigmatized groups are interacting with individuals who are thought to believe the negative stereotypes about their group, members of stigmatized groups may apply these negative group stereotypes to themselves (i.e., engage in self-stereotyping), particularly when they are highly motivated to form a social relationship with these individuals. Furthermore, Toni Schmader and Brian Lickel argue in the following chapter that in addition to influencing the way we *think* about ourselves, stereotype-confirmation can influence the way we *feel* about ourselves as well: Specifically, members of ethnic or racial groups are likely to feel a sense of shame when another member of their ingroup engages in behaviors that confirm a negative stereotype about their group and, as a consequence, will seek to distance themselves from the event and the stigmatized identity. Finally, Jennifer Crocker and Julie Garcia conclude this section and the volume as a whole by arguing that in the context of interactions between stigmatized and nonstigmatized individuals, potential threats to the self—either due to stigmatizing attributes or judgments that one is prejudiced—can lead to a destructive cycle that may only be broken when people focus outside themselves on learning goals, goals that include others, and goals that are larger than the self.

We hope this book will be a resource for students, a guide for future researchers, and a call to concerned citizens to use this wealth of information to guide their own efforts to mitigate the pernicious effects of stigma in their daily lives.

ACKNOWLEDGMENTS

We would like to acknowledge the many people who helped us put together the volume and the Twenty-First Annual Claremont Symposium on Applied Social Psychology, the one-day conference on stigma and group inequality at which all of the chapters of the book were presented. We are grateful to Professor Mark Costanzo of Claremont McKenna College for co-organizing the conference with us and to the School of Behavioral and Organizational Sciences at Claremont Graduate University for their generous financial support of the conference and working group. Many of the Claremont Colleges provided supporting funds for the conference, Claremont McKenna College provided physical facilities, and President Steadman Upham of Claremont Graduate University hosted a dinner for the speakers. With great diligence and enthusiasm, Winona Foote shouldered the major burden of getting and keeping the conference running smoothly and Bettina Casad provided technical support and organized the audiovisual materials. We would also like to thank the additional researchers who presented their work as part of the informal paper and poster session at the conference, and the many students in the social psychology program at Claremont Graduate University who volunteered their time to help us host the conference. We are most grateful to Debra Riegert at Lawrence Erlbaum Associates for her support of this project and Kerry Breen for keeping the editorial process on track. We would especially like to thank all of the authors who have worked with us for a number of years to make the larger project a great success.

REFERENCE

Allport, G. (1954). *The nature of prejudice.* New York: Doubleday Anchor.

CHAPTER

1

The Experience of Stigma: Individual, Interpersonal, and Situational Influences

Colette van Laar
Leiden University

Shana Levin
Claremont McKenna College

Social psychological research on stereotyping, prejudice, and discrimination has typically focused on the views and responses of members of dominant groups to members of minority groups. Recent efforts to focus attention on the perspective of stereotyped or stigmatized groups have led to a variety of theoretical and methodological innovations in the study of stigma. The authors in this volume have been on the forefront of these efforts. As a result, we have obtained a much deeper understanding of how stigma affects the stigmatized individual, his or her interaction partners, the stigmatized and nonstigmatized groups to which they belong, and relations between the groups. The volume as a whole examines many different forms of stigma, including stigma based on ethnicity, gender, sexual orientation, weight, eating disorders, mental and physical illness, and a history of incarceration. In particular, the volume addresses three main themes of research on stigma: (a) the effects of stigma and the processes that account for these effects; (b) the variables that moderate the effects of stigma on outcomes; and (c) the lessons that can be learned from this work to mitigate the negative effects of stigma at the individual, interpersonal, and structural or institutional levels.

THEMES OF THE VOLUME

Effects of Stigma

The research in this volume shows that stigma has profound effects across a wide range of outcomes, including well-being and self-esteem, self-perception, group identification, motivation, task performance, and social interaction. As the research shows, members of stigmatized groups may be devalued, ignored, and excluded. They may have difficulty establishing an accurate, stable, and clear self-concept, especially with regard to domains that are relevant to stereotypes about their group (Inzlicht & Good, chap. 7, this volume). As a result of interactions with others who are perceived to hold negative stereotypes about their group, members of stigmatized groups may perceive themselves in ways that are consistent with these stereotypes in an effort to socially tune and maintain relationships with them (Sinclair & Huntsinger, chap. 12, this volume). Repeated negative experiences with stigma can lead members of stigmatized groups to anxiously anticipate similar treatment in future situations, straining cognitive resources that would otherwise be devoted to other tasks (Mendoza-Denton, Page-Gould & Pietrzak, chap. 8, this volume). Such experiences with stigmatization also increase general anxiety and cardiovascular reactivity (R. Clark, Anderson, V. R. Clark, & Williams, 1999; Tomaka, Blascovich, Kelsey, & Leitten, 1993). Moreover, members of stigmatized groups are not only affected by their own experiences; the actions of their fellow group members may also reflect negatively on them, causing shame when these behaviors are perceived as confirming the negative stereotype that exists of their group (Schmader & Lickel, chap. 13, this volume).

So what do members of stigmatized groups do in the face of these challenges? Although research on the effects of stigma has shown broad and pervasive effects across a wide range of affective, cognitive, and behavioral outcomes, current work on stigma clearly indicates that there is much variability in responses across individuals, within individuals across time, and across situations. Also, the work clearly indicates that stigmatized individuals do indeed actively cope with the negative effects of stigma. Moving away from an early focus on members of stigmatized groups as passive victims of stigma and its consequences, the research in this volume demonstrates the flexibility and tenacity of members of stigmatized groups in responding to stigma, and the diversity in their responses as a result of their different goals, environments, and individual characteristics. Contrary to earlier perspectives, contemporary views of stigma are focused more centrally on the role of construals and goals in stigma processes. According to these emerging perspectives, any attempt to understand whether and how individuals of stigmatized groups cope with stigma needs to take into consideration both the stigmatized individuals' understanding of the situation and the goals that they have in that particular situation (Miller, chap. 2, this volume; Swim & Thomas, chap. 6, this volume). Although much of the early research focused on self-enhancement goals as the primary motives for members of devalued groups, more recent research shows that other goals may also be primary, among these the need to understand and control what happens to oneself and the need for a sense of belonging, each of which may sometimes be at odds with self-enhancement goals. Members of stigmatized groups, like people in general, prioritize the goal that they most want to accomplish in a situation and, to the degree that the situation allows them, act in ways to achieve it.

This focus on goal-directed behavior also emphasizes that there is not any one "optimal" coping response to stigma. The work by Kaiser (chap. 3, this volume) and by Shelton, Richeson, Salvatore, and Hill (chap. 4, this volume) provides fine examples of the need to consider the goals that members of stigmatized groups have when considering their optimal coping strategies. Both chapters address one of the key decisions facing members of stigmatized groups: whether to confront the injustice they face or whether to remain silent. They show that the avenue chosen by members of stigmatized groups depends on the intra- and interpersonal costs associated with their responses and the goals that they have in the situation. Kaiser shows that confronting the prejudiced behaviors of others often leads to derogation of the complainant and increased conflict, especially when the person accused of prejudice endorses beliefs that the world is a just place and that anyone can succeed through hard work and individual merit. Thus, when interpersonal and intergroup harmony are the primary goals, confronting prejudice may thwart these goals and may result in reduced well-being. However, as Shelton, Richeson, Salvatore, and Hill show in chapter 4, self-enhancement goals may also be thwarted by not confronting prejudice, particularly when stigmatized individuals are highly committed to confronting prejudice and as a result experience uncomfortable discrepancies between their behavior and their self-views when they do not confront. Moreover, the choices that members of stigmatized groups make have consequences not only for themselves and the immediate interaction but also for their larger social group and their group's relations with other groups. When members of stigmatized groups do not speak out against their unjust treatment, perpetrators of prejudice may not correct their biases and may continue to believe that the social structure is fair and permeable and feel no need to address group inequality. Failure to confront prejudice may also lead other members of the stigmatized group to underestimate the degree to which their sense of injustice is shared and undermine their sense of efficacy in responding more collectively to their shared injustice.

Variability in the Effects of Stigma

This volume also describes the huge leap forward the field has made in deepening our understanding of the variability in responses to stigma, and in identifying environmental and personal factors that explain these individual differences in responses to stigma. Taken together, the chapters in this volume show that variability in responses to stigma is shaped by the characteristics of the stigma, the characteristics of the person, and the characteristics of the situation.

Characteristics of the Stigma. One characteristic on which stigmas differ is in terms of how globally they involve devaluation of the stigmatized person (e.g., see Quinn, chap. 5, this volume). Although some stigmas are restricted to particular aspects of the person, such as being overweight or homosexual, other stigmas, such as mental illness, involve devaluation of a broad range of the person's characteristics. Individuals with more narrowly defined stigmas are likely to be able to escape the negative effects of stigma to a much greater extent than those with stigmas relevant to many characteristics. Quinn also shows how the stigma process depends on whether the stigma is concealable or not. Minority ethnicity may be a chronically accessible stigma that is difficult to conceal, but other stigmas, such as a history of eating disorders or mental illness, are easier to conceal. Compared to individuals with a chronically accessible stigma, individuals with a concealable stigma may be less likely to incorporate the stigmatized identity into their larger self-concept. Not incorporating a stigmatized identity into the self-concept may confer a disadvantage as such individuals are less able to make the ingroup comparisons and external attributions for prejudice that help protect the self from the negative effects of devaluation (Crocker & Major, 1989). Interpersonal interactions may also involve more decisions for individuals with concealable stigmas. Individuals with concealable stigmas have to choose when and to whom to reveal their stigma and may suffer from the potential guilt and loss of control associated with their stigma being exposed by others. Monitoring for signs of one's stigma being exposed and having to decide when and to whom to reveal the stigma can be anxiety provoking and place an extra cognitive burden on individuals with concealable stigmas.

Characteristics of the Stigmatized Individual. The effects of stigma also depend on the individual characteristics of the stigmatized individual. In the stress and coping model presented by Carol Miller (chap. 2, this volume), the coping process begins with appraisals of the threat and availability of coping responses. In this process, characteristics of the stigmatized individual may affect what is perceived as threatening and what resources the individual has and chooses to use in order to cope with the threat. Like Miller, Janet Swim and Margaret Thomas (chap. 6, this volume) argue that the goals of the stigmatized individual play a key role in determining the selection of coping responses and the evaluation of their effects for the individual. Thus one individual may be motivated to have the interaction go as smoothly as possible (see Sinclair & Huntsinger, chap. 12, this volume), whereas others may want to protect the self from negative stereotypes or evaluations (see Kaiser, chap. 3, this volume). Yet others may be concerned about failing to confront perpetrators of prejudice (see Shelton, Richeson, Salvatore, & Hill, chap. 4, this volume).

Prior experiences with stigma also affect the stigma process. Stigmatized individuals not only experience prejudice and discrimination directly, they are exposed to representations of their stigma in the dominant culture as well. Based on these prior experiences with stigma, members of stigmatized groups develop "collective representations," or shared feelings, beliefs, and expectations about their stigma and its potential effects (Major, chap. 10, this volume). Furthermore, individuals who have had much previous direct or vicarious experience with exclusion, prejudice, and discrimination are likely to perceive and react more strongly to an instance of prejudice than are those who have had few such previous experiences. Some individuals may be chronically more sensitive to instances of prejudice and discrimination. Mendoza-Denton, Page-Gould, and Pietrzak (chap. 8, this volume) show that individuals who are highly sensitive to status-based rejection are more likely to perceive discriminatory treatment and react more strongly and negatively when it occurs. Status-based sensitivity to rejection may also, however, have positive effects for the stigmatized group in that the higher salience of discrimination that results from status-based sensitivity to rejection may spur members of stigmatized groups to engage in collective action on behalf of their group.

Similar to this, group identification may play a part in influencing the effects of stigma (see Ellemers, Spears, & Doosje, 2002). Compared to low identifiers, individuals who are strongly identified with their stigmatized group may be more likely to perceive events as relevant to their stigma, be more attuned to such events, and react more strongly when they occur. At the same time, because the ingroup can be an important source of both practical and emotional support and provide a framework for understanding and negotiating the social world (see Branscombe, Schmitt, & Harvey, 1999), a strong group identity may also protect stigmatized group members from some of the negative effects of devaluation. As such, other stigmatized group members may provide both assistance in appraising an event as related to stigma and in coping with the event. However, identifying strongly with a group can also make members of stigmatized groups vulnerable to the actions of other ingroup members. In essence, the self is extended such that one may experience not only shame and guilt over one's own actions, but also over the actions of other ingroup members, especially to the extent that these actions are perceived to confirm existing negative stereotypes of the group (see Schmader & Lickel, chap. 13, this volume).

Characteristics of the Situation. Other chapters in this volume address the importance of situational variables in moderating the negative effects of stigma. Generally, this work notes that environmental cues that influence the salience of the stigmatized identity determine whether stigma affects outcomes in a particular setting. Inzlicht and Good (chap. 7) introduce the term *threatening environments* to describe settings in which members of stigmatized groups come to suspect that they may be devalued, stigmatized, or discriminated against because of their particular social identity. They note that such threatening environments compel individuals to think about their social identities and the stereotypes associated with these identities. Any environment that signals that the identity is not valued is likely to increase the negative effects of stigma. Heterogeneous settings that include people from many other groups may be particularly likely to form threatening environments for the stigmatized. Being outnumbered increases distinctiveness and self-consciousness, increases the salience of one's social identity, primes stereotypes, and increases anxiety and arousal among members of stigmatized groups. Tropp (chap. 9, this volume) shows how the repeated experience with threatening environments may make members of stigmatized groups less likely to show positive effects of known prejudice-reducing-strategies. Specifically, concerns about group status and discrimination against one's group may limit the potential for even positive intergroup contact to enhance positive attitudes toward outgroups among members of stigmatized groups. Interactions with outgroup members may also be damaging through self-stereotyping. The work by Sinclair and Huntsinger (chap. 12, this volume) shows that members of stigmatized groups may socially tune to the attitudes of members of the high-status group. Schmader and Lickel (chap. 13, this volume) suggest, in addition, that not only are members of stigmatized groups anxious about the actions of outgroup members in heterogeneous settings, but the actions of ingroup members may equally be a cause for concern, especially to the degree that these actions are perceived as confirming negative stereotypes of the group. Combining the work by Schmader and Lickel with that of Sinclair and Huntsinger suggests that interactions with ingroup members who hold negative stereotypes about their own group may actually be more harmful than interactions with prejudiced outgroup members. Because members of stigmatized groups may feel more close and safe with ingroup members and be more likely to socially tune with them, this may result in more negative self-stereotyping in interactions with ingroup members who hold negative group stereotypes than with outgroup members who hold negative group stereotypes.

Although the research on the impact of threatening environments highlights the negative effects of interactions with outgroup members, McLaughlin-Volpe (chap. 11, this volume) provides complementary evidence for the benefits of contact with outgroup members. Extending the self-expansion model (Aron & Aron, 1997) to intergroup relations, McLaughlin-Volpe argues that self-expansion through relations with higher status outgroup members is especially important for members of stigmatized groups, as such relations provide access to the physical and social resources of the higher status group. Together, this work suggests that the consequences of interactions with ingroup and outgroup members are contingent on the degree to which the interactions are close and free of negative stereotypes and expectations. When environments are safe and nonthreatening, both interactions with ingroup and outgroup members are likely to lead to positive self-expansion and social tuning, reduced prejudice and discrimination, and positive intergroup attitudes.

Strategies to Reduce the Negative Effects of Stigma

The contributions in this volume also provide suggestions regarding processes that may alleviate the negative effects of stigma on individuals, their groups, and on relations between groups. At the intrapersonal level, the work in this volume emphasizes the importance of considering which goal is primary for the stigmatized individual. Both Kaiser (chap. 3, this volume) and Shelton, Richeson, Salvatore, and Hill (chap. 4, this volume) note the importance of remaining true to the self and one's goals in maintaining personal well-being, positive interpersonal relations, or challenging injustice. Crocker and Garcia (chap. 14, this volume) note the benefits that may be gained by focusing on goals that are larger than the self, such as learning about the person with whom one is interacting or building a relationship with him or her.

Group identifications can also offer a solution to the dilemmas posed by stigma, with the perception of a collective union being a source of comfort and social support for the stigmatized individual at the same time that it provides a potential vehicle to challenge the low-status position of the group as a whole. Mendoza-Denton, Page-Gould and Pietrzak (chap. 8, this volume) show that ethnic identity may be a particularly important source of strength for individuals who are high in sensitivity to status-based rejection. Various other chapters also address the importance of supportive others in mitigating the negative effects of stigma. Inzlicht and Good (chap. 7, this volume) note that competent ingroup role models send the message that members of the ingroup are competent in a specific domain and signal that members of the group are respected. In addition to social support from ingroup members, McLaughlin-Volpe (chap. 11, this volume) shows how cross-group relations can be especially important for members of stigmatized groups in providing access to the social and physical resources of the high-status group and expanding the self to new levels. These cross-group friendships may be especially important for individuals high in status-based sensitivity to rejection by providing disconfirming evidence with regard to negative intergroup expectations (Mendoza-Denton, Page-Gould, & Pietrzak, chap. 8, this volume). For cross-group interactions to be effective, however, optimal contact conditions may not be sufficient; attention must also be devoted to concerns on the part of members of stigmatized groups about group status and discrimination (Tropp, chap. 9, this volume). Acknowledging and addressing these concerns will play an important role in dealing with stigma and group inequality in effective ways.

The work by Sinclair and Huntsinger (chap. 12, this volume) on the danger of social tuning to the attitudes of the outgroup among members of stigmatized groups also emphasizes the importance of active rejection of stereotypes by others in interactions. This is of course an especially difficult task, as negative stereotypes and attitudes are often implicit (Devine, 1989; Dovidio, Kawakami, & Gaertner, 2002). Failing the ability to control the attitudes of the other, members of stigmatized groups need to be careful with whom they develop relationships and can reduce the likelihood of negative social tuning by remaining interpersonally distant from those with stereotypic views. Increasingly, research also indicates that members of stigmatized groups may have developed considerable skills at identifying such individuals (e.g., see Dovidio et al., 2002).

The chapters in this volume also give several suggestions as to how stigma and its negative effects may be addressed at the institutional or structural level. First, many of the processes that have been identified at the interpersonal level as reducing the negative effects of stigma can also be structured more formally. For example, educational institutions can set up places where members of traditionally underrepresented groups can find a safe venue to interact and meet others. Such environments can already be seen in the formation of historically Black colleges and universities, Hispanic serving institutions, Latino and Black fraternities and sororities, and women's colleges and organizations. In these environments, members of stigmatized groups expect to be valued and treated with respect. More generally, the chapters call for the formation of nonthreatening environments in which important others clearly express counterstereotypic beliefs. Similarly, institutions can channel positive cross-group interactions in curricular and extracurricular activities. Mentorship programs can provide the role models that research has shown to be so important for members of stigmatized groups who find themselves in the numerical minority. Lastly, educational programs can educate individuals as to the processes of stereotyping and stigmatization and help individuals to develop skills to address these issues. For example, individuals who are in positions in which they regularly give feedback can be taught the "wise" feedback skills mentioned in the chapters by Inzlicht and Good (chap. 7, this volume) and Mendoza-Denton, Page-Gould, and Pietrzak (chap. 8, this volume). In addition, knowing that Mendoza-Denton and his colleagues have also shown that individuals high in status-based rejection sensitivity are likely to avoid various resources that an institution may offer, the institution can organize procedures by which this avoidance and its negative effects are minimized.

Reaching back to the importance of goals, a theme throughout the volume, Crocker and Garcia (chap. 14, this volume) provide a broad analysis of possible solutions to the dilemmas of stigma for members of stigmatized and nonstigmatized groups, noting that a solution to many of the issues addressed in the volume may be reached by reframing how we manage stigma and social inequality. They maintain that many of the negative effects of stigma result from the fact that stigma affects the "corporate image" of both members of stigmatized and nonstigmatized groups and that the downward spiral that follows is a result of an attempt by both sides to maintain or restore this corporate image. Crocker and Garcia suggest that this cycle can be broken by focusing on goals that are larger than the self, such as learning goals, inclusion goals, or superordinate goals. In their analysis, Crocker and Garcia move across the intrapersonal, interpersonal, and structural levels to suggest that individuals, interaction partners, and institutions should focus on what one can learn from the self and from the interaction partner, and should structure environments to be conducive to these learning and inclusion goals.

ORGANIZATION OF THE VOLUME

The chapters in the volume are divided into three sections. Part I focuses on responses to stigma in terms of confronting, concealing and coping with stigma; Part II explores the impact of the social context on stigma; and Part III addresses stigma and the social basis of the self.

Confronting, Concealing, and Coping: Responses to Stigma

Part I of the volume focuses on how members of stigmatized groups cope with and respond to stigma and discrimination. The chapters in this section discuss the potential costs and benefits associated with responding to stigma and discrimination, and how the goals and motives of the individual determine the responses that are chosen and their impact on the individual's feelings, cognitions, and behaviors. In chapter 2, Carol Miller begins with a historical focus on the work on stigma, emphasizing the shift that has occurred as researchers moved from a focus on the harm that stigma can inflict to the ways in which people actively cope with stigma. After discussing changes in the nature of prejudice that have affected the ways in which people cope with it, she introduces a stress and coping perspective on stigmatized people's reactions to prejudice, noting that coping is a dynamic process that involves tradeoffs between the costs and benefits of imperfect solutions. The coping process begins with appraisals of an event as threatening, appraisals of available resources to cope with the threat, and appraisals that the stressor is stigma related. She emphasizes that identification to the self, to other people, and by other people that prejudice has occurred can play an important role in both the appraisal of stigma-related stressors and the ways in which people cope with them. Miller makes a distinction between various forms of coping, paralleling the distinction between fight and flight responses in distinguishing coping responses that engage or approach the stressor from those that disengage or avoid the stressor.

In chapter 3, Cheryl Kaiser focuses on interpersonal reactions to discrimination claimants. Beginning with the finding that victims of unfair treatment often do not publicly acknowledge their discrimination, even when this discrimination is blatant, she shows that one reason for this is that victims of discrimination are derogated by others, even when others acknowledge that discrimination took place. Kaiser's analyses show that public attributions to discrimination serve as a source of ideological threat to observers—threatening dominant ideology beliefs such as individualism and the Protestant work ethic that contend that any individual can get ahead through hard work and merit—and therefore lead the observers to derogate the discrimination claimant. Furthermore, because those who most strongly endorse the dominant ideology are most likely to be threatened by claims of discrimination, they are most likely to respond by derogating the victim. Kaiser shows that the final outcome of this interpersonal interaction is that members of stigmatized groups may avoid confronting the discrimination that they face in an effort to avoid negative evaluations and intergroup conflict.

While Kaiser focuses on the interpersonal costs of confronting discrimination, J. Nicole Shelton, Jennifer Richeson, Jessica Salvatore, and Diana Hill emphasize the intrapersonal costs of not confronting discrimination. Specifically, in chapter 4, Shelton, Richeson, Salvatore and Hill present a self-discrepancy model to account for the intrapersonal consequences of not confronting perpetrators of prejudice. Although the interpersonal costs of confronting prejudice may be substantial, as Kaiser showed in chapter 3, Shelton, Richeson, Salvatore, and Hill show that not confronting prejudice can leave members of stigmatized groups with an inconsistency between their behaviors and self-standards, which can also have negative affective and cognitive consequences. Individuals of stigmatized groups may feel that they have transgressed a personal standard, that they have let down or "sold out" the group in order to make their lives easier, and may feel guilty and ruminate about their inaction, leading to cognitive distraction and decrements in performance, as well as intrusive and obsessive thoughts. Moreover, the authors show that these effects occur in particular for individuals who have a personal commitment to confront prejudice and discrimination; members of stigmatized groups who have no such personal commitment are protected from these adverse consequences. Together, the chapters by Kaiser and by Shelton, Richeson, Salvatore and Hill show that members of stigmatized groups appraise a prejudiced situation on the basis of their intrapersonal, interpersonal, and intergroup goals, and consider their response options in light of the costs and benefits associated with each option.

In chapter 5, Diane Quinn discusses the role that characteristics of the stigma play in the stigma process. Although members of many stigmatized groups find themselves in situations in which their stigma is chronically accessible to themselves and others, members of groups that have a stigma that is concealable face both a benefit and an extra burden in that they can and need to decide if and when to reveal their stigma to others. Quinn distinguishes these concealable stigmas from nonconcealable stigmas in terms of their emotional and behavioral demands. Using two potentially concealable stigmas as illustrations—a history of a mental illness and an eating disorder—she discusses some of the experiences unique to those with a concealable stigma, including deciding when and to whom to reveal, short- and long-term consequences of keeping an identity concealed, and concerns about the discovery of the stigma. Quinn shows how individuals with concealable stigmas are particularly affected by the salience of the stigma in different contexts and the resulting centrality of the stigma for the self. When the stigma is not salient, individuals with concealable stigmas are likely to have interactions that do not differ from those of the nonstigmatized. Those with concealable stigmas may be less competent, though, in situations in which their stigma is salient, having less experience in such interactions than those with chronically visible stigmas. Those with concealable stigmas also clearly face some other costs: the reactions of others who perceive them as dishonest or distrustful for not revealing their stigma and the danger that the stigma will reveal itself involuntarily at an inopportune moment. Quinn also highlights some of the benefits of concealability, noting that individuals with concealable stigmas can choose situations in which they feel comfortable to reveal their stigma, giving them an extra sense of control and the ability to "pass" in situations in which they do not want to reveal their stigma (Goffman, 1963).

Completing Part I of the volume, Janet Swim and Margaret Thomas (chap. 6) bring a goal perspective to the study of responses to stigma. They note that an understanding of the goals that members of stigmatized groups have is essential to an understanding of how individuals cope with stigma. Specifically, they place the selection of coping responses in a framework of self-regulation processes directed at achieving core social motives, arguing that an understanding of these processes helps clarify what is threatening or challenging about stigma, what motivates responses on the part of members of stigmatized groups, why members of stigmatized groups select particular coping responses, and how they appraise the effectiveness of their coping responses. Using Fiske's five core social goals (Fiske, 2003), Swim and Thomas argue that members of stigmatized groups have needs for self-enhancement, for trust, for understanding, for control and for belonging, and that the activation of these goals is situation-specific and varies across individuals. Swim and Thomas continue highlighting the theme prominent in this volume that coping involves tradeoffs and argue that goals determine not only what coping mechanisms are utilized but also the effects of these coping responses on stigmatized individuals' feelings, cognitions, and behaviors. An assessment of whether the coping response in a particular situation is beneficial or costly thus needs to take into consideration the goals and motives of the stigmatized person in that situation.

Stigma in the Social Context: Coping with Threatening Environments

Part II of the volume focuses on how the social context impacts the experience of stigma. The chapters in this section show that the effects of stigma are varied and depend on the characteristics of the stigmatized individual, the context surrounding the stigma, and the coping mechanisms marshaled in response to stigmatization.

In chapter 7, Michael Inzlicht and Catherine Good underscore the importance of situational and environmental factors for understanding the relationship between stigma and adjustment outcomes, and introduce the term *threatening environments* to discuss the role of context in the stigma process. Focusing on stereotype vulnerability in different contexts, Inzlicht and Good make the case that stereotype vulnerability threatens performance, the accuracy and stability of self-knowledge, and the sense of belonging that members of stigmatized groups feel in a domain. Using the case of women in the domain of math as an illustration, the authors argue that even small situational cues—for example, the ratio of men to women in a testing room—can have substantial effects on women's performance and engagement in the math domain. In order to overcome the threats posed by these environments, Inzlicht and Good suggest creating environments in which people are encouraged to view intelligence as malleable rather than fixed, to view negative group stereotypes as irrelevant to their own performance, and to view tests as less diagnostic of their ability in domains in which their group is negatively stereotyped.

In chapter 8, Rodolfo Mendoza-Denton, Elizabeth Page-Gould and Janina Pietrzak focus on the other side of the Person × Situation interaction, examining how individuals differ in their responses to similar environmental circumstances. They argue that prior experiences with discrimination lead people to anxiously anticipate similar treatment in future situations and make them especially vulnerable to the negative consequences of threatening environments. Mendoza-Denton, Page-Gould, and Pietrzak first review the conditions surrounding the development of such status-based rejection expectations and the consequences of these expectations. They then discuss how individuals may cope with status-based rejection at the intrapersonal and interpersonal levels and how institutions can establish procedures to manage status-based rejection and its effects.

In chapter 9, Linda Tropp reviews theory and research concerning the impact of stigma and status inequality on processes of intergroup contact. She summarizes results from studies on the expectations that members of minority and majority status groups have for intergroup contact and the outcomes of this contact, showing that experiences with prejudice and stigmatization can inhibit the potentially positive effects of contact in members of stigmatized groups. Specifically, she shows that concerns about group status and discrimination against one's group may play a more significant role in defining the intergroup interaction among members of minority status groups than among members of majority status groups. Tropp's analysis is an important extension of recent work on intergroup contact that focuses on the different concerns that members of minority and majority status groups have in intergroup interactions (e.g., see Devine, Evett, & Vasquez Suson, 1996). In addition, it extends one of the main themes of the volume in terms of the importance of considering the goals that individuals have in understanding processes of stigma and social inequality.

Concluding the section on stigma in the social context, Brenda Major (chap. 10) summarizes the core themes of the "New Look" in stigma research that has challenged traditional understandings of the effects of stigma. In contrast to traditional perspectives on stigma that focused on the internalization of stigma into chronic feelings of inferiority, contemporary perspectives on stigma assert that the effects of stigma are not uniformly or inevitably negative. Rather, these emerging perspectives emphasize the variability in responses to stigma across stigmatized groups, across individuals within stigmatized groups, and within individuals across different contexts, and seek to identity the factors that explain these sources of variability. Using a transactional model of responses to stigma, Major discusses the personal and situational factors that influence how stigmatized individuals cognitively appraise stigma-related events and cope with them when they are appraised as stressful.

Stigma and the Social Basis of the Self

Part III of the volume focuses on stigma and the social basis of the self. Each of the chapters in this section identifies ways in which social relationships with others influence the impact that stigma has on the lives of those who bear the stigmatized identity.

In chapter 11, Tracy McLaughlin-Volpe explores the benefits of self-expansion through interactions with members of outgroups. Taking a self-expansion perspective (A. Aron & E. N. Aron, 1997), which focuses on the importance of close relationships for personal growth, McLaughlin-Volpe extends the concept of self-expansion to intergroup relations. The chapter describes the self-expansion model and supporting research, shows how it is relevant to understanding the experiences of members of stigmatized groups, and discusses the role that the hypothesized self-expansion processes play in educational institutions. Consistent with the model, McLaughlin-Volpe provides evidence showing increased self-expansion when members of stigmatized groups have contacts with members of outgroups. This increased self-expansion is hypothesized to occur because members of outgroups are more different from the self than are ingroup members, having different knowledge, interests, and skills as a result of their different experiences. McLaughlin-Volpe concludes that these cross-group interactions are especially important for members of stigmatized groups because they provide members of stigmatized groups with access to the material and social resources of the higher status group.

While McLaughlin-Volpe concentrates on the benefits to be gained from interacting with others who are likely to provide extra avenues for self-expansion, the next two chapters in this section focus on the dangers that may result from such inclusion of others in the self. In chapter 12, Stacey Sinclair and Jeff Huntsinger focus on the consequences of including others in the self for self-stereotyping. They note that self-stereotyping will occur when members of stigmatized groups desire to form or maintain a relationship with a person who has negative views or stereotypes of their group. They argue that, in order to maintain a relationship with this other individual, stigmatized individuals will "socially tune" or adjust their social beliefs, including beliefs about the self, to those of their interaction partner. For members of stigmatized groups interacting with members of nonstigmatized groups, this can mean tuning to negative expectations and stereotypes held by the other person about their group, a process ultimately resulting in self-stereotyping. Sinclair and Huntsinger show that this phenomenon occurs even when this social tuning goes against other goals that the individual may have in the interaction, such as making a good impression or appearing competent. Together, the two chapters by McLaughlin-Volpe and by Sinclair and Huntsinger suggest that whether contacts with outgroup members are harmful or beneficial to the self will depend on the degree to which the interaction partner harbors negative stereotypes and expectations relevant to the stigma.

In chapter 13, Toni Schmader and Brian Lickel extend the discussion of the dangers of the inclusion of others in the self to contacts with ingroup members. They note that the inclusion of ingroup members in the self leads to a situation in which members of stigmatized groups are affected, not only by their own actions, but also by the actions of other members of their ingroup. Drawing on recent work on group-based emotion, Schmader and Lickel articulate why a person might feel threatened when someone other than the self confirms the negative stereotype about the group. They focus in particular on feelings of shame that may arise in response to actions by ingroup members that confirm the negative stereotype about the group, and link these emotional reactions to distinct action tendencies. They argue that members of stigmatized groups will respond very strongly to stereotypic actions by ingroup members, especially to the degree that the stigmatized identity is perceived to be "essentialized." *Essentialized identities* are those such as ethnicity and gender that are viewed by perceivers as being inalterable and deeply informative aspects of an individual (Rothbart & Taylor, 1992). Members of such essentialized groups are likely to be especially affected when members of their group behave in stereotypic ways. Although the chapter concentrates on feelings of shame, Schmader and Lickel also discuss other emotions that may result from stereotypic actions of ingroup members such as guilt, anger, sadness, and anxiety.

In the final chapter of Part III and the volume as a whole, Jennifer Crocker and Julie Garcia take a broad perspective on the dilemmas posed by stigma for members of stigmatized and nonstigmatized groups to call for a focus on goals that are larger than the self. They argue that many of the dilemmas posed by stigma occur because stigma affects the "corporate image" of both the stigmatized group member and his or her nonstigmatized interaction partner. The stigmatized person faces potential devaluation because of his or her stigmatizing attribute, whereas the nonstigmatized person faces the possibility of being judged as prejudiced or racist. In the context of social interactions, these potential self-threats can lead to mistrust, discomfort, anxiety, avoidance, and withdrawal, and eventually reinforce the negative views that each person in the interaction holds of the other. Sustaining the belief that the self is worthy and valuable becomes fundamentally difficult in such interactions between the stigmatized and the nonstigmatized. Examining this downward spiral, Crocker and Garcia argue that many of these negative outcomes may be reduced by focusing on goals to create something larger than the self, goals of learning rather than evaluation, and goals of inclusion and relationship-building rather than differentiation. In highlighting the dynamics and complexity of stigma effects, Crocker and Garcia present a thought-provoking analysis that suggests that a re-framing of goals in social interactions may provide a solution for the dilemmas faced by members of both stigmatized and nonstigmatized groups.

CONCLUSION

The theoretical and empirical work presented in this volume clearly indicates that individuals actively cope with stigma in ways that vary across stigmatized groups, across individuals within stigmatized groups, and within individuals across time and situations. As such, the chapters in the book demonstrate the resilience of members of stigmatized groups and the flexibility in their responses to stigma based on their different goals and other individual and contextual factors relevant to the stigmatizing situation. This work has helped to advance our understanding of how stigma affects the individual, his or her interaction partners, the stigmatized and nonstigmatized groups to which they belong, and relations between the groups. Together with the other contributors to the volume, we hope that these valuable findings will be used to inform future research, educate students, and move concerned citizens to apply them in their own life's settings to improve the outcomes of stigmatized and nonstigmatized individuals alike.

REFERENCES

Aron, A., & Aron, E. N. (1997). Self-expansion motivation and including other in the self. In S. Duck (Ed.), *Handbook of personal relationships: Theory, research and interventions* (2nd ed., pp. 251–270). New York: John Wiley & Sons.

Branscombe, N. R., Schmitt, M. T., & Harvey, R. D. (1999). Perceiving pervasive discrimination among African Americans: Implications for group identification and well-being. *Journal of Personality and Social Psychology, 77*(1), 135–149.

Clark, R., Anderson, N. B., Clark, V. R., & Williams, D. R. (1999). Racism as a stressor for African Americans: A biopsychosocial model. *American Psychologist, 54*(10), 805–816.

Crocker, J., & Major, B. (1989). Social stigma and self-esteem: The self-protective properties of stigma. *Psychological Review, 96*(4), 608–630.

Devine, P. G. (1989). Stereotypes and prejudice: Their automatic and controlled components. *Journal of Personality and Social Psychology, 56*(1), 5–18.

Devine, P. G., Evett, S. R., & Vasquez Suson, K. A. (1996). Exploring the interpersonal dynamics of intergroup contact. In R. M. Sorrentino & E. T. Higgins (Eds.), *Handbook of motivation and cognition, Vol. 3: The interpersonal context* (pp. 423–464). New York: Guilford.

Dovidio, J. F., Kawakami, K., & Gaertner, S. L. (2002). Implicit and explicit prejudice and interracial interaction. *Journal of Personality and Social Psychology, 82*(1), 62–68.

Ellemers, N., Spears, R., & Doosje, B. (2002). Self and social identity. *Annual Review of Psychology, 53*(1), 161–186.

Fiske, S. T. (2003). Five core social motives, plus or minus five. In S. J. Spencer & S. Fein (Eds.), *Motivated social perception: The Ontario Symposium, Vol. 9. Ontario Symposium on Personality and Social Psychology* (pp. 233–246). Mahwah, NJ: Lawrence Erlbaum Associates.

Goffman, E. (1963). *Stigma: Notes on the management of spoiled identity.* Englewood Cliffs, NJ: Prentice-Hall.

Rothbart, M., & Taylor, M. (1992). Category labels and social reality: Do we view social categories as natural kinds? In K. Fiedler & G. R. Semin (Eds.), *Language, interaction and social cognition* (pp. 11–36). Thousand Oaks, CA: Sage.

Tomaka, J., Blascovich, J., Kelsey, R. M., & Leitten, C. L. (1993). Subjective, physiological, and behavioral effects of threat and challenge appraisal. *Journal of Personality and Social Psychology, 65*(2), 248–260.

PART I

CONFRONTING, CONCEALING, AND COPING: RESPONSES TO STIGMA

CHAPTER

2

Social Psychological Perspectives on Coping With Stressors Related to Stigma

Carol T. Miller
University of Vermont

The defining characteristic of stigmatized people is that other people devalue them (Crocker, Major, & Steele, 1998). Devaluation exposes stigmatized people to a variety of stigma-related stressors (Allison, 1998; Meyer, 2003; Miller & Kaiser, 2001; Miller & Major, 2000). A *stressor* is an event in which environmental or internal demands tax or exceed the adaptive resources of the individual (Lazarus & Folkman, 1984). Stigma can create stress because other people have stereotyped expectancies about what stigmatized people are like, harbor prejudiced attitudes toward stigmatized people, and behave in a discriminatory manner toward stigmatized people (Fiske, 1998; Miller & Kaiser, 2001). The triumvirate of stereotypes, prejudiced attitudes, and discrimination, which throughout this chapter I refer to collectively simply as prejudice or stigma, can affect stigmatized people's access to educational and employment opportunities, the quantity and quality of health care they receive, and their acceptance by the communities in which they live (Allison, 1998; R. Clark, Anderson, V. R. Clark, & Williams, 1999; Meyer, 2003). Stigmatization also results in psychological stress responses such as anger, anxiety, hopelessness, resentment, and fear (R. Clark et al., 1999) and physiological stress responses such as increases in cardiovascular activity (R. Clark et al., 1999; Tomaka, Blascovich, Kelsey, & Leitten, 1993). Coping is a response to stress that draws on the individual's resources in an effort to meet the demands posed by a stressor (Lazarus & Folkman, 1984).

This chapter outlines why interest in coping with stigma is a relatively new development in the study of prejudice. It summarizes how modern incarnations of prejudice affect the types of stressors stigmatized people face due to their stigmatized status, and the way in which they cope with these stressors. It then describes three major components of a stress and coping perspective on reactions to prejudice: (a) appraisals of stigma-related stressors; (b) coping responses that are made to these stressors; and (c) related to both appraisals and coping, the identification to the self, to other people, and by other people that prejudice has occurred. The chapter concludes by emphasizing that coping with prejudice often involves making tradeoffs in which some goals may be sacrificed to achieve those that are most important to the stigmatized individual in a particular situation. It also reminds us of the importance of maintaining the perspective of stigmatized people to avoid making assumptions about how they "should" cope with prejudice or what their goals in a prejudice-tainted situation must be.

THE TARGET'S PERSPECTIVE AND COPING WITH PREJUDICE

Perhaps the most important single thing that can be said about how stigmatized people cope with stigma is that they do indeed cope. It took a surprisingly long time for the research community to recognize this simple fact. Even Allport's (1954) masterpiece, *The Nature of Prejudice*, which anticipated virtually every modern development in the study of prejudice, assumed that "Since no one can be indifferent to the abuse and expectations of others we must anticipate that ego defensiveness will frequently be found among members of groups that are set off for ridicule, disparagement, and discrimination. *It could not be otherwise*" (p. 139, emphasis in the original). Among the ego defenses Allport described were obsessive vigilance and hypersensitivity to prejudice, withdrawal and passivity, clowning, slyness and cunning, identification with the dominant group, self-hate, and neuroticism.

However, Allport's remarkable insights into the nature and consequences of prejudice also led him to point out that not all of these "persecution-based" traits are unpleasant. Stigmatized people also cope constructively, for example by showing enhanced striving in the face of prejudice. Allport also suggested that many people are able to avoid developing these "marks of oppression" even in the face of extreme prejudice.

Nonetheless, it is safe to say that research on stigmatized people has traditionally focused more on the harm that prejudice inflicts upon them than on the way stigmatized people cope with prejudice. There are a least three reasons for this. The first is that social scientists were intent on documenting the evils of prejudice. The notion that stigmatized people could cope with it did not fit well with this objective. Duckitt (1992) pointed out that in the United States prior to the 1920s, prejudice was not widely considered to be a social problem, because most people, including researchers at that time, assumed that prejudice was justified by the natural inferiority of certain groups. During the 1920s and 1930s, researchers began to identify prejudice as a social problem that could not easily be explained by the inferiority of certain groups. In the United States, this recognition reflected broad societal changes resulting from the Great Depression, worldwide challenges to colonialism, the influx of scholars into the social sciences who had direct experience with being stigmatized (e.g., Jewish scholars emigrating from Europe), and the growing influence of the civil rights movements (Duckitt, 1992).

Casting prejudice as a social problem led to efforts to document prejudice as the product of a variety of faulty cognitive processes and irrational personality dynamics (Duckitt, 1992). Entertaining the hypothesis that stigmatized people might be able to mitigate the effects of stereotyping, prejudice, and discrimination on their lives risked dismissing prejudice as a minor irritation rather than the major social problem that social scientists assumed it to be.

A second reason researchers have been a little slow to think about coping with prejudice is that a characteristic of human judgment is to assume that causes and their effects must be of roughly equal magnitude (Nisbett & Ross, 1980; Wegner & Wheatley, 1999). That is, dramatic effects must have equally dramatic causes and vice versa. A "big" problem such as prejudice is assumed to have "big" effects on its targets. The possibility that prejudice could pose extreme hardship on its targets without damaging their outcomes or characters seems to fly in the face of our common-sense understanding of the relationship between causes and their effects. As Allport (1954) explained, "One's reputation, whether false or true, cannot be hammered, hammered, hammered, into one's head without doing something to one's character" (p. 142).

Finally, research support for the assumption that prejudice damages its victims was has not been hard to find. To give just a few classic examples, social scientists in the United States marshaled an impressive array of evidence to help convince the Supreme Court that the "separate, but equal" doctrine that rationalized racial segregation in public schools was inherently unequal because segregation had adverse psychological, social, and academic effects on African Americans (see Zirkel & Cantor, 2004, for a recent review).

Several decades later, research on the self-fulfilling nature of teacher expectations about the educational promise of their students (Miller & Turnbull, 1986; Rosenthal & Rubin, 1978) was widely assumed to imply that race-based expectations could depress the academic performance of African Americans and other stigmatized groups. Contemporary research supports this view and indicates that even the suspicion of stereotyping can threaten the performance of stigmatized people (Inzlicht & Good, chap. 7, this volume; Steele, 1997). There is also evidence that for many stigmatized people, encounters with prejudice are common experiences, sufficiently prevalent to constitute "daily hassles" (Swim, Cohen, & Hyers, 1998). Such experiences have been implicated in cardiovascular and endocrine responses that may help explain the prevalence of health problems among members of stigmatized groups (R. Clark et al., 1999).

Empirical documentation of the adverse effects of prejudice was matched by the development of theories that explained the mechanics of how prejudice could create conditions that harmed the well-being of stigmatized people (Crocker & Major, 1989). Amid this impressive documentation of the power of prejudice and the establishment of theories that explained these findings, it is easy to understand why the idea that stigmatized people cope with prejudice did not readily spring to mind.

One set of findings that directly challenged the prevailing view of how prejudice affects stigmatized people was the finding that stigmatized people have levels of self-esteem that rival the levels of nonstigmatized people (Crocker & Major, 1989; Twenge & Crocker, 2000). As Crocker and Major (1989) pointed out, all the major theories of prejudice predict that stigmatized people should have poor self-esteem. Because the evidence that prejudice creates difficulties for stigmatized people is overwhelming, Crocker and Major concluded that something was happening that enabled stigmatized people to mitigate the effects of these prejudice-induced difficulties. They proposed that the "something" was a set of coping strategies that took advantage of special properties that being stigmatized conferred on stigmatized people. These coping responses included blaming poor outcomes on prejudice rather than personal shortcomings, devaluing domains and activities in which the stigmatized group is stereotyped as inferior, and limiting comparison of outcomes to other stigmatized people, thereby avoiding "upward" comparisons that might threaten self-esteem.

This landmark paper was published just as a number of researchers were beginning to emphasize the perspective of the targets of prejudice in their research rather than focusing on the perspective of the perpetrators (see Heatherton, Kleck, Hebl, & Hull, 2000; Shelton, 2000; Swim & Stangor, 1998, for reviews of much of this research). Almost as soon as researchers began to conceptualize stigmatized people as active agents who seek to control and better their outcomes rather than as passive victims of a society that devalues them, researchers recognized that stigmatized people can act both proactively and reactively to the predicaments posed by prejudice. This emphasis encouraged consideration of the ways in which stigmatized people may cope with prejudice.

CHANGES IN PREJUDICE THAT AFFECT COPING WITH IT

The nature of prejudice has altered in recent years as a result of changes in societal attitudes about the acceptability of prejudice (Crandall & Eshleman, 2003; Fiske, 1998; Gaertner & Dovidio, 1986). It is important to consider these changes because different types of prejudice may create different stressors for stigmatized people and may require different types of coping.

A large volume of research indicates that "old-fashioned" blatant prejudice is no longer socially or personally acceptable in many quarters. Theories about contemporary forms of prejudice generally assume that people are motivated to avoid being prejudiced either because of sincerely held egalitarian beliefs or because of social pressure (Crandall, Eshleman, & O'Brien, 2002). Consequently, prejudice now tends to be an ambivalent (Glick & Fiske, 2001; Katz & Haas, 1988), subtle (Gaertner & Dovidio, 1986), and sometimes even unconscious or automatic (Devine, 1989; Dovidio, Kawakami, & Gaertner, 2002) response to members of stigmatized groups. The difficulty for stigmatized people is that even people who aspire to be nonprejudiced may still (a) harbor ambivalent reactions to members of stigmatized groups; (b) experience negative affect when interacting with them; (c) have implicit stereotypes about them; (d) make judgments about stigmatized people that are unconsciously affected by prejudice; and (e) experience difficulty in acting normally when interacting with stigmatized people, especially with respect to nonverbal and other subtle behaviors that sometimes communicate more than a person intends (see Dovidio & Gaertner, 1998; Fiske, 1998, for reviews).

Expressions of old-fashioned blatant prejudice may create different stressors and require different coping strategies than do modern or subtle forms of prejudice (Barreto & Ellemers, in press). For example, blatant prejudice may lead to avoidance simply because the prospects of improving the situation are relatively poor. Stigmatized people may simply not care to expend their resources to deal with an out-and-out bigot, but may be more willing to work to establish a better situation with a less blatantly prejudiced person. However, some stigmatized people have expressed the view that it is easier to cope with blatant prejudice than it is to cope with subtle prejudice (Feagin & Sikes, 1994). At least they know where they stand with blatant prejudice, whereas it may be very difficult to identify what is going on when a person is subtly prejudiced or ambivalent about the stigmatized person. This can leave the stigmatized person with considerable ambiguity about what precisely is happening in a situation (Crocker & Major, 1989; Major, Quinton, & McCoy, 2002).

A STRESS AND COPING PERSPECTIVE ON STIGMATIZED PEOPLE'S REACTIONS TO PREJUDICE

There is a vast literature on coping with a wide variety of stressors (e.g., illness, bereavement, daily hassles), which has resulted in major theoretical, empirical, and methodological advances (Zeldner & Endler, 1996). Stigma researchers can profit greatly from the progress and problems that have occurred on the more general topic of how anybody copes with any kind of stressor (Allison, 1998; Major, chap. 10, this volume; Meyer, 2003; Miller & Kaiser, 2001; Miller & Major, 2000; Swim & Thomas, chap. 6, this volume). As shown in Fig. 2.1, there are three major components of coping with stigma, each of which is depicted by a triangle: appraisals of stigma-related stressors, coping responses, and related to both appraisals and coping, the identification of prejudice.

The coping process begins with a primary appraisal of an event as a personally relevant threat that may tax or exceed the person's resources for coping with it (see also Major, chap. 10, this volume; Swim & Thomas, chap. 6, this volume). This is accompanied by a secondary appraisal of whether sufficient resources can be called upon to cope with this threat (Lazarus & Folkman, 1984). As the bottom left triangle in Fig. 2.1 shows, a third important element that comes into play in the appraisal of stigma-related stressors is determining that the stressor is somehow related to or caused by the person's stigmatized status (Meyer, 2003).

Once an event as been appraised as a stigma-related stressor, stigmatized people are likely to have a variety of reactions to it. The vast literature

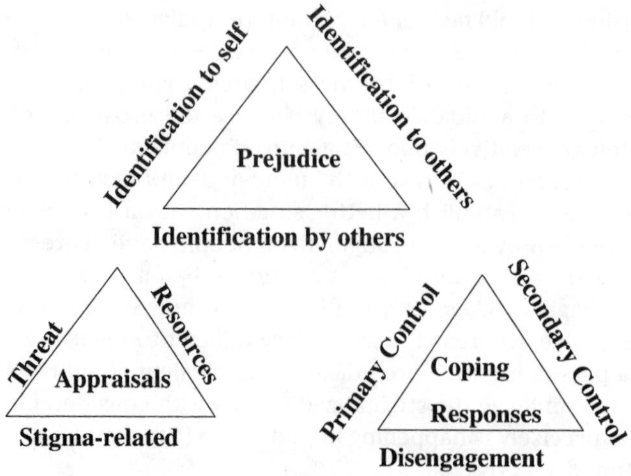

FIG. 2.1. Stress and coping model.

on coping with a wide variety of stressors (e.g., illness, bereavement, daily hassles) indicates that people have a myriad of physiological, cognitive, emotional, and behavioral responses to stress (Zeldner & Endler, 1996). In reviewing the diversity of ways in which stress responses and coping have been conceptualized and measured, Compas and his colleagues (Compas, Connor-Smith, Saltzman, Thompsen, & Wadsworth, 2001; Connor-Smith, Compas, Wadsworth, Thompsen, & Saltzman, 2000) recently proposed that the most fundamental distinction between different responses to stress is between voluntary coping responses and involuntary responses. This distinction emphasizes the fact that not everything a person does in response to stress constitutes coping. People may have involuntary emotional, behavioral, physiological, and cognitive responses to stress that do not serve to regulate or modify stressful experiences. The term *coping* is reserved for conscious volitional efforts to regulate emotion, thought, behavior, physiology, and the environment in response to stressful events or circumstances.

Compas and his colleagues (Compas et al., 2001; Conner-Smith et al., 2000) also suggested that coping responses can involve engagement or disengagement with the stressful event or problem. This distinction parallels traditional distinctions between fight versus flight responses and between approach and avoidance responses (Swim & Thomas, chap. 6, this volume). *Engagement coping* involves self-regulation efforts that engage with or approach the stressor in some way, whereas *disengagement coping* involves regulatory efforts that disengage from or avoid the stressor.

Engagement coping can be further distinguished by whether it is aimed at gaining primary or secondary control over the stressful event (Compas et al., 2001). Primary control coping includes efforts that are directed toward influencing objective events or conditions to enhance a sense of personal control over the environment and one's reactions (Compas et al., 2001). Secondary control coping, by contrast, involves efforts to adapt to the situation. It includes efforts to change the way one feels or thinks about the fact the stressful event. Primary and secondary control coping along with disengagement coping form the three sides of the coping triangle shown in Fig. 2.1.

Figure 2.1 also includes a triangle that represents the identification of prejudice. Prejudice identification refers to an inference that is made that prejudice is present or has an influence in a particular situation. Prejudice identification is depicted as hovering above appraisals (bottom left triangle) and coping responses (bottom right triangle) because the identification of prejudice can be important in both the appraisal of stigma-related stressors and the coping responses that are made to them.

In summary, this stress and coping perspective on reactions to stigma emphasizes the appraisal of stigma-related stressors, a hierarchically organized description of coping responses to these stressors, and consideration of the role of prejudice identification in both appraisals and coping.

Prejudice Identification Defined

Because nobody ever sees an act of prejudice directly, the identification of prejudice requires an inference that a threat is the result of prejudice. Both stigmatized people and other people use a variety of cues to make inferences about prejudice, including, for example, the nonstigmatized person's intentions with respect to the stigmatized person and the amount of harm the stigmatized person suffers (Swim, Scott, Sechrist, Campbell, & Stangor, 2003). There are three important ways in which prejudice can be identified. These are identification to the self that prejudice has occurred, identification to other people that prejudice has occurred, and identification by other people that prejudice has occurred. Identification of prejudice to the self that prejudice has occurred refers to an attribution or inference that stigmatized individuals make that they have been targeted by prejudice. Identification to other people that prejudice has occurred refers to instances in which stigmatized individuals communicate in words or actions to another person that they believe that they have been targeted by prejudice. Identification by other people that prejudice has occurred refers to instances in which other people draw their own inferences about whether stigmatized individuals have been targeted by prejudice. Inferences by other people about the occurrence of prejudice may be based on information from a variety of sources, including, for example, direct observation of events involving stigmatized individuals, hearsay from other people who have information about the event, or communications from the stigmatized individuals themselves.

Prejudice Identification and Appraisals of Stigma-Related Stressors

The appraisal of an event as a stigma-related stressor involves, at a minimum, the identification of prejudice to the self (Major et al., 2002). Without this identification, prejudice would not be appraised as the cause of the threatening event and thus the event would not be experienced as a stigma-related stressor (although it could be experienced as some other type of stressor). Some stressors that are a direct or indirect result of prejudice may not be recognized as such by stigmatized people. This can happen because stigmatized people may attribute an outcome that was actually the result of prejudice to some other cause (Crocker et al., 1998).

There are some situations in which virtually any stigmatized person will be highly aware of prejudice, for example when a stigmatized person is the only member of the stigmatized group present in a situation or when the situation emphasizes domains in which the stigmatized group is thought to perform poorly (Inzlicht & Good, chap. 7, this volume). There also are chronic individual differences between stigmatized people in how sensitive they are to the possibility that they will be stereotyped by others, a characteristic known as *stigma consciousness* (Pinel, 1999). Compared to stigmatized people who are not stigma conscious, highly stigma-conscious stigmatized people can provide more examples of situations in which they have been the targets of prejudice in the past and therefore anticipate more prejudice-based rejection (Pinel, 2002). Sensitivity to rejection in general and sensitivity to stigma-based rejection in particular also can affect the likelihood that stigmatized people will appraise an event as stigma related (thereby identifying to the self that prejudice has occurred) and the manner in which they will cope with rejection (Mendoza-Denton, Downey, Purdie, Davis, & Pietrzak, 2002; Mendoza-Denton, Page-Gold, & Pietrzak, chap. 8, this volume).

Prejudice Identification as a Cause of Stigma-Related Stressors

Prejudice identification to the self, to other people, and by other people can create different types of stressors for stigmatized people. For example, stigmatized people may consider themselves to be targeted by prejudice in a particular situation (identification to the self), but they may refrain from communicating this to others and thus may not be considered by others to have been targeted. The type of stressor that this is likely to create for stigmatized people is that they may be unfairly held accountable for events that resulted from prejudice.

Stigmatized people may also believe that they have encountered prejudice in a situation and may identify themselves as a target to other people, but these people and others who are present or who are informed about events may not accept the stigmatized person's construal of events. A stressor that this creates for stigmatized people is that they may be perceived as unfairly trying to blame prejudice for something for which they should be willing to take personal responsibility.

Identification by other people that prejudice has occurred also can create stressors for the stigmatized person. For example, even if they acknowledge that prejudice was present in a situation, other people may underestimate the effects it has on stigmatized people or may even have a tendency to engage in victim-blaming (Lerner & Miller, 1978; Miller & Krulewitz, 2003). Moreover, a hallmark of modern forms of prejudice is that nonstigmatized people often feel conflicted, upset, and anxious when prejudice surfaces (Devine, Monteith, Zuwerink, & Elliot, 1991; Dovidio et al., 2002), even when they were not personally responsible for the event. These negative feelings may be expressed in subtle ways that stigmatized people pick up on. In such situations, stigmatized people can wind up in a stressful prejudice-tainted interaction that is permeated with confusing and conflicting emotional and behavioral responses, without fully understanding why nonstigmatized people are so uncomfortable.

Prejudice Identification and Coping Responses

Prejudice identification also is an essential component of many coping responses to a stigma-related stressor. For example, the attribution of negative outcomes to prejudice, a method of coping that can protect the self-esteem of stigmatized people, requires identifying to oneself, that prejudice has occurred, but not necessarily identifying the occurrence of prejudice to other people. Identification of the occurrence of prejudice to other people is implicated in coping responses that involve confronting the perpetrator about his or her prejudice or communicating to other people about the situation (Kaiser, chap. 3, this volume; Shelton, Richeson, Salvatore, & Hill, chap. 4, this volume; Stangor et al., in press). Confronting prejudice obviously also requires that stigmatized people identify to the self that prejudiced has occurred as well. Identification by other people that prejudice has occurred can present stigmatized people with a different set of coping challenges. Coping responses that require identification of prejudice to the self will not be available when the stigmatized person is coping with stigma-related stressors that result from other people's (but not their own) identification that prejudice has occurred.

Consequences of Prejudice Identification

Prejudice identification in any of its forms is risky for stigmatized people because acknowledging the existence of prejudice challenges core beliefs about the fairness and justness of the world and the systems in which we live (see Kaiser, chap. 3, this volume, for a review). For example, self-identification as a target of prejudice can sometimes buffer self-esteem from the ravages of stigma because it provides the stigmatized person with an external reason for negative outcomes (see Major et al., 2002, for a review). However, identification of oneself as the target of prejudice could also lead to the belief that prejudice is pervasive and that the world is a cold and unjust place, and stigmatized people may suffer reduced psychological well-being as a result (Branscombe, Schmitt, & Harvey, 1999).

Identifying oneself as the target of prejudice to the perpetrator of that prejudice is likely to make the perpetrator feel accused, maligned, and in the case of subtle or unconscious forms of prejudice, misunderstood (Crocker & Garcia, chap. 14, this volume; Kaiser, chap. 3, this volume; Shelton, Richeson, Salvatore, & Hill, chap. 4, this volume). Stigmatized people may hope that communicating to people other than the perpetrator that one has been targeted by prejudice may enlist them as allies who could take remedial action to address the injustice. At the very least, identifying the prejudice to others should help them to understand why the stigmatized person's performance or outcomes were not as good as they could be.

Unfortunately, this rosy scenario may not be typical. For example, Kaiser and Miller (2001b; 2003) found that an African American who attributed a failing grade or failure to land a job to discrimination was perceived negatively by other people (see Kaiser, chap. 3, this volume, for a review). Even when it was virtually certain that the person who graded the test performance was prejudiced (because participants were told that 100% of the test evaluators discriminated against African Americans) or the job interviewer was prejudiced (because his written "interview notes" indicated that he had never hired a Black person and never would), study participants still formed relatively negative impressions of the African American who identified himself as a target of prejudice.

Prejudice identification to others can be problematic for the stigmatized person because he or she may stand in the role of accuser and/or excuse maker. What happens if instead other people reached their own conclusions about the presence of prejudice in a particular situation? The rosy scenario is that when other people themselves have drawn the inference that prejudice played a role in a particular situation, there should be no suspicion that self-interest or excuse making on the part of the stigmatized person explains the identification of prejudice. Consequently, other people should be driven to rectify things, confront the perpetrator themselves, or at least have sympathy and understanding for the stigmatized person. Unfortunately, being a "witness" to prejudice does not appear to prevent people from forming negative impressions of the targets of prejudice.

We (Miller & Krulewitz, 2003) investigated the impressions people formed of women who experienced an act of gender discrimination (sexual harassment) during a simulated job interview in which they participated as part of another study (Woodzicka & LaFrance, 2001). We played audiotapes of only the women's answers to scripted, job-appropriate questions (e.g., questions about qualifications and job-related experiences) that the interviewer had asked. People who listened to these responses without knowing the context in which the answers were given (i.e., whether or not the interviewer had sexually harassed the women) judged the harassed women as less competent and qualified for the job than nonharassed women. This result replicates Woodzicka and LaFrance's (2001) main finding—which was that sexual harassment has real and immediate negative effects on women's performance during a job interview.

Sadly, we also found that people who knew about the sexual harassment because they had seen a script of all of the questions that the interviewer had asked, including the sexually harassing questions, also rated the harassed women as less competent and qualified than nonharassed women. Even more sadly, people who were high in belief in a just world (Lerner & Miller, 1978) went one step further and evaluated harassed women more negatively when they knew that the women had been harassed—a striking example of victim derogation.

This experiment suggests that, at best, other people ignore the disadvantages prejudice causes for stigmatized people. This assumption of a "level playing field" puts stigmatized people at a severe disadvantage in any situation in which they are handicapped by the effects of prejudice, as, in fact, the harassed women in this experiment were. At worst, some people (i.e., those high in belief in a just world) not only fail to properly consider the role that prejudice may play in the behavior of stigmatized people, but may also derogate the victims of prejudice.

In sum, research on the identification of prejudice suggests that identifying prejudice may be threatening to stigmatized individuals and people to whom prejudice is identified, even if the stigmatized persons themselves had no hand in the identification of the prejudice. Kaiser (chap. 3, this volume) develops the theme that the reason prejudice identification is so threatening is that it challenges cherished beliefs about system fairness.

Effects of Prejudice on Resources Available to Stigmatized People

In the stress and coping literature, the appraisal of an event as a stressor involves not only the individual's appraisal of an event as a personally relevant threat, but it also involves an appraisal of whether he or she has sufficient resources to meet the demands of this threat (Meyer, 2003; Miller & Kaiser, 2001; Miller & Major, 2000). Resources include personal attributes such as optimism (Kaiser & Miller, in press), group identification (Branscombe et al., 1999), and interpersonal attributes such as social support, interpersonal skills, and prior experiences with coping with prejudice (Miller & Kaiser, 2001; Miller & Myers, 1998). Resources also can include economic security, status, education, and mobility. The stigmatized group itself may be a resource by providing safe avenues for affiliation, cohesiveness, and political and social influence (Branscombe & Ellemers, 1998; Meyer, 2003).

There is a complex interplay between stressors, resources, and coping. People with more resources generally face fewer stressors than those with fewer resources. This is partly because they are subjected to fewer potentially threatening events in the first place. For example, job-related stress is more prevalent among lower status workers, such as clerical staff, than higher status workers, such as executives, presumably because status affects how much control people have over events that occur in the workplace. When threats do occur, people with more resources are less likely to appraise them as stressful (i.e., something that will tax or exceed their resources) because they have sufficient resources to cope with the threats. Finally, people with more resources are better equipped to cope with threats that they do appraise as stressors (Meyer, 2003).

Prejudice affects the resources of stigmatized people in numerous ways. It can deny stigmatized people many of the educational, social, and economic opportunities that would provide them with resources that are needed for effective coping. Consequently, in many situations stigmatized people occupy low status roles and have little power (Fiske, Cuddy, Glick, & Xu, 2002).

Prejudice may deny some stigmatized people the opportunity to develop interpersonal skills that could be used to cope with prejudice (Miller & Myers, 1998). In experiments in which interaction partners rated the social skills and likability of stigmatized people with whom they conversed by telephone or intercom without being aware of their partner's stigmatized status, physically unattractive people (Goldman & Lewis, 1977) and women with heavy body weights (Miller, Rothblum, Barbour, Brand, & Felicio, 1990) were perceived as unlikable and lacking in social skill. These findings generally are interpreted as demonstrating that prejudice can affect the behavior of its targets via the operation of expectancy–confirmation processes (Miller & Turnbull, 1986) and denial of opportunities in social interactions.

Although stigma has a detrimental effect on many resources available to stigmatized people, the development of other resources actually depends on having experience with being stigmatized. Coping with prejudice can be likened to a skill that requires practice to develop (Miller & Myers, 1998; Miller, Rothblum, Felicio, & Brand, 1995). In the most widely cited studies of the way in which stereotypes can become self-fulfilling prophecies, the "stigmatized" people who participate are nonstigmatized people who have been assigned (without their knowledge) to be portrayed to other people as a member of a stigmatized group (Snyder, Tanke, & Berscheid, 1977; Word, Zanna, & Cooper, 1974). When nonstigmatized people are led to believe that they have been portrayed as a stigmatized person, their behavior exhibits considerable ineptness (Farina, Allen, & Saul, 1968; Kleck & Strenta, 1980). In contrast, studies of people who are actually stigmatized, including women (Kaiser & Miller, 2001a), overweight women (Miller et al., 1995), and African Americans (Shelton, 2003), showed that when stigmatized people know that others may be prejudiced against them, they tend to counteract stereotypes rather than confirm them and behave in a more socially skillful manner. In fact, the social skills "deficits" that are found when stigmatized people interact with someone who does not know about their stigmatized status (and the stigmatized people know this), disappear when stigmatized people think that other people do know about their stigmatized status (Miller et al., 1995). This suggests that when stigmatized people believe that prejudice threatens the outcome of their interactions, they marshal their interaction skills to counteract the effects that prejudice would otherwise have (Miller & Kaiser, 2001).

Coping Responses to Stigma-Related Stressors

There have been several efforts to identify dimensions that can be used to describe different types of coping with stigma. Some of these efforts have been developed specifically for stigma-related coping (Branscombe & Ellemers, 1998; Jacobson, 1977; Swim et al., 1998; Wright, Taylor, & Moghaddam, 1990). Many of these efforts are intuitively appealing, but lack empirical support and pay little heed to dimensions that have proved to be meaningful in the general stress and coping literature. Others have adapted dimensions of coping that have investigated in the general stress and coping literature (Major, chap. 10, this volume; Miller & Major, 2000; Miller & Myers, 1998). Miller and Kaiser (2001) adapted the Compas et al. model, already described, to integrate the existing research on coping with stigma (Compas et al., 2001; Connor-Smith et al., 2000).

In their model, they made the same distinction that Compas and his colleagues made between engagement and disengagement coping responses (see also Swim & Thomas, chap. 6, this volume). Recall that engagement coping involves self-regulation efforts that engage with or approach the stressor in some way, whereas disengagement coping involves regulatory efforts that disengage from or avoid the stressor. Recall also that engagement coping can involve seeking primary or secondary control over the stressful event. *Primary control coping* includes efforts that are directed toward influencing objective events or conditions to enhance a sense of personal control over the environment and one's reactions (Compas et al., 2001). Engagement control coping that is aimed at gaining primary control over the stressful event includes problem solving and efforts to directly regulate one's emotions or the expression of emotion. *Secondary control coping*, by contrast, involves efforts to adapt to the situation by changing the way one feels about or thinks about the stressful event. The major coping responses that fall into this coping domain are distraction, acceptance, positive thinking, and cognitive restructuring. Disengagement coping includes attempting to control thoughts and situations to avoid thinking about or encountering the stressor, denial that the stressor has occurred, and wishful thinking.

A growing body of research on how people cope with stigma has documented that stigmatized people do use primary and secondary control engagement coping and disengagement coping to protect themselves from the stressors that result from stigma (see Major et al., 2002; Miller & Kaiser, 2001, for reviews). Crocker and Major's (1989) pioneering article on the self-protective properties of stigma is largely a description of secondary control engagement coping strategies. They argued, for example, that stigmatized people protect self-esteem from the negative consequences of prejudice and discrimination by blaming poor outcomes on prejudice (Crocker & Major, 1989), a form of secondary control coping involving cognitive restructuring. Another type of secondary control engagement coping featured in Crocker and Major's analysis is the devaluation of domains on which the stigmatized group is stereotyped as performing poorly. For example, African Americans devalue academic achievement and women devalue the pursuit of mathematics and science—domains in which these groups are stereotyped as being inferior (Crocker et al., 1998). Devaluation can be conceptualized as a way of making stigmatized people (in this case, African Americans and women) feel better about the fact that their group has or is believed to have poor outcomes in a given domain, without changing the fact that these poor outcomes are associated with the stigmatized group.

Primary control coping has recently emerged as a focus of research. As was mentioned, the results of several experiments indicate when stigmatized people know that prejudice could affect their interactions with others, stigmatized people use problem-solving behavioral strategies that involve behaving in a more competent or socially skilled manner (Miller et al., 1995; Steckler & Rosenthal, 1985).

Another form of primary control coping is that stigmatized people may strategically present themselves to others in ways that confirm stereotypes about their group. This is especially likely to occur when the other people do indeed have stereotyped expectations and have power over the stigmatized individuals. For example, women job applicants dressed in a more traditionally feminine way and gave more stereotype-consistent answers to interview questions when they thought the interviewer had traditional views about women's role than when they thought he or she had liberal views (von Baeyer, Sherk, & Zanna, 1981). Sinclair and Huntsinger (chap. 12, this volume) suggest that self-stereotyping, a process in which stigmatized people actually perceive themselves to be consistent with stereotypes about them, may be used as a tool to help stigmatized people focus on those aspects of themselves that fit with other people's expectations about them. By sincerely believing (at least for the moment) that one *is* what the stereotype says one should be, stigmatized people may be better able to present themselves in ways that people who stereotype them expect, and consequently may enjoy more harmonious relationships with them.

Of course, sometimes stigmatized people have goals that encourage disconfirmation of stereotypes. In doing so they may sacrifice the goal of harmony with others, but achieve other goals that take precedence (Snyder & Haugen, 1995). For example, Kaiser and Miller (2001a) found that women who expected their performance on a measure of future career success to be evaluated by prejudiced evaluators wrote essays in response to test questions that were judged by people who read them as being counter to stereotypes about women compared to the essays written by women who were not expecting prejudiced evaluators. In the context of a test of career success, disconfirmation of gender stereotypes could be an asset, whereas a situation in which it is more important for people to get along could promote confirmation of gender stereotypes (Snyder & Haugen, 1995).

Primary control coping also may involve seeking out nonstigmatized people as mentors, friends, or other sources of social support. McLaughlin-Volpe (chap. 11, this volume) suggests that cross-group friendships can benefit stigmatized people by providing them access to resources (e.g., information about the situation) that might otherwise be denied them.

Much of the recent research on primary control coping has examined when and how stigmatized people confront prejudice (e.g., Kaiser, chap. 3, this volume; Shelton, Richeson, Salvatore, & Hill, chap. 4, this volume; Swim & Hyers, 1999). *Confrontation* is a general term that refers to behaviors or verbalizations that challenge the existence or expression of prejudice. Confronting prejudice can be a form of primary control coping because the hoped-for outcome is remedying the unjust situation either for the individual target of prejudice or for the stigmatized group as a whole.

There also is considerable evidence that stigmatized people use disengagement coping in response to stigma-related stressors. Disengagement often involves avoidance of social interactions with prejudiced people. For example, women avoid interacting with men who have reputations for being sexual harassers or sexists (Swim et al., 1998); women who expect that they will be stereotyped avoid interacting in situations in which gender stereotypes are applicable (Pinel, 1999); and college students who expect others to be prejudiced or to stereotype them avoid cross-group interactions (Mendoza-Denton, Page-Gould, & Pietrzak, chap. 8, this volume). Avoidance coping may not be feasible in situations in which stigmatized people typically are in the minority (Inzlicht & Good, chap. 7, this volume). For example, African American college students on a campus in which European Americans are the overwhelming majority may find it virtually impossible to use avoidance of interracial contact as a way of coping.

However, stigmatized people can also psychologically disengage from threatening situations even if they cannot actually avoid those situations. For example, there is abundant evidence that African Americans cope with stereotypes about their intellectual inferiority by disengaging from academic domains (Crocker et al., 1998; Major, Spencer, Schmader, Wolfe, & Crocker, 1998). Although physically present in academic settings, their self-esteem may be invested elsewhere. Of course, psychological disengagement can often result in leaving the stigma-threatened situation, as is the case, for example, when an African American drops out of school.

One common way in which some stigmatized people can avoid the consequences of their stigmatized status is to conceal their stigma from others (Crocker & Garcia, chap. 14, this volume; Crocker et al., 1998; Meyer, 2003; Quinn, chap. 5, this volume). Hiding one's stigmatized status avoids many of the stressors that result from stigma. If nobody knows about the stigmatized person's stigma, the stigmatized person will not have to deal with problems created by prejudice, stereotyping, and discrimination. Concealing a stigma or "passing" as a nonstigmatized person is a coping response that obviously is available only for certain kinds of stigmas. Stigmatizing conditions that are highly visible (e.g., ethnic group membership, gender, weight) cannot be concealed in any situation in which the stigmatized person is visible to others. Some behaviorally-based stigmas (e.g., severe alcoholism) also are virtually impossible to conceal successfully because the stigmatized person is unlikely to be able to control behaviors that signal the stigmatized state. Many other stigmas are potentially concealable even though it may take considerable effort to do so.

It is important to realize that a particular coping response may serve different goals depending on the goals the stigmatized person is seeking to achieve in a particular situation. For example, seeking social support can function as secondary control coping when it is aimed at helping the stigmatized person deal with the emotional and cognitive responses that they have to prejudice. Social support also can be used as a primary control coping response when, for example, stigmatized people band together to demand better treatment or seek out mentors and other advocates who will prevent others from acting on their prejudice. Similarly, emotional regulation is often the goal of secondary control coping. Stigmatized people may use distraction, wishful thinking, and cognitive reframing to help them feel good about themselves and avoid negative emotional states even though a prejudiced event has occurred. Emotional regulation also can help stigmatized people use primary control coping. Confronting prejudice, for example, may require either controlling or stoking the fires of one's anger at injustice, depending on the probable success of a cool-headed approach or a aggressive approach. Performing in a skillful manner that will overwhelm the other person's prejudice may require that stigmatized people be able to control their anxiety about the possibility that they may fall short and confirm the other person's stereotypes about them.

COPING WITH STIGMA INVOLVES TRADEOFFS

Coping is not a panacea. Although people often believe that they find meaning and gain strength through adversity, coping responses require a commitment of personal resources that could otherwise be used for other endeavors. This is true of coping with any type of stressor, and it is true of coping with stigma-related stressors as well. Consequently, it is not surprising that as soon as stigma researchers turned their attention to how people cope with stigma, they quickly discovered that coping with stigma often involves hard choices between imperfect options. Coping responses typically involve weighing the benefits of the response against the costs that will be incurred in making it (Kaiser & Miller, in press; Swim & Thomas, chap. 6, this volume).

For example, the negative reactions that others have to a stigmatized person who makes a claim of discrimination (Kaiser, chap. 3, this volume; Kaiser & Miller, 2001a, 2003; Shelton, Richeson, Salvatore, & Hill, chap. 4, this volume) may be offset by the possibility that challenging prejudice will help reduce it. Shelton and Stewart (in press) pointed out that although identification to others as a target of prejudice may be personally costly, the group as a whole may benefit when prejudice is challenged. They found that although a woman who confronted a male confederate about sexist behavior that was part of a script he was instructed to follow was evaluated negatively by him, his overall level of sexism declined after the confrontation. Thus, confrontation, although personally costly, may have considerable benefit for the stigmatized group as a whole.

There also is growing evidence that many nonstigmatized people are motivated not to be prejudiced and try not to let prejudice affect how they treat stigmatized people (Devine, 1989; Shelton, 2003). When they fail, they experience negative affect and try to compensate for this failure by bending over backwards not to be prejudiced in subsequent interactions (Devine et al., 1991). These findings suggest that at least some nonstigmatized people might ultimately appreciate having their prejudice pointed out to them, although in the short term they may have a tendency to "shoot the messenger" by having a negative reaction to the bearer of the bad news.

The primary control coping responses of self-stereotyping and stereotype-consistent self-presentation can promote interpersonal harmony (Sinclair & Huntsinger, chap. 12, this volume; Snyder & Haugen, 1995; von Baeyer et al., 1981), but they also may justify continued prejudice against stigmatized people. Stereotype confirmation can also depress the self-esteem of stigmatized people, particularly because stereotypes typically characterize stigmatized people in negative terms (Fiske, 1998; Steele, 1997). Even the suspicion that one might confirm a negative group stereotype can impair the performance of stigmatized people (Inzlicht & Good, chap. 7, this volume; Mendoza-Denton, Page-Gould, & Pietrzak, chap. 8, this volume; Steele, 1997). In addition, stereotype confirmation may be so threatening to stigmatized people that confirmation of a stereotype by other members of the stigmatized group causes stigmatized people to feel personally ashamed (Schmader & Lickel, chap. 13, this volume). Other forms of primary control coping also can exact costs on stigmatized people. Drawing on behavioral skills to compensate for prejudice uses cognitive, emotional, and behavioral resources that stigmatized people may need to achieve other goals (Miller & Myers, 1998). Other forms of problem solving such as taking collective action to reduce or outlaw discrimination (Branscombe & Ellemers, 1998) can be personally costly and are often dangerous.

The chief drawback of secondary control coping responses is that they make stigmatized individuals feel better about the fact that their outcomes are poor because of prejudice, but do nothing to prevent those outcomes from occurring. Some forms of secondary control coping can even exacerbate the situation. For example, when ethnic minority students cope with negative stereotypes about their academic promise by devaluing the pursuit of academic excellence, they cut themselves off from achievement in a domain that is critical in today's world (Crocker et al., 1998; Major et al., 1998; Mendoza-Denton, Page-Gould, & Pietrzak, chap. 8, this volume).

Disengagement coping also can have a number of pitfalls. In fact, research on coping with many types of stressors indicates that avoidance coping generally has a poor track record (Zeldner & Endler, 1996). The tendency to avoid interactions with nonstigmatized people may be counterproductive because an enormous volume of research indicates that prejudice against minority groups is reduced by intergroup contact (Tropp, chap. 9, this volume). There also are some major drawbacks to avoiding stressors by stigma concealment. Concealing the stigma often deprives the stigmatized person of social support from similarly stigmatized individuals (Major, Richards, Cooper, Cozzarelli, & Zubek, 1998). Concealment can result in suppression of thoughts about the stigma. Thought suppression is notorious for producing rebound effects in which the person experiences intrusive thoughts about the thought being suppressed (Wegner, 1994), and people who conceal their stigmas often do experience intrusive thoughts about the stigmatizing condition (Major et al., 1998; Smart & Wegner, 1999).

Consideration of the tradeoffs involved in coping with stigma suggests that there may be no easy or cost-free way to cope with it. However, stigma-related stress may be no different in this respect than any other type of stress. These tradeoffs do suggest that stigmatized people have to weigh the costs and benefits of a coping response. This involves considering what they most want to accomplish in a particular situation. This is likely to vary for different stigmatized individuals, in different situations, at different points in time. Thus, there is not likely to be any one "adaptive" coping response.

MAINTAINING THE PERSPECTIVE OF THE STIGMATIZED PERSON

Stigma researchers have been in the forefront of appreciating the stigmatized person's perspective in understanding the consequences of prejudice. This appreciation is what gave rise to research on coping with stigma and has led to important advances in our understanding of when and why stigmatized people are resilient or vulnerable to the effects of prejudice.

Keeping the perspective of stigmatized people in mind is critical in any discussion of the outcomes of coping with prejudice. Otherwise, it is tempting to try to identify what constitutes "good" or "effective" coping with stigma without considering the goals of the stigmatized person. For example, Pinel (2002) found that women high in stigma consciousness virtually sabotaged an interaction with a man whom they believed was a sexist, but who actually an innocuous fellow participant selected because he was not particularly sexist, by negatively evaluating his contributions to an experimental task before he had a chance to evaluate their own contributions. This effect was mediated by the women's expectations that the man would evaluate them negatively. When finally given a chance to evaluate the women's contributions to the task, the men responded in kind to the women's evaluations of their work, and the entire interaction entered a vicious cycle in which neither party ended up thinking highly of the other.

This unfortunate turn of events could be considered an example of spectacularly bad coping, because the stigma-conscious women's behavior left little room for the men to disconfirm the women's expectations. A better interpretation may be to consider this as an example of a stigmatized person deciding that she would rather not waste her time or energy earning the respect of someone whose regard she did not value anyway.

Like anyone else, stigmatized people have limited resources at their disposal. They face the same stressors that anyone faces, plus they have the additional stressors created by prejudice. Trying to cope with everything may leave stigmatized people unable to cope with anything. Consequently, they may have to set priorities that sacrifice some potentially important outcomes in order to achieve the goals that are most important to them.

Researchers are just beginning to give serious attention to the goals that stigmatized people may be attempting to achieve when they cope with prejudice. One important insight that is emerging from these efforts is a reminder that stigmatized people have the same basic motivations as anyone else does. Swim and Thomas (chap. 6, this volume) suggest that five core social motives (belonging, self-enhancement, control, trust, and understanding) that have been used to describe human social motivation in general (Fiske, 2003) can be usefully applied to stigmatized people. Other stigma theorists have placed more emphasis on a particular motive. For example, McLaughlin-Volpe (chap. 11, this volume) emphasizes control over resources whereas Crocker focuses on the self-enhancement goal (Crocker & Garcia, chap. 14, this volume; Crocker & Major, 1989).

This emphasis on goals that stigmatized people share with everyone else reminds us that stigmatized people are *people* who have been stigmatized by others. Conceptualizing people who are stigmatized primarily as *stigma-*

tized people risks thinking too narrowly about what their goals are in coping with prejudice. This can lead to the assumption stigmatized people are always or primarily concerned with goals that are directly related to their status as a stigmatized people (such as whether they are confirming or disconfirming stereotypes) and that the only goal of primary control coping is reducing or eliminating prejudice.

Crocker and Garcia (chap. 14, this volume) argue that stigmatized and nonstigmatized people too often approach interactions with each other in an ego-defensive manner. Stigmatized people define the situation as one in which they can accept their devalued status (and suffer a loss of self-esteem) or one in which they can maintain their self-worth by castigating the other person as prejudiced. Being suspected of prejudice makes nonstigmatized people anxious, uncomfortable, and perhaps even angry. This causes them to behave in ways that confirm the stigmatized person's fears about the interaction. According to Crocker and Garcia, this cycle of mistrust and suspicion can be broken if both stigmatized and nonstigmatized people focus on goals other than defending their egos, for example by focusing on (a) what can be learned in the situation, (b) how both parties can be included in each other's goals, and (c) striving for goals that are larger than the individual. Consideration of the variety of ways in which stigmatized people cope with stigma-related stressors and the way in which they tailor their responses to the situation at hand to achieve the goals that are most important to them suggests that many stigmatized people need no introduction to these ideas.

REFERENCES

Allison, K. W. (1998). Stress and oppressed social category membership. In J. K. Swim & C. Stangor (Eds.), *Prejudice: The target's perspective* (pp. 149–171). San Diego, CA: Academic Press.

Allport, G. (1954). *The nature of prejudice*. New York: Doubleday Anchor.

Barreto, M., & Ellemers, N. (in press). The perils of political correctness: Responses of men and women to old-fashioned and modern sexist views. *Social Psychology Quarterly*.

Branscombe, N. R., & Ellemers, N. (1998). Coping with group-based discrimination: Individualistic versus group-level strategies. In J. K. Swim & C. Stangor (Eds.), *Prejudice: The target's perspective* (pp. 243–266). San Diego, CA: Academic Press.

Branscombe, N. R., Schmitt, M. T., & Harvey, R. D. (1999). Perceiving pervasive discrimination among African Americans: Implications for group identification and well-being. *Journal of Personality and Social Psychology, 77,* 135–149.

Clark, R., Anderson, N. B., Clark, V. R., & Williams, D. R. (1999). Racism as a stressor for African Americans: A biopsychosocial model. *American Psychologist, 54*, 805–816.

Compas, B. E., Connor-Smith, J. K., Saltzman, H., Thompsen, A. H., & Wadsworth, M. E. (2001). Coping with stress during childhood and adolescence: Problems, progress and potential in theory and research. *Psychological Bulletin, 127*, 87–127.

Connor-Smith, J. K., Compas, B. E., Wadsworth, M. E., Thompsen, A. H., & Saltzman, H. (2000). Responses to stress in adolescence: Measurement of coping and involuntary stress responses. *Journal of Consulting and Clinical Psychology, 68*, 976–992.

Crandall, C. S., & Eshleman, A. (2003). A justification-suppression model of the expression and experience of prejudice. *Psychological Bulletin, 129*, 414–446.

Crandall, C. S., Eshleman, A., & O'Brien, L. (2002). Social norms and the expression and suppression of prejudice: The struggle for internalization. *Journal of Personality and Social Psychology, 82*, 359–378.

Crocker, J., & Major, B. (1989). Stigma and self-esteem: The self-protective properties of stigma. *Psychological Review, 96*, 608–630.

Crocker, J., Major, B., & Steele, C. (1998). Social stigma. In D. Gilbert, S. T. Fiske, & G. Lindzey (Eds.), *Handbook of social psychology* (4th ed., Vol. 2, pp. 504–553). New York: McGraw-Hill.

Devine, P. G. (1989). Stereotypes and prejudice: Their automatic and controlled components. *Journal of Personality and Social Psychology, 56*, 5–18.

Devine, P., Monteith, M., Zuwerink, J., & Elliot, A. (1991). Prejudice with and without compunction. *Journal of Personality and Social Psychology, 60*, 817–830.

Dovidio, J. F., & Gaertner, S. L. (1998). On the nature of contemporary prejudice: The causes, consequences, and challenges of aversive racism. In J. L. Eberhardt & S. T. Fiske (Eds.), *Confronting racism: The problem and the response* (pp. 3–32). Newbury Park, CA: Sage.

Dovidio, J. F., Kawakami, K., & Gaertner, S. L. (2002). Implicit and explicit prejudice and interracial interaction. *Journal of Personality and Social Psychology, 82*, 62–68.

Duckitt, J. (1992). Psychology and prejudice: A historical analysis and integrative framework. *American Psychologist, 47*, 1182–1193.

Feagin, J. R., & Sikes, M. P. (1994). *Living with racism: The Black middle-class experience*. Boston, MA: Beacon Press.

Farina, A., Allen, J., & Saul, B. (1968). The role of the stigmatized person in affecting social relationships. *Journal of Personality, 36*, 169–182.

Fiske, S. T. (1998). Stereotyping, prejudice, and discrimination. In D. T. Gilbert, S. T. Fiske, & G. Lindzey (Eds.), *Handbook of social psychology* (4th ed., Vol. 2, pp. 357–414). New York: McGraw-Hill.

Fiske, S. T. (2003). Five core social motives, plus or minus five. In S. J. Spencer, S. Fein, M. P. Zanna, & J. M. Olson (Eds.), *Motivated social perception: The Ontario symposium, Vol. 9* (pp. 233–246). Mahwah, NJ: Lawrence Erlbaum Associates.

Fiske, S. T., Cuddy, A. C., Glick, P., & Xu, J. (2002). The model of (often mixed) stereotype content: Competence and warmth respectively follow from perceived status and competition. *Journal of Personality and Social Psychology, 82*, 878–902.

Gaertner, S. L., & Dovidio, J. F. (1986). The aversive form of racism. In S. L. Gaertner & J. F. Dovidio (Eds.), *Prejudice, discrimination, and racism* (pp. 61–89). San Diego, CA: Academic Press.

Glick, P., & Fiske, S. T. (2001). An ambivalent alliance: Hostile and benevolent sexism as complementary justifications for gender inequality. *American Psychologist, 56*, 109–118.

Goldman, W., & Lewis, P. (1977). Beautiful is good: Evidence that the physically attractive are more socially skillful. *Journal of Experimental Social Psychology, 13*, 125–130.

Heatherton, T. F., Kleck, R. E., Hebl, M. R., & Hull, J. G. (Eds.). (2000). *The social psychology of stigma*. New York: Guilford.

Jacobson, C. K. (1977). Separatism, integrationism, and avoidance among Black, White, and Latin adolescents. *Social Forces, 55*, 1011–1027.

Katz, I., & Hass, R. G. (1988). Racial ambivalence and American value conflict: Correlational and priming studies of dual cognitive structures. *Journal of Personality and Social Psychology, 55*, 893–905.

Kaiser, C. R., & Miller, C. T. (2001a). Reacting to impending discrimination: Compensation for prejudice and attributions to discrimination. *Personality and Social Psychology Bulletin, 27*, 1357–1367.

Kaiser, C. R., & Miller, C. T. (2001b). Stop complaining! The social costs of making attributions to discrimination. *Personality and Social Psychology Bulletin, 27*, 254–263.

Kaiser, C. R., & Miller, C. T. (2003). Derogating the victim: The interpersonal consequences of blaming events on discrimination. *Group Processes and Intergroup Relations, 6*, 227–237.

Kaiser, C. R., & Miller, C. T. (in press). A stress and coping perspective on confronting sexism. *Psychology of Women Quarterly*.

Kleck, R. E., & Strenta, A. (1980). Perceptions of the impact of negatively valued physical characteristics on social interaction. *Journal of Personality and Social Psychology, 39*, 861–873.

Lazarus, R. S., & Folkman, S. (1984). *Stress, appraisal, and coping*. New York: Springer.

Lerner, M. J., & Miller, D. T. (1978). Just world research and the attribution process: Looking back and ahead. *Psychological Bulletin, 85*, 1030–1051.

Major, B., Quinton, W. J., & McCoy, S. K. (2002). Antecedents and consequences of attributions to discrimination: Theoretical and empirical advances. In M. Zanna (Ed.), *Advances in experimental social psychology* (Vol. 34, pp. 251–330). San Diego, CA: Academic Press.

Major, B., Richards, M. C., Cooper, M. L., Cozzarelli, C., & Zubek, J. (1998). Personal resilience, cognitive appraisals, and coping: An integrative model of adjustment to abortion. *Journal of Personality and Social Psychology, 74*, 735–752.

Major, B., Spencer, S., Schmader, T., Wolfe, C., & Crocker, J. (1998). Coping with negative stereotypes about intellectual performance: The role of psychological disengagement. *Personality and Social Psychology Bulletin, 24*, 34–50.

Mendoza-Denton, R., Downey, G., Purdie, V. J., Davis, A., & Pietrzak, J. (2002). Sensitivity to status-based rejection: Implications for African American students' college experience. *Journal of Personality and Social Psychology, 83*, 896–918.

Meyer, I. H. (2003). Prejudice, social stress, and mental health in lesbian, gay, and bisexual populations: Conceptual issues and research evidence. *Psychological Bulletin, 129*, 674–697.

Miller, C. T., & Kaiser, C. R. (2001). A theoretical perspective on coping with stigma. *Journal of Social Issues, 57*, 73–92.

Miller, C. T., & Krulewitz, J. (2003, October). *Identification to self and other as a victim of discrimination.* Paper presented at the Society of Experimental Social Psychology Self Pre-Conference, Boston, MA.

Miller, C. T., & Major, B. (2000). Coping with stigma and prejudice. In T. F. Heatherton, R. E. Kleck, M. R. Hebl, & J. G. Hull (Eds.), *The social psychology of stigma* (pp. 243–272). New York: Guilford.

Miller, C. T., & Myers, A. M. (1998). Compensating for prejudice: How obese people (and others) control outcomes despite prejudice. In J. K. Swim & C. Stangor (Eds.), *Prejudice: The target's perspective* (pp. 191–218). San Diego, CA: Academic Press.

Miller, C. T., Rothblum, E., Barbour, L., Brand, P., & Felicio, D. (1990). Social interactions of obese and nonobese women. *Journal of Personality, 58*, 365–380.

Miller, C. T., Rothblum, E., Felicio, D., & Brand, P. (1995). Compensating for stigma: Obese and nonobese women's reactions to being visible. *Personality and Social Psychology Bulletin, 21*, 1093–1106.

Miller, D. T., & Turnbull, W. (1986). Expectancies and interpersonal processes. *Annual Review of Psychology, 37*, 233–256.

Nisbett, R. E., & Ross, L. (1980). *Human inference: Strategies and shortcomings in social judgment.* Englewood Cliffs, NJ: Prentice-Hall.

Pinel, E. C. (1999). Stigma consciousness: The psychological legacy of social stereotypes. *Journal of Personality and Social Psychology, 76*, 114–128.

Pinel, E. (2002). Stigma consciousness in intergroup contexts: The power of conviction. *Journal of Experimental Social Psychology, 38*, 178–185.

Rosenthal, R., & Rubin, D. B. (1978). Interpersonal expectancy effects: The first 345 studies. *Behavioral and Brain Sciences, 3*, 377–386.

Shelton, J. N. (2000). A reconceptualization of how we study issues of racial prejudice. *Personality and Social Psychology Review, 4*, 374–390.

Shelton, J. N. (2003). Interpersonal concerns in social encounters between majority and minority group members. *Group Processes and Intergroup Relations, 6*, 171–185.

Shelton, J. N., & Stewart, S. (in press). Confronting sexism: The inhibitory role of social costs. *Psychology of Women Quarterly.*

Smart, L., & Wegner, D. (1999). Covering up what can't be seen: Concealable stigma and mental control. *Journal of Personality and Social Psychology, 77*, 474–486.

Snyder, M., & Haugen, J. A. (1995). Why does behavioral confirmation occur? A functional perspective on the role of the target. *Personality and Social Psychology Bulletin, 9,* 963–974.

Snyder, M., Tanke, E. D., & Berscheid, E. (1977). Social perception and interpersonal behavior: On the self-fulfilling nature of social stereotypes. *Journal of Personality and Social Psychology, 35*, 656–666.

Steckler, N. A., & Rosenthal, R. (1985). Sex differences in nonverbal and verbal communication with bosses, peers, and subordinates. *Journal of Applied Psychology, 70*, 17–163.

Steele, C. M. (1997). A threat in the air: How stereotypes shape intellectual identity and performance. *American Psychologist, 52*, 613–629.

Swim, J. K., Cohen, L. L., & Hyers, L. L. (1998). Experiencing everyday prejudice and discrimination. In J. K. Swim & C. Stangor (Eds.), *Prejudice: The target's perspective* (pp. 37–60). San Diego, CA: Academic Press.

Swim, J. K., & Hyers, L. L. (1999). Excuse me—What did you just say? Women's public and private responses to sexist remarks. *Journal of Experimental Social Psychology, 35*, 68–88.

Swim, J. K., Scott, E. D., Sechrist, G. B., Campbell, B., & Stangor, C. (2003). The role of intent and harm in perceptions of prejudice and discrimination. *Journal of Personality and Social Psychology, 84*, 944–959.

Swim, J. K., & Stangor, C. (Eds.). (1998). *Prejudice: The target's perspective*. San Diego, CA: Academic Press.

Tomaka, J., Blascovich, J., Kelsey, R. M., & Leitten, C. L. (1993). Subjective, physiological, and behavioral effects of threat and challenge appraisal. *Journal of Personality and Social Psychology, 65,* 248–260.

Twenge, J. M., & Crocker, J. (2000). Race and self-esteem: Meta-analyses comparing Whites, Blacks, Hispanics, Asians, and American Indians and comment on Gray-Little and Hafdahl (2000). *Psychological Bulletin, 128*, 371–408.

von Baeyer, C. L., Sherk, D. L., & Zanna, M. P. (1981). Impression management in the job interview: When the female applicant meets the male (chauvinist) interviewer. *Personality and Social Psychology Bulletin, 7,* 45–51.

Wegner, D. M. (1994). Ironic processes of mental control. *Psychological Review, 101*, 34–52.

Wegner, D. M., & Wheatley, T. (1999). Apparent mental causation: Sources of the experience of will. *American Psychologist, 54*, 480–492.

Woodzika, J. A., & LaFrance, M. (2001). Real versus imagined gender harassment. *Journal of Social Issues, 57,* 15–30.

Word, C. O., Zanna, M. P., & Cooper, J. (1974). The nonverbal mediation of self-fulfilling prophecies in interracial interaction. *Journal of Experimental Social Psychology, 10,* 109–120.

Wright, S. C., Taylor, D. M., & Moghaddam, F. M. (1990). Responding to membership in a disadvantaged group: From acceptance to collective protest. *Journal of Personality and Social Psychology, 35*, 68–88.

Zeldner, M., & Endler, N. S. (Eds.). (1996). *Handbook of coping.* New York: John Wiley & Sons.

Zirkel, S., & Cantor, N. (2004). 50 years after *Brown V. Board of Education*: The promise and challenge of multicultural education. *Journal of Social Issues, 60*, 1–15.

CHAPTER

3

Dominant Ideology Threat and the Interpersonal Consequences of Attributions to Discrimination

Cheryl R. Kaiser
Michigan State University

Although psychologists have studied prejudice for nearly a century, it has been only recently that attention has turned toward understanding the consequences of prejudice for its targets, those who are stigmatized (see Crocker, Major, & Steele, 1998; Major, Quinton, & McCoy, 2002, for reviews). *Stigmatized individuals* possess or are perceived to possess an attribute conveying a devalued social identity within a social context (Crocker et al., 1998). Examples of groups that are stigmatized in North America include racial and ethnic minorities, women, gay men and lesbians, people with heavy body weights, and individuals belonging to nontraditional religious groups. The stigmatized encounter discrimination in many domains including restricted access to resources such as employment, income, housing, and education (see R. Clark, Anderson, V. R. Clark, & Williams, 1999, for a review). Additionally, the stigmatized experience many forms of social threat, including being ignored, rejected, disrespected, and patronized (Hebl, Foster, Mannix, & Dovidio, 2002; Swim, Hyers, Cohen, & Ferguson, 2001). Thus, one important goal of research on stigma involves understanding how members of stigmatized groups cope with the predicaments posed by being the target of prejudice and discrimination (Miller, chap. 2, this volume; Swim & Thomas, chap. 6, this volume).

Attributing events to discrimination is a coping strategy that has received considerable attention in recent years (see Crocker & Major, 2003; Major et al., 2002; Major, McCoy, Kaiser, & Quinton, 2003; Schmitt & Branscombe, 2002b, for reviews). Attributions to discrimination are judgments of unfair treatment stemming from one's social identity (Major et al., 2002). In their seminal analysis of discrimination and self-esteem, Crocker and Major (1989) drew upon Kelley's (1973) discounting principle to argue that the awareness of being the target of discrimination offers members of stigmatized groups the opportunity to discount stable, internal, controllable attributes of the self as a cause of negative outcomes and can thus serve a self-esteem protective function. Crocker and Major's (1989) theoretical analysis has proven to be extremely generative and has provided the groundwork for many important theoretical and empirical advances on this topic (see Crocker & Major, 2003; Major et al., 2002; Major, McCoy, et al., 2003; Schmitt & Branscombe, 2002b, for reviews of this work).

However, despite the recent theoretical and empirical advances made in research on the consequences of attributions to discrimination, this work has remained almost exclusively focused on the intrapersonal consequences of these judgments. Although we now know quite a bit about the self-esteem and affective consequences of attributions to discrimination, we still know very little about other types of consequences these judgments might pose. In this chapter, I examine a less studied consequence of attributions to discrimination: the consequences of these judgments for interpersonal relationships.

The case of Bassem Youssef, a high-ranking Arab American FBI agent, who filed a discrimination lawsuit against the agency in 2002, illustrates these interpersonal consequences. Youssef, an American citizen who was born in Egypt, had worked with the agency for 15 years and had an excellent grasp of Arabic languages and Middle Eastern culture. Prior to the September 11, 2001, terrorist attacks on the United States, Youssef had worked extensively in counterterrorism, receiving consistently exceptional performance evaluations, commendation from both American and Arabic leaders, and a highly coveted Director of Central Intelligence Award. Youssef's discrimination claim states that after 9-11, he hit a glass ceiling and was blocked from counterterrorism assignments for which he was uniquely qualified, and that this negative treatment was due to his national origin. After Youssef discussed his perceived discriminatory treatment with his supervisor, he reported experiencing retaliation from the bureau. For example, Youssef learned at a public meeting that another agent would be taking over his job. Youssef also claimed that his responsibilities continued to be stripped from him, and that he was treated disrespectfully and was told that his actions disparaged the agency. This poor interpersonal treatment led Youssef to later add a charge of retaliation to his claim.

As this case illustrates, publicly claiming to be a target of prejudice can have negative interpersonal ramifications. Youssef's retaliatory experience is not uncommon. In 2002, retaliation charges represented over one quarter of the Equal Employment Opportunity Commission discrimination-related

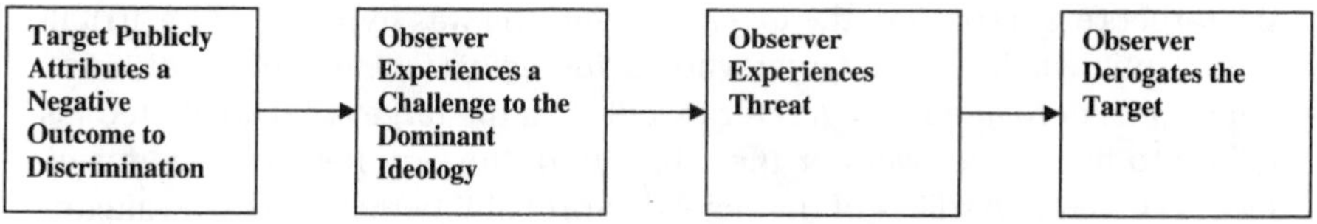

FIG. 3.1. Dominant ideology threat model of reactions to discrimination claimants.

charges (Nielson & Nelson, in press). In this chapter, I explore the interpersonal consequences of public attributions to discrimination. I first describe research demonstrating that attributions to discrimination are interpersonally costly. I then integrate these findings within a dominant ideology threat model of reactions to discrimination claims (see Fig. 3.1). This model argues that discrimination claims threaten core U.S. cultural beliefs, such as those contending that America is a fair place in which any individual or any group can get ahead through hard work and effort. Furthermore, individuals who strongly endorse this belief system or who are in situations where these beliefs are salient will feel threatened and will be particularly likely to derogate the discrimination claimant. I present research investigating these hypotheses and discuss the theoretical and applied implications of this research.

ATTRIBUTIONS TO DISCRIMINATION ARE INTERPERSONALLY COSTLY

Several studies demonstrate that individuals who publicly attribute events to discrimination incur negative interpersonal ramifications. Kaiser and Miller (2001) provided the first empirical test of the hypothesis that attributions to discrimination are interpersonally costly. They had predominantly White participants read a description of a Black man who had received a failing test grade. In addition, participants learned that the test administrator had informed the target person that either that there was no chance, a 50% chance, or a 100% chance that a racist White evaluator graded the target's test. Participants then examined a survey ostensibly completed by the target in which he indicated that his grade was due primarily to either discrimination, his inadequate test answers (an internal attribution), or to the difficulty of the test (an external attribution). Both internal and external attribution control groups were included because discrimination attributions have two loci of causality. They are internal because they implicate a part of the self (one's social identity) as the cause of negative feedback, and external because they implicate external factors (another person) as the cause of negative feedback (Major, Kaiser, & McCoy, 2003; Schmitt & Branscombe, 2002a). All participants then completed a measure of derogation of the target (e.g., ratings of the extent to which he was hypersensitive, irritating, a troublemaker). The target who attributed his failing grade to discrimination was derogated to a greater extent than the target who attributed his failure to his test answers or the difficulty of the test. Remarkably, this effect occurred regardless of the objective probability that a racist evaluator graded the target's test. In other words, the target who blamed a failure on discrimination experienced damage to his reputation even when prejudice was clearly responsible for the event (see Fig. 3.2).

Although the Kaiser and Miller (2001) experiment is consistent with the hypothesis that individuals who blame events on discrimination rather than other causes are derogated, participants in that experiment never saw direct evidence that the test grader was racist (i.e., participants received base rate information delivered by the test administer to the target person). Even though this second-hand base rate manipulation of prejudice was successful in establishing different levels of perceived prejudice in the experimental situation, it is possible that the participants' insensitivity to the amount of prejudice facing the target person occurred because this information lacked emotional saliency or credibility that might otherwise arise from seeing this information directly from the perpetrator of discrimination (e.g., Fazio & Zanna, 1978). Relative to information obtained indirectly, direct information is more confidently held, more cognitively accessible, and more likely to influence subsequent behavior (Fazio & Zanna, 1978, 1981).

In a subsequent experiment, Kaiser and Miller (2003) addressed this limitation by directly exposing participants to the source of prejudice. In this

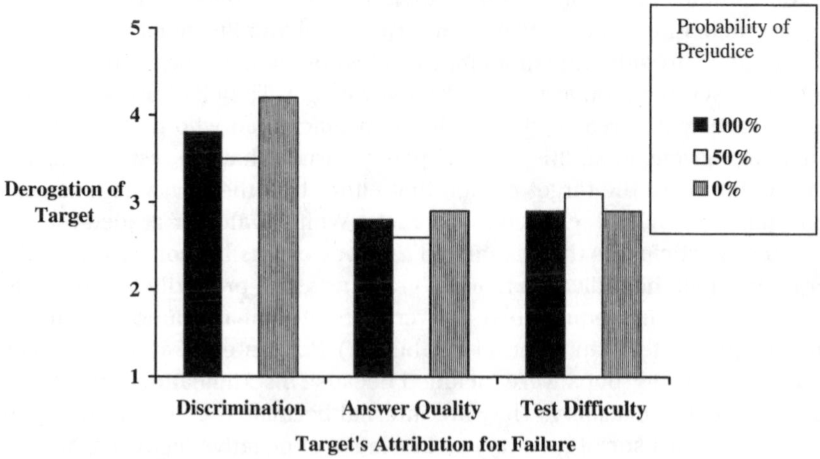

FIG. 3.2. Derogation of an African American target as a function of the target's attributions for failure and the chance of prejudice. Data from Kaiser and Miller (2001).

experiment, predominantly White college students participated in a study purportedly on employment processes. Participants reviewed the material of an African American job candidate (his race was conveyed by including a picture of a professionally dressed African American man) who failed to receive a job he desired. Participants then read comments purportedly made by the White interviewer in charge of the hiring decision that expressed either no animosity toward Blacks, moderate levels of racism, or blatant old-fashioned racism (i.e., he made statements such as "Black people are just not as smart as White people" and "I have never hired a Black person and I never will"). Participants then viewed a survey ostensibly completed by the job candidate in which he attributed his job rejection to discrimination, his poor interviewing skills, or the strong competition for the job. Consistent with Kaiser and Miller (2001), the applicant who blamed his rejection on discrimination still was derogated more than the applicant who blamed his rejection on other causes; even when he faced blatant old-fashioned racism.

These negative interpersonal reactions to discrimination claimants are not limited to Whites' reactions to Blacks. Shelton and Stewart (2004) demonstrated that women also incur negative interpersonal costs when they publicly acknowledge sexism. In this experiment, male participants were instructed to conduct job interviews with female participants. The men received a list of interview questions and were trained to behave consistently during the interviews. Half of the men were assigned to read a set of interview questions (which were adapted from Woodzicka & LaFrance, 2001) that contained several sexist questions ("Do you have a boyfriend?," "Do people find you desirable?," and "Do you think it is important for women to wear bras to work?") and the other half were assigned to read a set of questions that were rated as equally offensive as the former questions but irrelevant to sexism. The interviews were videotaped, and after the interviews were completed, the men completed dependent measures including the extent to which the women were complainers (i.e., perceived as argumentative, troublemakers, complainers). Raters then watched the videotaped interviews and indicated the extent to which the women job applicants confronted the men's sexist or offensive comments. When the women were asked sexist questions, the more they confronted the sexist remarks, the more the men who interviewed them saw them as complainers and perceived them less favorably. These relationships did not appear when women were subjected to offensive but nonsexist interview questions.

Likewise, Dodd, Giuliano, Boutell, and Moran (2001) examined participants' reactions to women who confronted or failed to confront a man who made sexist comments. In this study, participants read a scenario about a woman who was subjected to sexist comments and who either confronted or ignored the comments. Men who read about a woman who confronted sexist comments liked her less than when they read that she did not confront the comments. Although this study lacks a control group in which a woman makes a confrontation that is irrelevant to sexism, it does converge with studies showing that people who publicly acknowledge prejudice are disliked.

These laboratory experiments showing that people who publicly attribute events to prejudice are disliked are consistent with retrospective survey research. Survey research indicates that targets of prejudice believe that publicly claiming discrimination is socially costly and frequently anticipate being perceived as a troublemaker and targeted for retaliation when they do make such claims (Feagin & Sikes, 1994; Fitzgerald, Swan, & Fischer, 1995; Haslett & Lipman, 1997; Kaiser & Miller, 2004; Near & Jensen, 1983). For example, in a study of female attorneys' responses to sexism in the workplace, none of the women reported that confronting a peer's sexist behavior improved the relationship (Haslett & Lipman, 1997). At best the relationship remained the same and at worst the relationship deteriorated. In another study, 40% of women who brought sexual harassment allegations against their employers reported that the company responded by retaliating against them (Near & Jensen, 1983). Likewise, interviews with African Americans reveal that they anticipate social backlash from publicly attributing events to discrimination (Feagin & Sikes, 1994).

Having established that public attributions to prejudice are interpersonally costly, I next turn toward integrating this work within a dominant ideology threat theoretical framework (see Fig. 3.1). I begin by discussing U.S. dominant ideology and then explore the consequences of threats to this belief system. I then discuss research examining attributions to discrimination as a source of dominant ideology threat.

THE DOMINANT IDEOLOGY

Independence, the Protestant ethic, and the American dream are three pervasive values in the United States (de Tocqueville, 1840/1945; Plaut, Markus, & Lachman, 2002; Weber, 1904/1958). *Independence* involves the need for autonomy and the belief that success depends upon self-reliance and stamina (Triandis, 1995). The *Protestant ethic* is a moral imperative emphasizing the superiority of hard work, commitment, and industriousness (Weber, 1904/1958). The *American dream* combines notions about individualism, self-interest, and the Protestant ethic, and argues that the greatest good is to be individually successful and that almost anyone, regardless of his or her life circumstances, can get to the top through dedication, perseverance, and hard work (Hochschild, 1995; G. D. Spindler & L. S. Spindler, 1990). The collective endorsement of these values, norms, and beliefs in the United States has led this cultural belief system to be dubbed "the dominant ideology" (see Kluegel & Smith, 1986, for a review).

The dominant ideology has been theoretically conceptualized and empirically assessed with a number of related constructs, including individualism, the Protestant ethic, the belief in a just world, meritocracy beliefs, hierarchy enhancing beliefs, and individual mobility beliefs (e.g., Davey, Bobocel, Son Hing, & Zanna, 1999; Katz & Hass, 1988; Lerner, 1980; Major, 1994; Major, Kaiser, McCoy, & O'Brien, 2005; Quinn & Crocker, 1999; Sidanius & Pratto, 1999). The dominant ideology can also be manipulated with primes serving to activate these constructs (Biernat, Vescio, & Theno, 1996; Major et al., 2004; Quinn & Crocker, 1999). These beliefs share a common feature—they locate the causes of events internally within attributes of individuals and groups and hold individuals and groups responsible for their position in life. Thus, the dominant ideology creates the perception that individuals and groups who succeed in life are responsible for their success because they have worked hard; individuals and groups who experience failure are responsible for their outcomes because they simply have not worked hard enough.

Although the dominant ideology is part of a largely shared cultural value system, individuals do differ in the extent to which they endorse the ideology. Relative to weak endorsers of the dominant ideology, strong endorsers tend to (a) perceive the government as more fair, (b) place a high value on obedience, (c) accept inequalities in society as fair, (d) possess an internal locus of control, (e) possess a conservative political orientation, and (f) are less tolerant of members of stigmatized groups (see Furnham & Procter, 1989; Jost, Glaser, Kruglanski, & Sulloway, 2003; Lerner & Miller, 1978, for reviews). Among members of stigmatized groups, endorsing the dominant ideology is associated with lower self-esteem when faced with evidence of prejudice against their group (Major et al., 2005).

The dominant ideology serves several important functions for those who endorse it. First, it provides individuals with the perception that their social world is orderly, controllable, and predictable (Erickson, 1950; Greenberg, Solomon, & Pyszczynski, 1997; Jost & Banaji, 1994; Lerner, 1980), and these perceptions have a number of important benefits including enhanced motivation, performance, well-being, and mental health (Greenberg et al., 1997; Janoff-Bulman, 1989; Tomaka & Blascovich, 1994). Second, the dominant ideology provides individuals with the ability to make sense of negative events in their social world (Kluegel & Smith, 1986; Lerner & Miller, 1978). People and groups who experience negative outcomes have not worked hard enough and hence deserve their fate and are morally flawed. This explanatory style is adaptive because it provides individuals with a sense of hope about their future outcomes and protects them from feeling vulnerable to failure. As long as they work hard, they can achieve anything. Indeed, the more individuals endorse the dominant ideology, the more ambitious their life aspirations and goals (Mirels & Darland, 1990) and the less vulnerable they feel about experiencing a variety of negative events (Lambert, Burroughs, & Nguyen, 1999).

THREATS TO THE DOMINANT IDEOLOGY

What happens, however, when individuals encounter evidence that challenges the dominant ideology? A number of theoretical perspectives posit that individuals who have their worldviews challenged experience a heightened sense of fear, uncertainty, discomfort, and threat; and that one way to alleviate this discomfort is by punishing the source of the threat (Crocker & Garcia, chap. 14, this volume; Greenberg et al., 1997; Janoff-Bulman, 1989; Jost & Hunyady, 2002; Lerner, 1980). For instance, terror management theory argues that our cultural worldviews serve as the foundation for our self-esteem, and when these worldviews are threatened, we will experience discomfort and engage in behaviors to defend our worldview, such as punishing those who challenge our views and rewarding those who affirm our views (Greenberg et al., 1997). Likewise, Lerner's *just-world hypothesis* is predicated on the belief that innocent victims are so threatening to benevolent beliefs about the world that the more innocent they are, the more we convince ourselves that they deserve their fate so that we can protect ourselves from the distressing possibility that the world is not just and fair after all. Finally, *system justification theory* argues that individuals are motivated to justify existing beliefs and ideologies and will sometimes do so even when these beliefs contribute to the derogation and disadvantaged state of one's personal self and social groups (Jost & Banaji, 1994; Jost & Hunyady, 2002). These perspectives provide converging evidence that threats to one's worldview are indeed unsettling and motivate individuals to restore or reaffirm their belief systems.

A study by Kaiser, Vick, and Major (2004) demonstrated these psychological responses to threats against the worldview within the context of the 9-11 terrorist attacks against the United States. Kaiser and colleagues examined individuals' endorsement of just-world beliefs prior to the 9-11 terrorist attacks, an event which represented a severe challenge to this belief system, and then 2 months after the terrorist attacks examined the threat stemming from the attacks as well as the desire for revenge against the terrorists. Results revealed that the more individuals endorsed just world beliefs prior to September 11, 2001, the more threat they experienced after the terrorist attacks and the more they desired revenge against the terrorists. Furthermore, the relationship between just-world beliefs and the desire for revenge was mediated by threat. Thus, this study was consistent with theoretical perspectives arguing that worldview threat is distressing and can lead to restoration efforts through means such as punishing the source of the threat.

ATTRIBUTIONS TO DISCRIMINATION AS A SOURCE OF DOMINANT IDEOLOGY THREAT

Central to my argument is the notion that stigmatized group members' attributions to discrimination threaten the dominant ideology. These judgments call into question the basic assumptions upon which the dominant ideology is based, and thus serve as a source of ideology threat. Attributions to discrimination challenge the dominant ideology in a number of ways. These judgments threaten beliefs about autonomy, self-reliance, and personal control. That is, they communicate that effort and persistence are not sufficient to produce success and that even if we work hard, we will not always succeed. Attributions to discrimination also challenge prescriptive norms of the dominant ideology, which argue that individuals should take personal responsibility for their outcomes and should locate the causes of events internally, within personal attributes. Finally, attributions to discrimination convey that some groups in society are unable to obtain the American dream. In short, when individuals encounter stigmatized individuals who publicly blame events on discrimination, these accusations can undermine basic assumptions about the world, which can result in threat and distress.

This dominant ideology threat posed by discrimination claims is expressed by Shelby Steele (1990) in his essays, *The Content of Our Character:*

> The race-holder whines, or complains indiscriminately, not because he seeks redress, but because he seeks the status of a victim, a status that excuses him from what he fears. A victim is not responsible for his position, and by claiming a victim's status, the race-holder gives up a sense of personal responsibility he needs to better his condition. (p. 33)

Likewise, in his book, *A Nation of Victims*, Charles Sykes (1992) argued: "Unfortunately, that [perceived victimization] is a formula for social gridlock: the irresistible search for someone or something to blame colliding with unmovable unwillingness to accept responsibility" (p. 15). As these quotations illustrate, individuals who claim to be victims of discrimination threaten the dominant ideological premise that personal responsibility is the primary determinant of and proper route to success. Furthermore, because discrimination claims pose a threat to the important beliefs upon which U.S. culture rests, they by extension threaten the orderliness of the social world.

According to the dominant ideology threat model of reactions to discrimination claimants, challenges to the dominant ideology should be threatening and should motivate individuals to restore their faith in the worldview by finding fault in the character of those who threaten their belief system. This argument lends itself to the prediction that individuals who strongly endorse the dominant ideology or who are in situations in which these beliefs are salient will feel particularly threatened in the presence of stigmatized individuals who blame events on discrimination and will be especially likely to derogate those individuals (see Fig. 3.1). I next turn to reviewing empirical research that addresses these predictions.

THE MODERATING ROLE OF DOMINANT IDEOLOGY ENDORSEMENT

Perceived Threat

The model presented in Fig. 3.1 argues that attributions to discrimination will be threatening to individuals who strongly endorse the dominant ideology or who are in situations in which this belief system is salient. That is, discrimination claims should cause strong endorsers of the dominant ideology to feel anxious, uneasy, and on edge. Though few studies have directly tested this hypothesis, initial evidence appears to support the model. For instance, Kaiser (2005) primed undergraduate students with either the dominant ideology or neutral content and then examined how threatened they felt in the presence of a discrimination claimant. In this experiment, participants in the dominant ideology prime condition read a story in which a political leader selected an individual for a desirable promotion because that individual had worked hard and pulled himself up from poverty, and was the best qualified person for the job. In the control condition, participants read a neutral article about a tortoise species. After reading their respective article, participants read about an African American man who blamed a poor test grade given by a racist White evaluator on either discrimination, his test answers, or the difficulty of the test. Participants then completed a measure of threat (e.g., feeling nervous, anxious, distressed). Consistent with the dominant ideology threat hypothesis, relative to participants primed with neutral content, those primed with the dominant ideology experienced more threat in the presence of the African American man who blamed his failure on discrimination. The prime manipulation had no effect on self-reported threat when the African American target blamed his failure on either his test answers or the difficulty of the test.

Kaiser, Dyrenforth, and Hagiwara (2005, Experiment 2) replicated this threat effect in a study examining individual differences in chronic endorsement of the dominant ideology. In this study, participants who had previously completed a dominant ideology measure witnessed an African American man blame a failing test grade on a racist grader. Consistent with the priming study, the more participants endorsed the dominant ideology, the more threat they experienced when the target blamed his failure on a racist grader. Thus, this study demonstrates that individual differences in dominant ideology endorsement are associated with increased threat reactions when faced with individuals who make attributions to discrimination.

Interpersonal Outcomes

According to the dominant ideology threat model of reactions to discrimination claimants, individuals who chronically endorse the dominant ideology and those in situations in which this ideology is salient will not only feel more threatened in the presence of individuals who blame events on discrimination, they will be particularly likely to react negatively toward discrimination claimants as well. Several studies provide evidence consistent with this argument.

For example, Maass, Cadinu, Guarnieri, and Grasselli (2003) had male participants complete the Social Dominance Orientation Scale (e.g., "It's probably a good thing that certain groups are at the top and other groups are at the bottom"; Pratto, Sidanius, Stallworth, & Malle, 1994), a measure found to be related to dominant ideology endorsement (Sidanius & Pratto, 1999), and then interact via computer with a male and female confederate (the confederates were actually computer scripts). The female confederate's gender-related attitudes were manipulated so that half the time she was portrayed as a feminist who worked with a union that defends women's rights and half the time she was portrayed as traditionally feminine. In the former condition, one could readily infer that the woman attributes her group's disadvantage in society to sexism and she should thus pose a strong challenge to the dominant ideology. Under the guise that the study concerned visual memory, the men were instructed to send computer images to the women. Some of these images were hardcore pornographic in nature and others were not. During the interaction, the male confederate sent several hardcore pornographic images to the female confederate (who objected each time) and encouraged the male participant to do the same thing. The dependent variable of interest was sexual harassment of the female confederate by the male participant (assessed by the number and intensity of pornographic images he sent to the woman). Consistent with a dominant ideology threat perspective, the female confederate was harassed to a greater extent when she was portrayed as defending women's rights than when she was portrayed as feminine. Furthermore, across both the feminist and traditional woman conditions, the more participants endorsed social dominance orientation, the more they sexually harassed her. However, this relationship was particularly strong when the female confederate was portrayed as a feminist. This study provides important behavioral evidence that men treat women who publicly blame their gender group's outcomes on prejudice negatively, particularly if those men endorse the dominant ideology.

A study by Jost and Burgess (2000) also is consistent with the dominant ideology threat model of reactions to discrimination claimants. In this study, men and women read a newspaper story about a woman named Ann who was denied entry into her university's honors program (her qualifications were ambiguous). After learning that men were accepted into the program at a higher rate than women, Ann approached a school administrator who told her that this disparity reflected actual differences in qualification. Unsatisfied with this explanation, Ann brought a sexism lawsuit against the university. Participants then completed a number of measures including their attitudes toward Ann (e.g., "I feel proud of Ann"; "I feel that Ann has been unfair to the university" [reverse]). Additionally, participants completed the *Belief in a Just World Scale* (Rubin & Peplau, 1975), which assessed individual differences in the endorsement of the dominant ideology. Consistent with the dominant ideology threat approach, the more men endorsed the belief in a just world, the less favorably they evaluated Ann. The same relationship was observed for women, but it was not significant (although the relationship was not significantly different than the one observed for men).

Similarly, a study by Kaiser et al. (2004, Experiment 1) is consistent with the dominant ideology threat model. Participants in this study completed a just world beliefs measure prior to reading about an African American man who blamed a poor test grade given by a racist White evaluator on either discrimination, his test answers, or the difficulty of the test. The target of prejudice who blamed his failure on discrimination was derogated to a greater extent than the target who blamed his failure on other internal and external causes. Of importance, however, and consistent with the dominant ideology threat model, in the discrimination condition, the more participants endorsed just world beliefs, the more they derogated the African American man. This relationship was not observed when the target blamed his failure on his test answers or the difficulty of the test. This study provides important evidence that individuals who endorse the dominant ideology react negatively to African Americans who blame negative outcomes on discrimination.

SUMMARY

According to the dominant ideology threat model presented in this chapter, public attributions to discrimination serve as a source of dominant ideology threat. The model argues that strong endorsement of the dominant ideology leaves people feeling particularly threatened in the presence of discrimination claimants and likely to respond to this threat by derogating the discrimination claimant. The research reviewed in this chapter is consistent with this model. A number of studies utilizing a variety of research designs and stigmatized target groups demonstrate that individuals who blame negative outcomes on discrimination rather than other causes are derogated and treated negatively (e.g., Fitzgerald et al., 1995; Kaiser et al., 2005; Kaiser & Miller, 2001, 2003; Shelton & Stewart, 2004; Stangor et al., 2003). Of importance, individuals who chronically endorsed the dominant ideology or who were primed with this value system were particularly likely to experience threat in the presence of discrimination claimants and were more likely to respond negatively to individuals who blamed their failure on discrimination (Jost & Burgess, 2000; Kaiser, 2005; Kaiser et al., 2005; Maass et al., 2003). This research points to the importance of conceptualizing attributions to discrimination within a dominant ideology threat perspective. A next step in testing this model should involve examining whether threat mediates the relationship between dominant ideology endorsement and the derogation of discrimination claimants. This question is currently being addressed in my laboratory.

In the remainder of this chapter, I discuss the implications of this research for targets of prejudice and intergroup relations. This discussion focuses on how the interpersonal costs of claiming discrimination affect members of stigmatized groups' decisions about whether to publicly report prejudice as well as the personal, collective, and societal costs associated with these decisions.

THE TARGET'S DILEMMA

The research reviewed in this chapter highlights the interpersonal difficulties faced by individuals who claim to be targets of discrimination. Because claiming discrimination can be a negative experience for the claimant, individuals who experience discrimination face a difficult decision: Should they report it? The few studies to examine this decision show that even when faced with blatant discrimination, members of stigmatized groups often do not publicly acknowledge discrimination (Kaiser & Miller, 2004; Stangor et al., 2003; Stangor, Swim, Van Allen, & Sechrist, 2002; Swim & Hyers, 1999;

Woodzicka & LaFrance, 2001). For example, Swim and Hyers (1999) had undergraduate women engage in a group discussion in which a male confederate made a series of sexist or nonsexist comments. Although more than half (55%) of the women in the sexist comments condition did not respond to the discriminatory comments, private ratings made after the interaction revealed that 75% of these women who failed to respond rated the confederate as sexist and 91% had negative thoughts and feelings about him. Similarly, Woodzicka and LaFrance (2001) found that only a minority of women confronted a man who asked them sexually harassing questions during a laboratory-based interview. Furthermore, survey research on sexual harassment and discrimination demonstrates that fewer than half of women who experience sexual harassment respond by telling the perpetrator to discontinue his behavior (Fitzgerald et al., 1995; U.S. Merit System Protection Board, 1995).

Although deciding not to report discrimination can protect targets from experiencing retaliation for their claim, this decision can also have costs (Shelton, Richeson, Salvatore, & Hill, chap. 4, this volume; Swim & Thomas, chap. 6, this volume). For example, it is well established that the suppression of emotionally charged experiences has a number of serious detrimental effects on individuals, such as increased rumination about the experience, decrements in cognitive functioning, increased negative emotions, less successful social interactions, and increased sympathetic and cardiovascular responding (Butler et al., 2003; Gross, 1998; Quinn, chap. 5, this volume; Richards & Gross, 2000). When targets of prejudice do not disclose their perceptions of prejudice and related feelings, this could have harmful consequences for both their psychological and physical health. Indeed, African American women who reported accepting unfair treatment "as a fact of life" (Krieger & Sidney, 1996, p. 1373) had higher blood pressure than women who said they took some action. In short, repeated efforts to publicly suppress perceived discrimination could serve as a constant source of stress, thereby compromising mental and physical health (Sapolsky, 1998).

Deciding not to publicly acknowledge discrimination also can have harmful consequences for intergroup relations. When individuals remain silent in the face of prejudice, others may incorrectly assume that they do not perceive prejudice and are satisfied with how they are being treated and the outcomes they receive. Thus, when discriminatory events go uncorrected, discrimination will continue to exist because the perpetrators of prejudice may fail to recognize and correct their biases. In fact, recent research indicates that confronting prejudice is an effective means of reducing the perpetrator's prejudice (Czopp & Monteith, 2003; Czopp, Monteith, & Mark, 2005). Czopp and colleagues found that although individuals who were confronted about their prejudicial behavior did react negatively toward the person who confronted them, they simultaneously showed decreased stereotypic responding on a subsequent task. In other words, individuals who publicly acknowledge prejudice help to improve intergroup relations (unfortunately though, this occurs at a cost to the personal self).

The decision about whether to acknowledge prejudice also has implications for social policies and societal justice. If claims of discrimination are less frequent than objective levels of societal discrimination, members of stigmatized and nonstigmatized groups will have very different perceptions of societal (in)justice. If members of nonstigmatized groups are not fully aware of the extent to which stigmatized groups perceive discrimination and injustice (because the costs prevent them from speaking up), they may underestimate the extent to which discrimination is still a problem in society. Furthermore, this overly optimistic perception of societal outcomes may cause the nonstigmatized to downplay the importance and necessity of social policies aimed at reducing injustice. For example, if members of nonstigmatized groups believe that racial discrimination is rare in society, this perception can be used for justifying the elimination of affirmative action programs.

Infrequent claims of prejudice can also create a state of attributional ambiguity among the stigmatized. If objective encounters with prejudice are frequently denied because individuals fear retaliation, then the stigmatized may incorrectly come to assume that prejudice is decreasing and this perception can have negative consequences for self-esteem in some situations and can lead to the preservation of the status quo. For example, because speaking up about prejudice at work can have some severe costs, many members of targeted groups are likely to remain quiet when they perceive injustice. This silence may create pluralistic ignorance whereby employees belonging to stigmatized groups fail to correctly attribute their disadvantaged treatment to prejudice and instead wonder if there is something wrong with them or their group. This uncertainty is cognitively taxing and emotionally unpleasant. Furthermore, they may come to blame themselves and their group for outcomes for which they have little control and this could harm personal and collective self-esteem and prevent efforts aimed at changing a discriminatory culture (Crocker & Major, 1989; Major, Kaiser, et al., 2003).

Similarly, diminished public attributions to prejudice have implications for societal level collective action. Once discrimination is publicly acknowledged, other members of stigmatized groups (and their allies) have a forum for expressing their dissatisfaction. When groups of disenfranchised individuals come together with a common goal, such as reducing prejudice, this can result in social movements that bring about changes that actually affect how the group is treated. In short, publicly acknowledging discrimination can have tremendous societal benefits by exposing prejudice-based injustices and improving the group's social status (Crosby, 1993; Swim et al., 2001).

So how can the target's dilemma be resolved? The research reviewed in this chapter suggests that members of nonstigmatized groups should consider how their cultural belief systems influence their reactions toward members of stigmatized groups who blame events on discrimination (even when such attributions to discrimination are clearly warranted). By the same token, the research suggests that members of stigmatized groups should consider that attributions to discrimination may be especially costly interpersonally when they are identifying prejudice to those who endorse the dominant ideology. However, because identifying prejudice to these individuals might also be especially beneficial in terms of improving intergroup relations, the optimal reaction to perceived discrimination will likely depend on the stigmatized individual's goals in a particular situation (see also Miller, chap. 2, this volume; Swim & Thomas, chap. 6, this volume).

CONCLUSIONS

One of the defining features of stigmatization involves being the target of prejudice and discrimination. Although social psychologists have had a relatively long-standing interest in understanding the intrapersonal consequences of perceiving prejudice, we have just recently begun examining the interpersonal consequences of these perceptions. In this chapter, I adopted a dominant ideology threat theoretical framework that contends that individuals who publicly blame events on prejudice threaten core cultural values in the United States, such as the promise that any individual regardless of his or her life circumstances can get to the top through personal effort and self-reliance. When individuals experience a challenge to this belief system, they will experience threat and will derogate the source of the threat. The research reviewed in this chapter is consistent with this model, and makes important theoretical contributions to understanding the interpersonal consequences of attributions to discrimination. Research on the interpersonal consequences of attributions to prejudice has important implications for coping with prejudice, intergroup relationships, and social change.

ACKNOWLEDGMENTS

Preparation of this chapter was supported by a National Institute of Mental Health Behavioral Science Track Award for Rapid Transition (1R03MH071276). I am grateful to Shannon McCoy, Laurie O'Brien, and the Claremont Symposium participants for their thoughtful comments on this work.

REFERENCES

Biernat, M., Vescio, T. K., & Theno, S. A. (1996). Violating American values: A "value congruence" approach to understanding outgroup attitudes. *Journal of Experimental Social Psychology, 32,* 387–410.

Butler, E. A., Egloff, B., Wlhelm, F. H., Smith, N. C., Erickson, E. A., & Gross, J. J. (2003). The social consequences of expressive suppression. *Emotion, 3,* 48–67.

Clark, R., Anderson, N. B., Clark, V. R., & Williams, D. R. (1999). Racism as a stressor for African Americans: A biopsychosocial model. *American Psychologist, 54,* 805–816.

Crocker, J., & Major, B. (1989). Social stigma and self-esteem: The self-protective properties of stigma. *Psychological Review, 96,* 608–630.

Crocker, J., & Major, B. (2003). The self-protective properties of stigma: Evolution of a modern classic. *Psychological Inquiry, 14,* 232–237.

Crocker, J., Major, B., & Steele, C. (1998). Social stigma. In D. Gilbert, S. T. Fiske, & G. Lindzey (Eds.), *Handbook of social psychology* (4th ed., pp. 504–553). Boston, MA: McGraw-Hill.

Crosby, F. J. (1993). Why complain? *Journal of Social Issues, 49,* 169–184.

Czopp, A. M., & Monteith, M. J. (2003). Confronting prejudice (literally): Reactions to confrontations of racial and gender bias. *Personality and Social Psychology Bulletin, 29,* 532–544.

Czopp, A. M., Monteith, M. J., & Mark, A. Y. (2005). *Prejudice reduction through interpersonal confrontation: What happens when you speak out against prejudice?* Manuscript under review.

Davey, L. M., Bobocel, D. R., Son Hing, L. S., & Zanna, M. P. (1999). Preference for the Merit Principle Scale: An individual difference measure of distributive justice preferences. *Social Justice Research, 12,* 223–240.

de Tocqueville, A. (1945). *Democracy in America* (H. Reeve, Trans.). New York: Knopf. (Original work published 1840)

Dodd, E. H., Giuliano, T. A., Boutell, J. M., & Moran, B. E. (2001). Respected or rejected: Perceptions of women who confront sexist remarks. *Sex Roles, 45,* 567–577.

Erickson, E. H. (1950). *Childhood and society.* New York: Norton.

Fazio, R. H., & Zanna, M. P. (1978). On the predictive validity of attitudes: The roles of direct experience and confidence. *Journal of Personality, 46,* 228–243.

Fazio, R. H., & Zanna, M. P. (1981). Direct experience and attitude-behavior consistency. In L. Berkowitz (Ed.), *Advances in experimental social psychology* (Vol. 14, pp. 161–202). New York: Academic Press.

Feagin, J. R., & Sikes, M. P. (1994). *Living with racism: The Black middle-class experience.* Boston, MA: Beacon Press.

Fitzgerald, L. F., Swan, S., & Fischer, K. (1995). Why didn't she just report him? The psychological and legal implications of women's responses to sexual harassment. *Journal of Social Issues, 51,* 117–138.

Furnham, A., & Proctor, E. (1989). Belief in a just world: Review and critique of the individual difference literature. *British Journal of Social Psychology, 28,* 365–384.

Greenberg, J., Solomon, S., & Pyszczynski, T. (1997). Terror management theory of self-esteem and cultural worldviews: Empirical assessments and conceptual refinements. In M. P. Zanna (Ed.), *Advances in experimental social psychology* (Vol. 29, pp. 61–139). San Diego, CA: Academic Press.

Gross, J. J. (1998). Antecedent- and response-focused emotion regulation: Divergent consequences for experience, expression, and physiology. *Journal of Personality and Social Psychology, 74,* 224–237.

Haslett, B. B., & Lipman, S. (1997). Micro inequalities: Up close and personal. In N. V. Benokraitis (Ed.), *Subtle sexism: Current practice and prospects for change* (pp. 34–53). Thousand Oaks, CA: Sage Publications.

Hebl, M. R., Foster, J. M., Mannix, L. M., & Dovidio, J. F. (2002). Formal and interpersonal discrimination: A field study bias toward homosexual applicants. *Personality and Social Psychology Bulletin, 28,* 815–825.

Hochschild, J. L. (1995). *Facing up to the American dream: Race, class, and the soul of the nation.* Princeton, NJ: Princeton University Press.

Janoff-Bulman, R. (1989). Assumptive worlds and the stress of traumatic events: Applications of the schema construct. *Social Cognition, 7,* 113–136.

Jost, J. T., & Banaji, M. R. (1994). The role of stereotyping in system-justification and the production of false consciousness. *British Journal of Social Psychology, 33,* 1–27.

Jost, J. T., & Burgess, D. (2000). Attitudinal ambivalence and the conflict between group and system justification motives in low status groups. *Personality and Social Psychology Bulletin, 26,* 293–305.

Jost, J. T., Glaser, J., Kruglanski, A. W., & Sulloway, F. J. (2003). Political conservatism as motivated social cognition. *Psychological Bulletin, 129,* 339–375.

Jost, J. T., & Hunyady, O. (2002). The psychology of system justification and the palliative function of ideology. *European Review of Social Psychology, 13,* 111–153.

Kaiser, C. R. (2005). [Discrimination claims as a source of worldview threat]. Unpublished raw data.

Kaiser, C. R., Dyrenforth, P., & Hagiwara, N. (2005). *Why are attributions to discrimination interpersonally costly: A test of status legitimizing and group justifying motivations.* Manuscript submitted for publication.

Kaiser, C. R., & Miller, C. T. (2001). Stop complaining! The social costs of making attributions to discrimination. *Personality and Social Psychology Bulletin, 27,* 254–263.

Kaiser, C. R., & Miller, C. T. (2003). Derogating the victim: The interpersonal consequences of blaming events on discrimination. *Group Processes and Intergroup Relations, 6,* 227–237.

Kaiser, C. R., & Miller, C. T. (2004). A stress and coping perspective on confronting sexism. *Psychology of Women Quarterly, 28,* 168–178.

Kaiser, C. R., Vick, S. B., & Major, B. (2004). A prospective investigation of the relationship between just world beliefs and the desire for revenge post-September 11, 2001. *Psychological Science, 15,* 503–507.

Katz, I., & Hass, R. G. (1988). Racial ambivalence and American value conflict: Correlational and priming studies of dual cognitive structures. *Journal of Personality and Social Psychology, 55,* 893–905.

Kelley, H. H. (1973). The processes of causal attribution. *American Psychologist, 28,* 107–128.

Kleugel, J. R., & Smith, E. R. (1986). *Beliefs about inequality: Americans' view of what is and what ought to be.* Hawthorne, NJ: Aldine de Gruyer.

Krieger, N., & Sidney, S. (1996). Racial discrimination and blood pressure: The CARDIA Study of young Black and White adults. *American Journal of Public Health, 86,* 1370–1378.

Lambert, A. J., Burroughs, T., & Nguyen, T. (1999). Perceptions of risk and the buffering hypothesis: The role of just world beliefs and right-wing authoritarianism. *Personality and Social Psychology Bulletin, 25,* 643–656.

Lerner, M. J. (1980). *The belief in a just world: A fundamental delusion.* New York: Plenum Press.

Lerner, M. J., & Miller, D. T. (1978). Just world research and the attribution process: Looking back and ahead. *Psychological Bulletin, 85,* 1030–1051.

Maass, A., Cadinu, M., Guarnieri, G., & Grasselli, A. (2003). Sexual harassment under social identity threat: The computer harassment paradigm. *Journal of Personality and Social Psychology, 85,* 853–870.

Major, B. (1994). From social inequality to personal entitlement: The role of social comparisons, legitimacy appraisals, and group membership. In M. P. Zanna (Ed.), *Advances in experimental social psychology* (Vol. 26, pp. 293–348). San Diego, CA: Academic Press.

Major, B., Kaiser, C. R., & McCoy, S. K. (2003). It's not my fault: When and why attributions to prejudice protect well-being. *Personality and Social Psychology Bulletin, 29,* 772–781.

Major, B., Kaiser, C. R., McCoy, S. K., & O'Brien, L. T. (2005). *Legitimizing ideologies and the impact of prejudice on self-esteem.* Manuscript submitted for publication.

Major, B., McCoy, S. K., Kaiser, C. R., & Quinton, W. J. (2003). Prejudice and self-esteem: A transactional model. In W. Stroebe & M. Hewstone (Eds.), *European Review of Social Psychology, 14,* 77–104.

Major, B., Quinton, W. J., & McCoy, S. K. (2002). Antecedents and consequences of attributions to discrimination: Theoretical and empirical advances. In M. P. Zanna (Ed.), *Advances in experimental social psychology* (Vol. 34, pp. 251–330). New York: Academic Press.

Mirels, H. L., & Darland, D. M. (1990). The Protestant ethic and self-characterization. *Personality and Individual Differences, 11,* 895–898.

Near, J. P., & Jensen, T. C. (1983). The whistleblowing process: Retaliation and perceived effectiveness. *Work and Occupations, 10,* 3–28.

Nielsen, L. B., & Nelson, R. L. (in press). The legal construction of discrimination: A sociolegal model of employment discrimination law. In L. B. Nielsen & R. Nelson (Eds.), *Rights and realities: Legal and scientific approaches to employment discrimination.* New York: Kluwer.

Plaut, V. C., Markus, H. R., & Lachman, M. E. (2002). Place matters: Consensual features and regional variation in American well-being and self. *Journal of Personality and Social Psychology, 83,* 160–184.

Pratto, F., Sidanius, J., Stallworth, L. M., & Malle, B. F. (1994). Social dominance orientation: A personality variable predicting social and political attitudes. *Journal of Personality and Social Psychology, 67,* 741–763.

Quinn, D. M., & Crocker, J. (1999). When ideology hurts: Effects of belief in the Protestant ethic and feeling overweight on the psychological well-being of women. *Journal of Personality and Social Psychology, 77,* 402–414.

Richards, J. M., & Gross, J. J. (2000). Emotion regulation and memory: The cognitive costs of keeping one's cool. *Journal of Personality and Social Psychology, 79,* 410–424.

Rubin, Z., & Peplau, L. A. (1975). Who believes in a just world? *Journal of Social Issues, 31,* 65–89.

Sapolsky, R. M. (1998). *Why zebras don't get ulcers: An updated guide to stress, stress-related disease, and coping.* New York: W. H. Freeman.

Schmitt, M. T., & Branscombe, N. R. (2002a). The internal and external causal loci of attributions to prejudice. *Personality and Social Psychology Bulletin, 28,* 620–628.

Schmitt, M. T., & Branscombe, N. R. (2002b). The meaning and consequences of perceived discrimination in disadvantaged and privileged social groups. In W. Stroebe & M. Hewstone (Eds.), *European review of social psychology, Vol. 12* (pp. 167–199). Chichester, England: Wiley.

Shelton, J. N., & Stewart, B. (2004). Confronting perpetrators of prejudice: The inhibitory effects of social costs. *Psychology of Women Quarterly, 28,* 215–223.

Sidanius, J., & Pratto, F. (1999). *Social dominance: An intergroup theory of social hierarchy and oppression.* New York: Cambridge University Press.

Spindler, G. D., & Spindler, L. S. (1990). *The American cultural dialogue and its transmission.* New York: Falmer Press.

Stangor, C., Swim, J. K., Sechrist, G. B., Decoster, J., VanAllen, K. L., & Ottenbreit, A. (2003). Ask, answer, and announce: Three stages in perceiving and responding to prejudice. *European Review of Social Psychology, 14,* 277–311.

Stangor, C., Swim, J. K., Van Allen, K. L., & Sechrist, G. B. (2002). Reporting discrimination in public and private contexts. *Journal of Personality and Social Psychology, 82,* 69–74.

Steele, S. (1990). *Content of our character: A new vision of race in America.* New York: St. Martin's Press.

Swim, J. K., & Hyers, L. L. (1999). Excuse me—What did you say?!: Women's public and private responses to sexist remarks. *Journal of Experimental Social Psychology, 35,* 68–88.

Swim, J. K., Hyers, L. L., Cohen, L. L., & Ferguson, M. J. (2001). Everyday sexism: Evidence for its incidence, nature, and psychological impact from three daily diary studies. *Journal of Social Issues, 57,* 31–53.

Sykes, C. J. (1992). *A nation of victims: The decay of the American character.* New York: St. Martin's Press.

Tomaka, J., & Blascovich, J. (1994). Effects of justice beliefs on cognitive appraisal of and subjective physiological, and behavioral responses to potential stress. *Journal of Personality and Social Psychology, 67,* 732–740.

Triandis, H. C. (1995). *Individualism and collectivism.* Boulder, CO: Westview Press.

U.S. Merit System Protection Board. (1995). *Sexual harassment in the federal workplace: Trends, progress, and continuing challenges.* Washington, DC: Office of Policy & Evaluation.

Weber, M. (1958). *The Protestant ethic and the spirit of capitalism* (T. Parsons, Trans.). New York: Scribner. (Original work published 1904)

Woodzicka, J. A., & LaFrance, M. (2001). Real versus imagined gender harassment. *Journal of Social Issues, 57,* 15–30.

CHAPTER

4

Silence Is Not Golden: The Intrapersonal Consequences of Not Confronting Prejudice

J. Nicole Shelton
Princeton University

Jennifer A. Richeson
Dartmouth College

Jessica Salvatore
Diana M. Hill
Princeton University

When faced with prejudice and discrimination in interpersonal encounters, individuals must decide how to respond. They may decide to take one of the following two paths: either they confront the perpetrator and express their dissatisfaction, or they ignore the situation, letting their dissatisfaction go unnoticed. The decision is not likely to be an easy one (see Miller, chap. 2, this volume; Swim & Thomas, chap. 6, this volume, for goals and motives that may play a role in the decision). Moreover, these two reactions are likely to lead to strikingly different inter- and intrapersonal consequences. Researchers have recently turned their attention to understanding the *inter*personal costs targets of prejudice face when they make the decision to confront perpetrators of prejudice and discrimination (Dodd, Giuliano, Boutell, & Moran, 2001; Kaiser, chap. 3, this volume; Kaiser & Miller, 2001, 2003).

In this chapter, we examine the *intra*personal costs associated with *not* confronting perpetrators of prejudice and discrimination. Based on Higgins' (1987) self-discrepancy theory, we present a model (see Fig. 4.1) that suggests that targets of prejudice incur both affective and cognitive consequences as a result of not challenging prejudice, particularly when they think they should. Before discussing our model, however, we first provide

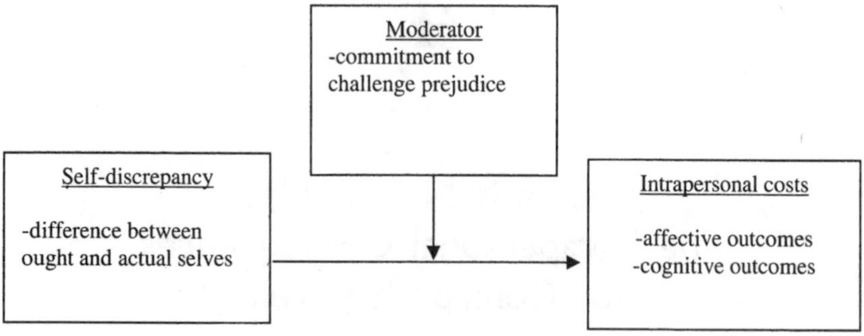

FIG. 4.1. Conceptual model of confronting perpetrators of prejudice.

a brief summary of research that has documented the interpersonal consequences of acknowledging that one has been the target of prejudice and discrimination. Next we briefly describe self-discrepancy theory in general and highlight how this theory has been applied to understand majority group members' attempts to curb prejudiced responding. We then discuss our model of the intrapersonal costs of not confronting prejudice, linking the consequences of failure to confront with perceived discrepancies between behavior and self-standards, and provide empirical support for this model from our laboratory. We conclude by considering the dilemma that targets of prejudice face as they decide between the interpersonal and intrapersonal costs of confronting and not confronting perpetrators of prejudice.

INTERPERSONAL CONSEQUENCES OF CHALLENGING PREJUDICE

A growing body of research suggests that it may be in the best interest of members of stigmatized groups to ignore perpetrators' prejudiced remarks and behaviors in order to avoid a host of negative consequences. Research on attributions to discrimination suggests that it may be best for individuals even to deny that they have experienced discrimination, even when there is good evidence that they have (see Kaiser, chap. 3, this volume). Kaiser and Miller (2001) illustrated, for example, that perceivers evaluated an African American student who attributed his failure on a test to discrimination as a "complainer and troublemaker," but not so for an African American student who attributed his failure to lack of effort. Kaiser and Miller (2003) replicated this finding in a job-interview setting by showing that perceivers evaluated an African American job candidate who attributed his rejection to discrimination more negatively than an African American who attributed his rejection to either his interviewing skills or to job competition. Across both studies, the derogation of the African American target occurred regardless of how blatant or subtle the discrimination. These findings suggest that in order to avoid interpersonal costs, stigmatized individuals should publicly minimize the amount of discrimination that they have encountered.

In addition to the research on attributions to discrimination, recent work finds that perceivers evaluate individuals who confront perpetrators of prejudice quite negatively. *Confronting*, in this context, is defined as verbally or nonverbally expressing one's dissatisfaction with prejudicial and discriminatory treatment to the person who is responsible for the remark or behavior. Dodd et al. (2001), for example, found that a woman reacting to a male's sexist comments about appropriate work for women was liked less by male perceivers when she expressed her dissatisfaction compared to when she did not. Similarly, Shelton and Stewart (2004) found that the more often women confronted a male interviewer who asked sexist questions, the more they were perceived as complainers. Taken together, this research suggests that stigmatized individuals can ill afford to claim, report, or confront the prejudice they face.

INTRAPERSONAL CONSEQUENCES OF NOT CHALLENGING PREJUDICE

Although the costs of confronting perpetrators of prejudice may be high, is *not* confronting really the best option for members of stigmatized groups? When making the decision of whether or not to confront a prejudiced person or situation, individuals must consider both the costs of doing so, as well as the potential costs of not doing so. Clearly, there are consequences associated with not confronting perpetrators of prejudice. For example, perpetrators who are not confronted are more likely to continue behaving in prejudiced ways if they are unaware of their wrongdoings and/or stigmatized individuals' discontent (Czopp & Monteith, 2003; Czopp, Monteith, & Mark, 2004). In addition, targets of prejudice may experience negative affect about letting prejudiced statements and behaviors pass without comment. For instance, they may feel that they have let down or "sold out" the group in order to make their lives easier. Furthermore, targets of prejudice may ruminate about their inaction, which could lead to cognitive distraction and decrements in performance. In other words, individuals may incur intrapersonal consequences when they do not express their dissatisfaction regarding an encounter that is tainted with prejudice.

A Self-Discrepancy Framework

Why would failing to confront a perpetrator of prejudice lead to affective and cognitive consequences? For many stigmatized groups, failing to confront a perpetrator's prejudiced comments will mean transgressing a personal standard for behavior. According to Higgins' self-discrepancy theory, transgressing a personal standard for behavior leads to negative affective consequences (Higgins, 1987). Higgins surmised that there are three basic domains of the self: the *actual self* (the self as it really is), the *ideal self* (the self as you would like it to be), and the *ought self* (the self as you believe it should be). When there is a discrepancy between these selves, individuals experience distinctive affective reactions. Of most importance to our work on the intrapersonal costs of not confronting prejudice is the discrepancy between one's actual self and one's ought self. Discrepancies between individuals' actual and their ought selves lead to agitation-related emotions. Specifically, individuals experience guilt, self-contempt, and uneasiness directed toward the self (Higgins, 1987).

Self-Discrepancy and Prejudice. Self-discrepancy theory has been applied to research within the prejudice domain when considering personal transgressions for members of dominant social groups. This research indicates that dominant group members (e.g., Whites, men, and heterosexuals) experience a *prejudice-related discrepancy* when their actual behavior toward stigmatized groups is at odds with their personal standards. Extensive research suggests that affective reactions to such perceived discrepancies can be quite aversive (e.g., Devine, Monteith, Zuwerink, & Elliot, 1991; Voils, Ashburn-Nardo, & Monteith, 2002; Zuwerink, Devine, Monteith, & Cook, 1996). Specifically, large prejudice-related discrepancies are accompanied by feelings of anger, discomfort, guilt, and self-criticism (Devine et al., 1991).

In additional work, Monteith (1993) demonstrated that when low-prejudiced individuals discriminate or otherwise behave in ways dissonant with their personal standards regarding prejudice, they experience an aversive self-discrepancy that over time functions to lower their level of prejudiced responding. Monteith (1993, 1996) provided extensive evidence that this self-regulatory cycle is largely driven by increased negative feelings toward the self, primarily compunction and guilt. Moreover, in some of her later work, Monteith (1996) indicated that the salience of prejudice-related standards moderated these affective reactions, such that those who had their standards made salient *after* discrepant responding experienced reduced guilt. In short, research on self-discrepancy and prejudice has demonstrated distinct affective consequences for those, primarily low-prejudiced individuals, who experience a discrepancy between their prejudice-related standards and their actual behavior toward stigmatized group members.

Although Higgins (1987) did not relate self-discrepancies to cognitive outcomes—only affective ones—some research on self-discrepancy and prejudice suggests that individuals who perceive a mismatch between their behavior and their self-standards will also incur cognitive costs. Monteith (1993), for example, found that low-prejudiced participants—exactly those for whom prejudiced responding violates an important self-standard and leads to guilt—also experienced increased self- and discrepancy-focused thoughts, and devoted increased attention to relevant information.

Self-Discrepancy Theory and Not Challenging Prejudice. Self-discrepancy theory has been successfully used in the past to examine individuals' reactions to their own prejudiced behavior, as just described. We now apply that same theory to the experiences of targets responding to others' prejudiced behavior. For some people, not confronting perpetrators of prejudice will lead to a discrepancy between their personal standards and actual behavior. That is, for some targets of prejudice, it will be a significant part of their ought self to challenge discrimination. If these individuals do not challenge the prejudice that they encounter, then their actual self will be dissonant with their ought self, resulting in a self-discrepancy. We propose that this discrepancy can have internal consequences for individuals: specifically, affective consequences (guilt) and cognitive consequences (obsessive thoughts). Moreover, similar to the work on self-discrepant prejudiced behavior by dominant group members, we propose that the relationship between the discrepancy and affective as well as cognitive consequences may be moderated by important individual difference and situational factors. In our work, we have been particularly interested in individual differences in the commitment to fight prejudice.

We believe that targets of prejudice who are committed to challenging prejudice are likely to be particularly vulnerable to the aforementioned consequences of failing to confront perpetrators. Research with women indicates that those who are committed to eliminating gender discrimination have internalized the importance of individual and collective action in fighting the mistreatment of women (Downing & Roush, 1985; O'Neil, Egan, Owen, & McBride-Murray, 1993). Not only are they identified with their gender group and dissatisfied with gender stereotypes, these individuals feel responsible for improving the treatment of women. At the societal level, this may involve behaviors such as filing a letter of complaint to a company about hiring practices or filing a gender discrimination lawsuit against a company. At the interpersonal level, standing up against gender discrimination may involve communicating, verbally or behaviorally, to other individuals in face-to-face interactions that their behavior is inappropriate. Research suggests that such an activist orientation is a better predictor of challenging perpetrators of prejudice than being identified with women or having positive attitudes toward women (Bargard & Hyde, 1991; Crosby, 1993; Swim & Hyers, 1998). But even these highly committed individuals may chose not to confront perpetrators of prejudice under conditions in which the interpersonal costs of doing so are particularly high (Shelton & Stewart, 2004).

Although the aforementioned research has focused on women, it is reasonable to consider that similar findings apply to other targets of prejudice, such as ethnic minorities, gays and lesbians, and the disabled. Similar to low-prejudice individuals, therefore, failing to confront perpetrators of prejudice should induce negative self-directed affect in targets of prejudice who have made a personal commitment to stand up against discrimination. Consistent with previous research examining prejudice with and without compunction, as well as self-discrepancy theory, we propose that targets of prejudice who are committed to challenging oppression and bias should experience negative self-directed affect when they violate personal standards by not confronting perpetrators of prejudice.

As noted previously, although self-discrepancy theory does not address cognitive consequences, there is reason to believe that individuals who perceive a mismatch between their behavior and their self-standards will also incur cognitive costs. These individuals are likely to be emotionally charged when they encounter discrimination, but must conceal their reactions from perpetrators. Concealing dissatisfaction from a perpetrator often consists of suppressing negative emotions, facial expressions, and, sometimes, even one's own thoughts. Research finds that suppressing facial displays of emotion, as well as thought suppression more generally, may come with cognitive baggage (Gross, 1998; Pennebaker, 1995; Wegner, 1994). For example, Richards and Gross (1999, 2000) demonstrated that emotion suppression is cognitively demanding and may impair individuals' memory for details of the emotional event. Additionally, Pennebaker (1995) and Wegner (1994) found that emotion and thought suppression often leads to intrusive and obsessive thoughts. For example, individuals who tried to suppress thoughts about their stigmatized identity had more obsessive thoughts about the identity compared to those who did not suppress such thoughts (Smart & Wegner, 1999). In sum, cognitive functioning may be impaired for individuals who violated their personal standards of not confronting perpetrators of prejudice.

EMPIRICAL SUPPORT

In our empirical work to date, we have sought preliminary support for our application of self-discrepancy theory to challenging perpetrators of prejudice. Specifically, we have tested the claim that there are negative self-directed affective consequences when individuals violate personal standards by not confronting perpetrators of sexism. We were particularly interested in the experience of people with a personal commitment to confronting prejudice. We predicted that this population would suffer the most intense consequences following a perceived discrepancy because they are not living up to a personal value. Moreover, we have tested the claim that there are cognitive costs of not confronting perpetrators of prejudice, especially when one is committed to challenging prejudice. Based on the work already reviewed, we predicted that women who are committed to challenging sexism who recalled a situation in which they failed to do so would report having obsessive thoughts about their inaction. We present two studies to support our claims. The first study focuses on the affective consequences, and the second study focuses on affective and cognitive consequences.

Study 1

In Study 1, in order to investigate the affective consequences of not confronting perpetrators of prejudice, we developed a discrepancy measure to assess the degree of inconsistency between women's actual responses and their personal standards for how they should respond toward perpetrators of prejudice. We adapted Devine et als.' (1991) should–would discrepancy questionnaire, which is used to measure prejudiced responses toward Blacks, to fit our purposes. Our should–would questionnaire consisted of three sections (i.e., should, would, and a measure of affect). Participants first reported their personal standards for how they should respond in six different situations involving gender discrimination. Specifically, the instructions read,

> Often times we set up personal standards or guidelines for evaluating our own behavior or responses to various groups of people. We usually phrase these guidelines in terms of how we believe we should respond or behave in various situations. Based on your own personal standards for how you should respond, consider the following situations. For each situation, circle the number between 1 (strongly disagree) and 7 (strongly agree) that best reflects your personal standard for how you should respond in the situation.

An example of a situation read as follows:

> Imagine that you have been treated unfairly by a teacher or professor because of your gender. You should confront your teacher or professor about this behavior.

Two of the six items focused on being treated unfairly by higher status individuals because of one's gender (i.e., being treated unfairly by professors and being denied a promotion or job by a supervisor). Two items focused on being treated unfairly by peers because of one's gender (i.e., being treated unfairly by fellow student or co-workers, and fellow students acting as if you need help on a challenging task). One item focused on hearing people making sexist jokes. The final item focused on hearing someone make sexist comments about the types of jobs women should or should not do. After completing how they should respond, participants answered how they actually would respond in those same six situations. Specifically, participants read,

> Although we set up personal standards for how we should respond, our actual responses may or may not be consistent with these standards or guidelines. Consider the six situations you responded to previously. You will now be presented with these same situations. But this time, report on the 1 to 7 scales below how you believe you would actually respond to the situations. Base these responses on your previous personal experiences. It is important to keep in mind that there are no right or wrong answers. Your responses may or may not be the same as the ones you gave earlier. It is also important that you be as honest and open as possible.

Participants answered in terms of how they would respond to the same six scenarios used for the should index.

Next participants indicated the extent to which 18 affect items described their feelings about how well their actual (would) responses matched their personal (should) standards. A principal components factor analysis with varimax rotation using the 18 items yielded four factors that accounted for 73% of the total variance. The first factor, *Negative Affect Toward the Self*, included the following 8 items that measure how much negative affect individuals felt toward the self: angry at myself, annoyed at myself, disappointed with myself, shame, self-critical, guilty, regretful, and disgusted with myself. The second factor, *General Positive Affect*, included: friendly, content, energetic, optimistic, happy, and good. The third factor, *Negative Affect Toward Others*, included the following three items that indicate negative feelings directed toward others: angry at others, disgusted with others, and irritated with others. The single item, *Embarrassed*, loaded separately as its own factor.

In addition to completing the should–would discrepancy and affect measures, our participants answered six questions to assess how responsible they felt for standing up against sexism. Examples of the questions include: "How committed are you to trying to fight gender discrimination?" and "How obligated do you feel to confront someone or something that is sexist?" The should–would measure and the commitment to fight sexism scale were embedded in a large questionnaire packet with other measures. These two sets of items were separated by some of the additional measures, and their presentation order was counterbalanced. The order of the sets of items did not influence the results.

In order to get a general sense of our participants' responses, first we conducted Pearson correlations to examine the relationships between the total "should" and total "would" ratings with the commitment to challenge discrimination scale. As expected, the more women felt committed to standing up against sexism, the more they thought they should ($r = .52$, $p < .001$) and would ($r = .62$, $p < .001$) confront the perpetrators in the scenarios. Additionally, the more women thought they should confront the perpetrators, the more they thought they would ($r = .73$, $p < .001$).

We then created a discrepancy index by subtracting participants' would rating from their should rating for each of the six situations and summing across the items. The discrepancy scores ranged from −6 to 18. Of our participants, 10% had a discrepancy score of 0, which indicates that their personal standards matched their actual responses. Additionally, 83% had positive discrepancy scores, which indicates their actual responses were lower than their personal standards (i.e., they thought they should respond but actually would not respond). Finally, 7% of the participants had negative discrepancy scores, which indicates they thought they should not respond but actually would respond. Similar to Devine et al. (1991), we deleted these latter participants from all analyses because their type of discrepancy is not the focus of the present research.

We conducted regression analyses to examine if individuals' discrepancy scores, level of personal commitment to fight sexism, and their interaction predicted their affective responses. In general, the results supported our prediction for negative self-directed affect associated with not confronting perpetrators of prejudice. The more women felt they should respond but would not actually respond, the more they experienced self-directed negative affect ($\beta = .19$, $p < .001$). Additionally, as predicted, the interaction between the discrepancy scores and commitment to challenge discrimination was significant for negative affect directed toward the self ($\beta = .07$, $p = .01$). Additional results revealed that at high levels of commitment, larger discrepancy scores were associated with more negative affect directed toward the self ($\beta = .18$, $p < .001$). Thus, for women who were committed to challenging discrimination, large discrepancies in how they would actually behave compared to how they felt they should behave when confronted with sexism resulted in negative feelings directed inward. In contrast, at lower levels of commitment, discrepancy scores were unrelated to negative affect toward the self ($\beta = .02$, $p = .63$). Thus, for women who are less committed to fighting discrimination, not behaving in a manner that is discrepant from their "should" standards has no bearing on how much shame and guilt they experience.

In addition, we conducted regression analyses to examine if individuals' discrepancy scores, level of personal commitment to fight sexism, and their interaction predicted individuals' positive affective responses. The results indicated that larger discrepancy scores were associated with feeling less positive affect ($\beta = -.11$, $p = .002$). These data show that participants with larger should–would discrepancies reported feeling less positively than women with smaller should–would discrepancies. Contrary to predictions, the main effect for commitment to fight discrimination and the interaction between commitment and should–would discrepancy were not statistically significant for positive affective responses. Hence, failing to confront sexism when they think they should seems to come with fewer positive affective consequences for many women, not just those committed to fighting discrimination.

We conducted similar regression analyses with negative affect toward others and embarrassment as the outcome variables. Given that the should–would discrepancy scores are based on individuals' internal standards for their lives, we did not expect these scores to be related to how they felt about others. Consistent with predictions, the discrepancy scores were unrelated to the amount of negative affect women felt toward others. The only (marginally) significant finding with this outcome variable is that the more women were committed to challenging discrimination, the more negative affect they experienced toward others ($\beta = .25$, $p = .09$). No effects (main effects nor interaction) emerged from the analysis of embarrassment.

Hence, the results of Study 1 suggest that women who felt they should confront perpetrators of prejudice, but knew they would not do so, experienced negative affective consequences. Specifically, women in the present study reported feeling less positively when they thought they would not confront perpetrators, but felt that they should. Furthermore, the adverse effect of not confronting perpetrators was particularly prominent for women who have made a personal commitment to take action against discrimination. That is, when women who felt personally responsible for challenging discrimination failed to do so, they reported heightened negative self-directed affect (e.g., shame, guilt, self-criticism). They reported feeling negatively about themselves for not following through with a value that is a central component of their identity. In contrast, when women who were less committed to fighting discrimination failed to challenge a perpetrator of prejudice, even if they thought they should, they were protected from these adverse self-directed affective consequences.

These findings offer initial support for the hypothesis that failing to confront perpetrators of sexism will have negative affective consequences for women who are committed to challenging sexism. However, several methodological limitations of the aforementioned study suggest caution regarding the interpretation of the data. First, participants were required to imagine how they would and should behave in hypothetical situations. It is likely that participants had differential degrees of actual experience in some, if not all, of the scenarios. Differential exposure would influence the ease and vividness with which participants could imagine the scenarios, and, furthermore, could influence their affective reactions to discrepancies between how they report they should and would actually behave.

Study 2

In Study 2, we sought to replicate the negative self-directed affect findings of Study 1 by having participants recall a situation in their actual lives involving sexism. Specifically, participants either recalled a situation involving sexism in which they should have responded to the perpetrator, but did not; or they recalled a situation involving sexism in which they should have responded to the perpetrator and did. Additionally, in order to make certain that not confronting sexism, rather than not confronting negative situations more generally, was the critical predictor of negative self-directed affect, we included a control condition in which participants recalled an offensive but nonsexist event to which they felt that they should have responded, but did not. In addition to these methodological changes, the primary goal of Study 2 was to extend the findings of Study 1 through an examination of potential cognitive costs of not confronting perpetrators of prejudice. We predicted that women who are committed to challenging sexism who recalled a situation in which they failed to do so would report having obsessive thoughts about their inaction.

We asked participants to describe a situation in their lives in which they had been treated in a negative manner because of their gender and they either did or did not confront the person who caused the event. The instructions read as follows,

> We would like for you to recall a situation in which you were treated in a negative manner because of your gender. If you cannot recall a situation in which you were personally involved, please recall a situation in which you witnessed another woman being treated negatively because of her gender. Regardless of whether the situation involved you personally or one in which you were the witness, it should be a situation in which you should have responded to the situation, but did not. That is, you did not confront the perpetrator nor let the perpetrator know how you felt even though you wanted to do so.

In the sexist situation in which women did confront the perpetrator, the instructions were the same except for the last two sentences, which we replaced with

> Regardless of whether the situation involved you personally or one in which you were the witness, it should be a situation in which you responded to the situation. That is, you either confronted the perpetrator or made it very clear how you felt.

In the offensive situation in which participants did not respond but wanted to do so, we used the same instructions except we told participants to recall a situation "in which someone did something negative to you. If you cannot recall a situation in which you were personally involved, please recall a situation in which you witnessed someone else being treated negatively."

After describing the situation in the space provided, participants completed items related to their affect and thoughts during the interaction. We composed a *negative affect toward the self* index by taking the average of participants' responses to six items, including "I was angry at myself," "I was annoyed at myself," and "I felt displeased with myself." Similarly, an *obsessive thoughts* scale was created in order to assess the extent to which women had obsessive thoughts about their behavior during the situation they recalled. The scale consisted of five items including, "I replayed the scene over and over in my mind," and "I ruminated about my behavior during the situation." In a separate testing session as a part of another study, participants completed the personal commitment to challenge discrimination scale used in Study 1.

Surprisingly, participants reported experiencing more negative affect toward the self after not responding to the offensive but nonsexist situation ($M = 2.36$, $SD = .91$) compared to not responding to the sexist situation ($M = 1.64$, $SD = .64$), $t(37) = -2.91$, $p = .01$, as well as compared to the sexist situation they did respond to ($M = 1.60$, $SD = 1.00$), $t(31) = -2.29$, $p = .03$. There was no significant difference in the amount of negative affect toward the self individuals experienced after not responding to the sexist situation and after responding to the sexist situation, $t(31) < 1.00$, *ns*. But more importantly, in addition to this main effect, the interaction between the commitment to challenge discrimination and the recalled situation approached conventional levels of statistical significance for negative self-directed affect ($\beta = -.22$, $p = .06$). For participants who recalled a sexist situation to which they should have responded but did not, the more committed they were to challenging discrimination, the more negative self-directed affect they experienced ($\beta = .24$, $p = .05$). In contrast, for participants who recalled a sexist situation in which they responded to the perpetrator, commitment to challenging discrimination was unrelated to negative self-directed affect ($\beta = -.23$, $p = .122$). Similarly, for participants who recalled an offensive situation that they should have responded to but did not, commitment to challenging discrimination was not related to negative self-directed affect ($\beta =$

−.19, $p = .31$). These data are consistent with the findings from Study 1 that among women who violated a personal standard by not confronting a perpetrator of prejudice, the more committed they were to challenging discrimination, the more they suffered the consequences of self-directed negative affect (e.g., shame, disappointment with the self).

In addition, the results generally support our prediction regarding the cognitive costs of remaining silent in the face of prejudice. The results revealed a significant interaction between the commitment to challenge discrimination and the recalled situation ($\beta = -.23$, $p = .03$). More specifically, for participants who recalled a sexist situation that they should have responded to but did not, the more they felt committed to challenge discrimination, the more obsessive thoughts they had during the situation ($\beta = .28$, $p = .07$). In contrast, for participants who recalled a sexist situation in which they responded, commitment to challenge discrimination was unrelated to obsessive thoughts ($\beta = -.04$, $p = .76$). Similarly, for participants who recalled an offensive situation in which they should have responded but did not, commitment to challenge discrimination was unrelated to obsessive thoughts ($\beta = -.17$, $p = .28$). Hence, these data suggest that women who are committed to challenging discrimination and recalled an instance in which they failed to do so, not only experienced negative affect but also ruminated and had obsessive thoughts about their behavior during the prejudiced encounter.

SILENCE IS NOT ALWAYS GOLDEN

A small, but rapidly growing, body of research is beginning to address the interpersonal costs of confronting perpetrators of prejudice (see Kaiser, chap. 3, this volume). In our research, we have been examining the flip side of this issue—the intrapersonal costs of not confronting perpetrators of prejudice. Our findings show that women who are committed to challenging discrimination experience guilt, regret, and disappointment with the self as a result of not confronting perpetrators of prejudice in situations where they thought they should have. Additionally, our results show that women suffer cognitively as a result of violating their personal standards by not confronting perpetrators of prejudice. Specifically, women experience obsessive thoughts and ruminate about their lack of confronting behavior. Taken together, these findings reveal that not confronting perpetrators of prejudice can be psychologically and cognitively costly for targets. In addition, these findings suggest that as targets of prejudice appraise a prejudiced situation and consider their response options (e.g., confront vs. not confront), the perceived inter- and intrapersonal costs associated with each option are likely to be shaped, in part, by their goals and motives in the situation (see Miller, chap. 2, this volume; Swim & Thomas, chap. 6, this volume).

Armed with this evidence, a number of future research directions become clear. First, more rigorous experimental studies are needed to examine these issues and provide stronger evidence regarding the affective and cognitive consequences of not confronting sexism that emerged in the present research. For instance, future research could manipulate individuals' beliefs regarding how they think they should behave or, even, how they think they would behave by manipulating the norms of the context or immediate situation. Moreover, future studies should constrain women's actual behavior such that they would not be able to confront a perpetrator of prejudice, and investigate the effects of this constraint on aspects of cognition and affect.

Further, in our work to date, we have focused exclusively on affective reactions and obsessive thoughts that occur as a result of remaining silent in the presence of prejudice. Are there other intrapersonal costs associated with not confronting perpetrators of prejudice? For instance, do individuals find it difficult to concentrate on or perform a task after they do not confront? Imagine the female employee who listens to her colleagues make sexist jokes or comments about women during a board meeting. Will this woman have trouble concentrating on her assignments if she decides not to express her dissatisfaction to her colleagues? The preliminary findings that we have presented in this chapter suggest that this may indeed be the case. This possibility has serious implications for the career success of targets of prejudice in the workplace, and should be pursued.

Finally, although we suspect that our findings would replicate to other targets of prejudice besides women, future research should explicitly address this issue. Do ethnic minorities who are committed to challenging discrimination experience self-directed negative affect and obsessive thoughts when they do not live up to their personal standards? Similarly, do members of dominant groups also experience similar affect when they fail to confront perpetrators of prejudice, particularly if they are committed to challenging discrimination? How might it differ for targets and nontargets? For instance, perhaps nontargets feel guilty and ashamed, but do not suffer any cognitive consequences. Future research is needed to isolate the extent to which these effects are exclusive to targets of prejudice and stereotyping.

Is Negative Self-Directed Affect Adaptive?

Although we acknowledge that the intrapersonal costs of not challenging discriminators are upsetting, we believe that they may play a functional role in encouraging targets to confront perpetrators. Many theorists have suggested that when people behave in ways that are discrepant from their personal standards, they become motivated to engage in discrepancy-reduction behaviors (Aronson, 1968; Duval & Wicklund, 1972; Festinger, 1957; Pyszczynski & Greenberg, 1987). The motivation arises because of the self-directed negative affect that accompanies the discrepancy. People are driven to reduce this negative affect. One way in which individuals could reduce the discrepancy between their behavior and values is by changing their future behavior so as to be more consistent with their values. Thus, individuals could decide to challenge discrimination in future situations in order to avoid feeling ashamed and guilty. This is not unlike cognitive dissonance theory, which also finds that individuals are driven to reduce negative affect by means of an attitude or behavior change when confronted with inconsistency between their thoughts and behavior (Festinger, 1957). In other words, one function of self-directed negative affect, therefore, is to motivate individuals to confront perpetrators more regularly. Of course, it will be necessary for individuals to weigh the group benefits and personal costs associated with this decision (see Miller, chap. 2, this volume). As opposed to motivating individuals to confront perpetrators more regularly, self-directed negative affect that results from self-discrepancies may motivate individuals to change their values so that the values are more in line with their behavior. For example, targets of prejudice who experience discrimination yet choose not to confront the perpetrator could change their values to match their behavior and decide that challenging discrimination is not important and then feel comfortable not confronting a perpetrator. According to the theoretical framework of our research, targets that engage in such a value change will not feel ashamed or guilty because their values and behaviors will be consistent. We hope, of course, that this attitude change is not the path that individuals decide to take.

FINAL THOUGHTS

We conclude with the question that probably plagues most targets of prejudice when they encounter interpersonal prejudice—to confront or not to confront? Previous research suggests that targets face a number of both affective and material consequences when they do confront perpetrators (Kaiser, chap. 3, this volume). In fact, these costs dissuade targets from doing just that (Shelton & Stewart, 2004). In the research presented in this chapter, we have shown that targets also face a number of both affective and cognitive consequences when they do not confront perpetrators. The interpersonal costs associated with confronting perpetrators of prejudice, and the intrapersonal costs associated with not confronting leave targets of prejudice in quite a dilemma. If they confront someone who behaves in a prejudiced manner, that person will dislike them. However, if they do not confront the person, they will dislike themselves at that moment.

Given this dilemma, to echo Czopp and Monteith (2003) in the words of Eberhardt and Fiske (1996), "What is a target to do?" There is, of course, no easy answer to this question. Situational and personality factors will determine which route (confront or not) targets will follow and the costs with which they will have to cope. For some targets, coping with the interpersonal costs will be so great that they will be willing to suffer the intrapersonal costs. For others, the opposite will be true—they will be willing to bear the interpersonal costs in order to feel good about themselves. When considering our research and Kaiser's research (chap. 3, this volume) in tandem, perhaps the following strategy is wise: Targets of prejudice should confront perpetrators when they are committed to fighting discrimination and they think they should confront in that particular situation. Targets should not confront perpetrators (even when they think they should) when the perpetrator endorses ideologies such as individualism and the Protestant ethic and the consequences of the perpetrators' evaluations are serious.

Thus, the decision to confront or not to confront will require a delicate balancing of both the interpersonal cost of confronting, as well as the intrapersonal costs of not confronting. The research presented in this chapter is offered as a first step toward identifying some of the intrapersonal costs associated with not confronting perpetrators of prejudice and discrimination. Coupled with research on the interpersonal costs of confronting perpetrators, we hope that this work will spark research aimed at understanding how targets of prejudice manage this balancing act in the face of discrimination in everyday life.

REFERENCES

Aronson, E. (1968). The theory of cognitive dissonance: A current perspective. In L. Berkowitz (Ed.), *Advances in experimental social psychology* (Vol. 4, pp. 1–34). San Diego, CA: Academic Press.

Bargard, A., & Hyde, J. S. (1991). Women's studies: A study of feminist identity development in women. *Psychology of Women Quarterly, 15,* 181–201.

Crosby, F. J. (1993). Why complain? *Journal of Social Issues, 49,* 169–184.

Czopp, A. M., & Monteith, M. J. (2003). Confronting prejudice (literally): Reactions to confrontations of racial and gender bias. *Personality and Social Psychology Bulletin, 29,* 532–544.

Czopp, A. M., Monteith, M. J., & Mark, A. Y. (2004). *Prejudice reduction through interpersonal confrontation: What happens when you speak out against prejudice?* Manuscript under review.

Devine, P., Monteith, M., Zuwerink, J., & Elliot, A. (1991). Prejudice with and without compunction. *Journal of Personality and Social Psychology, 60,* 817–830.

Dodd, E. H., Giuliano, T. A., Boutell, J. M., & Moran, B. E. (2001). Respected or rejected: Perceptions of women who confront sexist remarks. *Sex Roles, 45,* 567–577.

Downing, N. E., & Roush, K. L. (1985). From passive acceptance to active commitment: A model of feminist identity development for women. *The Counseling Psychologist, 13,* 695–709.

Duval, S., & Wicklund, R. A. (1972). *A theory of objective self-awareness.* San Diego, CA: Academic Press.

Eberhardt, J. L., & Fiske, S. T. (1996). Motivating individuals to change: What is the target to do? In C. N. Macrae, C. Stangor, & M. Hewstone (Eds.), *Stereotypes and stereotyping*. New York: Guilford Press.

Festinger, L. (1957). *A theory of cognitive dissonance*. Stanford, CA: Stanford University Press.

Gross, J. (1998). The emerging field of emotion regulation: An integrative review. *Review of General Psychology, 2*, 271–299.

Higgins, E. T. (1987). Self-discrepancy theory: A theory relating self and affect. *Psychological Review, 94*, 319–340.

Kaiser, C. R., & Miller, C. T. (2001). Stop complaining! The social costs of making attributions to discrimination. *Personality and Social Psychology Bulletin, 27*, 254–263.

Kaiser, C. R., & Miller, C. T. (2003). Derogating the victim: The interpersonal consequences of blaming events on discrimination. *Group Processes and Intergroup Relations, 6*, 227–237.

Monteith, M. J. (1993). Self-regulation of prejudiced responses: Implications for progress in prejudice reduction efforts. *Journal of Personality and Social Psychology, 65*, 469–485.

Monteith, M. J. (1996). Affective reactions to prejudice-related discrepant responses: The impact of standard salience. *Personality and Social Psychology Bulletin, 22*(1), 48–59.

O'Neil, J., Egan, J., Owen, S., & McBride-Murry, V. (1993). The gender role journal measure: Scale development and psychometric evaluation. *Sex Roles, 28*, 167–185.

Pennebaker, J. W. (1995). *Emotion, disclosure, and health.* Washington, DC: American Psychological Association.

Pyszczynski, T., & Greenberg, J. (1987). Self-regulatory perseveration and the depressive self-focusing style: A self-awareness theory of reactive depression. *Psychological Bulletin, 102*, 122–138.

Richards, J., & Gross, J. (1999). Composure at any cost? The cognitive consequences of emotion suppression. *Personality and Social Psychology Bulletin, 25*, 1033–1044.

Richards, J., & Gross, J. (2000). Emotion regulation and memory: The cognitive costs of keeping one's cool. *Journal of Personality and Social Psychology, 79*, 410–424.

Shelton, J. N., & Stewart, B. (2004). Confronting perpetrators of prejudice: The inhibitory effects of social costs. *Psychology of Women Quarterly, 28*, 215–223.

Smart, L., & Wegner, D. (1999). Covering up what can't be seen: Concealable stigma and mental control. *Journal of Personality and Social Psychology, 77*, 474–486.

Swim, J. K., & Hyers, L. L. (1998). Excuse me—What did you just say?! Women's public and private responses to sexist remarks. *Journal of Experimental Social Psychology, 35*, 68–88.

Voils, C. I., Ashburn-Nardo, L., & Monteith, M. J. (2002). Evidence of prejudice-related conflict and associated affect beyond the college setting. *Group Processes and Intergroup Relations, 5*(1), 19–33.

Wegner, D. M. (1994). Ironic processes of mental control. *Psychological Review, 101*, 34–52.

Zuwerink, J. R., Devine, P. G., Monteith, M. J., & Cook, D. A. (1996). Prejudice toward Blacks: With and without compunction? *Basic and Applied Social Psychology, 18*, 131–150.

CHAPTER

5

Concealable Versus Conspicuous Stigmatized Identities

Diane M. Quinn
University of Connecticut

A *social stigma* is defined as a negative attribute or identity that devalues a person within a particular context or culture (Goffman, 1963; Jones et al., 1984). In an attempt to define the different types, or dimensions, of stigma, Goffman discusses three main types—body disfigurements, blemishes of moral character, and "tribal" affiliations such as race or religion. Crossing these three main types, Goffman distinguishes between people who are already "discredited"—that is, their stigma is known to others either because it is immediately visible or because others have previous knowledge of the stigmatized status—or "discreditable"—those whose stigma is concealed. In a review of the stigma literature, Jones et al. (1984) suggested six important dimensions of stigma: visibility/concealability, origin/responsibility for stigmatized condition, aesthetics, peril (i.e., is the stigma perceived as dangerous to others), disruptiveness, and course of the mark (i.e., will it change over time). This search for a way to categorize types of stigma signifies how the experience and consequences of stigma defy a universal explanation. In order to understand the effects of a particular stigmatized status, more must be known about the type of stigma, how it affects the self, and its particular links to the social beliefs that make the mark stigmatizing. Crocker, Major, and Steele (1998) gave a very thorough overview of the current state of research on social stigma. Most of the research to date, however, has focused on the experience of people with a visible stigma. Thus, I limit this chapter to a consideration of some of the key differences between the experience of those with a concealed versus conspicuous stigma. For the purposes of this chapter, a *concealed stigma* is defined as a stigmatized identity that is not immediately knowable in a social interaction, such as a history of mental illness or incarceration. In the first section of the chapter, I discuss some of the experiences unique to those with a concealed stigma, including deciding when and to whom to reveal, short- and long-term consequences of keeping an identity concealed, and concerns about discovery. In order to highlight similarities and differences of concealed and conspicuous stigma, I then compare stereotype threat research examining gender, a conspicuous stigma, with work on mental illness, a concealed stigma.

SOME KEY QUESTIONS ABOUT CONCEALED STIGMA

When to Reveal? To Whom?

Unlike people with a conspicuous stigma, those with a concealed stigma usually have more control over when, or if, they reveal their status and to whom they reveal it. This level of control has some benefits. People with a concealed stigmatized identity can choose situations in which they feel comfortable and safe to reveal their identity. This can help to maintain personal boundaries and gives them control over levels of intimacy with others (Derlega & Chaiken, 1977; Kelly & McKillop, 1996). They can also choose to not reveal the stigmatized identity in contexts in which they are concerned about negative repercussions (such as in an interview or employment situation), and thus do not have to be constantly on the alert for prejudice and discrimination like a person with a conspicuous stigma. Jones and colleagues (1984) noted that people with a concealed stigma may have better initial interactions with others. They can "pass" in day-to-day activities (Goffman, 1963). Concealment may allow the person to proceed with acquaintance level relationships and activities with fewer burdens than a person with a visible devalued identity.

Once relationships progress beyond the initial interaction, however, a number of difficult issues arise for people with concealable stigmas. If a person has been maintaining their hidden identity but wants to reveal it, she or he must decide at what point in a relationship to reveal. If revealed too soon, the stigmatized person may worry about losing the relationship, and be concerned that the other person will break the confidentiality around the stigma (i.e., tell others). Research has shown that, overall, personal disclosure is related to greater liking, but there is some indication that people become uncomfortable when highly personal details are revealed too early in the relationship, perhaps because they feel they must reciprocate with intimate information of their own (Collins & Miller, 1994; Cozby, 1973). However, if the stigmatized person waits until a trusting relationship is formed before revealing, the relationship may be hurt because the stigmatized person is seen as not honest or trusting of the relationship enough to reveal earlier. Complicating this decision is research showing that people who are known to have something to hide, but who do not disclose, are liked less than those who do disclose (Jones & Archer, 1976). Yet, whether a person is seen as responsible for a negative personal plight also affects whether others like a person who reveals early in a relationship versus later. For example, Jones and Gordon (1972) found that a person who had been expelled from school due to cheating was liked more by participants if he revealed this information very early in an interaction—in a sense, he was seen as not trying to hide or misrepresent himself. However, if the person was forced to leave school due to parental divorce proceedings, he was liked more if he waited until late in an interaction to reveal this information. Perhaps if stigmatizing information is revealed too early in an interaction, the individual is perceived as trying to place blame on others for any misfortune and not take personal responsibility (something that goes against America's dominant ideology; see Kaiser, chap. 3, this volume).

Moreover, some concealed stigmas reveal themselves. For example, work on the stigma of epilepsy has shown that although many people with epilepsy keep their diagnosis a secret, they also worry about an unexpected epileptic seizure that might alert others to their condition—an involuntary disclosure of their stigma (see Jacoby, 2002, for a review). Likewise, other types of medical conditions can have uncontrollable side effects (e.g., shaking or vomiting) or concomitants that are difficult to hide (e.g., necessity of taking frequent medication). These types of stigma cues make it more difficult to conceal stigma and lessen the degree of comfort and control people have over their stigmatized identities (Golin, Isasi, Bontempi, & Eng, 2002). If stigma is revealed involuntarily, it also takes away the ability to choose to whom the identity is revealed.

Most experimental research on disclosure has been conducted with strangers or confederates in the laboratory, making it more difficult to gauge how people make the decision about to whom to disclose stigmatized identity. Not surprisingly, people report disclosing stigmatized identities primarily to close others, such as family or close friends. People with stigmatized identities who do reveal to others, however, risk negative or non-helpful responses and possible alienation (Kelly & McKillop, 1996). Therefore, being aware of (and correct about) who will or will not be supportive can have important psychological consequences. For example, research by Major and colleagues (Major et al., 1990) on psychological distress after abortion found that women who told a source (friend, family, or partner) but did not get complete support from them were more depressed and had lower coping self-efficacy postabortion than either women who told a supportive source or did not disclose at all. Thus, having a concealed versus conspicuous stigmatized identity gives a person more control over when to reveal, but this control comes with the cost of making difficult, and potentially costly, decisions about when and to whom to reveal.

Keeping It Concealed: What Are the Short- and Long-Term Consequences?

Perhaps the issue most dissimilar for those with concealable versus conspicuous stigmas is that people with a concealed stigma must worry about discovery: Will others find out? Am I leaking any cues that would make them suspect my status? Have they heard anything about me? This is Goffman's (1963) issue of being "discreditable." One may pass as nonstigmatized, but he or she then has the potential of being unmasked, discredited. The work required to keep a stigma concealed, and, thereby elude discovery, has been considered akin to an additional cognitive load. For example, research has shown that after a 5-minute conversation with a stranger, people with a concealable deviance were more likely than those with a visible deviance to report taking their partner's perspective (metaperspectives), taking particular notice of the interaction flow, and paying close attention to their partner's words (Frable, Blackstone, & Scherbaum, 1990). Frable and colleagues conclude that people with a deviant "master status" are more mindful in their interactions with others in order to be on the alert for cues of discrimination and devaluation. Likewise, research by Smart and Wegner (1999) examined the effect of keeping an eating disorder concealed. Except in the extremely underweight stage of anorexia, most eating disorders are not visible to strangers. In the Smart and Wegner studies, participants with and without an eating disorder were asked to role-play a person with or without an eating disorder while being interviewed by a study confederate. Participants who had an eating disorder but actively tried to conceal it during an interview that asked questions about eating and food reported that they worked harder to suppress thoughts of their disorder and were more concerned with secrecy than those not trying to conceal an eating disorder. They also reported increasing accessibility of eating-disorder thoughts over time, signifying that the more they tried to conceal their stigma, the more it was on their mind. Interestingly, in these particular studies, ratings of the participants attempting to keep their stigma concealed revealed that they did not seem more uncomfortable or neurotic than those without a concealed stigma. Thus, although maintaining a concealed stigma may add a cognitive and emotional burden, it did not seem to hinder an initial interaction, supporting Jones et al.'s (1984) contention that a concealed stigma leads to more positive social interactions than conspicuous stigma. Both the Frable et al. (1990) and the Smart and Wegner (1999) research point to the idea that people with concealed stigmas are quite facile at maintaining positive social interactions despite the additional cognitive burden. As Miller (chap. 2, this volume) notes, every stigma-coping strategy has both costs and benefits—by concealing their stigma, people reap the benefits of being considered unmarked in a social interaction, but incur the cost of an extra cognitive burden.

The aforementioned studies seem to suggest that the costs of maintaining a concealed identity are minimal. This may be true for initial, or short-term, interactions. The long-term effects of maintaining a concealed identity are likely to be more burdensome. Drawing on the work already mentioned showing that actively concealing an identity might lead to more intrusive thoughts, Major and Gramzow (1999) tested a model linking increased concealment of an abortion to distress in women 2 years postabortion. The results showed support for a model such that the more stigmatizing women felt abortion was, the more they attempted to keep their own abortion secret from others. Keeping the abortion secret was related to greater attempts at thought suppression, which led to more intrusive thoughts about the abortion. Intrusive thoughts were related to greater psychological distress. It is important to note that although almost half of the women in the study agreed that they would be stigmatized for having an abortion and they did feel the need to keep the abortion a secret from some close others, only around 6% reported suppressing thoughts of the abortion "quite a bit" or a "great deal." Thus, coping with a concealed stigma, particularly through thought suppression, is likely quite variable (see Miller, chap. 2, this volume; and Swim & Thomas, chap. 6, this volume, for reviews of types of coping with stigma).

Research on the long-term health effects of concealing sexual identity for gay men has linked increased concealment (self-reporting being half or mostly "in the closet") with higher rates of cancer and other infectious diseases (bronchitis, sinusitis; Cole, Kemeny, Taylor, & Visscher, 1996); and, for HIV-positive men, an accelerated progression of AIDS (Cole, Kemeny, Taylor, Visscher, & Fahey, 1996). These processes may be linked both to general issues related to inhibiting emotional expression and to increased loneliness or isolation. Members of visible stigmatized groups are able to easily seek each other out if they so choose. In contrast, people with a concealed stigma have a much more difficult time identifying similarly stigmatized others, and, therefore, may miss an avenue of strong social support and comfort. In an 11-day experience sampling study, Frable, Platt, and Hoey (1998) found that participants with concealable stigmas (sexual orientation, bulimia, or very low socioeconomic status) reported lower self-esteem and more instances of negative affect than participants with visible stigmas (ethnicity and weight). The participants reported an increase in mood when they were around similar others, but they were also the group least likely to spend time around similar others. In addition, maintaining a concealed identity may lead to people refusing to seek optimal medical care or other support. An HIV-positive individual who chooses not to disclose his or her status, may also skip doses of medication and/or not attend clinics or medical appointments in order to avoid inquiries from others that could lead to stigma revelation (Chesney & Smith, 1999).

What Is the Relationship Between Concealed Stigma and Self-Concept?

Crucial to research and understanding of conspicuous stigma is the extent to which the stigmatized identity becomes a central and integrated part of the self-concept. For example, scales exist to measure racial and ethnic identity (e.g., Cross, 1991; Phinney, 1992; Sellers, Rowley, Chavous, Shelton, & Smith, 1997) and gender identity (e.g., Gurin, 1985), and research has explored the extent to which racial and other collective identities are related to self-esteem, perceptions of prejudice, and coping (for reviews, see Ashmore, Deaux, & McLaughlin-Volpe, 2004; and Sellers, Smith, Shelton, Rowley, & Chavous, 1998). People with a visible stigmatized identity, perhaps because they must contend with negative stereotypes about their group on a daily basis, are assumed to incorporate their stigmatized identity into their larger self-concept. Incorporation of the stigmatized identity into the self-concept is considered positive and adaptive. As Crocker and Major (1989) pointed out, members of stigmatized groups may even use their stigma to help protect the self from the negative consequences of societal devaluation.

The distinct nature of concealable stigmas raises questions about how it differs from visible stigma for self-concept processes: To what extent does the concealed stigma become an essential part of one's self-concept and identity? Does the concealable nature of the stigma lead to a relative distancing of the stigma from the self-concept? And, if so, is this likely to lead to positive consequences for the self such that people are less likely to internalize stigmatized attributes and expectations? Or, does it lead to negative consequences for the self such as less protective attributions and more vulnerability to isolation and self-doubt? For concealed stigmas related to medical (or other variable) conditions, does the sense of stigmatized identity wax and wane with the activity or remission of the condition? Very little research has directly addressed these questions. There is some exploration of the experience of receiving a stigma label, such as obtaining a diagnosis of mental illness, cancer, epilepsy, or HIV. For example, Jacoby (2002) reported that at the time people received their initial diagnosis of epilepsy, approximately 25% reported feeling stigmatized. When followed up 2 years after diagnosis, the extent of feelings of stigma was strongly related to the severity of seizure experience. Those who had few seizures reported feeling less stigmatized.

Jacoby (1994) found that among people whose epilepsy was in remission for 2 or more years, self-identification as an "epileptic" dropped, and very few reported that they felt a stigmatized identity. Research on a diagnosis of mental illness, on the contrary, has shown that receiving the label of *mentally ill* is a source of enduring stigma (Link, Struening, Rahav, Phelan, & Nuttbrock, 1997). Perhaps because the negative stereotypes of mental illness are much more encompassing than those of epilepsy, the label of mental illness is more difficult to discard. Link, Cullen, Struening, Shrout, and Dohrenwend (1989) contended that one reason a label of mental illness is difficult for the self is because most people, prior to being labeled, know and, to some extent, endorse the stereotypes about the mentally ill. Once they, themselves, are diagnosed, they have the difficult set of beliefs that includes both that they are mentally ill and that others reject people with mental illness. Maintaining this set of beliefs leads to lower self-esteem and greater belief that one will be ostracized. In a sense, mental illness patients believe the stereotypes about the mentally ill before they become part of the devalued group. Note that this is different from racial and gender identities. Members of racial and gender groups know the stereotypes about their groups, but they are never in the position to be a nongroup member.

If people with concealed stigma do not integrate the stigmatized identity as part of their self-concept, they may be less able to use some of the coping mechanisms that people with visible stigmas utilize. For example, the three strategies Crocker and Major (1989) proposed for protecting self-esteem—attributing negative outcomes to prejudice, comparing to in-group members, and selectively valuing domains at which one's in-group succeeds—seem less available for those with a concealed stigma. If others are not aware of one's stigma, it is difficult to attribute negative life outcomes to prejudice. It is also difficult to find similar others with whom to compare (Frable et al., 1998). It may, however, still be possible to value and devalue particular domains (although support from one's in-group for doing so may not be available). These differences in identification with a stigmatized identity, as well as the breadth of stereotypes related to different types of stigma, and potential coping strategies available, will likely affect what types of situations will result in negative consequences for those with a concealed stigma. I return to this issue later in the chapter with a comparison of gender and mental-illness stigma.

What Are the Consequences of Discovery?

Obviously, the reason people with a concealed stigma are concerned with keeping it concealed is due to the perceived and actual consequences of discovery. People with concealed stigmas are concerned about others' prejudice. They experience anxiety and uncertainty about what the other person's reaction will be if they do discover the stigma. For example, in a study examining reasons why people with HIV decided to disclose or not disclose their status to others (Derlega, Winstead, Green, Serovich, & Elwood, 2002), participants' fear of rejection was correlated with not disclosing their status to parents and friends. Interestingly, in this study the participants also reported that protecting the other person was a reason not to tell parents or friends, as if they did not want close others to carry the burden or worry of their status. Moreover, the greater the amount of perceived HIV-related stigma, the less likely a participant was to disclose to his or her parents. People with a concealed stigma are also in the unique, and very uncomfortable, position of knowing exactly what close others think about their stigmatized identity. Unlike people with conspicuous stigmas, around whom others are likely careful to appear sensitive and nonprejudiced, people with concealed stigmas are likely to be in situations where others blatantly state their stereotypes and prejudiced attitudes. For example, in a survey study of undergraduates with a variety of concealed stigmatized identities, we (Quinn, Chaudoir, & Kallen, 2004) found that just over half of the respondents reported they had been in a situation in which others who were not aware of their concealed identity were derogating people with that identity.

Once a person with a stigmatized identity believes that their interaction partner knows about the stigma, they are placed in a situation more similar to people with a conspicuous devalued identity. Research has shown that when a person with a normally concealed stigma believes that an interaction partner knows about their stigma, they tend to act in less competent and more anxious ways. For example, Farina, Gliha, Boudreau, Allen, and Sherman (1971) conducted a study in which all of the participants were former patients of a psychiatric hospital. The participants interacted with a confederate whom they had been led to believe either knew about their patient status or believed they were medical patients. When participants thought the confederate knew of their psychiatric history, they spoke less often and performed worse on a joint task. They were also more visibly tense and anxious. As noted by Miller (chap. 2, this volume; Miller & Myers, 1998) coping strategies may evolve out of practice with stereotyping situations. If this is the case, people with normally concealed stigma who do not have as much experience coping with visible stigma, may have an added disadvantage when they do reveal.

USING AN IDENTITY THREAT MODEL TO CAPTURE THE SITUATIONAL NATURE OF STIGMA

As noted, one of the negative consequences of keeping a stigma concealed is the extra cognitive burden of maintaining the secret. An important question, however, is what are the conditions or situations in which the stigma is more or less salient for the individual? Although much of the research and theorizing assumes that the person with a concealed stigma is constantly worried about revealing it, this seems unlikely. If a stigma is well-concealed, and the situation is one in which it is unlikely to be revealed, it is reasonable to assume that in such situations, the person is unaffected by it. On the other hand, if the situation is one in which the stigmatized identity is likely to be activated—either through the content of the situation or an increased potential for discovery—then negative consequences may result. To date, because research has primarily focused on visible stigmas, the stigma is in the situation at all times. In a sense, for a person with a visible stigmatized identity, whenever they are with nonstigmatized others, they are alert to the possibility of stigmatization. This is not the case for people with a concealed stigma, but very little research has examined the boundaries of when a stigmatized identity will have an effect. Research on concealed stigma usually puts participants in situations in which the stigma will be salient (e.g., participants with eating disorders are asked to talk about food and diet during the study) or assumes that the concealed identity will always affect behavior (e.g., Frable et al., 1990). However, as noted in the work on abortion by Major and Gramzow (1999), only a small percentage of women reported chronically suppressing thoughts of the abortion. In our survey study, we (Quinn et al., 2004) found a great deal of variability, with approximately one third of the participants reporting they think about their concealed identity once a month or less, one third reporting they think about it once or a few times per week, and the final third thinking about it daily.

Recent theorizing on "stereotype threat" and a broader "identity threat" by Steele, Spencer, and Aronson (2002) may help to clarify some of the situational boundaries surrounding the saliency and consequences of concealed stigmas. Stereotype-threat research has shown that when people are in a situation in which a specific negative stereotype about their group performance is applicable, their behavior is affected. For example, Steele and Aronson (1995) reasoned that an intellectual testing situation is a context in which African American students are aware of a negative stereotype about their abilities. Part of the "Black" stereotype is less intelligence. Thus, whenever African American students are in a situation in which their intelligence is going to be judged, they may worry about that judgment. In a test of this hypothesis, Steele and Aronson found that African American students performed worse than European American students on a standardized test described as diagnostic of their intellectual abilities. When the same test was described as nondiagnostic of ability, African American and European American students performed equally. In an additional study, it was found that the African American students in the diagnostic condition had more thoughts about the racial stereotypes and their own ability on their mind, and avoided describing themselves in ways that could be construed as stereotypical. Thus, it was in a particular type of situation in which stigmatized identity had negative consequences.

In considering a broader definition of how stigmatized or stereotyped identities might affect behavior, Steele et al. (2002) speculated that people with a stigmatized identity will be alert to situational cues that signify that they may be devalued on the basis of their identity. Being on guard for such cues and trying to repudiate them if necessary is an extra burden that results for those who experience such "identity threat." Importantly, for both stereotype threat and identity threat, the threat is situationally bound. Particular situations raise particular threats. A person's stigmatized identity will not impinge on the self or behavior if it is not somehow relevant to the situation and activated in the person's mind. Thinking about the effects of stigmatized status in this way leads to some new ways to conceptualize when and how a concealed identity may affect the self and behavior.

Conspicuous Versus Concealed: An Example With Gender and Mental Illness

As an example of how identity threat can be used to explore the ramifications of different types of stigmatized identities, I am going to cite the research of my colleagues and me on the effects of threat on academic performance. In our research we have examined women as a stigmatized or stereotyped group, and, in separate research, we have examined people with a history of mental illness. Thinking about women as a stigmatized group points to the stickiness, or, contextuality, of defining *stigma*. Gender is always conspicuous, but it is not always stigmatized. Whether female gender is a devalued social identity is highly dependent on the context. In terms of Goffman's "character flaws," women are stereotypically portrayed to possess flaws such as being more narcissistic about their appearance, less intelligent, and less ambitious than men. Women in particular cultures and at particular times are deeply stigmatized for simply having a woman's body. Indeed, *objectification theory* (Fredrickson & Roberts, 1997) suggested that by constantly being bombarded with images of women's bodies as idealized sexual objects unrelated to the person, women learn to objectify themselves and experience distaste and revulsion for their own bodies (Fredrickson, Roberts, Noll, Quinn, & Twenge, 1998). Clearly, whether a woman's gender is linked to a devalued identity depends on situational cues indicating that she may be stereotyped or viewed through a stigmatizing mark or characteristic.

My own research has focused on the effects of stereotypes about women's math abilities on their math performance (Quinn & Spencer, 2001; Spencer, Steele, & Quinn, 1999). When women are taking a math test or are in a math class, they are in a situation in which a stereotype linked to their gender could be activated. Notably, gender itself is a visible characteristic. Thus, in this case, women's devalued identity is known to all in the situation. In trying to understand when women will be affected by their gender identity, the focus must turn to the content of the environment. Research on stereotype threat has shown that when (a) there is a negative stereotype in the culture about a group's intellectual performance (e.g., "Women are bad at math"); and (b) members of the stereotyped group are in a situation in which that stereotype could be used to evaluate them (e.g., performance on a diagnostic standardized test, such as the SAT); then (c) those group members tend to be negatively affected (e.g., through worse performance). However, when the situation is changed such that the stereotype is no longer relevant to judgment of the self or one's outcomes, members of stereotyped groups perform equally with their nonstereotyped peers. For example, Spencer and colleagues (Davies, Spencer, Quinn, & Gerhardstein, 2002; Quinn & Spencer, 2001; Spencer et al., 1999) found that when equally prepared men and women took a difficult math test, women tended to underperform in comparison to men. However, the performance difference disappears when men and women are led to believe that the same test had shown no gender differences in the past, thereby making the stereotype (and the women's identity) irrelevant to this situation. Inzlicht and Ben-Zeev (2000) showed that the gender make-up of the testing situation can make the stereotype more or less applicable. Women who took a math test when they were the minority (two other test takers were men) performed worse than when the other test takers were women. Moreover, in recent work (Quinn & Kallen, 2004), we found that even after receiving performance feedback (positive or negative) women reported feeling less comfortable and more concerned with bias in stereotype-threat situations compared to those described as gender fair. Considering how the situation can activate or deactivate particular stigmatized identities helps to define when an identity is likely to affect behavior and levels of comfort. Thus, in considering when members of different stigmatized groups may experience a threat of devaluation, the most important determinant may be whether they are in a situation in which they believe others know about and can use their stigmatized status to devalue them. With that in mind, I consider how identity threat might help shed light on when a concealed stigmatized identity—mental illness—might affect behavior.

Although various forms of mental illness are common in the population, having a mental illness is considered a highly socially stigmatizing condition. The stereotypes associated with being mentally ill devalue almost all aspects of a person and include being less socially acceptable, less intelligent, more unpredictable, mentally disorganized, dangerous, and dirty (Farina, Fischer, Boudreau, & Belt, 1996; Fracchia, Canale, Cambria, Ruest, &

Sheppard, 1976; Link et al., 1997; Nunnally, 1961). Stereotypes about mental illness not only affect the way that others treat those with mental illness (e.g., distancing, discriminating; see Corrigan & Penn, 1997; Link, 1987; Link et al., 1997), but may also affect the social expectations and beliefs about future social interactions of the mentally ill themselves (Farina & Ring, 1965).

The stigma of mental illness varies along a continuum of concealable to conspicuous. Whereas the large majority of people who get treated for such conditions as depression, anxiety, and phobias are not immediately identifiable as having a mental illness, people in the midst of a psychotic episode are easily recognized as having some mental problems. Even less conspicuous is the person who has undergone treatment for a mental illness in the past, but is no longer in the active stages of mental illness. In the research reported below, our participants were highly functioning university students who had been treated for a mental illness. For these students, the stigma of mental illness was concealable.

In comparing the stereotype-threat research on gender (a conspicuous stigmatized identity) to history of mental illness (a concealed stigma), several differences become apparent. Stereotype-threat research has examined groups with visible stigmas that have very specific stereotypes about their academic abilities linked to their group identities. For those with a mental illness history, however, the situation is different on both of these points (visibility and specific academic stereotypes). For example, because women's gender is conspicuous in the situation, the "control" or "baseline" condition for women taking a standardized math test should be to perform below their full potential. We have found that simply placing women in a standardized math testing situation leads to underperformance. There is no need to mention gender or gender differences (Quinn & Spencer, 2001; Spencer et al., 1999); the conspicuous identity combines with the stereotype-relevant situation. For people with a history of mental illness, a testing situation should be different. We hypothesized that the baseline for them would be to perform at their full ability. Their stigmatized identity is concealed and not likely to be known or applied within the testing situation. If there is no chance of anybody knowing their identity, there is no threat. If, however, their mental illness identity is revealed in a testing situation, they face a broader stigma than women in a math situation. The stigma of mental illness devalues at almost every level; those in need of treatment for mental illness are seen as inferior, incompetent, childlike, insecure, awkward, confused, and dangerous (e.g., Cohen & Struening, 1962; Sibicky & Dovidio, 1986). Thus, once a mental illness identity is revealed in a situation, that situation is likely to become threatening, in the sense that now a person must prove him or herself a competent, worthwhile human. Being in a situation of identity threat during a testing situation is likely to lead to lowered performance for those with a mental-illness stigma because the test performance is a means by which their competence and intelligence could be judged and found lacking.

We put this possibility to the test in several studies (see Quinn, Kahng, & Crocker, 2004), two of which are described here. In each of the experiments, we examined how revealing the normally concealed identity of a history of mental illness treatment affects test performance. For example, in one study (Quinn et al., 2004, Study 2), we brought college students into the lab to take a standardized test similar to the analytical section of the Graduate Record Exam. Several weeks prior to the laboratory session, participants had taken part in a mass prescreening session in which they completed questions about their mental health background. For this study, we selected participants for our "mental-illness history" group if they indicated that they had previously experienced psychological problems for which they had sought treatment (medication, counseling, or both), and that the type of psychological problem was related to depression. For our "no mental-illness history" group, we selected participants who had indicated that they had not had any major psychological problems and had never sought treatment of any kind. In this study, we chose depression both because it is a disorder that affects many people, thereby making our results generalizable to a larger population, and because it would be a stringent test of the hypothesis. Depression is arguably less stigmatizing than many other disorders (e.g., schizophrenia), and if a subtle manipulation such as ours initiates identity threat and affects performance, then the effects may be much larger for other mental-illness conditions (see Corrigan & Holtzman, 2001, for a theoretical discussion of how stereotype threat could affect cognitive deficits found with schizophrenia).

In order to manipulate whether the concealed identity is revealed or not during a testing situation, we had all participants complete a short background questionnaire before taking the standardized test. For half of the participants, the background questionnaire contained the same questions about mental-health history as in the prescreening. This was our "reveal" condition. For the other half of the participants, these questions were omitted. We hypothesized that when no mention of the stigmatized identity is made in a testing situation, participants with and without a history of mental illness will perform equally well. Because there is nothing to activate the concealed stigmatized identity, there is no reason it should impinge on performance. Note that this is different from stereotype-threat research on participants with conspicuous stigmatized identities such as gender and race. In those studies, the devalued identity is activated simply by the content of the testing situation. That is, a math situation automatically activates the gender and math stereotype leading women to score lower on a difficult math test than men (Spencer et al., 1999). In addition, unlike other research on concealed stigma, we are not assuming that people with concealed stigmas are perpetually aware of and harmed by their concealed identity. When participants do reveal their identity, we hypothesize that the situation becomes one of identity threat. The devalued identity is activated by the questions, the participants are aware that the experimenter will know their status, and they must contend with being negatively judged. We predicted that in this situation, participants with a history of mental illness would perform worse than in the no-reveal condition.

In addition, the study examined whether the evaluative pressure of the testing situation affected performance. Previous work on stereotype threat with both race and gender has shown that when the test is made nonevaluative by informing participants that the test is not diagnostic of ability, participants with stereotyped identities perform just as well as their nonstereotyped counterparts (Aronson, Quinn, & Spencer, 1998). That is, the stereotype-threat effect disappears when group members can no longer be judged and found lacking on the dimension specifically relevant to the stereotype. It is not clear that the process would be the same for people with a history of mental illness stigma. As already noted, the stigma attached to mental illness is very broad, devaluing almost every aspect of the person. Instead of one specific stereotype (e.g., "bad at math"), the stigma of mental illness questions the basic competence of the person. If this is the case, even when a test is described as nondiagnostic of abilities, a person who has just revealed their mental illness identity may still worry that they will be judged. To examine this possibility, all participants in the study completed two tests. The first was described as nondiagnostic (being used to "develop questions for future use"), the second as diagnostic (an "accurate indicator of a person's reasoning ability"). In sum, the design of the study was a 2 (history: no mental illness history vs. mental-illness history) by 2 (reveal or no reveal) by 2 (test description: nondiagnostic or diagnostic) with the test description a within-participants factor and history and reveal as between-participants factors.

As can been seen in Fig. 5.1, the results showed that participants with a history of mental illness performed worse when they revealed that history than when they did not reveal. This pattern was particularly strong on the diagnostic test, although it appears on both tests. For participants with no history of mental illness, there were no significant effects of being asked about their history, although in the diagnostic condition, there was a trend for them to do better in the reveal condition. In a recent meta-analysis of stereotype threat research, Walton and Cohen (2003) found a consistent pattern such that the nonstereotyped groups tend to get a performance lift when in the stereotype threat conditions, perhaps because they are reminded of their own superior status.

In comparing the experience of the participants in this study who had a normally concealed identity of mental illness with female participants in

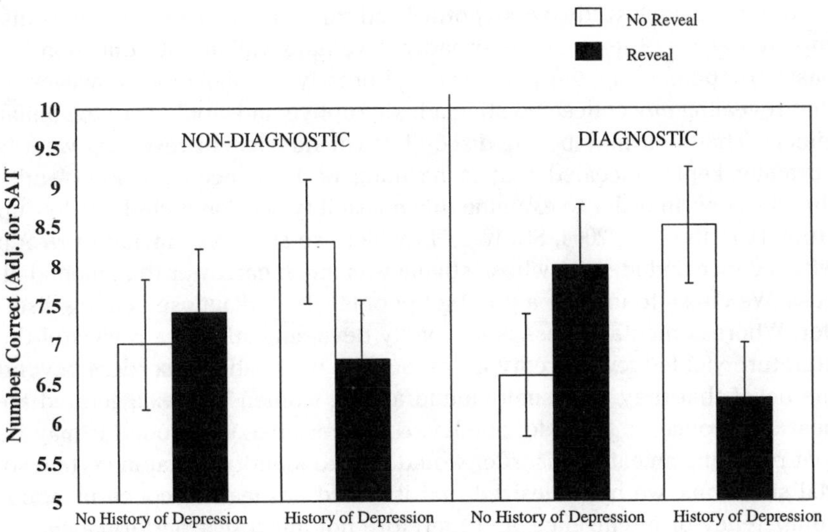

FIG. 5.1. Performance on reasoning test by depression treatment history and condition. From Quinn, Kahng, and Crocker, 2004, p. 809. Copyright © 2004 by Sage Publications. Reprinted with permission.

the stereotype-threat and math studies, we see both similarities and differences. As soon as women enter a math-testing situation, they are likely in an identity-threat situation; their gender is conspicuous and the math situation lends a devalued status to their gender. They are concerned about being judged on the stereotype-relevant performance and that concern translates to worse performance. The threat can be alleviated by changing the situation such that they no longer think the stereotype is applicable (e.g., the test is described as gender fair) or by taking away the possibility of evaluation (e.g., by describing the test as nondiagnostic of ability). In contrast, for people with a mental-illness history, their devalued identity is not automatically cued by a standardized-testing situation. Because the identity is normally concealed and there are no cues in the situation that would alert a person for identity threat, performance is not diminished. However, once the identity is revealed—in this case through simply noting their history in a questionnaire—the situation becomes one of identity threat. People with a mental-illness history now must be alert and concerned for evaluative judgment. Just as with the women taking a math test, this concern translates into lowered performance. But different from women, the performance decrement occurs in the nondiagnostic condition as well. The test is a clear way in which their competency can be judged, and they now have an extra burden of proving themselves worthy through their performance.

In the previous study, we hypothesized that mental-illness stigma is disruptive because the stigma is broadly devaluing, calling into question the basic competency of the person. An alternative explanation, however, is that revealing *any* concealed stigma is disruptive and would lead to similar effects. That is, it may be the discomfort (or novelty) of revealing what is normally kept concealed that is harming performance and not identity threat per se. In order to examine this possibility, we conducted a follow-up study (Quinn et al., 2004, Study 3), in which we sought to include a group with a concealed identity whose stigma was much narrower than mental illness. We chose to include a group of people with a diagnosed eating disorder. Whereas mental illness is a broadly devaluing stigma, a review of the literature yielded few stereotypes associated with eating disorders beyond the belief that they are usually found among women with exaggerated appearance concerns (Chiodo, Stanley, & Harvey, 1984). Although it may be that revealing an eating disorder would lead to identity threat in certain social situations, we hypothesized that it would not lead to concerns about competency or intelligence, and therefore not affect test performance.

The design of this study was a 3 (type of history: history of mental illness treatment vs. history of eating disorders vs. no history) by 2 (reveal vs. no reveal). We predicted that for participants with no history of mental illness or eating disorders, we would see a similar trend to the previous study, with slightly better performance in the reveal versus no-reveal condition. For participants with a history of mental illness, we predicted a replication of the previous study, with participants showing decreased performance after revealing their identity. For participants with a history of an eating disorder we predicted their performance would neither be hindered (as the mental illness participants) nor helped (as the no-history participants) by revealing their stigmatized identity. We used the same method, with the reveal questions embedded in a questionnaire given directly before the test. For all participants the test was described as diagnostic of reasoning ability. Participants with a history of mental illness were selected for study if they reported treatment for any type of psychological problem (not just depression) during the mass prescreening. The eating disorder participants were selected if they reported having a diagnosed eating disorder.

The results of the study supported our predictions. As can be seen in Fig. 5.2, the mental-illness history participants scored higher in the no-reveal than the reveal condition; whereas a nonsignificant reversal occurred for those with no mental-illness history. The performance of the participants with a history of eating disorders did not differ in reveal and no-reveal conditions. The pattern of results supports our hypothesis that revealing a mental illness identity is broadly devaluing and likely leads to concern over proving oneself competent and worthwhile in an evaluative situation such as taking a standardized test. A history of eating disorders, also a conceal-

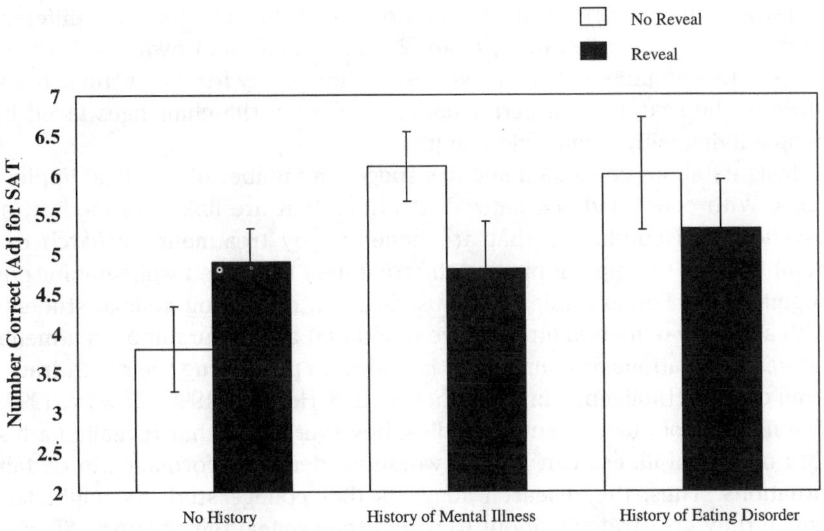

FIG. 5.2. Performance on reasoning test by treatment history and condition. From Quinn, Kahng, and Crocker, 2004, p. 812. Copyright © 2004 by Sage Publications. Reprinted with permission.

able stigma, does not carry the same negative connotations about basic competency and ability. Simply revealing this normally concealed identity did not lead to the same level of decrement in performance as revealing a history of mental illness.

Results of this study illustrate that in order to understand and predict the ramifications of different concealed stigmas, it is important to not only know if the concealed stigma is salient, but also whether the situation leads people to be concerned and wary of devaluation from others.

CONCLUSIONS

This chapter began with a list of key questions—by no means exhaustive—about the concerns and consequences unique to concealed stigma. How do people with a concealed stigma decide whom to tell and when to tell them? What are the consequences of concealing a stigma versus the consequences of revealing? Some research has started to answer these questions, but much more needs to be done. Recent work on the ramifications of conspicuous stigma, including most of the chapters in this book, has shed considerable light on the incredible number of ways that stigma affects people's lives and interactions. Future research might focus on the applicability of these frameworks to concealable stigma, noting where they intersect and where they diverge. Current work on the costs and benefits of different coping strategies (see Miller, chap. 2, this volume and Swim & Thomas, chap. 6, this volume) will also give researchers many fruitful avenues to explore in the search for a better understanding of the challenges faced by people living with a concealed stigma.

Insights about concealed stigmas suggest a number of practical implications. With concealed stigmatized identities that are linked to medical or psychological conditions that are benefited by treatment, research can point to ways to help people find the treatment they need while minimizing stigma costs. For example, previous research examining college students with a history of mental illness have noted that active pursuit of treatments (either medications or counseling) is critical in preventing their withdrawal from college (Heiligenstein, Guenther, Hsu, & Herman, 1996; Illovsky, 1997). The findings of our presented studies, however, show that revealing a history of mental illness can lead to worse academic performance in certain situations. Thus, the research suggests that college students might fare best if they are strategic about to whom they reveal their history. Sharing the history with close supportive others and with therapists may lesson the cognitive load and lead to helpful treatment options; whereas sharing the history with teachers or classmates should be undertaken with care. The findings of these studies also provide implications for counselors and teachers who work with students with concealed identities, such as learning disorders, history of mental illness, or history of family abuse. Teachers and counselors need to be particularly careful that they do not maximize stigma by pulling students out of class at odd times or otherwise highlighting the students' differences and taking away the control the student has over when and how to disclose.

REFERENCES

Aronson, J., Quinn, D. M., & Spencer, S. J. (1998). Stereotype threat and the academic underperformance of minorities and women. In J. K. Swim & C. Stangor (Eds.), *Prejudice: The target's perspective* (pp. 83–103). San Diego, CA: Academic Press.

Ashmore, R. D., Deaux, K., & McLaughlin-Volpe, T. (2004). An organizing framework for collective identity: Articulation and significance of multidimensionality. *Psychological Bulletin, 130*(1), 80–114.

Chesney, M. A., & Smith, A. W. (1999). Critical delays in HIV testing and care: The potential role of stigma. *American Behavioral Scientist, 42*(7), 1162–1174.

Chiodo, J., Stanley, M., & Harvey, J. H. (1984). Attributions about anorexia nervosa and bulimia. *Journal of Social and Clinical Psychology, 2*(3), 280–285.

Cohen, J., & Struening, E. L. (1962). Opinions about mental illness in the personnel of two large mental hospitals. *Journal of Abnormal and Social Psychology, 64*, 349–360.

Cole, S. W., Kemeny, M. E., Taylor, S. E., & Visscher, B. R. (1996). Elevated physical health risk among gay men who conceal their homosexual identity. *Health Psychology, 15*(4), 243–251.

Cole, S. W., Kemeny, M. E., Taylor, S. E., Visscher, B. R., & Fahey, J. L. (1996). Accelerated course of human immunodeficiency virus infection in gay men who conceal their homosexual identity. *Psychosomatic Medicine, 58*(3), 219–231.

Collins, N. L., & Miller, L. C. (1994). Self-disclosure and liking: A meta-analytic review. *Psychological Bulletin, 116*(3), 457–475.

Corrigan, P. W., & Holtzman, K. L. (2001). Do stereotype threats influence social cognitive deficits in schizophrenia? In P. W. Corrigan & D. L. Penn (Eds.), *Social cognition and schizophrenia* (pp. 175–192). Washington, DC: American Psychological Association.

Corrigan, P. W., & Penn, D. L. (1997). Disease and discrimination: Two paradigms that describe severe mental illness. *Journal of Mental Health, 6*, 355–366.

Cozby, P. C. (1973). Self-disclosure: A literature review. *Psychological Bulletin, 79*, 73–91.

Crocker, J., & Major, B. (1989). Social stigma and self-esteem: The self-protective properties of stigma. *Psychological Review, 96*, 608–630.

Crocker, J., Major, B., & Steele, C. (1998). Social stigma. In D. Gilbert, S. T. Fiske, & G. Lindzey (Eds.), *The handbook of social psychology* (4th ed., Vol. 2, pp. 504–553). New York: McGraw-Hill.

Cross, W. E. (1991). *Shades of Black: Diversity in African-American identity.* Philadelphia: Temple University Press.

Davies, P. G., Spencer, S. J., Quinn, D. M., & Gerhardstein, R. (2002). Consuming images: How television commercials that elicit stereotype threat can restrain women academically and professionally. *Personality and Social Psychology Bulletin, 28*(12), 1615–1628.

Derlega, V. J., & Chaiken, A. L. (1977). Privacy and self-disclosure in social relationships. *Journal of Social Issues, 33*(3), 102–115.

Derlega, V. J., Winstead, B. A., Green, K., Serovich, J., & Elwood, W. N. (2002). Perceived HIV-related stigma and HIV disclosure to relationship partners after finding out about the seropositive diagnosis. *Journal of Health Psychology, 7*(4), 415–432.

Farina, A., Fischer, E. H., Boudreau, L. A., & Belt, W. E. (1996). Mode of target presentation in measuring the stigma of mental disorder. *Journal of Applied Social Psychology, 26*(24), 2147–2156.

Farina, A., Gliha, D., Boudreau, L. A., Allen, J. G., & Sherman, M. (1971). Mental illness and the impact of believing others know about it. *Journal of Abnormal Psychology, 77*, 1–5.

Farina, A., & Ring, K. (1965). The influence of perceived mental illness on interpersonal relations. *Journal of Abnormal Psychology, 70*(1), 47–51.

Frable, D. E. S., Blackstone, T., & Scherbaum, C. (1990). Marginal and mindful: Deviants in social interactions. *Journal of Personality and Social Psychology, 59*(1), 140–149.

Frable, D. E. S., Platt, L., & Hoey, S. (1998). Concealable stigmas and positive self-perceptions: Feeling better around similar others. *Journal of Personality and Social Psychology, 74*(4), 909–922.

Fracchia, H., Canale, D., Cambria, E., Ruest, E., & Sheppard, D. (1976). Public views of ex-mental consumers: A note on perceived dangerousness and unpredictability. *Psychological Reports, 38*, 495–498.

Fredrickson, B. L., & Roberts, T. A. (1997). Objectification theory: Towards understanding women's lived experience and mental health risks. *Psychology of Women Quarterly, 21*, 173–206.

Fredrickson, B. L., Roberts, T. A., Noll, S. M., Quinn, D. M., & Twenge, J. M. (1998). That swimsuit becomes you: Sex differences in self-objectification, restrained eating, and math performance. *Journal of Personality and Social Psychology, 75*(1), 269–284.

Goffman, E. (1963). *Stigma: Notes on the management of spoiled identity.* Englewood Cliffs, NJ: Prentice Hall.

Golin, C., Isasi, F., Bontempi, J. B., & Eng, E. (2002). Secret pills: HIV-positive patients' experiences taking antiretroviral therapy in North Carolina. *AIDS Education and Prevention, 14*(4), 318–329.

Gurin, P. (1985). Women's gender consciousness. *Public Opinion Quarterly, 49*(2), 143–163.

Heiligenstein, E., Guenther, G., Hsu, K., & Herman, K. (1996). Depression and academic impairment in college students. *Journal of American College Health, 45*, 59–64.

Illovsky, M. (1997). Effects of counseling on grades and retention. *Journal of College Student Psychotherapy, 12*(1), 29–44.

Inzlicht, M., & Ben-Zeev, T. (2000). A threatening intellectual environment: Why females are susceptible to experiencing problem-solving deficits in the presence of males. *Psychological Science, 11*(5), 365–371.

Jacoby, A. (1994). Felt versus enacted stigma: A concept revisited: Evidence from a study of people with epilepsy in remission. *Social Science and Medicine, 38*(2), 269–274.

Jacoby, A. (2002). Stigma, epilepsy and quality of life. *Epilepsy and Behavior, 3*(6), 10–20.

Jones, E. E., & Archer, R. L. (1976). Are there special effects of personalistic self-disclosure? *Journal of Experimental Social Psychology, 12*(2), 180–193.

Jones, E. E., Farina, A., Hastorf, A. H., Markus, H., Miller, D. T., & Scott, R. A. (1984). *Social stigma: The psychology of marked relationships*. New York: Freeman.

Jones, E. E., & Gordon, E. M. (1972). Timing of self-disclosure and its effects on personal attraction. *Journal of Personality and Social Psychology, 24*(3), 358–365.

Kelly, A. E., & McKillop, K. J. (1996). Consequences of revealing personal secrets. *Psychological Bulletin, 120*(3), 450–465.

Link, B. G. (1987). Understanding labeling effects in the area of mental disorders: An assessment of the effects of expectations of rejection. *American Sociological Review, 52*, 96–112.

Link, B. G., Cullen, F. T., Struening, E., Shrout, P. E., & Dohrenwend, B. P. (1989). A modified labeling theory approach to mental disorders: An empirical assessment. *American Sociological Review, 54*, 400–423.

Link, B. G., Struening, E. L., Rahav, M., Phelan, J. C., & Nuttbrock, L. (1997). On stigma and its consequences: Evidence from a longitudinal study of men with dual diagnoses of mental illness and substance abuse. *Journal of Health and Social Behavior, 38*, 177–190.

Major, B., Cozzarelli, C., Sciacchitano, A. M., Cooper, M. L., Testa, M., & Mueller, P. M. (1990). Perceived social support, self-efficacy, and adjustment to abortion. *Journal of Personality and Social Psychology, 59*(3), 452–463.

Major, B., & Gramzow, R. H. (1999). Abortion as stigma: Cognitive and emotional implications of concealment. *Journal of Personality and Social Psychology, 77*(4), 735–745.

Miller, C. T., & Myers, A. M. (1998). Compensating for prejudice: How heavyweight people (and others) control outcomes despite prejudice. In J. K. Swim & C. Stangor (Eds.), *Prejudice: The target's perspective* (pp. 191–218). San Diego, CA: Academic Press.

Nunnally, J. (1961). *Popular conceptions of mental health, their development and change.* New York: Holt.

Phinney, J. S. (1992). The multigroup ethnic identity measure: A new scale for use with diverse groups. *Journal of Adolescent Research, 7*, 156–172.

Quinn, D. M., Chaudoir, S. R., & Kallen, R. W. (2004). *Understanding concealed identity.* Unpublished data, University of Connecticut, Storrs, CT.

Quinn, D. M., Kahng, S. K., & Crocker, J. (2004). Discreditable: Stigma effects of revealing a mental illness on test performance. *Personality and Social Psychology Bulletin, 30*(7), 803–815.

Quinn, D. M., & Kallen, R. W. (2004). *Reducing threat, increasing comfort: Stereotype threat and perceptions of the test-taking situation*. Unpublished manuscript, University of Connecticut, Storrs, CT.

Quinn, D. M., & Spencer, S. J. (2001). The interference of stereotype threat with women's generation of mathematical problem-solving strategies. *Journal of Social Issues, 57*(1), 55–71.

Sellers, R. M., Rowley, S. A. J., Chavous, T. M., Shelton, J. N., & Smith, M. A. (1997). Multidimensional inventory of Black identity: Preliminary investigations of reliability and construct validity. *Journal of Personality and Social Psychology, 73*(4), 805–815.

Sellers, R. M., Smith, M. A., Shelton, J. N., Rowley, S. A. J., & Chavous, T. M. (1998). Multidimensional model of racial identity: A reconceptualization of African American racial identity. *Personality and Social Psychology Review, 2*(1), 18–39.

Sibicky, M., & Dovidio, J. F. (1986). Stigma of psychological therapy: Stereotypes, interpersonal reaction, and the self-fulfilling prophecy. *Journal of Counseling Psychology, 33*(2), 148–154.

Smart, L., & Wegner, D. M. (1999). Covering up what can't be seen: Concealable stigma and mental control. *Journal of Personality and Social Psychology, 77*(3), 474–486.

Spencer, S. J., Steele, C. M., & Quinn, D. M. (1999). Stereotype threat and women's math performance. *Journal of Experimental Social Psychology, 35*(1), 4–28.

Steele, C. M., & Aronson, J. (1995). Stereotype threat and the intellectual test performance of African Americans. *Journal of Personality and Social Psychology, 69*(5), 797–811.

Steele, C. M., Spencer, S. J., & Aronson, J. (2002). Contending with group image: The psychology of stereotype and social identity threat. In M. P. Zanna (Ed.), *Advances in experimental social psychology* (Vol. 34, pp. 379–440). San Diego, CA: Academic Press.

Walton, G. M., & Cohen, G. L. (2003). Stereotype lift. *Journal of Experimental Social Psychology, 39*(5), 456–467.

CHAPTER

6

Responding to Everyday Discrimination: A Synthesis of Research on Goal-Directed, Self-Regulatory Coping Behaviors

Janet K. Swim
Margaret A. Thomas
The Pennsylvania State University

A dominant theme in the previous chapters is the interpersonal and intrapersonal cost-benefit trade off targets face when considering possible coping responses to actual or anticipated discrimination. For instance, after identifying an incident as discriminatory to the self, one specific way of responding to discrimination is to identify the discrimination to others by way of confronting a perpetrator. If this identification challenges an audience's (e.g., a perpetrator's or an observer's) ideology, the audience will feel distress and may cope by derogating the confronter (Kaiser, chap. 3, this volume). However, if the target of the discrimination feels committed to challenging discrimination but does *not* challenge the discrimination, perhaps to avoid derogation, the stigmatized individual will feel worse about her or himself than if they had confronted, and have intrusive thoughts due to discrepancies between her or his actual and ought self (Shelton, Richeson, Salvatore, & Hill, chap. 4, this volume). Cost-benefit considerations also occur when considering the coping response of hiding a stigma. Hiding a stigma to avoid discrimination can result in intrusive thoughts regarding the stigma and long-term negative health effects, but revealing it can result in stereotype-threat responses (Quinn, chap. 5, this volume).

Given these tradeoffs, how do targets of prejudice decide how to cope with actual or potential discrimination? The previous chapters point to some important issues to consider when answering this question. First, targets are not simply faced with the decision to confront or not to confront discrimination or to reveal or not reveal a stigma. Decisions about how to cope with discrimination or potential discrimination are done within the context of selecting among a number of different possible coping responses (Miller, chap. 2, this volume; see also Miller & Kaiser, 2001, Swim, Johnston, & Pearson, 2005).

Second, targets' evaluations of their options and the consequences of their responses are likely to be goal driven (Miller, chap. 2, this volume). Goals will determine whether anticipated and actual consequences of coping responses are judged as desirable or problematic. For example, those who have the goal of challenging discrimination suffer more negative consequences for not confronting than those who do not share this goal (Shelton, Richeson, Salvatore, & Hill, chap. 4, this volume.)

Third, whether a response is interpersonally costly will depend on the goals and response of the audience. For instance, confrontation will likely be interpersonally costly if a perpetrator has the goal of maintaining belief systems (Kaiser, chap. 3, this volume). But if the perpetrator or observers are more open to change, confronting may alter their behaviors or beliefs (e.g., Czopp & Monteith, 2003). In the remainder of this chapter, we elaborate on the role that goals likely play in targets' evaluation and selection of coping responses and how these goals and others' responses impact targets evaluation of the consequences of their coping responses.

SCOPE AND OVERVIEW OF THE CHAPTER

In this chapter we examine proactive and reactive coping responses within the context of everyday forms of discrimination—routine encounters with another's prejudice and discriminatory behavior that pervade people's daily social interactions. We have found that these forms of discrimination are relatively common; people report about two to three of these incidents per week in diary studies (Swim, Hyers, Cohen, & Ferguson, 2001; Swim, Hyers, Cohen, Fitzgerald, & Bylsma, 2003; Swim et al., 2004). Despite the emphasis in psychology on subtle and covert forms of discrimination, everyday discrimination runs the entire spectrum from subtle and covert discrimination to blatant discrimination, particularly from the target's perspective. Even considering this broad spectrum, however, we and others in this book are not addressing institutional or cultural forms of discrimination. Plus, we only address a subset of coping responses because we focus on individual rather than collective action.

We are particularly interested in the role that targets' goals have on their evaluation and selection of coping responses. As illustrated in the previous chapters, researchers studying coping with discrimination have argued that consideration of interpersonal and intrapersonal goals influence target's selection of coping responses. Moreover, adopting a stress and coping framework can also aid in understanding processes involved in coping with discrimination (Miller, chap. 2, this volume; Miller & Kaiser, 2001; Miller & Major, 2000). Although we agree with this assessment, we believe it is useful to place these considerations within the framework of self-regulation processes and core social goals. Understanding self-regulation processes and core goals can help clarify (a) what is threatening or challenging about discrimination, (b) what motivates targets' responses, (c) why targets select particular coping responses, and (d) how targets' evaluate the consequences of their coping responses.

Carver and Scheier's (1998) cybernetic, self-regulation model provides a useful starting point for our discussion of coping with discrimination. This model, presented in Fig. 6.1, indicates that self-regulation processes begin when people compare their perceptions (i.e., inputs) with their goals, standards, or references. A comparison that reveals a discrepancy between inputs and desired goals, standards, or references creates motivation to reduce the discrepancy. These comparison processes can also be framed in reference to *antigoals*, or undesirable end states. Just as people are moti-

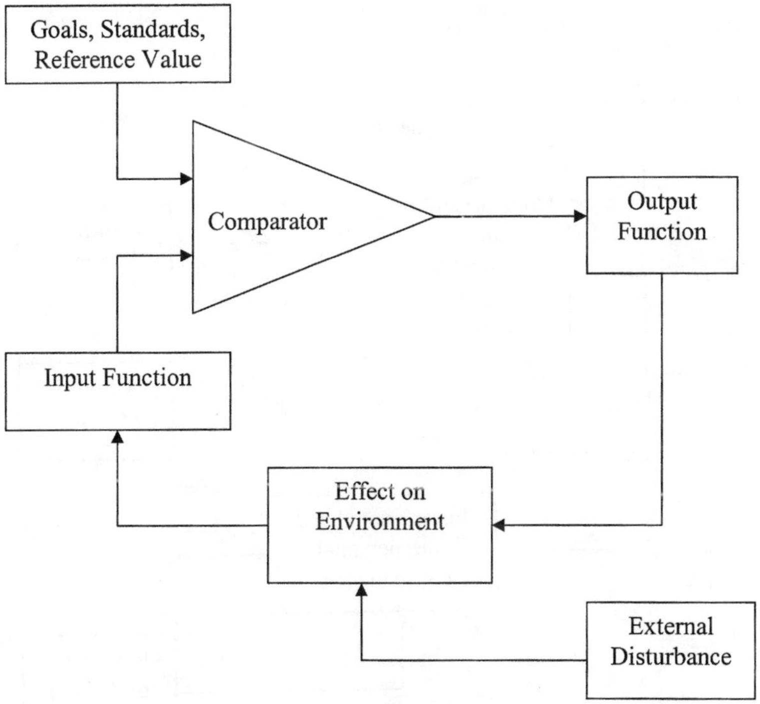

FIG. 6.1. Carver and Scheier's (1998, 2002) self-regulation model. Reprinted with permission of Lawrence Erlbaum Associates.

vated to achieve goals, they are motivated to avoid antigoals. A comparison that indicates closeness to an antigoal creates motivation to increase distance from the antigoal. These motivational states result in outputs that are selected to reduce the discrepancy from goals and increase distance from antigoals. These outputs, as well as external disturbances, influence one's external environment. The effect on the environment leads to a new input and comparison to determine whether one is successfully on the path to reaching a goal or avoiding an antigoal.

Figure 6.2 integrates this self-regulation model and elements from stress and coping models and applies the modified model to voluntary responses to discrimination. The initial input in the self-regulation model becomes an individual's self-identification of actual or potential discrimination (see Stangor et al., 2003, for a discussion on identification of discrimination; also Miller, chap. 2, this volume) and this input is compared with individuals' goals. The goals in self-regulation models range from very situation specific goals to abstract goals. Similarly, a variety of types of goals will also be relevant to appraising experiences with discrimination (Miller, chap. 2, this volume). In the present chapter, however, we consider the role of abstract

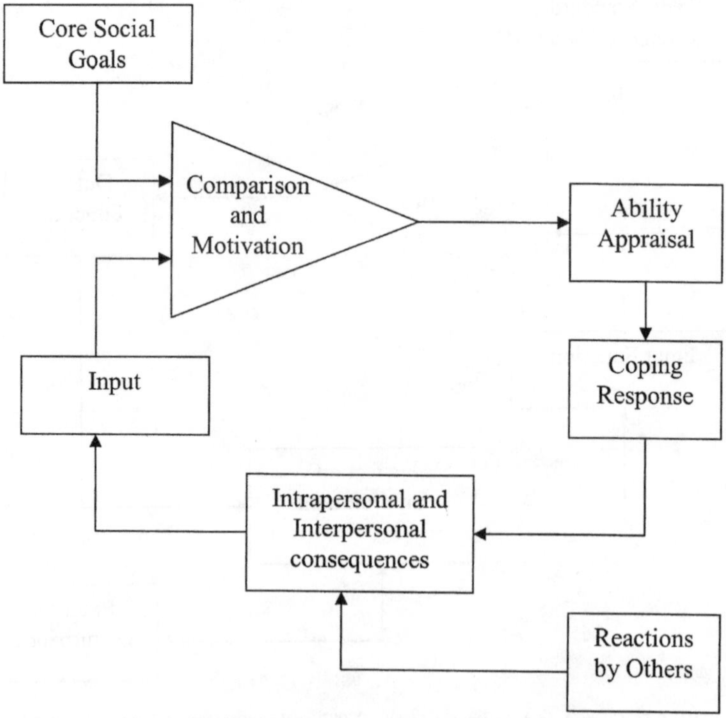

FIG. 6.2. Self-regulation processes in response to discrimination.

goals in terms of core social goals in self-regulation processes. The comparison between the actual or potential discrimination and core social goals can be thought of as an appraisal of the situation, similar to primary appraisals or threat appraisals as described in the health psychology literature. Primary appraisals consist of an assessment of the damage that has already been done by an event and the threat of future damage (Lazarus & Folkman, 1984). Similarly, threat appraisals consist of an assessment of one's vulnerability or susceptibility to a threat and the perceived severity of the threat (Rogers, 1975; Rogers & Prentice-Dunn, 1997). A comparison that indicates that anticipated or actual discrimination blocks goals or matches antigoals creates motivation to consider and select strategies that restore goals or avoid antigoals.

The health psychology literature points to another important type of appraisal to be considered, an appraisal of one's ability to engage in responses that address the situation. These appraisals have been termed *secondary appraisals* or *coping appraisals*. They consist of assessments of one's personal ability to engage in a behavior (i.e., self-efficacy), the ability of a behavior to result in the desired outcome (i.e., response efficacy), and constraints on response options (Lazarus & Folkman, 1984; Rogers, 1975; Rogers & Prentice-Dunn, 1997). Together the comparison process (i.e., primary or threat appraisals) and resultant motivation and the perceived ability to respond (i.e., secondary or coping appraisals) will impact the selection of a coping response (Mallett, 2004).[1] This response as well as possible responses made by others will then influence the social environment. The effect on the social environment can be considered the interpersonal consequences of coping responses. Many coping responses reflect efforts to change the self instead of changing the situation (Rothbaum, Weisz, & Snyder, 1982; Weisz, Rothbaum, & Blackburn, 1984). Therefore, coping responses can potentially have intrapersonal consequences as well interpersonal consequences. These consequences then consist of new input in the self-regulation process, replacing the initial perception of discrimination. Depending on the reevaluated distance from goals and antigoals, the person may consider additional coping responses or exit this particular feedback loop.

As an example, an interaction between two people could look something like the following. While at a party, a female athlete is leading a conversation about women's sports with a few individuals. A male interjects in the conversation, "Although you seem like you know a lot about women's

---

[1]This model indicates that comparison processes precede ability appraisals, which then influence engagement in coping responses selected. However, both processes may independently influence engagement in coping responses. In addition, ability appraisals as well as comparisons could affect motivation (Mallett & Swim, 2004).

sports, I bet you don't know anything about men's sports, and that's what counts" (discrimination). The athlete had been in control of the conversation, and feels as though this comment diminished her control (comparison). This loss of control bothers her and she wants to regain control (motivation). She considers possible responses she can make (ability appraisal) in light of her goal to regain control of the conversation. The woman decides to respond by saying, "Actually, I'd be willing to match wits against you in a contest about sports trivia of *all* kinds" (coping response). She feels good about having stood her ground (intrapersonal consequences). Others present also decide to make comments as well (reactions by others). As a result of her response and other's responses, the male commentator falls silent (interpersonal consequence). She regained control of the situation and was able to leave this feedback loop.

In the remainder of the chapter, we elaborate on the model presented in Fig. 6.2 by discussing: (a) core social goals, (b) discrimination as a potential threat or challenge to core social goals at the comparison stage, (c) evaluation and selection of coping responses in light of core social goals and framing of goals, and (d) the interpersonal and intrapersonal consequences of responses and whether the consequences help targets reach core goals or avoid antigoals.

CORE SOCIAL GOALS

In the present chapter, we consider five core social motives outlined by Fiske (2004). Her organization encompasses several other motivational frameworks and highlights a variety of goals that are likely to be important when considering experiences with discrimination. Although it is possible to argue for other core goals, needs, or motives, it is likely that many of these could be interpreted within these five goals. These five core social goals are the need for self-enhancement, the need to trust others, the need for understanding, the need for control, and the need to belong.

Self-enhancement has been described as a universal human goal that appears in various forms cross-culturally (Sedikides, Gaertner, & Toguchi, 2003). The need for self-enhancement occurs in many frameworks of basic psychological goals, including self-determination theory (Deci & Ryan, 1985, 2000) and is important to research on stigmatized individuals' experiences with discrimination (see Crocker & Garcia, chap. 14, this volume). According to Fiske (2004), the desire to maintain self-esteem and the desire to improve as an individual is encompassed in the need for self-enhancement. Essentially, people like to feel good about themselves (Taylor & Brown, 1988), thus the characterization of self-enhancement as an affective goal. Intrapersonally, self-enhancement involves self-esteem, personal growth, and self-efficacy; we are motivated to feel good about ourselves, maintain that good feeling, and find ways to improve our outlook of ourselves. The need to improve underlies the need for achievement, a goal that has a long history of psychological research (e.g., McClelland, Atkinson, & Clark, 1949). Although primarily self-directed, self-enhancement has an interpersonal aspect as well. Interpersonally, self-enhancement addresses the perception of the public's interpretation and presentation of the self.

A second affective goal is the need for trust, which is primarily an other-directed or interpersonal goal. The need for trust involves seeing the world as a benevolent place. We are motivated to believe that other people are basically good, that they will not purposely hurt us, and that we can depend on them. This motivation is reflected in the belief that the world is just (Lerner & Miller, 1978) and has related justice-based ideologies (Mallett, Huntsinger, & Swim, 2004).

The five core goals also include cognitive goals, the first of which is the reflective goal of understanding. Intrapersonally, this goal includes seeking explanations for other's behavior, a central part of early research on attribution (e.g., Kelley, 1967). Interpersonally, we are driven to have shared meanings with others and to share other relevant individuals' understanding of events or situations. For instance, groups will share information with each other, which serves to reinforce worldviews (Larson, Foster-Fishman, & Keys, 1994). This motivation may be a reason why stigmatized individuals self-stereotype to increase shared reality (Sinclair & Huntsinger, chap. 12, this volume). The drive for shared meaning suggests that the goal of understanding can be considered as a need to understand others and to be understood by others.

The second cognitive goal, the need for control, reflects being active in the world. Individuals are driven to be effective and have control over their actions. We seek a link between our behaviors and what happens to us. Control is both intrapersonal (self-directed) and interpersonal (other directed); we seek to control our own actions and the actions of others. Intrapersonally, the need for control encompasses not only a need for competence, but also a need for autonomy, for instance, in terms of desiring the ability to make choices about one's own behavior, as described in self-determination theory (Deci & Ryan, 1985). Interpersonally, our need for control is in play when we try to persuade our friends, family, or co-workers to do things our way or perceive the world as we see it.

The final goal is the need to belong. This goal includes the need for strong stable relationships with others and a need to have frequent, positive interactions with a few others (Baumeister & Leary, 1995). Fiske (2004) proposed that this goal underlies the other four social goals. The need to belong is posited as a core goal in nearly all psychological research addressing psychological goals (e.g., Deci & Ryan, 2000; Glasser, 1998) and has been argued to be the most basic and fundamental psychological goal (Baumeister & Leary, 1995). The need for affiliation (i.e., belonging) is one of the core motivators for social identification with others (Brewer, 1991) and has a long history in social psychology; for example, research on need for affiliation reaches back at least to the 1950s (e.g., Shipley & Veroff, 1952).

Tying these goals to self-regulation processes, we propose that these five core social goals can be framed as goals or antigoals. For instance, the need to belong could translate into seeking inclusion or avoiding exclusion. Reflecting a desire to be included, one gay male noted that he hid his stigma because "You had to put on the act at the time . . . so people would accept you" (Rivers & D'Augelli, 2001, p. 208). Trying to prevent exclusion, another gay individual commented, "I didn't come out and tell my parents, certainly, because I was still living at home. . . . As long as your parents didn't know that part of you, they wouldn't reject you" (Weston, 1991, p. 63). The other core social goals can also be framed in terms of goals and antigoals. The need for self-enhancement could translate into seeking self-enhancement or avoiding self-diminishment. The need for trust could translate into desiring trust or avoiding mistrust. The need for understanding could translate into desiring to understand and be understood or avoiding confusion and misunderstanding. Finally, the need for control could translate into desiring self-control or avoiding loss of control.

DISCRIMINATION AS A THREAT OR CHALLENGE TO CORE SOCIAL MOTIVES

We propose that comparisons between anticipated or actual discrimination and core social goals will motivate individuals to generate, evaluate, and engage in coping responses. This comparison will indicate that core social goals are or will be blocked or that core social antigoals are or will be met. The appraised distance between one's current state and one's goals or antigoals will predict the strength of the threat or challenge to one's goals and predict the resulting motivation to protect one's self from current or future harm. Because individuals likely have multiple goals, these appraisals could also determine which goals (including goals not highlighted by experiences with discrimination) are perceived as most in need of being addressed.

Precedence for predicting that discrimination threatens or challenges core social motives can be found in research on reactions to ostracism. *Ostracism* can be defined as "any act or acts of ignoring and excluding of an individual or group by an individual or group" (Williams, 2001, p. iv). Discrimination can take the form of ostracism when ostracism is based upon a person's group membership or discrimination can feel like ostracism when it creates or reinforces social distance from others. Research on ostracism demonstrates that being ignored or excluded threatens a need to belong, need for self-esteem, and need for control (Williams, Case, & Govan, 2003).

Thus, discrimination, perhaps via ostracism, may directly threaten or challenge a core need to belong by activating a belief that one is not accepted or valued by a group or does not fit into a group. For instance, when discrimination comes in the form of patronizing behavior, low-power targeted individuals feel marginalized (Vescio, Snyder, & Gervais 2004; see also Foschi, 2000).

Also like ostracism, discrimination may threaten or challenge self-esteem, or more generally self-enhancement. Self-esteem maintenance has been central to research on stigmatized individual's responses to prejudice and discrimination (Crocker & Garcia, chap. 14, this volume). Although being in a stigmatized group is not necessarily associated with lower personal self-esteem (Crocker & Major, 1989), particular stigmatized groups do have relatively low personal self-esteem (Twenge & Crocker, 2002) and experiences with discrimination for those not identified with a group can threaten personal self-esteem (Branscombe, Schmidt, & Harvey, 1999). Moreover, discrimination can also threaten public self-esteem while leaving personal self-esteem intact (Swim et al., 2005). The impact on public and not personal self-esteem can be seen in one Black American's description of his experiences with discrimination, "[t]he way things are done now is that everything that a Black person does . . . they try to discount it, say it's not as good, which is not true" (Feagin & Sikes, 1994, p. 297). Consistent with this comment, we have found that the more incidents of heterosexist hassles lesbian, gay, and bisexual individuals report during a day, the more they perceive that others negatively evaluate their group; however, these experiences do not influence personal state self-esteem (Swim et al., 2001, 2004). Discrimination could also potentially convey specific stereotypic beliefs about groups and, depending upon the particular group; this could result in believing that others think that they are incompetent or not likeable (Fiske, Xu, Cuddy, & Glick, 1999).

Again, like ostracism, discrimination can potentially threaten or challenge the goal of control. Discrimination can be perceived as blocking one's ability to obtain important intrapersonal and interpersonal outcomes (Sechrist, Swim, & Stangor, 2004). For instance, the following recollection of experiences with racism on a school bus relays the sense of personal loss of control and inability to control a situation. "The kids always teased and hit me as I sat on the bus totally helpless. Many of the people who were against me didn't even know me. So I just sat there while everyone stared and laughed" (retrieved June 7, 2004, from http://collections.ic.gc.ca/sharing/racism2_e.html).

Experiencing prejudice can also threaten or challenge an individual's goal to trust others. Consistent with this, Janoff-Bulman (1992) found that seeing antigay campaign materials made many lesbian and gay individuals question their belief that the world was safe and that others were good. Discrimination can decrease feelings of trust in others, particularly the perpetrator and those perceived to be associated with or similar to the perpetrator. For instance, Blacks' cultural mistrust (F. Terrell & S. L. Terrell, 1981) and a greater tendency to believe in conspiracies against Blacks (Crocker, Luhtanen, Broadnax, & Blaine, 1999) are attributable at least in part to their group's past and present experiences with discrimination (Feldman & Swim, 1998). Experiences with discrimination may also indicate or remind some stigmatized individuals that the world is not just (Mallett et al., 2004). Depending on the type of discrimination experienced, discrimination can threaten one's belief in distributive justice (outcomes were distributed fairly), procedural justice (the process of distributing outcomes was fair), or interaction justice (they were treated with dignity and respect and given appropriate information about procedures that influence them) (Mitchell & Daniels, 2003).

Finally, experiences with discrimination can influence one's need to understand. If discrimination comes unexpectedly, it could prompt attributions to help targets explain and understand such events (Hastie, 1984). Moreover, discriminatory actions suggest that perpetrators do not understand targets and they do not share the same understanding of social reality. A Black social worker described difficulties with sharing an understanding of discrimination with White individuals: "And what disturbed me and continues to disturb me is that Whites will try to tell you that they're not being racist, when they can't tell you what you perceive, or how you've experienced something" (Feagin & Sikes, 1994, p. 282). Mismatches in understanding may be a result of differences in access to or emphasis on information regarding the role of intent and harm on judgments of discrimination (Swim, Scott, Sechrist, Campbell, & Stangor, 2003). Mismatches could also occur if stigmatized group members make attributions for their social status to individual, institutional, or cultural discrimination while nonstigmatized group members make attributions to stigmatized group members' behaviors.

Although discrimination can potentially threaten all five core social goals, all five goals may not be activated in the face of discrimination, nor will the same goals be activated for every person. In general, goal activation can be situation specific, such as a need to self-enhance at one's job, and can vary across individuals, such as individual differences in need for affiliation. These goals may be supplanted, accentuated, or simultaneously considered by goals activated by discrimination. People likely balance responses to the activation of multiple goals in terms of the strength of competing goals and their perception of their ability to address the goals. For instance, some have noted that a reason they did not confront discrimination was that it would interrupt the task at hand (Hyers, 2005) suggesting that goals driven by the task at hand were deemed more important than those activated by discrimination. Interestingly, similar responses may be made to offensive but nondiscriminatory behaviors if the behaviors threaten or challenge the same goals. Similar responses may also occur if different goals are activated but similar responses are perceived to be effective at addressing the different goals.

EVALUATION AND SELECTION OF COPING RESPONSES

Matching Coping Appraisals and Goals

Strength of activation and weighted importance of goals is likely insufficient to determine the selection of coping responses. One must also consider the ability to generate possible responses and the appraisal of these responses. The possible set of responses to be appraised could be based on the target's own past experiences, observations of others, social skills, or creativity, as examples. The ability to generate coping responses may be limited by factors such as a target's mood state (Gasper & Clore, 1998; Vickers et al., 2003), the perceived need to generate responses quickly (Kowalski, 1996), or cognitive load. Additionally, the goal that is threatened may focus attention only on those responses that could possibly address the goal.

Appraisal of one's ability to engage in responses (self-efficacy) and the ability of a response to address goals (response efficacy) will likely be considered in reference to perceived situational constraints (Lazarus & Folkman, 1984; Rogers, 1975; Rogers & Prentice-Dunn, 1997). Response efficacy involves anticipating the consequences of coping responses and is therefore the appraisal that is tied most closely to goals. Reflecting this goal based appraisal, one Black hospital administrator said, "[w]hen [discrimination] *does* happen . . . you have to formulate a plan of action to still accomplish your goal and let that be your number one priority" (Feagin & Sikes, 1994, p. 274). Anticipated consequences that lead toward the satisfaction of a social goal or the avoidance of an antigoal can be expected to be beneficial. Anticipated consequences that hinder the satisfaction of the social goal or avoidance of an antigoal can be expected to be costly. Individuals presumably prefer responses that are primarily beneficial. Thus, goals can potentially influence the selection of coping response either by guiding a search for possible responses or by representing standards for evaluating the potential costs and benefits of responses being considered. We now consider how different coping responses might be appraised in light of the five core social goals, starting with confronting.

Much of the past discussions about the role of interpersonal goals on decisions about confronting may specifically be concerns about belonging and public self-enhancement. Confronters could be seen as a deviant if others do not support them. They could then be rejected or ostracized from a group because of this deviance (Schacter et al., 1954; Williams, 2001). Indeed, laboratory studies demonstrate that self-presentation concerns inhibit stigmatized individuals' public labeling of incidents as discrimination (Stangor, Swim, VanAllen & Sechrist, 2002; Sechrist et al., 2004). Plus, stigmatized individuals are more likely to make public attributions to discrimination when in the presence of ingroup rather than outgroup members (Stangor et al., 2002), perhaps due to fewer concerns about rejection from ingroup rather than outgroup members.

Although fear of loss of more control could inhibit confronting, confronting can also reflect attempts to gain control over others in a situation. For instance, women in a diary study on confronting reported that they selected responses that served the goal of changing perpetrators' behaviors (e.g., "I wanted them to leave me alone" or "I wanted him to stop saying those things"; Hyers, 2005, p. 20). Confronting can also be a means of achieving a sense of control over the self and increasing personal self-enhancement. When confronting allows one to be true to the self, confronting can reduce intrusive thoughts or rumination and avoid negative self-evaluations that come from self-discrepancy with beliefs about how one ought to behave (Shelton, Richeson, Salvatore, & Hill, chap. 4, this volume). Similarly, public attributions to discrimination can allow targets to regain the sense of loss of control over future outcomes by placing blame for negative outcomes on a transient cause and allowing one to remain confident in one's own control over future outcomes (e.g., Sechrist et al., 2004).

Although confronting is often treated as if people either confront or do not confront, people have multiple ways in which they can confront and these different manifestations of confronting may reflect different goals. One of the most frequent means of confronting others is by asking others to explain their behavior (Shelton & Stewart, 2004; Swim & Hyers, 1999). The perpetrator's explanations or apologies that could follow this form of confrontation could allow the targeted individual to trust or better understand the perpetrator. Other forms of confronting could also address the goal of understanding. For instance, a desire to educate a perpetrator is one of the prime motivators women reported for confronting sexism, racism, anti-Semitism, and heterosexism (Hyers, 2005). The resulting social influence attempts could be driven by a desire to be understood by others or a desire to have a shared understanding of situations. Conversely, a common reason people give for not confronting discrimination is that they perceived that confronting would not change an actor's opinions (Hyers, 2005). In the latter situation, targets appear to be appraising confronting in terms of their ability to socially influence the perpetrator rather than in terms of other goals such as regaining control or self-enhancement.

Other coping responses can also be considered in terms of their relation to each of the core goals. Much of the early research on coping with discrimination was framed in terms of responses to protect self-esteem (Crocker & Major, 1989). Responses such as making attributions to discrimination (Major, Kaiser, & McCoy, 2003), making within group comparisons (Bylsma & Major, 1994), and devaluing domains and activities where one's group is stereotyped as inferior (Schmader, Major, Eccleston, & McCoy, 2001), have been argued to be responses that protected self-esteem. Additionally, many coping responses have been classified in the stress and coping literature in terms of attempts at control, both in terms of the goal of controlling situations to suit the self and controlling the self to suit situations (Rothbaum et al., 1982; Weisz et al., 1984.)

The aforementioned responses reflect reactive coping. Yet, proactive coping responses aimed at preventing discrimination can also address different core social goals. For instance, hiding one's stigma could prevent stigma-based ostracism and subsequent threats or challenges to the goals of belonging, self-enhancement, and control. Although hiding a stigma may protect these goals, hiding a stigma may also threaten or challenge goals. If stigmatized individuals who hide their stigma believe that they are not being true to themselves, the lack of authenticity may threaten personal self-enhancement and threaten the goal of being understood by others. Additionally, hiding one's stigma might highlight one's lack of trust in others and threaten the belief that the world is benevolent. Finally, hiding stigma can potentially result in thought intrusions due to monitoring whether other's detect one's stigma (Frable, Blackstone, & Scherbaum, 1990) or in feeling a loss of control due to the distraction of rebound effects while suppressing one's identity (Smart & Wegner, 2000).

Thus, different coping responses and manifestations of coping responses (such as different ways to confront) may be expected to be more or less effective at addressing the goals and antigoals that are activated by discrimination. Accordingly, these goals will influence the appraisal of coping strategies. The extent to which a response is appraised as effectively addressing a goal or avoiding an antigoal likely will influence whether the response is given.

Framing and Affect

Targets framing of goals is another potentially important predictor of the selection of coping responses (see Table 6.1). One outcome of primary appraisals has been described as establishing whether one is threatened or challenged by a stressor (Lazarus & Folkman, 1984). Threat and challenge

TABLE 6.1
Comparison of Different Framing Orientations and Foci Toward Situations and Affective and Behavior Consequences of These Framing Orientations and Foci

Framing	*Threat* *Prevention*	*Challenge* *Promotion*
Concern or focus	Avoid loss	Seek gain
	Avoid antigoal	Seek goal
	Avoid costs	Seek benefits
Affect	Anxiety	Anger
	Behavioral inhibition system	Behavioral approach system
Coping responses	Avoidance	Approach
	Disengagement	Engagement/Effort
	Secondary coping responses	Primary coping responses

may be related to prevention and promotion motivational principles (Higgens, 1998). That is, feeling threatened is similar to being prevention focused because both represent a focus on avoiding losses. On the other hand, feeling challenged is similar to being promotion focused because they both represent a focus on seeking gains. Moreover, these foci can be tied to Carver and Scheier's (1998) self-regulation model because avoiding losses is akin to avoiding antigoals and approaching gains is akin to approaching goals. For instance, responses to the possibility of being stereotyped can come in the form of stereotype threat or stereotype challenge (also known as stereotype reactance; see Kray, Thompson, & Galinsky, 2001). Stereotype-threat responses may be a result of a prevention orientation aimed at avoiding the antigoal of self-diminishment that can come from confirming the stereotypes. In contrast, stereotype challenge responses may be a result of a promotion orientation aimed at attaining the goal of self-enhancement by illustrating one's competence. Additionally, tying these terms to cost-benefit analyses that have been used to describe targets' consideration of responses to discrimination, avoiding costs may be thought of as avoiding losses or antigoals and seeking benefits may be thought of as seeking gains or approaching goals.

These different types of framing and foci have implications for affective responses to incidents (Carver, 2004; Carver & Scheier, 1998). Approaching antigoals results in anxiety and avoiding antigoals produces relief. In contrast, approaching goals results in joy or happiness, whereas discrepancies from goals results in anger.[2] Affective reactions are important to consider

[2]Sadness is another emotion that can emerge if behaviors do not increase an ability to reach goals. Sadness or depression has been associated with more reported experiences with discrimination (Landrine & Klonoff, 1996; Russell & Richards, 2003). Yet, in our diary studies we have found that experiences with discrimination affect anger and anxiety and not depression. Sad-

when reflecting on experiences with discrimination; we have found that daily experiences with everyday discrimination are associated with increased anxiety and anger (Swim et al., 2001; Swim, Hyers et al., 2003; Swim et al., 2005). Increased anxiety would suggest that experiences with discrimination have activated concerns about approaching antigoals. Conversely, increased anger would suggest that experiences with discrimination have activated concerns about blockage of goals. Thus, people may feel either anxious or angry when they experience discrimination, dependent on their framing of the situation.

It is also possible that they may feel both angry and anxious in a particular interaction. The simultaneous occurrence of anger and anxiety responses may reflect concerns about more than one type of core social goal. For example, individuals may be concerned about being excluded while simultaneously wanting to gain control. Alternatively, feeling both angry and anxious during an interaction could also be a result of fluxing between two different framing orientations. For example, Carver and Scheier (1998) argued that antigoals and goals can be linked. That is, the same goal may be thought about in terms of how close one is to a goal (e.g., close to being included) or how far away one is from the same goal (e.g., distance from exclusion). Although avoidance responses to antigoals are not limited by natural ending points, approach responses to goals are limited by reaching the goal itself. Yet, in practice, goals may provide limits to antigoals; one may stop avoiding an antigoal when they have reached the goal. For instance, one might stop worrying about exclusion after one feels assured that they are included.

Different affective responses have implications for the selection of coping responses (see Table 6.1). Anxiety is associated with the Behavioral Inhibition System and avoidance behaviors. In contrast, anger is associated with the Behavioral Approach System and approach behaviors (Harmon-Jones & Allen, 1997, 1998; Harmon-Jones & Sigelman, 2001). Consistent with these associations between affect and behavior, Carver and Scheier (1998) argued that approaching antigoals is associated with disengagement responses and moving away from goals is associated with effort.

The inhibition and activation systems and resultant avoidant and approach behaviors parallel the classification of coping responses in the stress literature as either disengagement/avoidance or engagement/approach responses (Compas, Connor-Smith, Saltzman, Thomsen, & Wadsworth, 2001; Connor-Smith, Compas, Wadsworth, Thomsen, & Saltzman,

---

ness may differ from anger because sadness may not reflect initial reactions to discrimination but may instead reflect repeated experiences with discrimination interfering with core social goals. Yet, if sadness does emerge, we would anticipate that it would be related to coping responses tied to behavioral inhibition systems.

2000). Plus, parallels between coping responses to discrimination and engagement and disengagement responses have been made (Miller, chap. 2, this volume; Miller & Kaiser, 2001). There are also other ways to classify coping responses that share similarities with inhibition responses and approach-related behaviors. For example, responses aimed at changing a situation to fit the self (primary control responses) could be considered approach related whereas responses made with the goal of changing the self to fit the situation could be considered inhibitory responses (Rothbaum et al., 1982; Weisz et al., 1984).[3] Examples of approach responses to discrimination that could be related to attempts to achieve goals include attempts at social influence, expression of moral outrage, or anger, revenge (e.g., Hyers, 2005), and compensatory behavior (Miller & Myers, 1998). Examples of inhibitory responses to discrimination that could be related to avoiding antigoals include avoiding groups (e.g., Cohen & Swim, 1995), hiding stigma (Quinn, chap. 5, this volume), self-silencing (Swim, Quinliven, Ferguson, & Eyssel, 2004), dis-identification with groups (Major & Schmader, 1998), or devaluing threatened attributes (Schmader et al., 2001). Other coping responses to discrimination could be also be considered inhibitory responses because they do not directly address discrimination. Yet, unlike the other inhibitory responses listed, they could still be related to active attempts to reach goals rather than avoid antigoals. These responses include: preferring within-group comparison (Bylsma & Major, 1994); shifting one's social identity to nonthreatened group identities to increase belonging (Mussweiler, Gariel, & Bodenhausen, 2000); strengthening ingroup identification to increase feelings of belonging (Branscombe et al., 1999; Jetten, Branscombe, Schmitt, & Spears, 2001); or focusing on task completion to increase self-control (Hyers, 2005). Research is needed to establish whether different coping responses emerge dependent on how situations are framed (e.g., threat vs. challenge), the concern highlighted (e.g., avoid less vs. seek gains), and the type of affect generated (e.g., anger vs. anxiety).

CONSEQUENCES OF COPING RESPONSES

As the previous chapters illustrate, coping responses can have intrapersonal consequences, for instance, in terms evaluations of the self based upon whether one is acting in line with one's beliefs (Shelton, Richeson,

[3]Responses have also been differentiated into voluntary coping responses (those discussed here) and involuntary responses. Both may be a result of comparison processes and both may have an impact on one's social environment. For instance, involuntary responses of rumination and intrusive thoughts may decrease task performance. The difference between voluntary coping responses and involuntary responses may be that the latter are not influenced by coping appraisals.

Salvatore, & Hill, chap. 4, this volume) or stereotype-threat responses if one's stigma is revealed (Quinn, chap. 5, this volume), as well as interpersonal consequences, for instance, in terms of other's defensive reactions to confronting (Kaiser, chap. 3, this volume) or rejection after a stigma is revealed (Quinn, chap. 5, this volume). Thus, it is important to remember that consequences of coping responses are partially out of targets' control because interpersonal consequences depend on how others respond to targets' coping responses. Targets', perpetrators', and observers' behaviors are linked such that each other's behavior can become inputs into others' self-regulation processes (Carver & Scheier, 1998). Thus, targets overt coping responses may influence perpetrators' or observers' social goals and subsequently, their behaviors. Additionally, other people may respond independently of targets' responses and these responses may influence the social environment. Both the intrapersonal and interpersonal consequences of responses to discrimination become new input to be compared to core social goals.

This new comparison and reappraisal will determine the target's assessment of the overall success of a coping response in light of the target's personal goals. For instance, confronting may appear to be ineffective because it does not alter an actor's opinions and, worse yet, may result in retaliatory behavior. However, from the target's point of view, if the goal of confronting was to self-validate, then the response may be perceived as effective. Even so, discrimination can threaten many goals and it is likely that many responses will satisfy certain goals while simultaneously aggravating other goals. The balance between the costs and benefits across goals will likely influence the subsequent comparison and reappraisal processes.

The reappraisal of threatened or challenged goals can have multiple outcomes. Reappraisal may indicate that discrepancies between an individual's current state and goals no longer exist and individuals may exit from the cycle. However, the reappraisal may also indicate that the discrepancies still exist or highlight new discrepancies that may have emerged, perhaps as unanticipated consequences of the coping responses. Alternative coping responses or means of enacting the selected coping responses may be generated and appraised. Targets may find that they are unable to engage in other coping responses; for instance, this would occur if the interaction has ended or timing within the interaction is critical. They may find other ways to meet core social goals through other interactions such as increased belonging and enhancement through other groups. Additionally, the consequences of a coping response may inform their self-efficacy and response efficacy in future situations where they encounter discrimination.

Finally, the consequences we consider here reflect immediate effects of coping responses. Long-term effects may differ from immediate effects (Quinn, chap. 5, this volume). For instance, individuals who reveal a hidden stigma may be appreciated for their honesty in the moment. However, revealing the stigma may result in unanticipated long-term consequences such as a person avoiding them in the future. At this later time, the individual may need to engage in other means of self-regulation processes to deal with these later threats.

SUMMARY AND CONCLUSIONS

We began this chapter by asking the question: How do targets of prejudice decide how to respond to discrimination? We have attempted to provide answers to this question by considering research and theory on self-regulation processes, core social goals, stress and coping, and everyday discrimination. The combination of these different literatures leads us to the model presented in Fig. 6.2. To summarize, we propose that experiencing discrimination motivates the generation and selection of coping because it threatens or challenges core social goals in the form of discrepancies from goals or matches with antigoals. Voluntary coping responses are selected after the generation of possible coping responses and ability appraisals, including appraising the ability of the response to approach a goal or avoid an antigoal. Plus, framing of incidents in terms of goals and antigoals may influence the type of affect one experiences which in turn may influence the types of coping responses considered and selected. The classification of responses that follow anxiety and anger into inhibitory and approach responses is consistent with other classifications of coping responses from the stress and coping literature. This classification suggests that the type of affect people often experience in response to discrimination may also play an important role in their selection of coping responses. The responses selected will have intrapersonal and interpersonal consequences and these consequences then become reappraised in terms of comparisons with core social goals.

Understanding how targets respond to discrimination in a particular situation is complex and multifaceted. Targets are not passive recipients of discrimination. Their responses are likely influenced by the activation and prioritizing of goals and their appraisals of themselves, the situation, and response options in light of their goals. They have a large repertoire of response options, some of which help them avoid antigoals and associated costs and others that help them approach goals and associated benefits. Responding to discrimination is intrapersonally and interpersonally dynamic; it can be influenced by previous experiences with discrimination, the salience and prioritizing of goals within a situation, and self-regulatory adjustments made during an interaction and the responses made by others.

REFERENCES

Baumeister, R. F., & Leary, M. R. (1995). The need to belong: Desire for interpersonal attachments as a fundamental human motivation. *Psychological Bulletin, 117*(3), 497–529.

Branscombe, N. R., Schmitt, M. T., & Harvey, R. D. (1999). Perceiving pervasive discrimination among African Americans: Implications for group identification and well-being. *Journal of Personality and Social Psychology, 77*(1), 135–149.

Brewer, M. B. (1991). The social self: On being the same and different at the same time. *Personality and Social Psychology Bulletin, 17*(5), 475–482.

Bylsma, W. H., & Major, B. (1994). Social comparisons and contentment: Exploring the psychological costs of the gender wage gap. *Psychology of Women Quarterly, 18*(2), 241–249.

Carver, C. S. (2004). Negative affects deriving from the behavioral approach system. *Emotion, 4*(1), 3–22.

Carver, C. S., & Scheier, M. F. (1998). *On the self-regulation of behavior.* New York: Cambridge University Press.

Carver, C. S., & Scheier, M. F. (2002). Control processes and self-organization as complementary principles underlying behavior. *Personality and Social Psychology Review, 6*(4), 304–315.

Cohen, L. L., & Swim, J. K. (1995). The differential impact of gender ratios on women and men: Tokenism, self-confidence, and expectations. *Personality and Social Psychology Bulletin, 21*(9), 876–884.

Compas, B. E., Connor-Smith, J. K., Saltzman, H., Thomsen, A. H., & Wadsworth, M. E. (2001). Coping with stress during childhood and adolescence: Problems, progress and potential in theory and research. *Psychological Bulletin, 127*, 87–127.

Connor-Smith, J. K., Compas, B. E., Wadsworth, M. E., Thomsen, A. H., & Saltzman, H. (2000). Responses to stress in adolescence: Measurement of coping and involuntary stress responses. *Journal of Consulting and Clinical Psychology, 68*(6), 976–992.

Crocker, J., Luhtanen, R., Broadnax, S., & Blaine, B. E. (1999). Belief in U. S. government conspiracies against Blacks among Black and White college students: Powerlessness or system blame? *Personality and Social Psychology Bulletin, 25*(8), 941–953.

Crocker, J., & Major, B. (1989). Social stigma and self-esteem: The self-protective properties of stigma. *Psychological Review, 96*(4), 608–630.

Czopp, A. M., & Monteith, M. J. (2003). Confronting prejudice (literally): Reactions to confrontations of racial and gender bias. *Personality and Social Psychology Bulletin, 29*(4), 532–544.

Deci, E. L., & Ryan, R. M. (1985). The general causality orientations scale: Self-determination in personality. *Journal of Research in Personality, 19*(2), 109–134.

Deci, E. L., & Ryan, R. M. (2000). The "what" and "why" of goal pursuits: Human needs and the self-determination of behavior. *Psychological Inquiry, 11*(4), 227–268.

Feagin, J. R., & Sikes, M. P. (1994). *Living with racism: The Black middle-class experience.* Boston, MA: Beacon Press.

Feldman, L. B., & Swim, J. K. (1998). Appraisals of prejudice and discrimination. In J. K. Swim & C. Stangor (Eds.), *Prejudice: The target's perspective* (pp. 11–36). San Diego, CA: Academic Press.

Fiske, S. T. (2004). *Social beings: A core social motives approach to social psychology.* Hoboken, NJ: Wiley & Sons.

Fiske, S. T., Xu, J., Cuddy, A. C., & Glick, P. (1999). (Dis)respecting versus (dis)liking: Status and interdependence predict ambivalent stereotypes of competence and warmth. *Journal of Social Issues, 55*(3), 473–489.

Foschi, M. (2000). Double standards for competence: Theory and research. *Annual Review of Sociology, 26*, 21–42.

Frable, D. E., Blackstone, T., & Scherbaum, C. (1990). Marginal and mindful: Deviants in social interactions. *Journal of Personality and Social Psychology, 59*(1), 140–149.

Gasper, K., & Clore, G. L. (1998). The persistent use of negative affect by anxious individuals to estimate risk. *Journal of Personality and Social Psychology, 74*(5), 1350–1363.

Glasser, W. (1998). *Choice theory.* New York: Harper Collins.

Harmon-Jones, E., & Allen, J. J. B. (1997). Behavioral activation sensitivity and resting frontal EEG asymmetry: Covariation of putative indicators related to risk for mood disorders. *Journal of Abnormal Psychology, 106*(1), 159–163.

Harmon-Jones, E., & Allen, J. J. B. (1998). Anger and frontal brain activity: EEG asymmetry consistent with approach motivation despite negative affective valence. *Journal of Personality and Social Psychology, 74*(5), 1310–1316.

Harmon-Jones, E., & Sigelman, J. (2001). State anger and prefrontal brain activity: Evidence that insult-related relative left-prefrontal activation is associated with experienced anger and aggression. *Journal of Personality and Social Psychology, 80*(5), 797-803.

Hastie, R. (1984). Causes and effects of causal attribution. *Journal of Personality and Social Psychology, 46*(1), 44–56.

Higgens, E. T. (1998). Promotion and prevention: Regulatory focus as a motivational principle. In M. P. Zanna (Ed.), *Advances in experimental social psychology* (Vol. 30, pp. 1–46). New York: Academic Press.

Hyers. L. L. (2004). *Challenging everyday prejudice: The personal and social implications of women's assertive responses to interpersonal incidents of anti-Black racism, anti-semitism, heterosexism, and sexism.* Manuscript under review.

Janoff-Bulman, R. (1992). *Shattered assumptions: Towards a new psychology of trauma.* New York: Free Press.

Jetten, J., Branscombe, N. R., Schmitt, M. T., & Spears, R. (2001). Rebels with a cause: Group identification as a response to perceived discrimination from the mainstream. *Personality and Social Psychology Bulletin, 27*(9), 1204–1213.

Kelley, H. H. (1967). Attribution theory in social psychology. *Nebraska Symposium on Motivation* (pp. 192–238). University of Nebraska Press.

Kowalski, R. M. (1996). Complaints and complaining: Functions, antecedents, and consequences. *Psychological Bulletin, 119*(2), 179–196.

Kray, L J., Thompson, L., & Galinsky, A. (2001). Battle of the sexes: Gender stereotype confirmation and reactance in negotiations. *Journal of Personality and Social Psychology, 80*(6), 942–958.

Landrine, H., & Klonoff, E. A. (1996). The schedule of racist incidents: A measure of racial discrimination and a study of its negative physical and mental health consequences. *Journal of Black Psychology, 22*, 144–168.

Larson, J. R., Foster-Fishman, P. G., & Keys, C. B. (1994). Discussion of shared and unshared information in decision-making groups. *Journal of Personality and Social Psychology, 67*(3), 446–461.

Lazarus, R. S., & Folkman, S. (1984). *Stress, appraisal, and coping.* New York: Springer.

Lerner, M. J., & Miller, D. T. (1978). Just world research and the attribution process: Looking back and ahead. *Psychological Bulletin, 85*(5), 1030–1051.

Major, B., Kaiser, C. R., & McCoy, S. K. (2003). It's not my fault: When and why attributions to prejudice protect self-esteem. *Personality-and-Social-Psychology-Bulletin, 29*(6), 772–781.

Major, B., & Schmader, T. (1998). Coping with stigma through psychological disengagement. In J. K. Swim & C. Stangor (Eds.), *Prejudice: The target's perspective* (pp. 219–241). San Diego, CA: Academic Press.

Mallett, R. K., Huntsinger, J., & Swim, J. K. (2004). *They saw an injustice: The role of perceived injustice in predicting social policy support.* Manuscript under review.

Mallet, R. K., & Swim, J. (2005). *Bring it on: Proactive coping with discrimination.* Submitted for review.

McClelland, D. C., Atkinson, J. W., & Clark, R. A. (1949). The projective expression of needs: III. The effect of ego-involvement, success, and failure on perception. *Journal of Psychology: Interdsciplinary and Applied, 27*, 311–330.

Miller, C. T. & Kaiser, C. R. (2001). A theoretical perspective on coping with stigma. *Journal of Social Issues, 57*(1), 73–92.

Miller, C. T., & Major, B. (2000). Coping with stigma and prejudice. In T. F. Heatherton & R. E. Kleck (Eds.), *The social psychology of stigma* (pp. 243–272). New York: Guilford Press.

Miller, C. T., & Myers, A. M. (1998). Compensating for prejudice: How heavyweight people (and others) control outcomes despite prejudice. In J. K. Swim & C. Stangor (Eds.), *Prejudice: The target's perspective* (pp. 191–218). San Diego, CA: Academic Press.

Mitchell, T. R., & Daniels, D. (2003). Motivation. In W. C. Borman & D. R. Ilgen (Eds.), *Handbook of psychology: Industrial and organizational psychology, Vol. 12* (pp. 225–254). New York: John Wiley & Sons.

Mussweiler, T., Gariel, S., & Bodenhausen, G. V. (2000). Shifting social identities as a strategy for deflecting threatening social comparisons. *Journal of Personality and Social Psychology, 79*(3), 398–409.

Rivers, I., & D'Augelli, A. R. (2001). The victimization of lesbian, gay, and bisexual youths. In A. R. D'Augelli & C. J. Patterson (Eds.), *Lesbian, gay, and bisexual identities and youth* (pp. 199–223). New York: Oxford University Press.

Rogers, R. W. (1975). A protection motivation theory of fear appeals and attitude change. *Journal of Psychology, 91*(1), 93–114.

Rogers, R. W. & Prentice-Dunn, S. (1997) Protection motivation theory. In D. S. Gochman (Ed.), *Handbook of health behavior research 1: Personal and social determinant* (pp. 113–132). New York: Plenum Press.

Rothbaum, F., Weisz, J. R., & Snyder, S. S., (1982). Changing the world and changing the self: A two-process model of perceived control. *Journal of Personality and Social Psychology, 42*(1), 5–37.

Russell, G. M., & Richards, J. A. (2003). Stressor and resilience factors for lesbians, gay men, and bisexuals confronting antigay politics. *American Journal of Community Psychology, 3*(3–4), 313–328.

Schacter, S, Nuttin, J., De-Monchaux, C., Maucorps, P. H., Osmer, D., Duijker, H., Rommetveit, R., & Israel, J. (1954). Cross-cultural experiments on threat and rejection. *Human Relations, 7*, 403–440.

Schmader, T., Major, B., Eccleston, C. P., & McCoy, S. K. (2001). Devaluing domains in response to threatening intergroup comparisons: Perceived legitimacy and the status value asymmetry. *Journal of Personality and Social Psychology, 80*(5), 782–796.

Sechrist, G. B., Swim, J. K., & Stangor, C. (2004). When do the stigmatized make attributions to discrimination occurring to the self and others? The roles of self-presentation and need for control. *Journal of Personality and Social Psychology, 87*(1), 111–122.

Sedikides, C., Gaertner, L., & Toguchi, Y. (2003). Pancultural self enhancement. *Journal of Personality and Social Psychology, 84*(1), 60–79.

Shelton, J., & Stewart, R. E. (2004). Confronting perpetrators of prejudice: The inhibitory effects of social costs. *Psychology of Women Quarterly, 28*(3), 215–223.

Shipley, T. E., Jr., & Veroff, J. (1952). A projective measure of need for affiliation. *Journal of Experimental Psychology, 43*, 349–356.

Smart, L., & Wegner, D. (2000). The hidden costs of hidden stigma. In T. F. Heatherton & R. E. Kleck (Eds.), *The social psychology of stigma* (pp. 220–242). New York: Guilford Press.

Stangor, C., Swim, J. K., Sechrist, G. G., DeCoster, J., Van Allen, K. L., & Ottenbreit, A. (2003). Ask, answer and announce: Three stages in perceiving discrimination. *European Review of Social Psychology, 14*, 277–311.

Stangor, C., Swim, J. K., Van Allen, K. L., & Sechrist, G. B. (2002). Reporting discrimination in public and private contexts. *Journal of Personality and Social Psychology, 82*(1), 69–74.

Swim, J. K., & Hyers, L. L. (1999). Excuse me—What did you just say?!: Women's public and private responses to sexist remarks. *Journal of Experimental Social Psychology, 35*(1), 68–88.

Swim, J. K., Hyers, L. L., Cohen, L. L., & Ferguson, M. J. (2001). Everyday sexism: Evidence for its incidence, nature, and psychological impact from three daily diary studies. *Journal of Social Issues, 57*(1), 31–53.

Swim, J. K., Hyers, L. L., Cohen, L. L., Fitzgerald, D. C., & Bylsma, W. H. (2003). African American college students' experiences with everyday racism: Characteristics of and responses to these incidents. *Journal of Black Psychology, 29*(1), 38–67.

Swim, J. K., Johnston, K. E. & Pearson, N. B (2005). *Hidden stigma and social constraints on coping with everyday discrimination.* Manuscript submitted for review.

Swim, J. K., Quinliven, E., Ferguson, M., & Eyssell, K. (2004). *Self-silencing and avoidance of confrontation.* Unpublished manuscript, The Pennsylvania State University.

Swim, J. K., Scott, E. D., Sechrist, G. B., Campbell, B., & Stangor, C. (2003). The role of intent and harm in judgments of prejudice and discrimination. *Journal of Personality and Social Psychology, 84*(5), 944–959.

Taylor, S. E., & Brown, J. D. (1988). Illusion and well-being: A social psychological perspective on mental health. *Psychological Bulletin, 103*(2), 193–210.

Terrell, F., & Terrell, S. L. (1981). An inventory to measure cultural mistrust among Blacks. *Western Journal of Black Studies, 5*(3), 180–184.

Twenge, J. M., & Crocker, J. (2002). Race and self-esteem: Meta-analyses comparing Whites, Blacks, Hispanics, Asians, and American Indians and comment on Gray-Little and Hafdahl (2000). *Psychological Bulletin, 128*(3), 371–408.

Vescio, T. K., Snyder, M., & Gervais, S. J. (2004). Power, stereotyping, and social influence: The dynamics of interactions between the powerful and the powerless. Chapter invited for consideration for publication in M. Hewstone & W. Stroebe (Eds.), *European Review of Social Psychology.* London, UK: Frances & Taylor.

Vickers, K. S, Patten, C. A., Lane, K., Clark, M. M., Croghan, I. T., Schroeder, D. R., & Hurt, R. D. (2003). Depressed versus nondepressed young adult tobacco users: Differences in coping style, weight concerns and exercise level. *Health Psychology, 22*(5), 498–503.

Weisz, J. R., Rothbaum, F. M., & Blackburn, T. C. (1984). Swapping recipes for control. *American Psychologist, 39*(9), 974–975.

Weston, K. (1991). *Families we choose: Lesbians, gays, kinship.* New York: Columbia University Press.

Williams, K. D. (2001). *Ostracism: The power of silence.* New York: Guilford Press.

Williams, K. D., Case, T. I., & Govan, C. L. (2003). Impact of ostracism on social judgments and decisions: Explicit and implicit responses. In J. P Forgas & K. D. Williams (Eds.), *Social judgments: Implicit and explicit processes* (pp. 325–342). New York: Cambridge University Press.

PART II

STIGMA IN THE SOCIAL CONTEXT: COPING WITH THREATENING ENVIRONMENTS

CHAPTER

7

How Environments Can Threaten Academic Performance, Self-Knowledge, and Sense of Belonging

Michael Inzlicht
University of Toronto

Catherine Good
Columbia University

"Like many other Blacks," recounted African American tennis great, Arthur Ashe, "when I find myself in a new public situation, I will count" (Ashe, 1993, p. 131). Ashe–who played a sport that was and still is dominated by Whites–counted his "Blackness" frequently. By "counting," Ashe was referring to the difficulty he encountered as a member of a group that is outnumbered and devalued in American society; he counted the number of Black faces in a room to determine how well his social identity was valued and represented. It turns out that many of us engage in a similar, albeit less conscious, form of mental arithmetic. We scan the environment and count those features about ourselves that stand out. When those features are related to a stigmatized social identity, we, like Ashe, may be distressed and burdened by negative stereotypes associated with our identity. For the past few years, our research has focused on the burdens of being immersed in environments that compel us to count our social identity–borne not only by African Americans, but by anyone who is the target of stereotypes based on race, gender, sexual orientation, or religious affiliation. Much of this research has focused on what we call *threatening environments*, which are environments that can activate social identities and the relevant negative stereotypes about them. The aim of this chapter is to describe this research, and in so doing, illustrate what it means to belong to a group with a "spoiled identity" (Goffman, 1963).

Although individuals belonging to stigmatized groups now occupy positions in schools, employment settings, and legislative bodies that were once reserved for White men, research continues to paint a discouraging portrait of underrepresentation for these individuals. Women, for example, still comprise only 38% of the faculty in American universities, 16% of the corporate officers in America's largest companies, and 13% of senators in the 107th U.S. Congress (Business and Professional Women/USA, 2003). Observations about people of color show a similar pattern of underrepresentation. Clearly, these individuals are immersed in social milieus compelling them to count their social identities and the stereotypes associated with them (W. I. McGuire, C. V. McGuire, Child, & Fujioka, 1978). Being outnumbered, though, is not the only way environments activate social identities and stereotypes. Hearing about the latest reality TV show with 20 beautiful women chasing after a rich bachelor, watching a commercial showing a woman getting excited about a kitchen cleaner, or even taking a class with a White instructor are all ways the environment can conspire to make us think about our social identities.

So what are the effects of being in environments that compel us to count our group? How does a salient social identity affect the way we behave, feel, and think? These questions are important because our world is increasingly becoming a mosaic of different cultures, races, and religions, and so introduces environments that regularly make us think about our identities and their associated stereotypes.

In this chapter, we explore how social factors can create threatening environments and come to affect intellectual performance, academic self-concept, and feelings of belonging. First, we review research showing how being in the numerical minority can impact intellectual performance. We describe, for example, how being outnumbered by Whites can activate negative race stereotypes and undermine African Americans' standardized test performance through a psychological process known as *stereotype threat.* Second, we explore how specific environments can make people apprehensive about being the targets of prejudice, which in turn can pose problems for their academic self-concepts. That is, we show how viewing the world through the lens of social identity—or being in environments that compel one to do so—can rob people of valuable self-relevant information and so foster inaccurate self-knowledge and an unstable self-concept. Third, we examine how threatening environments convey exclusionary messages by signaling that certain groups have only marginal status in the setting and so are not as valued as other groups. In so doing, these settings can hamper feelings of belonging, acceptance, and comfort, especially when they communicate that ability and intelligence are fixed qualities. Finally, we discuss what we can do to disarm these harmful environments so that people can succeed and prosper in them. Specifically, we suggest that we can inure people against the threatening features of an environment by convincing them that ability and intelligence are malleable. We begin by introducing the concept of threatening environments.

THREATENING ENVIRONMENTS

Threatening environments can be thought of as settings where people come to suspect that they could be devalued, stigmatized, or discriminated against because of a particular social identity. These settings compel individuals to think about their particular social identities and, in addition, the stereotypes associated with them. For individuals belonging to stigmatized groups, these stereotypes are negative, and any cues that signal that one's group is treated with ill will, is not valued socially, or is marginalized in any way, should increase one's vigilance for prejudice, foster mistrust, and create a threatening environment (Steele, Spencer, & Aronson, 2002). After watching the film *White Men Can't Jump*, for example, a normal game of pick-up may become threatening to a White basketball player playing with his Black friends (e.g. Stone, Lynch, Sjomeling, & Darley, 1999). Similarly, the boardroom may become threatening for a female executive who becomes aware that the corporation she works for values men more than women and hires them almost exclusively (e.g. Kray, Thompson, & Galinsky, 2001). Once people belonging to stigmatized groups start thinking about their social identities in such threatening contexts, these thoughts can trigger a chain of events leading to underperformance, feelings of rejection, and feelings of doubt about why they receive the outcomes they do.

Settings that include people from more than one social group—heterogeneous ones—may be particularly likely to form threatening environments among the stigmatized. This may be especially true for settings where stigmatized groups are outnumbered by the more dominant group, as is the case, say, for an African American medical student who finds herself outnumbered by her White classmates. According to distinctiveness theory (W. J. McGuire et al., 1978), we are selective self-perceivers and attend to those aspects of ourselves that are distinct and peculiar in our immediate social context. Thus, our medical student will tend to notice and think about her "Blackness" in her White classroom, but in a different setting, say a class full of men, her race loses salience and she will become more conscious of being a woman. In one study, W. J. McGuire and his colleagues (W. J. McGuire et al., 1978) found that high-school students were more likely to spontaneously self-define as a member of their racial group when that group formed a minority rather than a majority in their classrooms. Further, this feeling of distinctiveness increased as the proportion of their race decreased in the classroom (cf. W. J. McGuire, C. V. McGuire, & Winton,

1979). And when people feel distinct, they may feel self-conscious. For example, when asked to imagine that they were taking an oral exam in front of a group that was of a different race, African Americans responded that they would feel uncomfortable being seen as a representative of their group (as cited in Thompson and Sekaquaptewa, 2002). Mixed-group settings, then, can compel people to count and become aware of the representation of their group, and this tendency becomes more marked when people need only a few fingers to do so.

Environments can also become threatening by dint of stereotype activation. When members of stigmatized groups are outnumbered, they tend to notice their social identity; and once this happens, they may start ruminating about the stereotypes about their group. Inzlicht, Aronson, Good, and McKay (in press), for example, discovered that Black participants were more likely to think about stereotypes about their race when Whites outnumbered them. In their study, Black participants took a test with two other people—two other Blacks, two Whites, or one Black and one White. Before taking the test, participants completed a measure of stereotype activation, which consisted of 36 word fragments, twelve of which could be completed with, among other words, words associated with the African American stereotype (e.g., B R _ _ _ _ _ [BROTHER], or W E L _ _ _ _ [WELFARE]). The premise behind this task is that participants for whom the Black stereotype is activated should be more likely to make stereotypic completions than participants for whom the stereotype is not activated (Gilbert & Hixon, 1991; Steele & Aronson, 1995). In accordance with distinctiveness theory (W. J. McGuire et al., 1979), stereotypes should be more active for the Black participants the less their race was represented in the group (i.e., the more distinct they were). Results confirmed predictions. The more participants were outnumbered, the more stereotypic completions they made. Our point here is that being outnumbered can increase awareness of one's group and of the stereotypes associated with one's group, and, ultimately, create a threatening environment where people expect stereotypes to be used against them.

ENVIRONMENTS CAN THREATEN INTELLECTUAL PERFORMANCE

Stereotype Threat

Environments that activate stereotypes might threaten intellectual performance via a motivational phenomenon known as stereotype threat (Aronson, 2002; Aronson et al., 1999; Spencer, Steele & Quinn, 1999; Steele, 1997; Steele & Aronson, 1995). Stereotype threat is the discomfort individuals feel when they are at risk of fulfilling a negative stereotype about their group. The possibility that they may confirm the stereotype—in their own and other people's eyes (Inzlicht & Ben-Zeev, 2003)—causes anxiety that is experienced as heightened physiological arousal (Ben-Zeev, Fein, & Inzlicht, 2005; Blascovich, Spencer, Quinn, & Steele, 2001; O'Brien & Crandall, 2003). Ultimately this arousal may deplete working memory (Schmader & Johns, 2003) and result in suboptimal performance, especially when individuals are highly identified with success and achievement in the stereotyped domain (Aronson et al., 1999). For instance, when faced with the stereotype that their group is not proficient in academic tests, African Americans may feel anxious about being judged along stereotypical lines, and behave in a way that ironically confirms the very stereotype they were trying to refute; they may underperform. Interestingly, stereotype threat does not necessarily spring from actually being stereotyped and can occur even in the absence of stereotypical treatment. The key is holding a negative meta-stereotype about future treatment (Vorauer, Main, & O'Connell, 1998), or put another way, expecting to be stereotyped.

Women are also exposed to negative stereotypes about their group and are threatened by them accordingly. In math and science, for example, women have to contend with stereotypes alleging inferiority to men (Davies, Spencer, Quinn, Gerhardstein, 2002; Quinn & Spencer, 2001; Schmader, 2002; Spencer et al., 1999). Further, women often find themselves in the minority in math and science domains; although they account for well over half of the student body, women form only a small minority of college students in the physical and computer sciences (National Science Foundation, 2000). Given that minority environments[1] can activate negative stereotypes, it follows that they should also trigger stereotype threat and lead to depressed intellectual performance for women in math. Inzlicht and Ben-Zeev (2000) conducted two studies to find out if this was indeed the case.

Minority Environments

In the first study (Inzlicht & Ben-Zeev, 2000, Study 1), women participated in a focus-group study on test strategies. Participants were seated with two other people—either two other women or two men—and told that they would take a

[1]Researchers have used the terms *token*, *solo-status*, and *minority environment* somewhat interchangeably to denote being outnumbered in an environment. Although similar, these terms have different meanings. Kanter (1977) defined the term token to denote individuals who belong to subgroups that comprise less than 15% of the superordinate group. Furthermore, this term implies that one is chosen out of some symbolic gesture. Solo-status implies that one is the only member of one's group. Finally, the term minority is often used to describe any nondominant racial or ethnic group; in the strictest sense, however, the terms minority and minority environment denote numerical inferiority and are the terms we prefer.

math test, the results of which would be publicly discussed in the focus group. For women taking the test with two men, the mere distinctiveness of being in the minority should focus their attention on their gender, and along with it, the negative stereotypes about women and math. Conversely, women in the majority group should be less likely to spontaneously notice their gender and related stereotypes. In other words, being in the presence of two men should be enough to cause stereotype threat and lead to lower performance among women in a minority environment compared to women in a same-gender environment. This is precisely what happened. A second study revealed that women performed worse when they were in the presence of even one man (Inzlicht & Ben-Zeev, 2000, Study 2). Because social identity and stereotypes become more salient with increases in the relative number of out-group members in the environment (Inzlicht et al., in press; W. J. McGuire et al., 1979), it follows that women's math performance would drop in relation to the number of men in the room. Figure 7.1 shows that when women took the math test in mixed-gender majority environments (with one other women and one man), they performed worse than women in a same-gender environment but better than women in a minority one. Therefore a seemingly innocuous contextual cue—the number of men in a room—can create a threatening intellectual environment and affect women's math test performance. Similar results have been found with other stigmatized groups (e.g. Sekaquaptewa & Thompson, 2002).

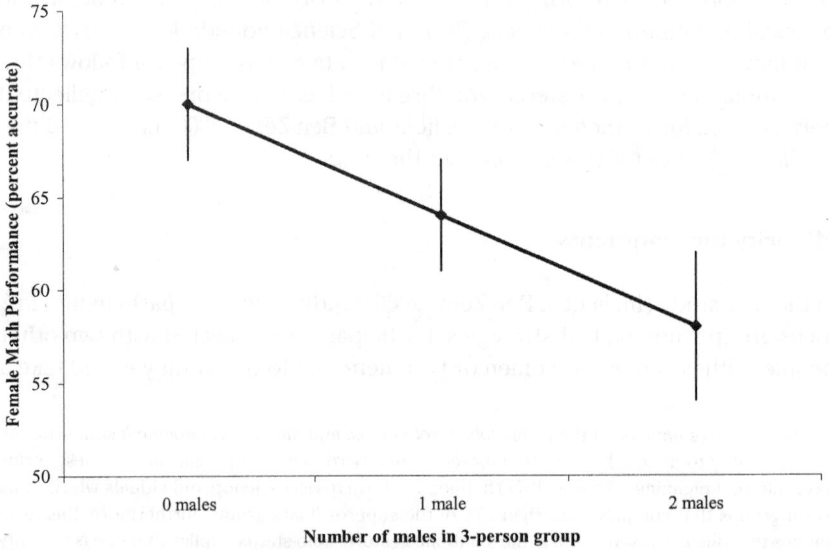

FIG. 7.1. Women's math performance as a function of the number of men in a 3-person group. Error bars represent standard error.

So how, then, do minority environments threaten intellectual performance? One possibility is that being outnumbered can increase the distinctiveness of one's social identity, activate negative stereotypes, and then increase arousal. In other words, being outnumbered may increase feelings of apprehension, stoke the fires of arousal, and as a result lead to underperformance. Using the classic misattribution paradigm (e.g. Zanna & Cooper, 1974), Ben-Zeev and her colleagues (2005; Study 2) found that arousal—and an individual's construal of arousal—was a key ingredient linking minority environments to underperformance. In their study, women took a math test with either two men or two women. Half of the participants were also given the opportunity to attribute the negative arousal presumably triggered by the threat to a benign source—in this case, a subliminal tone. As expected, women in the minority environment performed worse on the math test than women in the same-sex environment. These minority performance deficits, however, were attenuated when the participants were given an opportunity to misattribute their arousal to an external source. When participants were told that a subliminal noise might make them feel anxious, minority participants performed as well as same-gender ones. Arousal, and the manner in which arousal is attributed, can therefore play an important role in mediating minority underperformance effects.

Threatening environments can also lower performance via lower performance expectations. In a study reported by Sekaquaptewa and Thompson (2003), women and men placed in virtual minority or same-gender groups were asked to estimate their performance before taking a math test. Results showed that women in the minority group had lower performance expectations than those in a same-gender group; men's performance expectations, in contrast, did not differ. Furthermore, the effect of minority environments on women's math performance was partly mediated by these lower expectations. Minority environments, therefore, may impugn intellectual performance by raising arousal and by lowering performance expectations.

Importantly, the effects of threatening minority environments on intellectual performance may be limited to groups operating in stereotyped domains. For example, even though a White man may be more likely to notice his race in a group of Black men and his gender in a group of White women, the stereotypes that these social identities are likely to activate may not be negative or threatening. Tokenism theory (Lord & Saenz, 1985; Saenz & Lord, 1989), on the other hand, suggests that being in the minority can cause cognitive deficits in all domains and for all groups, presumably as an outgrowth of the self-consciousness it causes. Performance deficits, in other words, are caused by feelings of general self-consciousness and not from stereotype activation. Although research supports both models, there is now converging evidence that minority situations are most threatening to groups dealing with negative stereotypes. Thus, although women and African Americans do worse when outnumbered by White men, White men are unaffected when the situation is reversed (e.g. Inzlicht & Ben-Zeev, 2000; Thompson & Sekaquaptewa, 2002). Similarly, although businesswomen (Kanter, 1977) and policewomen (Ott, 1989) suffer as a result of being in the numerical inferiority, male nurses, librarians, and elementary school teachers, who are not stereotyped to be inferior, do not (Williams, 1992).

Other Devaluing Environments

Thus far we have focused on the environmental threats posed by the gender or race of fellow test takers. Equally threatening is the race or gender of classroom instructors (Marx & Roman, 2002). For instance, on noticing that most of their high school's math and science teachers are men, girls in a math class might wonder whether gender and science are intricately connected and ask if math and science are male centered. For these girls, this "male-centeredness" may signal that their social identity has only marginal value and so may transform their class into a threatening environment (Steele et al., 2002). Marx and Roman (2002) tested this idea by examining whether a testing environment could become threatening by the mere presence of a male experimenter. In their first study, a competent experimenter, who was either a man or a woman, administered a difficult math test to individual male and female participants. The presence of a competent male experimenter, it was hypothesized, would reinforce participants' notion of math as falling under the dominion of men and lead to impaired performance for women. On the other hand, the presence of a competent female experimenter would provide a counterexample to the stereotype about women's alleged difficulties in math and protect women's math performance. Experimenter gender, then, can signal how much import is placed on women's contributions and so can determine whether an environment is threatening and performance impugning. Results confirmed predictions: Women did worse with a male experimenter than with a female one, whereas men were unaffected by experimenter's gender. A second study conducted by Marx and Roman (2002) suggested that female experimenters were only effective in protecting women's math performance to the extent that they were perceived as competent and intelligent in math. It appears that a competent female experimenter—or instructor—sends the message that women can excel in domains in which they are negatively stereotyped, signals that women are clearly respected and esteemed in the setting, and disarms potentially threatening environments.

However, one does not need to take a class with a male instructor or attend a mostly White college to find threatening environments. One, in fact, need go no further than the living room for the pleasure of such an experience. For those households that indulge in a heavy diet of television consumption, one's own home can become threatening. A quick glance at the TV is all one needs to be inundated with images that reinforce racial, ethnic, and gender stereotypes. It is no surprise, then, that compared to light viewers, heavy television viewers believe that women have less ability, fewer interests, and fewer career options than men (Gerbner, Gross, Morgan, & Signorielli, 1993). Watching TV—or reading magazines, listening to radio, or surfing the Internet—can therefore foster threatening environments and impugn intellectual performance as a result. Davies and his colleagues (2002) examined this idea in a study on the effects of television commercials on intellectual performance. Men and women watched a set of either stereotypic commercials (e.g., a commercial portraying a woman "drooling" with anticipation to try a new brownie mix) or counterstereotypic commercials (e.g., a woman speaking intelligently about health care concerns) and then took a difficult math test. Before taking the test, but after watching the commercials, participants also completed a measure of stereotype activation. Even though the stereotypic commercials made no reference to the alleged difference in math ability, results revealed that women who watched stereotypic commercials did worse on the math test than women who watched the counterstereotypic commercials or than men more generally. Men, in contrast, were unaffected by the type of commercial they had seen. Furthermore, these test results were mediated by stereotype activation; the women who watched stereotypic commercials thought more about negative female stereotypes and did worse on the test as a consequence. Threats to performance, therefore, can literally be broadcast in the air.

ENVIRONMENTS CAN THREATEN ACADEMIC SELF-CONCEPT

Watching a stereotypical TV commercial, being outnumbered, or being taught by a member of the dominant group are not the only ways that environments threaten stereotyped individuals; and decreased performance is not the only way threat can manifest itself. Environments can also increase people's suspicions that they are being evaluated on the social prejudices that others hold against their group (Crocker & Major, 1989), and in the long run, become detrimental to the development of accurate, realistic, and stable knowledge about one's strengths and weaknesses (Aronson & Inzlicht, 2004).

Discounting Feedback

Environments can increase people's *prejudice apprehension*, which is the extent to which a person anxiously expects, readily perceives, and intensely reacts to rejection that may be due to discrimination (Mendoza-Denton,

Downey, Purdie, Davis, & Pietrzak, 2002). In a study by Inzlicht (2004), for instance, when Black participants were in three-person groups, they felt more apprehensive about being discriminated against the less their social group was represented in the group. In this study, Black participants took a test as either one of one, two, or three Black participants in a three-person group. After the test, they completed a measure of prejudice apprehension (see Mendoza-Denton, Page-Gould, & Pietrzak, chap. 8, this volume). Results showed that participants were more likely to expect and be bothered by discrimination the more Whites there were in the room. Thus, being outnumbered may enable suspicions of bias and discrimination, and lead people to be uncertain as to whether they are being devalued, marginalized, or discriminated against because of their social identity.

In their landmark paper on stigma, Crocker and Major (1989) called this state of uncertainty *attributional ambiguity* and defined it as the doubt that people have about the causes of their performances and the feedback they receive. For example, after failing a paper, a Black student may wonder whether he actually deserves the poor grade or discount it because he thinks his professor is racist. Because there are multiple possible reasons as to why he got the grade he did, he can discount internal attributions and minimize self-blame (Kelley, 1973; Major, Quinton, & McKoy, 2002).

Blaming one's shortcomings on prejudice and discrimination can buffer people from many of the negative affective consequences of poor outcomes. In one study, Crocker, Voelkl, Testa, and Major (1991) had Black and White college students participate in a study on "friendship development" with a same-gender White partner. Participants completed a self-description that was ostensibly given to their partner and then received either positive or negative interpersonal feedback. Half of the participants sat in a room with the blinds on a one-way mirror partially raised, whereas the blinds were down for the other half of the participants. Being in a room with blinds raised, it was hypothesized, would increase the visibility of the participant, subtly communicate group membership, and so increase the possibility that Black participants would attribute their outcome to prejudice against their group. In contrast, being in a room with blinds down would make it impossible for the White partner to know the participant's race and thus would minimize the possibility that Black participants would feel like they were targets of discrimination. This is just what happened. Among Black participants, attributions to discrimination were higher if they thought their partner could see them and know their race than if their race was unknown. Furthermore, after getting negative feedback, they actually felt better about themselves—as reflected in self-esteem—if they could attribute the feedback to prejudice. White participants, on the other hand, were not affected by their visibility. Environments that signal that people may be judged along the basis of their social identity—threatening environments—can increase prejudice apprehension and therefore lead people to discount feedback and so become unaffected by it.

Inaccurate and Unstable Self-Knowledge

Although suspecting that the negative feedback one receives reflects prejudice and discrimination can protect self-esteem, it may also have negative consequences for self-knowledge. Specifically, it may also lead individuals to disregard potentially instructive feedback, which can rob them of opportunities to learn about themselves from valuable sources of information. The more frequently one discounts feedback or writes off test scores as invalid, the less one can learn about one's underlying abilities. The uncertainty of attributionally ambiguous environments means that individuals belonging to stigmatized groups may have a difficult time developing a *clear self-concept*—that is, a stable and accurate conception of one's strengths and weaknesses (Major et al., 2002).

Aronson and Inzlicht (2004) tested this idea in a series of correlational studies. In their first study, Aronson and Inzlicht hypothesized that individuals who are high in prejudice apprehension would make assessments of their performances that are poorly "calibrated" with reality (Lichtenstein & Fischhoff, 1977). That is, those individuals who anxiously expect and readily perceive discrimination should judge their abilities in a way that corresponds very little with their actual abilities; those who expect and perceive less bias should judge their abilities more accurately. Black participants who were high or low in prejudice apprehension and White participants took a test composed of ten verbal items and then indicated the probability that each of their answers was correct. Results confirmed expectations. Black participants who were prejudice apprehensive were overconfident and had estimates of their ability that were more miscalibrated with reality than either Blacks who did not expect prejudice or than Whites more generally. Black students who have a history of discounting feedback, in other words, may not have the benefit of learning from feedback and thus remain overconfident and miscalibrated. Being wary of discrimination, then, is associated with inaccurate academic self-knowledge.

Another way to examine the self-knowledge hypothesis is to examine self-knowledge over time. People who have unclear academic self-knowledge do not really know how good or bad their academic skills are and may experience temporally unstable self-knowledge as a result (Kernis, Cornell, Sun, Berry, & Harlow, 1993; Wright, 2001). Aronson and Inzlicht (2004) therefore conducted a second study where Black participants who were high or low in prejudice apprehension and White participants completed diary measures of academic self-efficacy twice daily for 2 weeks. Being apprehensive for prejudice, they suspected, would be related to impaired self-knowledge, and along with it, unstable academic self-efficacy. In other words, because they do not really know how skilled they are, prejudice apprehensive individuals should have highly variable feelings of self-efficacy, sometimes feeling confident and other times not. In contrast, Black participants who are not prejudice apprehensive—or Whites more generally—should have feelings of self-efficacy that are more stable over time.

This is exactly what happened: Black participants who were prejudice apprehensive experienced more ups and downs in their feelings of academic competence than any of the other participants. Figure 7.2 shows, however, that apprehensive participants only experienced heightened instability in self-concepts related to stereotyped domains (i.e., academic performance). They did not suffer instability in nonstereotyped domains, such as in athletic self-efficacy.

Combined, these two studies show that although sensitivity to discrimination can protect self-esteem, it can harm the development of accurate and stable self-knowledge, both of which may be vital components of intelligence and goal setting (e.g., Gardner, 1999; Sternberg, 1996). Further, given that minority environments can enable suspicions of bias and discrimination (Inzlicht, 2004), it follows that they may also allow people to discount negative feedback and so may threaten the accuracy and stability of self-knowledge as a result. Future research needs to examine this possibility.

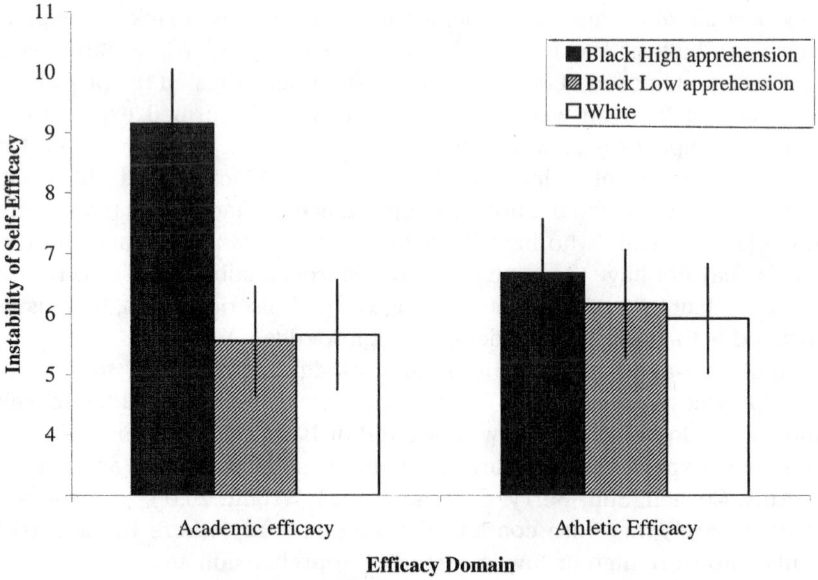

FIG. 7.2. Instability of self-efficacy as a function of group and domain. Higher values denote greater instability. Errors bars represent standard error.

ENVIRONMENTS CAN SEND EXCLUSIONARY MESSAGES

Thus far, we have seen how threatening environments can affect people's intellectual performance and, possibly, their academic self-knowledge. They can also, however, increase people's suspicions that they do not belong. Current research shows that environments that activate negative stereotypes can make people feel like outsiders and that their contributions do not matter. This is especially so when these stereotypic messages are coupled with messages about the immutability and fixedness of intelligence (Good & Dweck, 2003a), which can spring forth from the individuals who hold positions of authority in the environments; for example, from teachers in classrooms (Good & Dweck, 2003b).

Sense of Belonging

Building on research by Dweck and her colleagues on implicit theories of intelligence (see Dweck, 1999, for a review), Good and Dweck (2003a) wondered whether academic environments that suggest that intelligence is fixed could constitute a double threat to individuals who must also contend with negative stereotypes about their abilities, and thus foster feelings of unease and rejection. When a learning environment conveys the message of fixed intelligence, any failure within that environment is seen as a reflection of true ability, which makes stereotypes implying low ability more pejorative and more harmful to a feeling that one's social identity is valued and respected. Alternatively, contexts that portray skills as acquirable may create resiliency to the negative stereotype's debilitating message and send inclusionary, as opposed to exclusionary, messages. If the environment portrays the view that skills can be acquired through effort over time, then the stereotype of lesser underlying ability may become less credible and, consequently, less threatening (cf. Hong, Chiu, Dweck, Linn, & Wan, 1999; Mueller & Dweck, 1998).

Furthermore, academic contexts that focus on fixed ability could, like stereotypes, undermine students' sense of belonging–their feelings that they are valued members of the academic community. These environments may insinuate that only those with high ability will be seen as valued members whose presence and contributions matter. And any slip in achievement or performance may be taken to indicate that a student is in fact inherently lower in ability and consequently does not really belong to the academic community in which they are stereotyped. On the other hand, environments that foster the belief that competencies can be developed over time through effort may create room for many more people to be valued members, perhaps because a secure sense of belonging may depend more on one's interest, commitment, and progress and less on one's perceived ability (c.f. Butler, 2000; Hong et al., 1999).

To test these hypotheses, Good and Dweck (2003a) conducted a longitudinal study of calculus students in which participants completed the Sense of Belonging to Math Scale at the beginning and end of the semester. The questionnaires also included measures of students' perceptions of whether their math classes sent messages of fixed views of math ability and gender stereotyping about math ability. Results showed that at the beginning of the semester, the most important determinant of women's sense of belonging to math was their prior math ability. Specifically, women with higher SAT scores reported a greater sense of belonging to math than did those with lower SAT scores. Over time, however, prior ability played less of a role and the educational environment played a larger one. By the end of the semester, women's perceptions of both the amount of stereotyping in their environment and the extent to which the environment was focused on fixed ability each independently undermined their sense of belonging to math. That is, female students with either of these perceptions felt less accepted, felt that others had lower expectations for them, felt a greater desire to fade into the woodwork, felt less trust of their learning environment, and had lower confidence in their abilities.

Although perceptions of gender stereotyping and perceptions of a fixed-ability learning environment each independently lowered women's sense of belonging to math, Fig. 7.3 shows that together they interacted to constitute a double threat. Women who perceived both a fixed-ability learning environment and high gender stereotyping not only had to contend with messages of fixed ability implied by the stereotype, but also messages of fixed ability fostered by the environment. It was precisely these students who were most susceptible to a lowered sense of belonging to math, regardless of their prior ability. Environments that portrayed skills as acquirable and expandable, however, created resiliency to the negative stereotypes' debilitating message. Learning environments that communicate that math ability is acquirable helped women maintain a sense of belonging to math even when they perceived their environment as highly gender-stereotypical. Thus, by the end of the semester, the effect of gender stereotyping on sense of belonging was moderated by the types of messages the environment communicated about math intelligence—fixed-ability environments aggravated the effect and malleable-ability environments muted it.

Importantly, these results were based on women's perceptions of their environment and not on an objective measure of whether that environment actually promoted gender stereotypes or communicated that math intelligence is fixed. The point here is that regardless of their actual environments, women's subjective appraisals of those environments influenced their vulnerability to a decreased sense of belonging. The good news is that

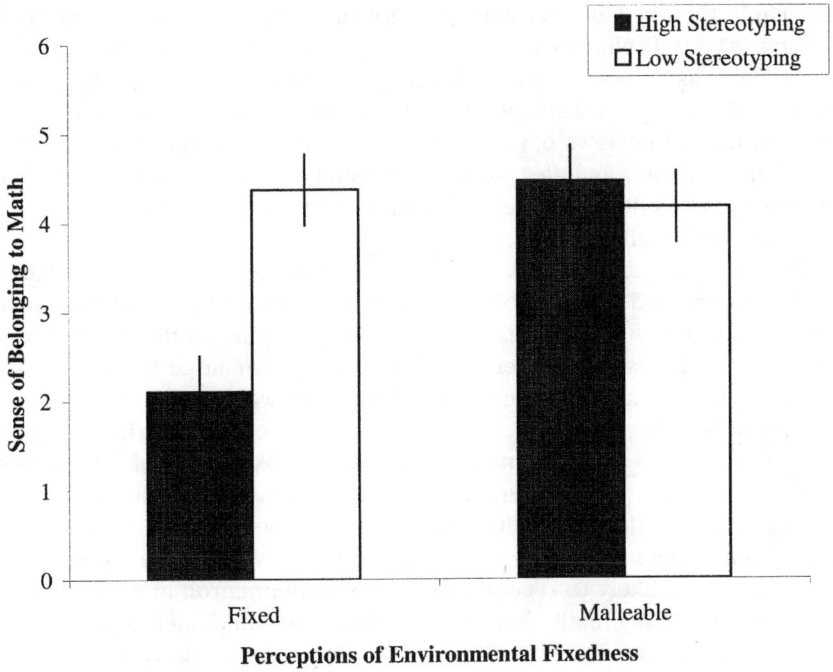

FIG 7.3. Sense of belonging to math as a function of perceptions of environmental stereotyping and fixedness. Error bars represent standard error.

changing people's perceptions of their environment can be an effective tool to counter the effects of stereotype threat. For example, it may be possible to buffer the effects of stereotypes on a sense of belonging by having people perceive their environment in a more benign way, say, by seeing that it promotes a malleable view of math intelligence. We examine this and other possibilities later in the chapter.

How Environments Send Threatening Messages

Whether an environment portrays the view that ability is fixed or malleable can determine whether it is seen as threatening or benign. But, how exactly do they convey such messages? One way to tackle this question is to look at the people who are in positions of authority in a given environment to see what types of messages they send. In a classroom, for example, we might examine what teachers say and think about intelligence to see how it affects students' perceptions of the environment. If teachers send the message that intelligence is malleable as opposed to fixed, perhaps this can create a safe environment where students reap the rewards conferred by a malleable theory. This possibility is currently being investigated (Good & Dweck, 2003b). Preliminary results suggest that when a novel math lesson includes a discussion about the hard work and effort that go into mathematical discovery, students perceive the instructor and the environment as holding malleable views of math intelligence. Alternatively, when the same novel math lesson includes statements about the genius of mathematical discovery, students perceive the environment as communicating a fixed view of math intelligence.

In a second study (Good & Dweck, 2003b), college students were primed with either a fixed or malleable view of intelligence and then asked to take the perspective of a math teacher who was returning math exams to students. Participants read a scenario about either a female or male math student and were asked to indicate how likely they would be to implement a variety of pedagogical practices for the student in question. Preliminary results suggest that participants primed with the fixed view of intelligence had pronounced gender stereotyping that was expressed through their pedagogical practices. Participants primed with the malleable view, in contrast, showed less gender stereotyping. Fixed-ability participants, for example, were more likely to recommend that a student enroll in a gifted math program and join a math club when the hypothetical student was male as opposed to female. Participants primed with the malleable view, however, were just as likely to make these recommendations to males and females.

These results underscore the subtle ways in which a teacher's implicit theory of intelligence can direct the degree to which stereotyping is conveyed and so affect whether a classroom environment is seen as threatening or not. In combination, both studies show that teachers holding a fixed view of intelligence not only communicate that ability is fixed but also that they have different expectations for males and females. And as discussed earlier, holding gender stereotypes and a fixed view of intelligence forms a deadly combination by creating an environment that can affect motivational states—such as a decreased sense of belonging—and perhaps even performance (Good & Dweck, 2003a). There is, however, a silver lining to all of this: Given that malleable-intelligence environments can buffer people from threats posed by negative stereotypes, it follows that instructors who teach this malleable view can foster an accepting and inclusionary learning environment and thus reduce students' vulnerability to stereotype threat. This possibility is currently being investigated (Good & Dweck, 2003b).

OVERCOMING THREATENING ENVIRONMENTS

In this chapter, we've spent most of our time—perhaps even too much time (Seligman, 2002)—discussing how environments can hurt, threaten, and impede. For example, we discussed how minority environments can evoke stereotype threat, how perceiving a fixed-ability learning environment can hurt feelings of belonging, and how being stereotype vulnerable—or possibly being in an environment that fosters stereotype vulnerability—can threaten self-knowledge. But what can we do to help people overcome these threats? How can we neutralize threats present in the environment?

Learning About the Malleability of Intelligence

One possibility, which builds on Carol Dweck's work on implicit theories of intelligence (see Dweck, 1999), is to create environments where people are encouraged to view intelligence as a malleable quantity. A number of studies have addressed this possibility. In one study, for example, Aronson, Fried, and Good (2002) conducted an intervention in which college students were encouraged to adopt a malleable mindset about intelligence. In this study, both African American and White participants were randomly assigned to one of three groups. The first group received training in order to view intelligence as something that can grow and increase with effort—the *malleable view*. To foster this view, they watched a film illustrating that the brain forms new connections and literally changes whenever you learn something new. Furthermore, they participated in a pen-pal program in which they wrote a letter to a struggling junior high-school student and emphasized in their letters the idea that intelligence is expandable and increases with mental work. In the control groups, participants either received no treatment or a treatment about the many forms of ability. At the end of the semester, the group receiving the malleable intervention reported greater enjoyment of their academic work and greater valuing of academics in general. In addition, this group showed a clear gain in grade-point average over the other groups. Although these gains were apparent for all students in the study (both Whites and African Americans), the gains were largest for the African American students.

In a second study, Good, Aronson, & Inzlicht (2003) designed a similar intervention to investigate whether teaching junior-high students about the malleable nature of intelligence could be used to reduce their vulnerability to stereotype threat and increase their standardized test performance. Specifically, boys and girls in the seventh grade of a low-income, predominantly Hispanic school participated in a year-long intervention where they were mentored by college students who taught them either that intelligence is expandable (experimental group) or about the perils of drug use (control group). At the year's end, the two groups' math and reading performance on a state-wide standardized achievement test was compared. Results indicated that the students in the malleable group received higher standardized test scores in both math and reading than students in the control group. Although the malleable intelligence manipulation helped all students, it was particularly beneficial for the stigmatized students—the Hispanic students in reading and the females in math. For example, in the malleable condition, the gender gap in math, evident in the control group, disappeared. These two studies therefore provide good evidence that interventions directed at students' key motivation-relevant beliefs could pay off by boosting intellectual performance.

Other Interventions

There are, of course, other remedies to the effects of threatening environments. Steele et al. (1997), for example, designed a "wise" schooling intervention for first-year students at the University of Michigan. Using mixed-race groups, students were "honorifically" recruited to the program by emphasizing that they had survived a very competitive admission process at the school, and that the University recognized their strong potential and had high expectations for them—all things that signal the insignificance of negative group stereotypes. Once in the program, students were reminded of these high expectations and challenged with weekly workshops on advanced material that went beyond material presented in most freshman classes. Several years of the program demonstrated that such practices can substantially increase the school performance of African Americans. Uri Treisman's Emerging Scholars Program is another possible remedy. In this program, underrepresented groups in mathematics, such as females, attend math workshops (in addition to their regular math lectures) that specifically redress some of the factors that make math threatening. The Emerging Scholars Program fosters an environment where students feel safe to explore new and unfamiliar ideas in math, the results of which are increases in performance and retention for women and other underrepresented populations (see College Board, 2001, for a review). Other things teachers can do include reducing the apparent diagnosticity of tests (Steele & Aronson, 1995) and increasing the number of minority teachers and role models (Marx & Roman, 2002; see Aronson, 2002, for a review).

CONCLUSION

Social psychological research shows us that our environments can be threatening. They can remind us of our social identities, activate negative stereotypes, and otherwise communicate that our groups are marginalized, devalued, and not accepted. When this happens people must cope with these pejorative messages, and the skill with which this is done can influence a number of important outcomes, including academic and intellectual performance, feelings of trust and belonging, and the accuracy and stability of self-knowledge. The good news that we hope has come through in this chapter is that the effects of threatening environments can be mitigated and that there is much that educators and policy makers can do to help. Once this is done, counting one's social identity—as Arthur Ashe did—will no longer have the same negative repercussions.

ACKNOWLEDGMENTS

This chapter was written in part by the support of a SPSSI Grants-In-Aid Award and a Spencer post-doctoral fellowship to Michael Inzlicht and an NSF grant to Catherine Good. We thank Josh Aronson, Carol Dweck, Talia Ben-Zeev, Steve Fein, Linda McKay, and Naomi Sarah Ball for valuable insights. We also acknowledge support from New York University's Center for Research on Culture, Development, and Education. Correspondence concerning this chapter should be addressed to Michael Inzlicht, Department of Life Sciences, University of Toronto at Scarborough, 1265 Military Trail, Toronto, Ontario M1C 1A4, Canada (E-mail: michael.inzlicht@utoronto.ca).

REFERENCES

Aronson, J. (2002). Stereotype threat: Contending and coping with unnerving expectations. In J. Aronson (Ed.), *Improving academic achievement: Impact of psychological factors on education* (pp. 279–301). San Diego, CA: Academic Press.

Aronson, J., Fried, C., & Good, C. (2002). Reducing the effects of stereotype threat on African American college students by shaping theories of intelligence. *Journal of Experimental Social Psychology, 38*, 113–125.

Aronson, J., & Inzlicht, M. (2004). The ups and downs of attributional ambiguity: Stereotype vulnerability and the academic self-knowledge of African American college students. *Psychological Science, 15,* 829–836.

Aronson, J., Lustina, M. J., Good, C., Keough, K., Steele, C. M., & Brown, J. (1999). When white men can't do math: Necessary and sufficient factors in stereotype threat. *Journal of Experimental Social Psychology, 35*, 29–46.

Ashe, A. (1993). *Days of grace.* New York: Alfred A. Knopf.

Ben-Zeev, T., Fein, S., & Inzlicht, M. (2005). Arousal and stereotype threat *Journal of Experimental Social Psychology, 41*, 174–181.

Blascovich, J., Spencer, S. J., Quinn, D., & Steele, C. (2001). African Americans and high blood pressure: The role of stereotype threat. *Psychological Science, 12*, 225–229.

Business and Professional Women/USA. (2003). *101 facts on the status of working women.* Retrieved September 9, 2004, from http://www.bpwusa.org/content/PressRoom/101Facts/101Facts.htm

Butler, R. (2000). Making judgments about ability: The role of implicit theories of ability in moderating inferences from temporal and social comparison information. *Journal of Personality and Social Psychology, 78*, 965–978.

College Board. (2001). *Calculus and community: A history of the emerging scholars community.* Retrieved September 9, 2004, from http://www.collegeboard.com/repository/calcandcomm_3947.pdf

Crocker, J., & Major, B. (1989). Social stigma and self-esteem: The self-protective properties of stigma. *Psychological Review, 96,* 608–630.

Crocker, J., Voelkl, K., Testa, M., & Major, B. (1991). Social stigma: The affective consequences of attributional ambiguity. *Journal of Personality and Social Psychology, 60,* 218–228.

Davies, P. G., Spencer, S. J., Quinn, D. M., & Gerhardstein, R. (2002). Consuming images: How television commercials that elicit stereotype threat can restrain women academically and professionally. *Personality and Social Psychology Bulletin, 28,* 1615–1628.

Dweck, C. (1999). *Self-theories: Their role in motivation, personality, and development.* Philadelphia: Psychology Press.

Gardner, H. (1999). *Intelligence reframed: Multiple intelligences for the 21st century.* New York: Basic Books.

Gerbner, G., Gross, L., Morgan, M., & Signorielli, N. (1993). Growing up with television: The cultivation perspective. In J. Bryant & D. Zillman (Eds.), *Media effects: Advances in theory and research.* Hillsdale, NJ: Lawrence Erlbaum Associates.

Gilbert, D. T., & Hixon, J. G. (1991). The trouble of thinking: Activation and application of stereotypic beliefs. *Journal of Personality and Social Psychology, 60,* 509–517.

Goffman, E. (1963). *Stigma: Notes on the management of spoiled identity.* Englewood Cliffs, NJ: Prentice-Hall.

Good, C., Aronson, J., & Inzlicht, M. (2003). Improving adolescents' standardized test performance: An intervention to reduce the effects of stereotype threat. *Journal of Applied Developmental Psychology, 24,* 645–662.

Good, C., & Dweck, C. (2003a). *The effects of stereotypes and fixed-views of intelligence on students' sense of belonging to math.* Unpublished manuscript, Columbia University.

Good, C. & Dweck, C. (2003b). *How teachers inadvertently send messages about the nature of intelligence.* Unpublished manuscript, Columbia University.

Hong, Y. Y., Chiu, C., Dweck, C. S., Linn, D., & Wan, W. (1999) Implicit theories, attributions, and coping: A meaning system approach. *Journal of Personality and Social Psychology, 77,* 588–599.

Inzlicht, M. (2004). *When being alone increases suspicions of prejudice.* Unpublished manuscript, New York University.

Inzlicht, M., Aronson, J., Good, C., & McKay, L. (in press). A particular resiliency to threatening environments. *Journal of Experimental Social Psychology.*

Inzlicht, M., & Ben-Zeev, T. (2000). A threatening intellectual environment: Why females are susceptible to experiencing problem-solving deficits in the presence of males. *Psychological Science, 11,* 365–371.

Inzlicht, M., & Ben-Zeev, T. (2003). Do high-achieving female students underperform in private? The implications of threatening environments on intellectual processing. *Journal of Educational Psychology, 95,* 796–805.

Kanter, R. M. (1977). *Men and women of the corporation.* New York: Basic Books.

Kelley, H. H. (1973). The process of causal attribution. *American Psychologist, 28,* 107–128.

Kernis, M. H., Cornell, D. P., Sun, C. R., Berry, A. J., & Harlow, T. (1993). There's more to self-esteem than whether it is high or low: The importance of stability of self-esteem. *Journal of Personality and Social Psychology, 65,* 1190–1204.

Kray, L. J., Thompson, L., & Galinksy, A. (2001). Battle of the sexes: Gender stereotype confirmation and reactance to negotiations. *Journal of Personality and Social Psychology, 80,* 942–958.

Lichtenstein, S., & Fischoff, B. (1977). Do those who know more also know more about how much they know? *Organizational Behavior and Human Performance, 20,* 159–183.

Lord, C. G., & Saenz, D. S. (1985). Memory deficits and memory surfeits: Differential cognitive consequences of tokenism for tokens and observer. *Journal of Personality and Social Psychology, 49,* 918–926.

Major, B., Quinton, W. J., & McCoy, S. K. (2002). Antecedents and consequences of attributions to discrimination: Theoretical and empirical advances. In M. Zanna (Ed.), *Advances in Experimental Social Psychology* (Vol. 34, pp. 251–330). San Diego, CA: Academic Press.

Marx, D., & Roman, J. S. (2002). Female role-models: Protecting women's math test performance. *Personality and Social Psychology Bulletin, 28,* 1183–1193.

McGuire, W. J., McGuire C. V., Child, P., & Fujioka, T. (1978). Salience of ethnicity in the spontaneous self-concept as a function of one's ethnic distinctiveness in the social environment. *Journal of Personality and Social Psychology, 36,* 511-520.

McGuire, W. J., McGuire, C. V., & Winton, W. (1979). Effects of household sex composition on the salience of one's gender in the spontaneous self-concept. *Journal of Experimental Social Psychology, 15,* 77–90.

Mendoza-Denton, R., Downey, G., Purdie, V. J., Davis, & Pietrzak, J. (2002). Sensitivity to status-based rejection: Implications for African American students' college experience. *Journal of Personality and Social Psychology, 83,* 896–918.

Mueller, C. M., & Dweck, C. S. (1998). Intelligence praise can undermine motivation and performance. *Journal of Personality and Social Psychology, 75,* 33–52.

National Science Foundation. (2000). *Women, minorities, and persons with disabilities in science and engineering: 2000* (NSF Publication No. 00–327). Arlington, VA: Author

O'Brien, L. T., & Crandall, C. S. (2003). Stereotype threat and arousal: Effects on women's math performance. *Personality and Social Psychology Bulletin, 29,* 782–789.

Ott, E. M. (1989). Effects of the male–female ratio at work. *Psychology of Women Quarterly, 13,* 41–57.

Quinn, D. M., & Spencer, S. J. (2001). The interference of stereotype threat with women's generation of mathematical problem-solving strategies. *Journal of Social Issues, 57,* 55–71.

Saenz, D. S., & Lord, C. G. (1989). Reversing roles: A cognitive strategy for undoing memory deficits associated with token status. *Journal of Personality and Social Psychology, 56,* 698–708.

Schmader, T. (2002). Gender identification moderates stereotype threat effects on women's math performance. *Journal of Experimental Social Psychology, 38,* 194–201.

Schmader, T., & Johns, M. (2003). Converging evidence that stereotype threat reduces working memory capacity. *Journal of Personality and Social Psychology, 85,* 440–452.

Sekaquaptewa, D., & Thompson, M. (2002). The differential effects of solo status on members of high and low-status groups. *Personality and Social Psychology Bulletin, 28,* 694–707.

Sekaquaptewa, D., & Thompson, M. (2003). Solo status, stereotype threat, and performance expectancies: Their effects on women's performance. *Journal of Experimental Social Psychology, 39,* 68–74.

Seligman, M. E. P. (2002). Positive psychology, positive prevention, and positive therapy. In C. R. Snyder & S. Lopez (Eds.), *Handbook of positive psychology* (pp. 3–12). Oxford, England: Oxford University Press.

Spencer, S. J., Steele, C. M. & Quinn, D. (1999). Stereotype threat and women's math performance. *Journal of Experimental Social Psychology, 35,* 4–28.

Steele, C. M. (1997). A threat in the air: How stereotypes shape intellectual identity and performance. *American Psychologist, 52,* 613–629.

Steele, C. M. & Aronson, J. (1995). Stereotype threat and the intellectual test performance of African Americans. *Journal of Personality and Social Psychology, 69,* 797–811.

Steele, C. M., Spencer, S., & Aronson, J. (2002) Contending with images of one's group: The psychology of stereotype and social identity threat. In M. Zanna (Ed.), *Advances in Experimental Social Psychology* (Vol. 34, pp. 379–440). San Diego, CA: Academic Press.

Steele, C. M., Spencer, S. J., Hummel, M., Carter, K., Harber, K., Schoem, D., & Nisbett, R. (1997). *African-American college achievement: A "wise" intervention.* Unpublished manuscript, Stanford University.

Sternberg, R. J. (1996). *Successful intelligence.* New York: Simon & Schuster.

Stone, J., Lynch, C. I., Sjomeling, M., & Darley, J. M. (1999). Stereotype threat effects on Black and White athletic performance. *Journal of Personality and Social Psychology, 77*, 1213–1227.

Thompson, M., & Sekaquaptewa, D. (2002). When being different is detrimental: Solo status and the performance of women and racial minorities. *Analyses of Social Issues and Public Policy, 2*, 183–203.

Vorauer, J. D., Main, K. J., & O'Connell, G. B. (1998). How do individuals expect to be viewed by members of lower status groups? Content and implications of meta-stereotypes. *Journal of Personality and Social Psychology, 75*, 917–937.

Williams, C. L. (1992). The glass escalator: Hidden advantages for men in the "female" professions. *Social Problems, 39*, 253–267.

Wright, R. (2001). Self-certainty and self-esteem. In T. J. Owens, S. Stryker, & N. Goodman (Eds.), *Extending self-esteem theory and research: Sociological and psychological currents* (pp. 101–134). New York: Cambridge University Press.

Zanna, M. P., & Cooper, J. (1974). Dissonance and the pill: An attribution approach to studying the arousal properties of dissonance. *Journal of Personality and Social Psychology, 29*, 703–709.

CHAPTER

8

Mechanisms for Coping With Status-Based Rejection Expectations

Rodolfo Mendoza-Denton
University of California, Berkeley

Elizabeth Page-Gould
University of California, Berkeley

Janina Pietrzak
University of Warsaw

"Ask yourself," Gordon Allport invited readers in his 1954 classic, *The Nature of Prejudice*, to consider, "what would happen to your personality if you heard it said over and over again that you were lazy . . . and had inferior blood" (p. 138). Although the study of prejudice and discrimination has historically been dominated by research from the perspective of the perpetrator (Oyserman & Swim, 2001), the past 15 years in particular have witnessed an explosion of research that yields initial answers to Allport's question. Collectively, this research suggests that the effects of stigma on adjustment and adaptation are varied, and depend on the stigmatized characteristic, the context surrounding the stigma, and the coping mechanisms marshaled in response to stigmatization (Puhl & Brownell, 2003). Consistent with stress and coping frameworks for understanding stigma (see Major, chap. 10, this volume; Swim & Thomas, chap. 6, this volume), the chapters in this volume illustrate well the heterogeneity and contextual specificity of targets' responses to stigma. Given that the experience of stigmatization can vary widely, any one coping mechanism is not a panacea for all groups—or all individuals within groups.

In this chapter, we review a growing body of research documenting the development and consequences of *status-based rejection expectations*. Rejection plays a central role in the experience of stigmatization (Branscombe, Schmitt, & Harvey, 1999; Miller and Kaiser, 2001; Root, 1992) and characterizes an important aspect of threat-related dynamics that include stereotype threat (Aronson, 2002; Steele, 1997), stigma consciousness (Pinel, 1999; 2002), and race-based rejection sensitivity (Mendoza-Denton, Downey, Purdie, Davis, & Pietrzak, 2002; Pietrzak, Mendoza-Denton, & Downey, 2004). First, we review the conditions surrounding and consequences that follow from expectations of status-based rejection. Although such expectations can arise from situational pressures alone (see Inzlicht & Good, chap. 7, this volume), evidence also suggests that in certain situations, some people are more likely than others to experience threat or apprehension on the basis of status characteristics (Brown & Pinel, 2003; Mendoza-Denton et al., 2002). Further, not everybody who fears and expects rejection experiences similar outcomes (Ayduk et al., 2000; Freitas & Downey, 1998). We argue here that variability in outcomes related to status-based rejection expectations is dependent on individual cognitions and affects that constitute peoples' coping mechanisms in the face of such rejection.

The latter half of this chapter explores these coping mechanisms at three levels: the intrapersonal, the interpersonal, and the institutional or structural. At the intrapersonal level, we review burgeoning research on personal strengths that individuals can marshal to cope with rejection expectations. These include (among many others) beliefs about the malleability of intelligence (Aronson, Fried, & Good, 2002), ethnic identity (Pietrzak et al., 2004), and proactive social activism for positive social change (see Deaux & Ethier, 1998). At the interpersonal level, we focus on the effect of cross-race relationships (McLaughlin-Volpe, Mendoza-Denton, & Shelton, in press; see also McLaughlin-Volpe, chap. 11, this volume) and on the quality of mentoring relationships (Cohen, Steele, & Ross, 1999). Finally, we turn to mechanisms at the structural or institutional level; namely, those procedures and steps institutions can take to gain the trust of individuals historically marginalized by the institution.

THEORETICAL FRAMEWORK: THE COGNITIVE–AFFECTIVE PROCESSING SYSTEM

Although research on the effects of stigma on adjustment and well-being have traditionally focused on between-group differences, more recently researchers have investigated within-group variability in outcomes as well (Major, chap. 10, this volume; Major, Quinton, McCoy, & Schmader, 2000). Consistent with this view, our own analysis is framed within Mischel & Shoda's (1995, 1999) Cognitive-Affective Processing System (CAPS) framework. From the CAPS perspective, a person's characteristic responses are mediated by his or her unique network of *cognitive-affective units* (CAUs)—construals, expectations/beliefs, affects, and goals—activated in particular situations. The organization of these CAUs (the network), which reflects the social-cognitive history of the individual (Shoda & Mischel, 1998), guides and constrains the activation of cognitions, affects, and potential behaviors while an individual processes situational features. Our analysis of coping mechanisms is framed within this broad framework, such that a person's behavioral responses are influenced not only by the activation of race-based rejection expectations, but also by a host of other mechanisms in the network. These mechanisms can reflect individual differences (e.g., ethnic identity) as well as environmental influences (e.g., outgroup friendships).

As the individual grows, learns, and gains life experience, an increasingly rich and complex network of CAUs develops. Some CAUs are acquired through the unique experience of the individual, whereas others are shared among members of cultural groups (Mendoza-Denton, Shoda, Ayduk, & Mischel, 1999). Other CAUs can come to be shared as a result of having similar experiences specific to one's cultural group—as when, for example, a shared group characteristic (e.g., skin color) makes a group significantly more likely to experience negative treatment, discrimination, or stigmatization.

A central emphasis of CAPS theory is that the effect of context and situations is mediated by the individual's cognitions and affects, activated in specific situations. As such, we emphasize that people are not the passive recipients of contexts and situations, but are active participants in the construction and management of their environment (Kelly, 1955). In sum, we frame our analysis of the effect of stigma on the individual within a constructivist, Person X situation framework, rather than viewing the phenomenon as being caused by either situational causes or dispositional causes alone. In this view, the question posed at the beginning of this chapter is not an invitation to an analysis of immutable dispositions or characteristics, but rather to an understanding of the psychological process that represents a person's coping repertoire in response to a particular challenge—the challenge of being a target of stereotypes and prejudice.

EXPERIENCING STEREOTYPES AND PREJUDICE: A COPING CHALLENGE

Returning to the question Allport posed half a century ago: what happens to a person when one is told over and over that one is lazy and is of inferior blood? Historically, psychologists have understandably been reluctant to answer this question in characterological terms, preferring instead to analyze outcomes related to stigma in terms of situational pressures (Major et al., 2000). Research on stereotype threat (Aronson, 2002; Steele, 1997) is one such example. In the classic demonstration of the stereotype-threat phenomenon, Steele and Aronson (1995) presented African American students with questions similar to those found in standardized achievement tests. A simple yet powerful experimental manipulation was introduced: in one condition, students were told that the researchers were interested in measuring their verbal ability, and were thus being tested with items diagnostic of their ability. In the other condition, the students were told that the (same) questions were being used to understand the psychological processes associated with problem solving, but that the researchers would not be evaluating the participants' ability. The former condition framed the experimental test questions similarly to the achievement tests widely used in America's educational system. The latter condition framed the test questions with the intention of lifting the students' concerns that their ability was under suspicion or scrutiny as members of a negatively stereotyped group. As hypothesized, the White students performed comparably regardless of experimental condition. The African American students, however, underperformed relative to White students in the "ability diagnostic" condition but performed just as well as the White students in the "nondiagnostic" condition. In other words, African American participants' performance on the same set of questions was significantly affected by a small—but psychologically critical—framing of the test. Other studies have shown that stereotype-relevant intrusive ideation and concerns about fulfilling the stereotype (Steele & Aronson, 1995), and the cognitive busyness that results (Croizet & Després, 2003), help explain this underperformance effect. To the degree that schooling in general, and standardized testing in particular, emphasize the diagnosis of ability as a gateway for tracking, college admissions, and other future opportunities, the implications of stereotype threat in relation to minority student achievement are profound.

Research on stereotype threat provides compelling evidence that even small changes in the framing of a testing situation can have significant effects on the performance of minority students in the classroom (see also Inzlicht & Good, chap. 7, this volume). This research has had wide impact, in part, because it provides a testable psychological account of the contextual and societal forces that can account for the Black–White academic achievement gap (College Board, 1999), and provides a powerful, experimentally validated alternative to biological explanations for achievement differences between groups (e.g., Herrnstein & Murray, 1994).

Race-Based Rejection Expectations

Within social psychology, a distinction has been made between *stereotypes*, the cognitively based belief systems associated with particular groups, and *prejudice*, the affectively based attitudes that people hold toward other groups (e.g., Franzoi, 1996). Independent of negative stereotypes and their influence on their targets, another critical dimension of the experience of being stigmatized is the affectively charged, general dislike held and expressed toward members of one's group by outgroup members—in other words, the problem of prejudice.

But if not through stereotype threat, how can one quantify and psychologically assess the impact of prejudice on its targets? Recent research on African American students' apprehensive anticipation of prejudice (Mendoza-Denton et al., 2002) yields some insight into this issue. According to Mendoza-Denton and colleagues, direct or vicarious experiences of exclusion, discrimination, and prejudice can lead people to anxiously anticipate that they will be similarly treated in new contexts where the possibility of such treatment exists. These expectations are activated in intergroup situations where race-based rejection is possible, leading people to perceive discrimination more readily and to react to such race-based rejection more intensely. Mendoza-Denton and colleagues refer to this processing dynamic (expectations, perceptions, intense reactions) as *race-based rejection sensitivity* (RS-race). This process has also been referred to as *prejudice apprehension* to reflect the notion that individuals can develop expectations about others' prejudice and discrimination unmediated by their fears about confirming stereotypes (Mendoza-Denton & Aronson, in press).

Evidence from other lines of research is consistent with the notion that anxious expectations of status-based rejection can have a detrimental effect on academic outcomes. Independent of psychiatric symptoms, expectations of status-based rejection among those labeled mentally ill have been found to undermine well-being and social functioning (Link, Cullen, Frank & Wozniak, 1987). Similarly, individual differences in stigma consciousness have been related to women's avoidance of situations where gender stigmatization is possible (Pinel, 1999), and to disruptive social interactions with outgroup members (Pinel, 2002). Broader constructs such as intergroup anxiety (W. G. Stephan & C. W. Stephan, 2000) and cultural mistrust (F. Terrell & S. Terrell, 1981), which are also characterized by anticipatory anxiety in relation to intergroup contact, have been related to wariness in anticipation of interaction and avoidance of intergroup contexts.

Testing the Links of the RS-Race Dynamic

To operationalize the construct for African Americans, Mendoza-Denton et al. (2002) first developed and validated the RS-race Questionnaire, a measure that assesses anxious expectations of rejection in situations where race-based rejection is both applicable and personally salient (Higgins, 1996) for African Americans (e.g., a roadblock where police are randomly pulling people over). African Americans scored higher overall on the measure than Asian Americans or Whites, although, as expected, there was substantial within-group variability among African Americans. Consistent with the model, individual differences in anxious expectations of race-based rejection were related to a higher frequency of perceiving racial discrimination and prejudice in a series of cross-sectional and longitudinal studies. Also consistent with the model, students high in RS-race reported greater levels of rejection and alienation following a negative race-related experience than those who were low in RS-race. Together, these results lend empirical support to the conceptualization of RS-race as a cognitive-affective processing dynamic (Mischel & Shoda, 1995) to anxiously expect, readily perceive, and intensely react to race-based rejection.

RS-Race and the Transition to College

Having established a valid and reliable measure of RS-race, the researchers then addressed the questions of central concern to their research program: Do individual differences in RS-race help explain why some African American students view their college experience as alienating and undermining whereas others do not? In particular, does RS-race influence African American students' initial college experiences in ways that have long-lasting implications? The researchers reasoned that preexisting fears about race-based rejection might play a formative role in students' overall college experience by influencing the quality of the relationships they form with professors and peers and the sense of belonging they feel during the first weeks of college.

To examine these questions, RS-race was assessed prior to the beginning of classes in two cohorts of incoming African American students at the university. Participants then completed a structured daily diary for the first 3 weeks of classes. Controlling for interpersonal rejection sensitivity, African American students preidentified as anxiously expectant of race-based rejection experienced a heightened sense of alienation on the typical day of the diary period. They also felt less welcome at their new university, had greater difficulties with their roommates, and formed a less positive view of their professors than their low RS-race counterparts.

Consistent with the model's predictions, students high in RS-race felt less trust and obligation toward the university at the end of their first year in college. As sophomores and juniors, they also reported decreased attendance at academic review sessions, as well as increased anxiety about approaching professors and TAs with academic problems. RS-race was predictive of participants' change in grade-point average (GPA) over the first five semesters of college, such that students high in RS-race were particularly likely to experience a decrease in their grades over time.

Mendoza-Denton et al. (2002) also tracked the development of participants' social relationships during the transition to college in relation to RS-race. At the end of their first year of college, participants were asked to report on the number, age, and race of new friends they made in college. Students high on RS-race reported having fewer White friends at the end of their first year in college than their counterparts low in RS-race. These results also held when controlling for number of Black friends and sensitivity to rejection based on personal characteristics (Downey & Feldman, 1996). Demonstrating the specificity of the construct as a dynamic that motivates people to avoid those who are more likely to reject them on the basis of race, but not necessarily to approach other ethnic minority ingroup members, RS-race was unrelated to the number of ingroup friends that participants reported. This is important because it distinguishes RS-race from a more generalized social anxiety or tendency to avoid social contact (see also Major, Quinton, & McCoy, 2002).

MECHANISMS FOR COPING

As previously noted, not everyone who develops or has anxious expectations is necessarily doomed to negative adjustment or poor intergroup outcomes. As the CAPS model reminds us, anxious expectations are only one aspect of a person's CAPS network, and interact with other CAUs in the system (Ayduk et al., 2000). We refer here to psychological mechanisms that facilitate coping by allowing people to flexibly encode, transform, and interpret stimuli and events as operating at the intrapersonal level.

We now review in some detail recent research shedding light on the interactive effects of ethnic identity and race-based rejection sensitivity on institutional identity as one example of coping at the intrapersonal level. We also discuss social activism as an example of a proactive coping mechanism. Although its effects are interpersonal, we place social activism as an intrapersonal coping response to emphasize its cognitive and affective benefits for the individual. Another example of a coping mechanism at this level, reviewed in more detail by Inzlicht and Good (chap. 7, this volume), is holding a belief in the malleability of intelligence in the face of stereotype threat (Aronson et al., 2002; Good, Aronson, & Inzlicht, 2003).

Given the inherently interactive nature of the CAPS system, whereby a person's stable CAUs are not only activated by specific situations but also developed and maintained by one's social cognitive learning past and current history, mechanisms at two other levels (at least) are also possible, and explored here—the interpersonal and the institutional. At the interpersonal level, we describe how positive intergroup contact can have a significant impact on the outcomes associated with race-based rejection expectations (see also Tropp, chap. 9, this volume, and McLaughlin-Volpe, chap. 11, this volume). We describe an ongoing research program suggesting that cross-race friendships may foster positive academic outcomes, particularly among those who expect rejection the most. At the structural or institutional level, certain practices or structures set up by the institution are also reviewed.

Intrapersonal Level

Ethnic Identity. In recent work, Pietrzak et al. (2004) examined the interactive effects of ethnic identity and RS-race for institutional affiliation and well-being within the college setting. Our interest in ethnic identity stemmed in part from our observation that research on the effects of ethnic identity on adjustment outcomes has yielded somewhat contradictory results, sometimes associated with positive outcomes and sometimes with negative outcomes. As such, we proposed that status-based rejection expectations might help account for some of the variation in these findings.

Several researchers (e.g., Ogbu, 1991, 1994; Parham, 1989) argued that ethnic and institutional identities are associated with conflicting values for minority students. Whereas identifying with one's ethnic group involves taking pride in and having respect for the customs and history of one's ethnic group, identifying with the university may mean implicitly turning a blind eye towards a history of discrimination and exclusion of one's ethnic group by the university and its representatives. Accordingly, ethnic identity within the context of a predominantly White institution has been linked to reduced identification with the institution (Ogbu, 1994; Phinney, Horenczyk, Liebkind, & Vedder, 2001), as well as with greater perceptions of discrimination within the institution (Operario & Fiske, 2001). In a related vein, McCoy and Major (2003) found that individuals highly identified with a particular ingroup were more prone to negative emotions following events perceived as discriminatory. In sum, research from this avenue suggests that ethnic identity stands in opposition to the development of an institutional identity, and as such could contribute to negative intergroup relations and to a greater sense of alienation from the institution (see Sidanius & Petrocik, 2001, for a broader discussion of the negotiation of superordinate and ethnic identities).

At the same time, a number of studies have linked identification with an ethnic or minority group to positive outcomes, including high self-esteem (Phinney, 1992; Roberts et al., 1999; Wright, 1985), academic persistence and efficacy (Bennett & Okinaka, 1990; Jo, 1999; Oyserman, Harrison, & Bybee, 2001), and general well-being (Contrada et al., 2001; Cross, Parham, & Helms, 1991; Roberts et al., 1999). This research, though not related to institutional identification specifically, nevertheless suggests that ethnic identity may not always be in conflict with institutional values and identity.

Pietrzak and colleagues (2004) hypothesized that the effects of ethnic identity on institutional belonging should be different depending on whether a person expects to be rejected on the basis of their race. In other words, one's ethnic identity should be in conflict with one's institutional identity only when one expects that the institution and its members are likely to reject and devalue one's ethnicity. In the absence of anxious rejection expectations, however, the researchers hypothesized that ethnic and institutional identity should be orthogonal; given that the outgroup is less likely to be seen as a devaluator, a person may be able feel a sense of pride and belonging both as a member of the institution and as a member of one's ethnic group without experiencing dissonance.

Three studies were conducted to test these hypotheses—one correlational, one longitudinal, and one experimental (in which participants' ethnic identity was experimentally manipulated). Across all three studies, the hypothesized pattern emerged. Among individuals low on RS-race, no relationship (and in one study, even a positive relationship) was found between the two identities. Among participants high in RS-race, however, the greater one's ethnic identity, the lower one's institutional identity (Pietrzak et al., 2004). This pattern of results suggests that when a person is concerned about being devalued on the basis of their race, identity may indeed become a salient feature of social interaction (Ethier & Deaux, 1994), and ethnic identity may be developed in oppositional terms to the university as a protective identity (Parham, 1989).

Of note is the finding that among those individuals high in RS-race, there was also a negative relationship between ethnic identity and reports of somatic symptoms (headaches, stomachaches) following negative racial incidents. In other words, ethnic identity seemed to serve as a source of strength for individuals high in RS-race, taking some of the sting out of negative race-related incidents. Individuals high in RS-race but low in ethnic identity, on the other hand, reported greater institutional identity, but also greater vulnerability to somatic symptoms in the face of discrimination. In the face of RS-race, people who do not feel close to their ethnic group may in fact embrace their institutional identity even more, leaving them vulnerable to the pain of rejection. These findings illustrate well the notion that coping mechanisms often function as a system of tradeoffs, rather than as purely beneficial (see also Miller, chap. 2, this volume).

Participation in Social Activism. Another way of coping with RS-race in particular, and expectations of status-based rejection more generally, may be to engage in collective social action to combat discrimination. Numerous researchers have posited a link between stigmatized social status and participation in social movements (Duncan, 1999; Gamson, 1992; Luhtanen, 1996; Puhl & Brownell, 2003; Zurcher & Snow, 1981), particularly in the face of immutable stigmas (Deaux & Ethier, 1998). Participation in social action or movements provides a proactive coping mechanism for counteracting discriminatory attitudes (Siegal, Lune, & Meyer, 1998), increasing one's social connections (Puhl & Brownell, 2003), validating one's experiences of stigmatization (Gamson, 1992), and enhancing group consciousness (Duncan, 1999).

There is some suggestive data to support the notion of a link between status-based rejection expectations and social action. Bowen and Bok (1998) found that African American students who attended historically White universities were much more likely to participate in social activism and be involved in their community years later than their White counterparts. Looking only at African Americans, advanced degree holders tended to be more involved in the community. This suggests that people exposed to decreasingly diverse institutions in the journey through higher education were increasingly motivated to take social action. In the words of one participant:

> What we found when we got there—when we got all the way up the ladder—is that there isn't a lot of difference. People still see you first of all as Black. Because you get that rude awakening, I think you end up feeling that you better hold on to those things that you knew before. And some part of that is what leads us back, to make sure that we keep roots in the community and keep this thing going. Like the people who helped us. (quoted in Bowen & Bok, 1998, p. 172)

In another study, Kaplan and Liu (2001) followed a group of over 4,000 adolescents through 30 years, and found that those adolescents who reported feeling stigmatized or rejected were most likely to be involved in social movements in their thirties. Kaplan and Liu found this relationship to be moderated by both self-efficacy with regard to social change and by the presence of others also engaged in social action. Although the authors did not differentiate between rejection based on personal versus status characteristics, it nevertheless suggests a relationship between social action and the broader construct of rejection.

In sum, expectations of race-based rejection may spur people toward social action by making the pervasiveness of discrimination—and thus the need for action—more salient. A promising avenue for new research is to draw a more explicit link between prior experiences of stigmatization, future expectations of stigma-based rejection, and social action. Coping through social action provides one example of how people are active participants in the construction and management of their social environment in the face of stigma (Kelly, 1955; see also Deaux & Ethier, 1998)—and how their coping strategies can have important positive ramifications.

Interpersonal Level

One of the basic premises of the RS-race model, and of CAPS theory more generally, is that expectations of race-based rejection develop out of prior experiences of discrimination (either direct or vicarious) with outgroup members. Therefore, it makes sense that positive intergroup contact may have a beneficial effect on race-based rejection expectations by providing disconfirming evidence with regard to such expectations. Positive intergroup contact may help prevent the generalization of rejection expectations to all outgroup members. In recent research, our lab has been focusing specifically on the impact of cross-race friendships on minority students' academic adjustment and intergroup relations. Although even relatively superficial intergroup contact has been found to be generally beneficial for reducing prejudice (Pettigrew & Tropp, 2000), the effects of this type of contact are substantially weaker for low-status relative to high-status groups (Tropp, chap. 9, this volume). We propose that clear, unambiguous signs of relational positivity may be necessary to witness the positive effects of intergroup contact for stigmatized group members, and in particular for those who have anxious expectations of rejection. Because ambiguous cues are more likely to confirm a person's rejection schema, repeated gestures of closeness—such as those expressed in burgeoning friendships—may help to attenuate expectations of stigma-based rejection.

Cross-Group Friendships. Although establishing a cross-group friendship may be difficult and needs to overcome substantial barriers of anxiety and suspicion (Frable, Blackstone, & Scherbaum, 1990; Ickes, 1984; W. G. Stephan & C. W. Stephan, 2000), research suggests that its benefits may be substantial. Notably, in Pettigrew and Tropp's (2000) meta-analysis of intergroup contact, the inverse relationship between contact and prejudice was clearly strongest in studies examining intergroup friendship. Similarly, a recent study by McLaughlin-Volpe (chap. 11, this volume) concludes that the effect of intergroup contact on prejudice is not contingent on amount of interaction per se, but rather on how much those interactions lead to closeness between members of different groups, or inclusion of the outgroup other in the self (also see A. Aron, E. N. Aron, & Smollan, 1992). In a powerful demonstration of the strength of the effects of contact on prejudice, Wright, Aron, McLaughlin-Volpe, and Ropp (1997) found that the mere knowledge of an ingroup member's cross-race friendship fostered positive intergroup affect—termed the *extended contact effect.*

As Mary McPherson, president of Bryn Mawr College, noted in *The Shape of the River* (Bowen & Bok, 1998): "Since students have only a limited amount of time and emotional energy, those able to concentrate on their academic tasks, without constant concern about their place on the campus and their relationships to others, are most likely to do well academically" (p. 82). Although ingroup friends provide "safe havens" where low-status group members do not have to be "on guard" (Crocker, Major, & Steele, 1998), outgroup friendships may actively help change beliefs about one's acceptance by the majority group and one's belonging within the institution. Through repeated exposure to a nondiscriminatory outgroup member, students high in RS-race may begin to see more heterogeneous possibilities for treatment by outgroup members, including professors and institutional policymakers.

To test the aforementioned ideas, Mendoza-Denton and Page-Gould (2002) examined the moderating effect of White friends on the relationship between RS-race and adjustment outcomes among the participants of the same longitudinal study described in Mendoza-Denton et al. (2002). To increase our confidence in the causal nature of the effects being investigated, we took advantage of three different stages of data collection. Specifically, a number of longitudinal outcomes collected 3 to 4 years after the beginning of the study were analyzed as functions of RS-race and cross-race friendships, both measured at least 1 year earlier. The analyses controlled for participants' scores on the outcome measures at the end of their freshman year of college, thus allowing us to look at the predictive power of our independent variables (RS-race, cross-race friends) on change in our dependent variables. The dependent measures examined were anxiety about speaking with peers about academic problems and satisfaction with the university. The overall pattern of results suggests that having outgroup friends serves a positive, beneficial function for students high in RS-race. Controlling for interpersonal rejection sensitivity, self-esteem, and ethnic identity, we found that students high in RS-race who had few outgroup friends reported the highest anxiety about sharing academic problems, and the greatest dissatisfaction with the university. Given the longitudinal nature of the design, and the fact that we controlled for students' initial scores on the dependent variables, these findings are supportive of the idea that there may be a causal effect of number of outgroup friends on the relationship between RS-race and subsequent feelings of satisfaction within the institution. In current research, we are attempting to replicate these findings by manipulating friendship (see A. Aron, Melinat, E. N. Aron, & Vallone, 1997), responding in part to a call for experimental research to establish a causal link between cross-race friendship and positive outcomes (Levin, van Laar, & Sidanius, 2003; Pettigrew, 1997).

Mentoring Relationships. In addition to cross-race friendships, a second type of interpersonal relationship that can help one cope with status-based rejection expectations on the college campus is the mentoring relationship. For example, Cohen, Steele, and Ross (1999) showed the influence of different types of mentoring feedback on minority students' motivation and impressions of bias. Although there is often a premium placed on emotion-free critical analysis in our culture (Cosmides, Tooby, & Barkow, 1992), Cohen and colleagues' research suggests that when it comes to mentoring across the racial divide, minority students' discomfort and apprehension must be actively addressed.

In their study, Cohen and colleagues (1999) invited African American and White university students to write an essay for possible publication in a university magazine. All students were given feedback on their essay 1 week later, and were led to believe that a White university professor (the purported editor of the magazine) was the one who provided the feedback. Unbeknown to the students, the experimenters manipulated the way in which the feedback was given. Participants received one of three different feedback types: (a) "criticism only"—students received critical feedback on their essay in the form of red markings along the margins (e.g., "unclear," "awkward"), two checkmarks for good points, plus specific suggestions; (b) "criticism plus high standards"—students received critical feedback, but the professor also wrote "Remember, I wouldn't go through the trouble of giving you this feedback if I weren't committed to the quality of this journal—I want to uphold the highest standards for what I consider a suitable entry"; and, (c) "criticism plus high standards plus assurance"—the professor provided similarly critical feedback but additionally wrote: "Remember, I wouldn't go through the trouble of giving you this feedback if I didn't think, based on what I've read in your letter, that you are capable of meeting the higher standard I mentioned."

The results from this study clearly showed that African American students' motivation to revise the essay, based on the professor's feedback, was the greatest in the "wise" criticism condition—that is, criticism + high standards + assurance. By contrast, the "criticism only" condition led to the lowest task motivation, and identification with the writing task, and the greatest ratings of perceived bias (for most of these dependent variables, "criticism plus high standards" fell between the two other conditions). These results suggest that there may be negative motivational consequences, particularly for African American students, in the face of pointed, unmitigated criticism. Such negative effects were not observed among the White students, who were less sensitive to the experimental manipulations. Consistent with the arguments presented here, those students most likely to have doubts about their professors' attitudes toward them benefited the most from the "wise" feedback, implying that professors may be able to motivate students who are concerned about being treated negatively on the basis of race by framing critical feedback in a constructive and supportive manner.

Institutional Level

Mechanisms at the institutional level can also have a significant impact on the outcomes associated with race-based rejection expectations. Academic abilities are nurtured and developed through pedagogical, social, and institutional supports—a type of developmental "scaffolding" around and within which students can grow and find support (Gordon & Bridglall, 2003). The research mentioned suggests that beyond the achievement of numerical diversity, educators—and the institutions that they represent—must work toward the achievement of relational diversity (Fine, Weis, & Powell, 1997). By *relational diversity*, we mean a type of diversity where institutions are not merely filling numerical quotas, but are instead actively working to secure the trust and confidence of all students. As research on RS-race shows, concerns about one's belonging can directly impact one's achievement by leading people to avoid various resources that the institution may offer, such as a professor's office hours and academic counseling. Although this self-protective strategy minimizes the possibility of rejection and future prejudice, it also reduces the number of resources and support systems one can count on when faced with the same difficulties that all students face.

How do institutions build bridges allowing all of their members to succeed and to achieve the goals they arrived at the institution to realize? One suggestive finding comes from Mendoza-Denton et al. (2002), who found that students who anxiously expected rejection at the university felt an increased sense of belonging at the university following days in which they had had a positive race-related experience. Examples of positive race-related experiences included speaking with another student about the experience of being Black at the university, as well as having attended a meeting of the Black Student Organization at the university. This finding provides initial evidence for the beneficial effect of having institutionally sanctioned events and organizations that foster positive race-related experiences. When universities explicitly value and support such organizations and events, they may disconfirm negative expectations about the institution's lack of support, and foster a sense that the institution is attentive to the needs of all its members. Thus, in contrast to the perception that student groups organized around ethnicity lead to balkanization, these findings suggest that such organizations may lead to greater institutional belonging. These findings await replication and expansion; however, a task for future research remains to identify institutional arrangements that can aid—or hinder—the realization of true relational diversity (Fine et al., 1997).

SUMMARY

Despite the removal of legal and institutional barriers to achieving diversity, clear disparities remain in educational achievement outcomes between minority and White students (Bowen & Bok, 1998). In this chapter, we argued that expectations of race-based rejection are an important factor in understanding these disparities, noting that status-based rejection describes well the phenomenology captured by the constructs of stereotype threat, stigma consciousness, cultural mistrust, and RS-race. Although expectations of race-based rejection can arise solely out of situational pressures, not everyone responds similarly to such rejection. The CAPS framework emphasizes that expectations of rejection interact with other dynamics to determine behavior, which is consistent with a stress and coping framework. We have reviewed examples of coping mechanisms at three levels—intrapersonal, interpersonal, and institutional—to illustrate the within-group diversity that characterizes stigmatized groups. This view adds one layer of complexity to analyses of stigma focused on between-group differences, and allows us to emphasize the cognitive and affective processes involved in answering Allport's (1954) observation that "one's reputation, whether true or false, cannot be hammered, hammered, hammered into one's head without doing something to one's character" (pp. 138–139). We have reviewed recent research relevant to this question to better understand the experience of being stigmatized. With such an understanding, we are better prepared to develop effective interventions at various levels.

REFERENCES

Allport, G. W. (1954). *The nature of prejudice*. Oxford, England: Addison-Wesley.

Aron, A., Aron, E. N., & Smollan, D. (1992). Inclusion of the other in the self scale and the structure of interpersonal closeness. *Journal of Personality and Social Psychology, 63*, 596–612.

Aron, A., Melinat, E., Aron, E. N., & Vallone, R. D. (1997). The experimental generation of interpersonal closeness: A procedure and some preliminary findings. *Personality and Social Psychology Bulletin, 23*(4), 363–377.

Aronson, J. (2002). Stereotype threat: Contending and coping with unnerving expectations. In J. Aronson (Ed.), *Improving academic achievement: Impact of psychological factors on education*. San Diego, CA: Academic Press.

Aronson, J., Fried, C. B., & Good, C. (2002). Reducing the effects of stereotype threat on African American college students by shaping theories of intelligence. *Journal of Experimental Social Psychology, 38*(2), 113–125.

Ayduk, O., Mendoza-Denton, R., Mischel, W., Downey, G., Peake, P., & Rodriguez, M. (2000). Regulating the interpersonal self: Strategic self-regulation for coping with rejection sensitivity. *Journal of Personality and Social Psychology, 79*, 776–792.

Bennett, C., & Okinaka, A. M. (1990). Factors related to persistence among Asian, Black, Hispanic, and White undergraduates at a predominantly White university: Comparison between first and fourth year cohorts. *Urban Review, 22*(1), 33–60.

Bowen, W. G., & Bok, D. (1998). *The shape of the river: Long-term consequences of considering race in college and university admissions*. Princeton, NJ: Princeton University Press.

Branscombe, N. R., Schmitt, M. T., & Harvey, R. D. (1999). Perceiving pervasive discrimination among African Americans: Implications for group identification and well-being. *Journal of Personality and Social Psychology, 77*, 135–149.

Brown, R. P., & Pinel, E. C. (2003). Stigma on my mind: Individual differences in the experience of stereotype threat. *Journal of Experimental Social Psychology, 39*(6), 626–633.

Cohen, G. L., Steele, C. M., & Ross, L. D. (1999). The mentor's dilemma: Providing critical feedback across the racial divide. *Personality and Social Psychology Bulletin, 25*, 1302–1318.

College Board. (1999). *Reaching the top: A report of the National Task Force on Minority High Achievement*. New York: The College Board.

Contrada, R. J., Ashmore, R. D., Gary, M. L., Coups, E., Egeth, J. D., Sewell, A., Ewell, K., Goyal, T. M., & Chasse, V. (2001). Measures of ethnicity-related stress: Psychometric properties, ethnic group differences, and associations with well-being. *Journal of Applied Social Psychology, 31*, 1775–1820.

Cosmides, L., Tooby, J., & Barkow, J. H. (1992). The psychological foundations of culture. In J. H. Barkow, L. Cosmides, & J. Tooby (Eds.), *The adapted mind*. Oxford, England: Oxford University Press.

Crocker, J., Major, B., & Steele, C. (1998). Social stigma. In D. T. Gilbert & S. T. Fiske (Eds.), *The handbook of social psychology* (4th ed., pp. 504–553). New York: McGraw-Hill.

Croizet, J.-C., & Desprès, G. (2003, February). *How does stereotype threat undermine performance?* Paper presented at the Annual Meeting of the Society for Personality and Social Psychology, Los Angeles, CA.

Cross, W. E., Parham, T. A., & Helms, J. E. (1991). The stages of Black identity development: Nigresence models. In R. L. Jones (Ed.), *Black psychology* (3rd ed., pp. 319–338). Berkeley, CA: Cobb & Henry.

Deaux, K., & Ethier, K. A. (1998). Negotiating social identity. In J. K. Swim, & C. Stangor (Eds.), *Prejudice: The target's perspective* (pp. 301–323). San Diego, CA: Academic Press.

Downey, G., & Feldman, S. (1996). Implications of rejection sensitivity for intimate relationships. *Journal of Personality and Social Psychology, 70*, 1327–1343.

Duncan, L. E. (1999). Motivation for collective action: Group consciousness as mediator of personality, life experiences, and women's rights activism. *Political Psychology, 20*, 611–635.

Ethier, K., & Deaux, K. (1994). Negotiating social identity when contexts change: Maintaining identification and responding to threat. *Journal of Personality and Social Psychology, 67*, 243–251.

Fine, M., Weis, L. & Powell, L. C. (1997). Communities of difference: A critical look at desegregated spaces created for and by youth. *Harvard Educational Review, 67*, 247–284.

Frable, D. E., Blackstone, T., & Scherbaum, C. (1990). Marginal and mindful: Deviants in social interactions. *Journal of Personality and Social Psychology, 59*, 140–149.

Franzoi, S. L. (1996). *Social psychology*. Madison, WI: Brown & Benchmark.

Freitas, A. L., & Downey, G. (1998). Resilience: A dynamic perspective. *International Journal of Behavioral Development, 22*, 263–285.

Gamson, W. (1992). The social psychology of collective action. In A. Morris & C. Mueller (Eds.), *Frontiers of social movement theory* (pp. 53–76). New Haven, CT: Yale University Press.

Good, C., Aronson, J., & Inzlicht, M. (2003). Improving adolescents' standardized test performance: An intervention to reduce the effects of stereotype threat. *Journal of Applied Developmental Psychology, 24*(6), 645–662.

Gordon, E. W., & Bridglall, B. L. (2003, March). The idea of supplementary education. *Pedagogical Inquiry and Praxis*, 4.

Herrnstein, R. J., & Murray, C. A. (1994). *The bell curve: Intelligence and class structure in American life*. New York: Free Press.

Higgins, E. T. (1996). Knowledge activation: Accessibility, applicability, and salience. In E. T. Higgins & A. W. Kruglanski (Eds.), *Social psychology: Handbook of basic principles* (pp. 133–168). New York: Guilford Press.

Ickes, W. (1984). Compositions in Black and White: Determinants of interaction in interracial dyads. *Journal of Personality and Social Psychology, 47*(2), 330–341.

Jo, H. (1999). The influence of African American urban high school students' ethnic identity and coping strategies on academic involvement and psychological adjustment. *Dissertation Abstracts International 59*(7-1) (UMI: 2361).

Kaplan, H. B., & Liu, X. (2001). Adolescent self-rejection and adult social action: A conditional relationship. *Social Science Quarterly, 82*, 701–715.

Kelly, G. A. (1955). *A theory of personality: The psychology of personal constructs*. New York: Norton.

Levin, S., van Laar, C., & Sidanius, J. (2003). The effects of ingroup and outgroup friendship on ethnic attitudes in college: A longitudinal study. *Group Processes & Intergroup Relations, 6*(1), 76–92.

Link, B. G., Cullen, F. T., Frank, J., & Wozniak, J. F. (1987). The social rejection of ex-mental patients: Understanding why labels matter. *American Journal of Sociology, 92*, 1461–1500.

Luhtanen, R. K. (1996). Identity, stigma management and psychological well-being in lesbians and gay men. *Dissertation Abstracts International: Section B: The Sciences & Engineering, 56*(10-B), 5773.

Major, B., Quinton, W. J., & McCoy, S. K. (2002). Antecedents and consequences of attributions to discrimination: Theoretical and empirical advances. In M. P. Zanna, (Ed.), *Advances in experimental social psychology* (Vol. 34, pp. 251–330). San Diego, CA: Academic Press.

Major, B., Quinton, W. J., McCoy, S. K., & Schmader, T. (2000). Reducing prejudice: The target's perspective. In S. Oskamp (Ed.), *Reducing prejudice and discrimination: The Claremont Symposium on Applied Social Psychology* (pp. 211–237). Mahwah, NJ: Lawrence Erlbaum Associates.

McCoy, S. K., & Major, B. (2003). Group identification moderates emotional responses to perceived prejudice. *Personality and Social Psychology Bulletin, 29*(8), 1005–1017.

McLaughlin-Volpe, T., Mendoza-Denton, R., & Shelton, J. N. (in press). Including out-group others in the self: Implications for coping with race-based rejection and alienation among minority students. In G. Downey, C. S. Dweck, J. Eccles, & C. Chatman (Eds.), *Social identity, coping and life tasks*. New York: Russell Sage.

Mendoza-Denton, R., & Aronson, J. (in press). Making the pinnacle possible: Psychological processes associated with minority students' achievement. In E. W. Gordon & B. L. Bridglall (Eds.), *The affirmative development of academic ability*. Lanham, MD: Rowman & Littlefield.

Mendoza-Denton, R., Downey, G., Purdie, V. J., Davis, A., & Pietrzak, J. (2002). Sensitivity to status-based rejection: Implications for African American students' college experience. *Journal of Personality and Social Psychology, 83*(4), 896–918.

Mendoza-Denton, R., & Page-Gould, E. (2002). Cross-race friendships moderate the link between anxious rejection expectations based on race and adjustment outcomes. Unpublished data, University of California, Berkeley.

Mendoza-Denton, R., Shoda, Y., Ayduk, O., & Mischel, W. (1999). Applying cognitive-affective processing system (CAPS) theory to cultural differences in social behavior. In W. J. Lonner & D. L. Dinnel (Eds.), *Merging past, present, and future in cross-cultural psychology: Selected papers from the Fourteenth International Congress of the International Association for Cross-Cultural Psychology* (pp. 205–217). Bristol, PA: Swets & Zeitlinger.

Miller, C. T., & Kaiser, C. R. (2001). Implications of mental models of self and others for the targets of stigmatization. In M. R. Leary (Ed.), *Interpersonal rejection* (pp. 189–212). London: Oxford University Press.

Mischel, W., & Shoda, Y. (1995). A cognitive-affective system theory of personality: Reconceptualizing situations, dispositions, dynamics and invariance in personality structure. *Psychological Review, 102*, 246–268.

Mischel, W., & Shoda, Y. (1999). Integrating dispositions and processing dynamics within a unified theory of personality: The cognitive affective personality system (CAPS). In L. Pervin & O. John (Eds.), *Handbook of personality: Theory and research* (pp. 197–218). New York: Guilford Press.

Ogbu, J. U. (1991). Minority coping responses and school experience. *The Journal of Psychohistory, 18*, 433–456.

Ogbu, J. U. (1994). Understanding cultural diversity and learning. *Journal for the Education of the Gifted, 17*, 354–383.

Operario, D., & Fiske, S. T. (2001). Ethnic identity moderates perceptions of prejudice: Judgments of personal versus group discrimination and subtle versus blatant bias. *Personality and Social Psychology Bulletin, 27*, 550–561.

Oyserman, D., Harrison, K., & Bybee, D. (2001). Can racial identity be promotive of academic efficacy? *International Journal of Behavioral Development, 25*, 379–385.

Oyserman, D., & Swim, J. K. (2001). Stigma: An insider's view. *Journal of Social Issues, 57*(1), 113–128.

Parham, T. (1989) Cycles of psychological nigrescence. *The Counseling Psychologist, 17*, 175–182.

Pettigrew, T. F. (1997). Generalized intergroup contact effects on prejudice. *Personality and Social Psychology Bulletin, 23*(2), 173–185.

Pettigrew, T. F., & Tropp, L. R. (2000). Does intergroup contact reduce prejudice: Recent meta-analytic findings. In S. Oskamp (Ed.), *Reducing prejudice and discrimination: The Claremont Symposium on Applied Social Psychology* (pp. 93–114). Mahwah, NJ: Lawrence Erlbaum Associates.

Phinney, J. S. (1992). The multigroup ethnic identity measure: A new scale for use with diverse groups. *Journal of Adolescent Research, 7*, 156–176.

Phinney, J. S., Horenczyk, G., Liebkind, K., & Vedder, P. (2001). Ethnic identity, immigration, and well-being: An interactional perspective. *Journal of Social Issues, 57*, 493–510.

Pietrzak, J., Mendoza-Denton, R., & Downey, G. (2004, January). *A clash of identities: Racial rejection sensitivity moderates the effect of ethnic identity on institutional identity.* Poster presented at the annual convention of the Society for Personality and Social Psychology, Austin, TX.

Pinel, E. C. (1999). Stigma consciousness: The psychological legacy of social stereotypes. *Journal of Personality and Social Psychology, 76*(1), 114–128.

Pinel, E. C. (2002). Stigma consciousness in intergroup contexts: The power of conviction. *Journal of Experimental Social Psychology, 38*(2), 178–185.

Puhl, R., & Brownell, K. D. (2003). Ways of coping with obesity stigma: Review and conceptual analysis. *Eating Behaviors, 4*, 53–78.

Roberts, R. E., Phinney, J. S., Masse, L. C., Chen, Y. R., Roberts, C. R., & Romero, A. (1999). The structure of ethnic identity of young adolescents from diverse ethnocultural groups. *The Journal of Early Adolescence, 19*, 301–322.

Root, M. P. (1992). Reconstructing the impact of trauma on personality. In L. S. Brown & M. Ballou (Eds.), *Personality and psychopathology: Feminist reappraisals* (pp. 229–266). New York: Guilford.

Shoda, Y., & Mischel, W. (1998). Personality as a stable cognitive-affective activation network: Characteristic patterns of behavior variation emerge from a stable personality structure. In S. Read & L. C. Miller (Eds.), *Connectionist models of social reasoning and social behavior* (pp. 175–208). Mahwah, NJ: Lawrence Erlbaum Associates.

Sidanius, J., & Petrocik, J. R. (2001). Communal and national identity in a multiethnic state: A comparison of three perspectives. In R. D. Ashmore & L. Jussim (Eds.), *Rutgers series on self and social identity (Vol. 3): Social identity, intergroup conflict, and conflict reduction* (pp. 101–129). London: Oxford University Press.

Siegal, K., Lune, H., & Meyer, I. H. (1998). Stigma management among gay/bisexual men with HIV/AIDS. *Qualitative Sociology, 21*, 3–24.

Steele, C. M., & Aronson, J. (1995). Stereotype threat and the intellectual performance of African Americans. *Journal of Personality and Social Psychology, 69,* 797–811.

Steele, C. M. (1997). A threat in the air: How stereotypes shape intellectual identity and performance. *American Psychologist, 52*(6), 613–629.

Stephan, W. G., & Stephan, C. W. (2000). An integrated threat theory of prejudice. In S. Oskamp (Ed.), *Reducing prejudice and discrimination: The Claremont Symposium on Applied Social Psychology* (pp. 23–45). Mahwah, NJ: Lawrence Erlbaum Associates.

Terrell, F., & Terrell, S. (1981). An inventory to measure cultural mistrust among Blacks. *The Western Journal of Black Studies, 5*, 180–185.

Wright, B. (1985). The effects of racial self-esteem on the personal self-esteem of Black youth. *International Journal of Intercultural Relations, 9*, 19–30.

Wright, S. C., Aron, A., McLaughlin-Volpe, T., & Ropp, S. A. (1997). The extended contact effect: Knowledge of cross-group friendships and prejudice. *Journal of Personality and Social Psychology, 73*(1), 73–90.

Zurcher, L., & Snow, D. (1981). Collective behavior: Social movements. In M. Rosenberg & R. Turner (Eds.), *Social psychology: Sociological perspectives*. New York: Basic Books.

CHAPTER

9

Stigma and Intergroup Contact Among Members of Minority and Majority Status Groups

Linda R. Tropp
Boston College

For decades, researchers in the social sciences have sought to identify strategies that would be effective in reducing prejudice and promoting positive intergroup relations. In his monograph, *The Reduction of Intergroup Tensions*, Williams (1947) suggested that the "mere giving of objective general information" (p. 64) about an outgroup would likely do little to reduce intergroup hostility. Instead, he proposed that certain kinds of contact between groups could facilitate the development of positive intergroup attitudes. Allport (1954) concurred with this view, stating that contact under optimal conditions could reduce intergroup prejudice and improve relations between groups.

Guiding these authors' views was an understanding that intergroup relationships are often marked by some degree of hostility or conflict, and contact therefore holds the potential to either enhance or diminish prejudice between groups (Allport & Kramer, 1946; Williams, 1947). Hence, they focused their attention on positive conditions of the contact situation designed to ensure that intergroup contact would lead to reductions in prejudice. In particular, Williams emphasized that intergroup contact would maximally reduce prejudice when the groups share similar status, interests, and tasks, and the contact situation fosters intimate relations between the groups. Extending the work of Williams, Allport (1954) specified four optimal conditions that would be effective in reducing prejudice when implemented within the contact situation. First, Allport stressed the importance of establishing *equal status between the groups within the contact situation.*

Thus, even though the groups may be accorded different statuses in the larger society, they should be regarded as equal in status within the contact situation. Allport also noted the importance of *authority sanction*, such that the contact—and the equal status nature of that contact—would be supported by institutional authorities, laws, or customs. Additionally, Allport emphasized that the groups should work toward *common goals*, and that they should do so in *cooperation* and not in competition, such that the groups would work together and rely on each other in order to achieve their shared goals.

Since Allport's time, investigations of contact effects have flourished, with hundreds of studies being conducted across a wide range of social groups, contexts, and societies (Pettigrew & Tropp, 2000, in press-a). Early field studies showed that equal status contact between racial groups can contribute to more positive intergroup attitudes (Deutsch & Collins, 1951; Wilner, Walkley, & Cook, 1955; Works, 1961). And a half century later, we now have substantial evidence from longitudinal (Levin, van Laar, & Sidanius, 2003), experimental (Wright et al., 2004), and meta-analytic studies (Pettigrew & Tropp, in press-a) suggesting that intergroup contact can lead to significant reductions in intergroup prejudice.

Still, intergroup contact theory has persisted as a fairly general conceptualization of what occurs when members of different groups interact. Indeed, only recently have researchers begun to consider the distinct ways in which members of minority and majority status groups are likely to respond to intergroup contact, given their differing histories of experiences within the broader society (see Devine & Vasquez, 1998). It is the goal of this chapter to link intergroup contact theory to recent perspectives on group differences in status, to evaluate the likely effectiveness of contact for improving relations between members of minority and majority status groups.

A SHIFTING FOCUS FOR CONTACT RESEARCH: OBJECTIVE CONDITIONS TO SUBJECTIVE RESPONSES

In line with Allport's original approach, intergroup contact research has traditionally focused on establishing optimal conditions within the contact situation, toward the ultimate goal of achieving broad-scale reductions in intergroup prejudice (see Cook, 1984; Hewstone & Brown, 1986; Pettigrew, 1998). As such, contact research has highlighted the importance of objective conditions of the contact situation, with relatively little attention to group members' subjective responses to those contact situations. Moreover, with its traditional focus on prejudice reduction, studies of intergroup contact have overemphasized the perspectives and attitudes of members of majority status groups, to the relative neglect of the perspectives of members of minority status groups (Devine & Vasquez, 1998; Shelton, 2000).

Emerging contact research has begun to address these shortcomings by assessing minority and majority group members' experiences during intergroup contact, along with the beliefs and expectations they bring to the contact situation. This work suggests that members of both minority and majority status groups have challenges with which they must contend as they approach cross-group interactions (see Devine & Vasquez, 1998). Generally, members of minority and majority status groups both have concerns about how they are likely to be perceived by the other groups (Sigelman & Tuch, 1997; Vorauer, Main, & O'Connell, 1998), and they are both likely to feel anxious about engaging in cross-group interactions (Plant & Devine, 2003; W. G. Stephan & C. W. Stephan, 1985; Tropp, 2003). Nonetheless, research suggests that their anxieties may be based in largely different sets of concerns. In particular, members of majority status groups are likely to experience anxiety about being perceived as prejudiced, whereas members of minority status groups tend to be anxious about potentially becoming the target of prejudice (Devine & Vasquez, 1998; W. G. Stephan & C. W. Stephan, 1985).

EXAMINING CONTACT EFFECTS IN TERMS OF STATUS RELATIONS BETWEEN THE GROUPS

These perspectives offer important advances for our understanding of group members' subjective experiences in intergroup contexts, and the dimensions that are likely to be of concern to minority and majority group members during contact. But beyond these concerns in the immediate contact situation, we must also consider whether there are broader differences in minority and majority group members' views regarding the role that group status plays in defining relations between their groups (see Blumer, 1958; Bobo, 1999). Other work has shown contrasting bases of intergroup prejudice among members of minority and majority status groups, such that majority attitudes are linked to support for their privileged status, while minority attitudes are often based in the anticipation of prejudice from the majority group (see Livingston, Brewer, & Alexander, 2004; Monteith & Spicer, 2000). Additionally, due to their privileged position, members of majority status groups are generally less inclined to reflect on their group's status (Leach, Snider, & Iyer, 2002), or to think of themselves in terms of their group membership (Kim-Ju & Liem, 2003; Pinel, 1999), unless it is required by demands of the immediate social context (W. McGuire, C. McGuire, Child, & Fujioka, 1978). By contrast, members of minority status groups are often acutely aware of their group's devalued status (Jones et al., 1984) and that they are likely to be seen and evaluated in terms of their devalued group membership (Crocker, Major, & Steele, 1998; Goffman, 1963; Mendoza-Denton, Downey, Purdie, Davis, & Pietrzak, 2002; Pinel, 1999). Consequently, they live with a constant threat of becoming targets of prejudice and discrimination (Crocker et al., 1998), and worse still, they are often confronted with prejudice and discrimination due to their devalued group membership (Feagin & Sikes, 1994; Swim, Cohen, & Hyers, 1998; Swim, Hyers, Cohen, Fitzgerald, & Bylsma, 2003). As such, these regular reminders of their group's devalued status may become concrete features of the intergroup relationship from the perspective of members of minority status groups, while these features may be less likely to be perceived as intrinsic to the intergroup relationship among members of the majority status group.

Recent polls reveal trends that are consistent with this analysis. Overall, Black Americans perceive significantly more racial discrimination against their group than do White Americans (National Conference for Community and Justice, 2000), at the same time as most White Americans believe Blacks in their communities are treated as well as Whites (Gallup Organization, 2001). Correspondingly, relative to White Americans, Black Americans tend to see racial tensions as a bigger problem in our society, and they tend to be more pessimistic about the potential for American race relations to improve in the future (Gallup Organization, 2001; National Conference for Community and Justice, 2000). Thus, concerns about group status and discrimination against one's group may play a more significant role in defining the intergroup relationship among members of minority status groups, relative to the role they play among members of majority status groups.

Given these trends, it is perhaps not surprising that American race relations are typically characterized in terms of racial distrust (Dovidio, Gaertner, Kawakami, & Hodson, 2002), particularly so when viewed from the perspective of members of minority status groups. Stigmatization understandably impedes the development of trust (Cohen & Steele, 2002; Kramer & Wei, 1999; Pinel, 2002; see also Inzlicht & Good, chap. 7, this volume; McLaughlin-Volpe, chap. 11, this volume; Mendoza-Denton, Page-Gould, & Pietrzak, chap. 8, this volume). Thus, members of minority status groups may be especially vigilant in their relations with the majority outgroup until they feel outgroup members are worthy of their trust (Brown & Dobbins, 2004; Steele, Spencer, & Aronson, 2002). Cohen, Walton, and Garcia (2004) recently examined these issues among ethnic minority and majority students in a high school context. These authors found that ethnic minority and majority students reported similar levels of concern about their academic abilities, as well as comparable levels of social anxiety. Still, ethnic minority students reported substantially greater racial mistrust and perceptions of bias against their ethnic group relative to ethnic majority students.

Cohen et al.'s (2004) findings reveal that members of both minority and majority status groups are likely to have multiple concerns about how they will be perceived and evaluated in intergroup contexts. Moreover, their findings suggest that a continual recognition of devalued group status and discrimination against one's group may constitute an added negative factor with which minority group members must contend in intergroup contexts, whereas such a factor may not be operating for members of majority status groups. A constant awareness of devaluation could make minority group members especially motivated to avoid intergroup contact to keep from exposing themselves to prejudice and discrimination from the majority group (see Crocker et al., 1998; Goffman, 1963; Mendoza-Denton et al., 2002; W. G. Stephan & C. W. Stephan, 1985). But we can also consider the broader implications of this tendency for achieving positive relations between members of minority and majority status groups. It is likely that long-standing histories of devaluation and discrimination against one's group would seriously inhibit the potential for enhancing positive feelings about intergroup relationships among members of minority status groups, relative to the effects that might be observed among members of majority status groups. This possibility is considered throughout the remainder of this chapter, in reference to samples of data gathered from meta-analytic, survey, and experimental studies on intergroup contact.

CONTACT EFFECTS FOR MINORITY AND MAJORITY STATUS GROUPS: META-ANALYTIC COMPARISONS

These issues are first examined using data from a recent meta-analysis of intergroup contact effects (see Pettigrew & Tropp, in press-a, in press-b; Tropp & Pettigrew, in press). For this analysis, we retrieved hundreds of papers on intergroup contact through intensive searches of multiple research literatures. As we located these papers, we then checked to see whether each met the four criteria we determined for inclusion in the meta-analysis.

First, because our analysis focused on the effects of intergroup contact, we considered only those cases in which intergroup contact could act as an independent variable for predicting intergroup prejudice. These studies included both experimental studies testing for the effects of contact on prejudice, and correlational studies in which contact was used as a correlate or predictor for intergroup prejudice. Second, we included only studies that involved contact between members of clearly defined groups to ensure that we examined intergroup—rather than interpersonal—outcomes. Third, the studies had to involve some degree of direct contact between members of the different groups, which could either be observed by others or reported by the participants themselves. This criterion excludes studies that attempted to gauge contact using indirect measures such as information about an outgroup, as well as studies in which participants were categorized into groups without opportunities for actual cross-group interactions. Finally, to be included, the outcome measures had to be collected on individuals rather than assessed on an aggregate level, and some type of comparative data had to be available to evaluate variability in prejudice in relation to the contact (see Pettigrew & Tropp, in press-a, for an extended discussion).

From a 5-year search, we uncovered 516 studies (including 715 independent samples) examining relationships between contact and prejudice that met these inclusion criteria. The studies were conducted between the early 1940s through the year 2000, spanning many disciplines and involving contact between members of a wide range of groups. Together, the studies include responses from 250,555 individuals in 38 countries.

In conducting our analysis, we used two indicators of effect size (Cohen's *d* and Pearson's *r*), with larger effect sizes signifying stronger relationships between intergroup contact and prejudice. We also examined contact–prejudice effects at distinct levels of analysis. Analyses conducted at the level of studies represent the overall effects for all data reported in each paper. Analyses at the level of samples represent the overall effects for each independent sample reported in each paper. Because studies often include multiple samples, analyzing data at the level of samples offers larger numbers of cases for conducting more detailed comparisons of effects (see Pettigrew & Tropp, in press-a).

Overall, results from the meta-analysis reveal that greater levels of intergroup contact are typically associated with lower levels of intergroup prejudice. These patterns of effects are consistent across analyses by studies and samples (in each case, mean $d = -.43$, mean $r = -.21$). Moreover, additional analyses suggest that these results are unlikely to be due to participant selection or publication biases, and the more rigorous research studies also reveal stronger contact–prejudice effects (Pettigrew & Tropp, in press-a).

We then examined patterns of contact–prejudice effects among members of minority and majority status groups. Here, we coded samples as to whether participants in the contact situation belonged to a devalued, lower status group (i.e., minority status), or a dominant, higher status group (i.e., majority status). As a first step in our analysis, we tallied the number of samples that examined relationships between contact and prejudice among members of minority and majority status groups. This comparison clearly reveals the relative scarcity of research on intergroup contact from the perspectives of members of minority status groups (see Devine & Vasquez, 1998; Shelton, 2000). Indeed, of the 715 samples included in our full analysis, only 142 samples examined contact outcomes among members of minority status groups, whereas an overwhelming 505 samples examined contact outcomes among members of majority status groups.

We then proceeded to compare the magnitudes of the contact–prejudice relationships among members of minority and majority status groups (see Tropp & Pettigrew, in press). Overall, we found that the relationship between contact and prejudice is significantly weaker among members of minority status groups (mean $d = -.38$, mean $r = -.19$) relative to the effects obtained for members of majority status groups (mean $d = -.44$, mean $r = -.22$; $p < .001$ for the difference between effect sizes). Thus, although significant contact–prejudice relationships were observed in both cases, the magnitudes of these relationships still appear to vary among members of minority and majority status groups.

As we interpret these findings, we must recognize that there are several possible reasons for this pattern of results. For example, it could be that because minorities are fewer in number, and are regularly exposed to the majority group, any single contact experience would have less of an impact on their attitudes, thereby producing less change in their feelings toward the majority group as a whole. Additionally, it might be that members of minority status groups generally report lower levels of prejudice than members of majority status groups, which could limit the degree to which their prejudices could be reduced further through intergroup contact.

Alternatively, it could be that these patterns of effects are associated with the different perceptions that group members have about intergroup contact, based on the broader relationships between their groups in the larger society (Bobo, 1999; Livingston et al., 2004; Monteith & Spicer, 2000). Indeed, members of minority status groups are well aware of the devaluation that surrounds their group membership (Pinel, 1999), along with the possibility that they might become the targets of prejudice (Crocker et al., 1998). Thus, with good reason, minority group members' responses to intergroup contact may be colored by a persisting recognition of their group's devaluation, which could inhibit the potential for achieving positive contact outcomes.

SURVEY OF CONTACT–PREJUDICE RELATIONSHIPS AMONG MINORITY AND MAJORITY STATUS GROUPS

To examine these possibilities, we conducted a secondary analysis of survey responses gathered by the National Conference for Community and Justice (2000; see also Tropp, 2005). These survey responses resulted from telephone interviews conducted between January, 2000, and March, 2000, with a nationally representative sample of approximately 2,500 adults in the continental United States. Oversamples of racial and ethnic minority respondents were drawn, such that the sample included responses from 995 White Americans and 709 Black Americans.

Responses from these participants have been reanalyzed in an attempt to replicate findings from the meta-analysis, and to provide more insights regarding possible interpretations of its results. Testing for replication in a single study that uses identical procedures across all participants offers an important extension of our meta-analytic research, since meta-analyses are often criticized for including comparisons across studies where variables, samples, and testing procedures are not uniform (see Rosenthal, 1991, for an extended discussion).

In this survey, participants were asked to indicate their contact experiences and feelings of intergroup closeness with respect to a wide variety of groups. For the present analysis, reported experiences with and closeness to Blacks were used as measures of intergroup contact and prejudice among White respondents. Similarly, reported experiences with and closeness to Whites were used as measures of intergroup contact and prejudice among Black respondents.

First, respondents provided "yes" or "no" responses to a general contact measure, in which they indicated whether they "now have contact or not with a person who is (White/Black)." Respondents also responded to a general measure of intergroup closeness, by reporting "how close they feel to (Whites/Blacks)" on a 5-point scale, with recoded responses ranging from 1 (*very far*) to 5 (*very close*). Reported feelings of intergroup closeness can be an especially useful indicator of intergroup prejudice, because affective responses to the outgroup typically show stronger relationships with intergroup contact than other sorts of prejudice indicators (see Tropp & Pettigrew, 2005).

As a first step in our analysis, we examined the overall relationships between intergroup contact and prejudice, to see whether we would obtain the same results as what we observed in the meta-analysis (see Tropp, 2005). Here, we conducted bivariate correlations between contact and intergroup closeness, as well as partial correlations controlling for demographic variables such as level of education, socioeconomic status, political ideology, age, and gender. As in the meta-analysis, we found significant overall relationships between contact and closeness both with and without controlling for the demographic variables, $r = .17$, partial $r = .17$, $p < .001$. Moreover, we also found that the relationships between contact and closeness were significantly weaker among Black participants, $r = .08$, partial $r = .06$, $p < .05$, relative to the effects obtained for White participants, $r = .22$, partial $r = .24$, $p < .001$; $p < .01$ for the difference between effect sizes.

Subsequent analyses examined the obtained patterns of effects in relation to three possible interpretations growing from our meta-analytic results. First, we considered whether the patterns of effects might be due to a tendency for White and Black respondents to differ in their levels of intergroup contact. Specifically, a chi-square analysis tested whether White and Black respondents were more or less likely to have contact with the outgroup. The chi-square analysis was not significant, $\chi^2(1) = 2.01$, $p > .10$, suggesting that White and Black respondents did not meaningfully differ in the extent to which they had contact with the outgroup. Thus, it seems unlikely that initial differences in the amount of contact with the outgroup would account for the weaker contact–prejudice effects observed among Black respondents in this sample, or among minority status groups in the meta-analysis.

Additional analyses then examined whether White and Black respondents generally differed in the extent to which they reported feeling close to members of the outgroup. Results indicate that White and Black respondents did not significantly differ in their overall feelings of intergroup closeness ($M = 3.63$ and 3.68, respectively), $F(1, 1654) = 1.54$, $p > .10$. Thus, initial differences in levels of intergroup closeness as a measure of prejudice cannot explain the divergent contact–prejudice relationships observed between White and Black respondents in the present sample, and are therefore unlikely to explain the differing contact–prejudice relationships observed between minority and majority status groups in the meta-analysis.

We then sought to test whether the differences in patterns of effects among White and Black participants might be associated with distinct views of the intergroup relationship. Because members of minority groups anticipate being targeted by prejudice and discrimination to a greater extent than members of majority groups (e.g., Cohen et al., 2004), we focused our analysis on group members' perceptions of discrimination against their group. Specifically, we used respondents' answers to a separate item concerning "how much discrimination there is against (Whites/Blacks) in our society today," with reverse-coded responses of 1 (*none at all*), 2 (*only a little*), 3 (*some*), and 4 (*a great deal*).

As might be expected, preliminary analyses showed that Black respondents perceived significantly more discrimination against their group ($M = 3.43$) relative to the discrimination perceived by White respondents against their group ($M = 2.37$), $F(1, 1691) = 619.60$, $p < .001$. More importantly, however, we find that perceiving discrimination bears different relationships with reports of intergroup closeness among White and Black respondents. Specifically, greater perceived discrimination against one's group relates significantly to lower feelings of intergroup closeness among Black respondents, $r = -.12$, partial $r = -.12$, $p < .01$, whereas the relationship between perceived discrimination and intergroup closeness is not significant among White respondents, $r = .03$, partial $r = .03$, $p > .30$.

We also find some evidence that perceived discrimination moderates the relationship between intergroup contact and closeness among Black respondents, whereas such moderation does not occur for White respondents. Table 9.1 presents bivariate and partial correlations between contact and closeness for Black and White respondents who perceive varying degrees of discrimination against their group. These analyses indicate that the relationship between intergroup contact and closeness is consistently strong for White respondents, regardless of the degree to which they perceive discrimination against their group. However, among Black respondents, the relationship between contact and closeness differs substantially depending on the degree to which they perceive discrimination against their group. Specifically, the relationship between contact and closeness is significant among Black respondents who perceive only a moderate amount of discrimination against their group, yet contact and closeness are not significantly related among Black respondents who perceive a great deal of discrimination against their group. It is also important to note that over half of the Black respondents reported that they perceived a great deal of discrimination against their group ($n = 387$, 56.6%), whereas most of the remaining Black respondents perceived a moderate amount of discrimination against their group ($n = 272$, 39.8%). Together, these findings suggest that the more members of minority status groups perceive discrimination against their groups, the weaker their contact–prejudice relationships will tend to be. The one exception to this trend involved the small number of Black respondents who reported absolutely no discrimination against their group ($n = 25$, 3.6%). These respondents reported high feelings of intergroup closeness whether they did ($M = 4.12$) or did not ($M = 4.00$) have contact with the outgroup. Moreover, taken together, their mean reports of intergroup closeness were significantly higher ($M = 4.08$) than those reported

TABLE 9.1
Perceived Discrimination as Moderator for Relationship Between Contact and Intergroup Closeness Among Black and White Respondents

Perceived Discrimination	*Black Respondents*			*White Respondents*		
	r	*partial r*	*n*	*r*	*partial r*	*n*
A Great Deal	.06	.02	387	.34**	.29*	72
Some/Only A Little	.18**	.18**	272	.17***	.19***	664
None At All	.06	−.08	25	.29***	.32***	227

Note. r = Pearson correlation coefficient; *partial* r = Pearson correlation coefficient controlling for level of education, socioeconomic status, political ideology, age, and gender; n = number of respondents.

$^*p < .05$. $^{**}p < .01$. $^{***}p < .001$.

by all other Black respondents in this sample ($M = 3.66$), $t(682) = 2.52$, $p = .01$. Thus, it could be that because they already have quite positive orientations toward the outgroup, there are limits on the degree to which intergroup contact could further enhance their feelings of intergroup closeness.

Overall, these patterns of findings provide important insights into the nature of contact–prejudice relationships among members of minority and majority status groups, which can aid in our interpretation of results from the meta-analysis. For members of minority status groups, perceiving discrimination against one's group exists as a powerful, negative force that permeates the intergroup relationship, although this force appears to be largely irrelevant to the intergroup relationship from the perspective of members of majority status groups. As such, contact–prejudice relationships are likely to vary depending on the degree to which minority group members perceive discrimination against their groups, although such effects are less likely to be observed among members of majority groups. Thus, although positive intergroup outcomes can often be achieved through intergroup contact (Pettigrew & Tropp, in press-a), the negative presence of discrimination as a feature of the intergroup relationship is likely to restrain the potentially positive effects of contact for members of minority status groups.

EXPERIMENTAL EFFECTS OF PREJUDICE ON FEELINGS TOWARD CROSS-GROUP INTERACTIONS

In sum, findings from the survey indicate that perceiving discrimination against one's group will likely inhibit feelings of intergroup closeness among members of minority status groups. Thus far, these relationships have been examined using survey data, showing that greater perceptions of discrimination correspond with reduced feelings of closeness toward the majority outgroup as a whole. But some experimental evidence also suggests that exposure to prejudice can lead members of minority status groups to feel less positively about relations with the majority group.

Specifically, studies involving both laboratory and real groups have examined how an expression of prejudice from an outgroup member would affect minority group members' expectations for cross-group interactions (see Tropp, 2003). In one of these studies (Tropp, 2003, Study 2), participants from two ethnic minority groups (Latinos and Asian Americans) were initially informed that the study concerned "communication styles" among members of different ethnic groups. After completing a filler task and a personal information form, participants then learned that they were randomly assigned to interact with a White person, and they were given a photograph and personal information form for a White partner. In actuality, the person believed to be the White partner was a confederate working with the research team.

To manipulate participants' exposure to an expression of prejudice, participants then overheard one of two scripted dialogues between the confederate and the experimenter while seated on the other side of a partition. In the prejudice condition, participants overheard the confederate ask if he could switch partners because he would rather not be matched with a (Latino/Asian) person. Instead, in the neutral condition, participants overheard the confederate ask a benign question concerning whether the study would take over an hour to complete. It should also be noted that the confederate actually making these comments was a native English-speaking Asian American, rather than the White person who participants believed was their partner. This procedure was used to ensure that, through the debriefing process, participants would be confident that the White person they saw in the photograph did not actually express or endorse prejudice against their ethnic group.

Following these procedures, participants completed a brief questionnaire packet as they anticipated an interaction with their partner. To assess their orientations toward the outgroup, this packet asked participants to report the extent to which they expected to get along with, trust, feel comfortable with, enjoy interacting with, and have a lot in common with their outgroup partner, and with outgroup members in general (αs ranging from .89 to .97). Results from this study revealed that participants exposed to prejudice from an outgroup member had significantly less positive orientations toward the outgroup partner, and they also tended to have less positive orientations toward outgroup members in general.

These findings offer important insights regarding the roles that prejudice and discrimination may play in shaping understandings of intergroup relationships among members of minority status groups. In particular, exposure to even a single instance of prejudice from an outgroup member may lead members of minority status groups to anticipate less trust and closeness in their relations with the outgroup. Given that members of minority status groups are regularly confronted with prejudice in their everyday lives (Swim et al., 1998, 2003), we must consider the broader detrimental effects that repeated exposure to prejudice is likely to have on minority group members' feelings toward relations with the majority outgroup.

The varied research findings presented thus far indicate that devalued group status and discrimination against one's group play important roles in defining the nature of intergroup relationships among members of minority status groups. We have observed that the positive effects of intergroup contact tend to be diminished among members of minority status groups, relative to the effects observed for members of majority status groups (Tropp & Pettigrew, in press). We also find significant relationships between perceiving discrimination and reduced feelings of intergroup closeness among members of minority status groups, although these relationships are not significant among members of majority status groups; moreover, contact-prejudice relationships tend to be weak among members of minority status groups who perceive a great deal of discrimination against their groups (Tropp, 2005). Experimental findings also suggest that exposure to even a single instance of prejudice can lead minority group members to feel less positively about interacting with members of the majority outgroup (Tropp, 2003). In sum, these collected findings suggest that intergroup contact may generally be a less effective means for promoting positive intergroup outcomes among members of minority status groups, to the extent that prejudice and discrimination act as negative forces curbing contact's positive effects.

EFFECTS OF OPTIMAL CONTACT CONDITIONS AMONG MINORITY AND MAJORITY STATUS GROUPS

Relating these findings to the broader framework of intergroup contact theory (Allport, 1954; Hewstone & Brown, 1986; Pettigrew, 1998), we must therefore question whether establishing Allport's optimal conditions within the contact situation can sufficiently alleviate these negative forces to allow positive contact outcomes to emerge among members of both minority and majority status groups. Indeed, many researchers have noted that conditions of equal status may be defined and interpreted in a number of ways (Cohen, 1982; Foster & Finchilescu, 1986; Riordan, 1978), and members of different status groups may not always agree about the extent to which equal status has been achieved within the contact situation (Robinson & Preston, 1976). Thus, even when objective attempts are made to establish such conditions as equal status, group members' subjective responses to intergroup contact may still vary depending on the perceptions and experiences that inform their understanding of the intergroup relationship (see Cohen, 1982; Livingston et al., 2004). As such, implementing optimal conditions within the contact situation may not necessarily be enough to ensure positive contact outcomes among members of both minority and majority status groups.

We returned to our meta-analytic data to pursue a preliminary test of these ideas (see Tropp & Pettigrew, in press). Specifically, we sought to examine whether samples from minority and majority status groups would still show different patterns of contact–prejudice relationships even in those cases where the contact situation was purposely designed to maximize positive intergroup outcomes. To guide this investigation, we focused heavily on Allport's proposed conditions for optimal intergroup contact because they have played such a pivotal role in prior contact research. We began by attempting to rate each of Allport's conditions individually for each sample, but this approach proved impossible due to the limited information available in most of the research reports. We therefore shifted our approach and rated each sample as to whether the contact situation was explicitly structured to approximate Allport's conditions for optimal intergroup contact. These global ratings actually offer a more direct test of Allport's contentions than our original approach because Allport held that his four conditions should be implemented together to maximize positive intergroup outcomes.

As a general test of the effectiveness of Allport's conditions, we then compared samples that corresponded with our ratings, such that the contact situation either was or was not explicitly structured in line with Allport's conditions (see Pettigrew & Tropp, in press-a, in press-b). Overall, we found that samples with contact structured in line with Allport's conditions yielded significantly stronger contact–prejudice effects (mean $d = -.58$, mean $r = -.28$) relative to the effects obtained for the remaining samples (mean $d = -.42$, mean $r = -.21$; $p < .0001$ for the difference between effect sizes).

We then turned to focus our analysis on whether Allport's conditions would be comparably effective in promoting strong contact–prejudice relationships among members of minority and majority status groups (see Tropp & Pettigrew, in press). We examined this issue by comparing the effect sizes for minority and majority samples that either were or were not structured to meet Allport's conditions. Among majority status groups, the 98 samples with contact structured in line with Allport's conditions showed significantly stronger contact–prejudice effects (mean $d = -.67$, mean $r = -.32$), relative to the remaining majority samples (mean $d = -.43$, mean $r = -.21$; $p < .0001$ for the difference between effect sizes). However, among minority status groups, the 13 samples with contact situations structured in line with Allport's conditions did not show substantially stronger contact–prejudice effects (mean $d = -.46$, mean $r = -.22$), relative to the other minority samples (mean $d = -.38$, mean $r = -.19$; $p > .30$ for the difference between effect sizes). In part, the lack of statistical significance in the minority context could reflect the relatively small number of studies included in this comparison. Nonetheless, given the difference in magnitude of the effects in the minority and majority contexts, these patterns suggest that members of minority and majority status groups may still show different responses to intergroup contact, even when the contact situation is explicitly structured to maximize positive intergroup outcomes. Specifically, it may be that establishing Allport's conditions within the contact situation can enhance the positive effects of contact among members of majority status groups although these conditions may not significantly enhance the positive effects of contact among members of minority status groups.

As suggested previously, we believe these findings may grow from general differences in perspective regarding the nature of relationships between the groups (see Bobo, 1999; Livingston et al., 2004). Members of minority status groups are likely to perceive prejudice and discrimination as integral to the intergroup relationship, although these may be less prominent features of the intergroup relationship in the minds of members of majority status groups. As such, the effects of positive conditions within the intergroup context may be diluted for members of minority status groups, as their feelings about relations with the majority group are constructed in conjunction with long-standing histories of devaluation. Thus, even when attempts are made to establish positive norms of tolerance and mutual acceptance, these efforts may not be sufficient to fully counter the negative effects of discrimination on minority group members' feelings about relations with the majority group.

Related to this point, we have recently gathered responses to a survey in which we assess ethnic minority and majority group members' perceptions of societal norms, perceptions of discrimination, and orientations toward outgroup members (see Tropp, 2004). To date, our sample includes responses from 153 undergraduate participants (84 ethnic minority, 69 ethnic majority), with ages ranging from 17 to 32 years (mean age = 19.20 years). With these data, we compare how group members' feelings toward relations with outgroup members correspond with perceived norms of tolerance in the broader society and perceived discrimination against their ethnic groups.

To prepare for this analysis, we averaged responses to two items concerning norms of tolerance, in which participants indicated the extent to which they believe "efforts (are) made to establish norms of tolerance and acceptance among different ethnic groups" and "people acknowledge and promote ethnic diversity" in American society ($\alpha = .74$ and .84 among ethnic minority and majority participants, respectively). Using a single item, participants also reported the extent to which they perceive discrimination against their ethnic group as a whole. These items were scored on 7-point scales ranging from 1 (not at all/strongly disagree) to 7 (very much/strongly agree).

As a first step in our analysis, we correlated scores on these measures with an indicator of perceived inclusion of one's ethnic group. Specifically, participants reported the degree to which they perceive their ethnic group as being "included" in American society, with scores ranging from 1 (not included at all) to 7 (completely included). Among ethnic minority participants, perceiving norms of tolerance was positively associated with the

TABLE 9.2
Correlating Perceived Norms of Tolerance and Discrimination
With Feelings Toward Intergroup Relationships
Among Members of Ethnic Minority and Majority Groups

	Norms of Tolerance		*Discrimination*	
	Minority	*Majority*	*Minority*	*Majority*
Orientations toward Outgroup Members	.23*	.14	−.24*	.24*
Warmth toward Outgroup Members	.24*	.15	−.32**	.11
Proportions of Outgroup Friends	.28**	.11	−.35**	17

*$p < .05$. **$p < .01$.

sense that one's group is included in American society, $r = .28$, $p = .01$, whereas perceiving discrimination was negatively associated with perceived ingroup inclusion, $r = -.26$, $p < .05$. At the same time, neither perceiving norms of tolerance nor perceiving discrimination were significantly related to perceptions of ingroup inclusion among ethnic majority participants, $r = .10$ and −.11, respectively, $p > .30$.

We then examined how perceiving norms of tolerance and discrimination related to feelings about relations with the outgroup across a number of indicators. Participants reported their general orientations toward interacting with outgroup members (Tropp, 2003), along with feelings of warmth toward outgroup members and their proportions of outgroup friends. Table 9.2 provides correlations between these indicators and the norms of tolerance and discrimination measures for ethnic minority and majority participants.

Thus far, responses from ethnic minority participants show that perceiving norms of tolerance typically corresponds with more positive orientations toward outgroup members, greater warmth, and greater proportions of outgroup friends. At the same time, perceived discrimination corresponds with significantly less positive orientations toward outgroup members, less warmth, and smaller proportions of outgroup friends among ethnic minority participants. Additionally, when entered simultaneously as predictors, both norms of tolerance and discrimination emerge as significant predictors for each indicator, yet perceived discrimination tends to be a stronger predictor than perceived norms of tolerance.[1] By contrast, among ethnic majority participants, there are no significant relationships between perceiving norms of tolerance and these indicators, and only one

[1]Standardized regression coefficients (β) for perceived discrimination were −.22 when predicting orientations toward outgroup members, $p = .05$; −.30 when predicting warmth, $p = .005$; and −.32 when predicting proportions of outgroup friends, $p = .002$. Standardized regression coefficients for perceived norms of tolerance were .20 when predicting orientations toward outgroup members, $p = .06$; .21 when predicting warmth, $p = .05$; and .25 when predicting proportions of outgroup friends, $p = .02$.

indicator reveals a significant relationship with perceived discrimination; greater perceptions of discrimination correspond with more positive orientations toward outgroup members, $r = .24$, $p < .05$.

Taken together, these findings suggest that members of minority and majority status groups generally differ in the extent to which they see norms of tolerance and discrimination as relevant to their intergroup relationships. Perceiving norms of tolerance can encourage greater feelings of inclusion and more positive orientations toward cross-group interactions among members of minority status groups. At the same time, however, perceiving discrimination acts as a persisting negative force in the intergroup relationship from the perspective of members of minority status groups, whereas neither norms of tolerance nor perceived discrimination contribute substantially to majority group members' feelings about their intergroup relationships.

It may be that members of majority status groups enjoy the privilege of not having to think about their group's status as they reflect on the broader intergroup relationship (see Leach et al., 2002), unless such reflection is induced by demands of the immediate social context (see Devine & Vasquez, 1998). By contrast, considerations of group status and discrimination appear to be of great importance to members of minority status groups, such that these considerations permeate their feelings about relations with the majority status group. Moreover, given that members of minority status groups are often met with prejudice and discrimination against their groups (Swim et al., 1998), perceived discrimination is likely to operate as a perpetual negative force in their views of the intergroup relationship although such a consistent negative force may not be operating among members of the majority status group.

These patterns of findings appear to diverge somewhat from the traditional emphasis of *intergroup contact theory*, which suggests that positive intergroup attitudes can be enhanced by emphasizing equal status between groups within the contact situation (Allport, 1954; Pettigrew, 1998). As such, the results may reflect distinctions between what people report in relatively abstract contexts, as compared to what they would likely experience in actual contact situations (see Levy, Freitas, & Salovey, 2002, for a related discussion). But these findings also point to broader issues we must consider regarding the approaches we use to achieve positive intergroup relations in the larger society.

CONCLUSIONS

Together, these combined findings suggest that our traditional focus on establishing optimal conditions within the intergroup context may not be enough to promote positive intergroup relations among members of both minority and majority status groups. Beyond emphasizing conditions of the contact situation, we must also recognize that group members have histories of perceptions and experiences that are likely to inform their understanding of the intergroup relationship (Cohen et al., 2004; Livingston et al., 2004), and their responses to cross-group interactions (Devine & Vasquez, 1998; Plant & Devine, 2003; Tropp, 2003). Indeed, even when objective attempts are made to establish optimal conditions within the contact situation, group members' subjective responses to contact may still be guided by their long-standing views of the intergroup relationship (see Cohen, 1982; Robinson & Preston, 1976).

Consistent with this view, the research presented in this chapter indicates that members of minority status groups not only contend with prejudice and discrimination (Crocker et al., 1998; Swim et al., 1998), but these factors can also contribute negatively to their feelings about intergroup relations (Tropp, 2003), in ways beyond those that are likely to be detected among members of the majority group (Tropp & Pettigrew, in press). As such, we must extend our understanding of intergroup contact theory to acknowledge how differing histories of experiences may lead members of minority and majority status groups to show different responses to intergroup contact, and to recognize the important role that prejudice and discrimination can play in shaping minority group members' feelings toward intergroup relationships.

Thus, as we look to future research on intergroup contact, we must look beyond establishing a set of objective conditions within the contact situation to promote positive intergroup outcomes, corresponding to the approach that has commonly been used in the past (see Allport, 1954; Pettigrew, 1998; Williams, 1947). Rather, we must also take into account the subjective perspectives of the different groups involved and attempt to address concerns that are particularly relevant to their conceptions of the intergroup relationship. Because prejudice and discrimination can curb the potentially positive effects of contact, we must work to create environments that members of minority status groups feel they can trust (Cohen & Steele, 2002; Steele et al., 2002), and in which they can feel confident that prejudice and discrimination will not affect how they will be perceived and treated (Crocker et al., 1998). At the same time, we must not only curb the endorsement of prejudice among members of majority status groups, but we must also encourage them to recognize the significance of prejudice and discrimination in minority group members' views of the intergroup relationship. Perhaps through such a sharing of perspectives, we can achieve more common understandings of intergroup relationships among group members on both sides, along with promoting the kinds of mutual trust and openness that can facilitate positive relations between members of minority and majority status groups.

REFERENCES

Allport, G. W. (1954). *The nature of prejudice*. Reading, MA: Addison-Wesley.

Allport, G. W., & Kramer, B. M. (1946). Some roots of prejudice. *Journal of Psychology, 22*, 9–39.

Blumer, H. (1958). Race prejudice as a sense of group position. *Pacific Sociological Review, 1*, 3–7.

Bobo, L. D. (1999). Prejudice as group position: Microfoundations of a sociological approach to racism and intergroup relations. *Journal of Social Issues, 55*, 445–472.

Brown, L. M., & Dobbins, H. (2004). Students' of color and European American students' stigma-relevant perceptions of university instructors. *Journal of Social Issues, 60*, 157–174.

Cohen, E. G. (1982). Expectation states and interracial interaction in school settings. *Annual Review of Sociology, 8*, 209–235.

Cohen, G. L., & Steele, C. M. (2002). A barrier of mistrust: How negative stereotypes affect cross-race mentoring. In J. Aronson (Ed.), *Improving academic achievement: Impact of psychological factors on education* (pp. 303–327). San Diego, CA: Academic Press.

Cohen, G., Walton, G. M., & Garcia, J. (2004, January). *The trust gap: The effect of stigmatization on academic experience*. Paper presented at the annual meeting of the Society for Personality and Social Psychology, Austin, TX.

Cook, S. W. (1984). Cooperative interaction in multiethnic contexts. In N. Miller & M. B. Brewer (Eds.), *Groups in contact: The psychology of desegregation* (pp. 155–185). Orlando, FL: Academic Press.

Crocker, J., Major, B., & Steele, C. M. (1998). Social stigma. In D. T. Gilbert, S. T. Fiske, & G. Lindzey (Eds.), *Handbook of social psychology* (4th ed., pp. 504–553). Boston, MA: McGraw-Hill.

Deutsch, M., & Collins, M. (1951). *Interracial housing: A psychological evaluation of a social experiment.* Minneapolis: University of Minnesota Press.

Devine, P. G., & Vasquez, K. A. (1998). The rocky road to positive intergroup relations. In J. L. Eberhardt & S. T. Fiske (Eds.), *Confronting racism: The problem and the response* (pp. 234–262). Thousand Oaks, CA: Sage.

Dovidio, J. F., Gaertner, S. L., Kawakami, K., & Hodson, G. (2002). Why can't we just get along? Interpersonal biases and interracial distrust. *Cultural Diversity and Ethnic Minority Psychology, 8*, 88–102.

Feagin, J. R., & Sikes, M. P. (1994). *Living with racism: The Black middle class experience*. Boston, MA: Beacon Press.

Foster, D., & Finchilescu, G. (1986). Contact in a "non-contact" society: The case of South Africa. In M. Hewstone & R. Brown (Eds.), *Contact and conflict in intergroup encounters* (pp. 119–136). Cambridge, England: Blackwell.

Gallup Organization. (2001, July). *Black–White relations in the United States: 2001 update*. Washington, DC: Author.

Goffman, E. (1963). *Stigma: Notes on the management of spoiled identity*. Englewood Cliffs, NJ: Prentice-Hall.

Hewstone, M., & Brown, R. (1986). Contact is not enough: An intergroup perspective on the 'Contact Hypothesis.' In M. Hewstone & R. Brown (Eds.), *Contact and conflict in intergroup encounters* (pp. 1–44). Oxford, England: Basil Blackwell.

Jones, E. E., Farina, A., Hastorf, A. H., Markus, H., Miller, D. T., & Scott, R. A. (1984). *Social stigma: The psychology of marked relationships*. New York: Freeman.

Kim-Ju, G. M., & Liem, R. (2003). Ethnic self-awareness as a function of ethnic group status, group composition, and ethnic identity orientation. *Cultural Diversity and Ethnic Minority Psychology, 9*, 289–302.

Kramer, R. M., & Wei, J. (1999). Social uncertainty and the problem of trust in social groups: The social self in doubt. In T. R. Tyler, R. M. Kramer, & O. P. John (Eds.), *The psychology of the social self* (pp. 145–168). Mahwah, NJ: Lawrence Erlbaum Associates.

Leach, C. W., Snider, N., & Iyer, A. (2002). Poisoning the consciences of the fortunate: The experience of relative advantage and support for social equality. In I. Walker & H. J. Smith (Eds.), *Relative deprivation: Specification, development, and integration* (pp. 136–163). Cambridge, England: Cambridge University Press.

Levin, S., van Laar, C., & Sidanius, J. (2003). The effects of ingroup and outgroup friendship on ethnic attitudes in college: A longitudinal study. *Group Processes and Intergroup Relations, 6*, 76–92.

Levy, S. R., Freitas, A. L., & Salovey, P. (2002). Construing action abstractly and blurring social distinctions: Implications for perceiving homogeneity among, but also empathizing with and helping, others. *Journal of Personality and Social Psychology, 83*, 1224–1238.

Livingston, R. W., Brewer, M. B., & Alexander, M. G. (2004, January). *Images, emotions, and prejudice: Qualitative differences in the nature of Black and White racial attitudes.* Paper presented at the annual meeting of the Society for Personality and Social Psychology, Austin, TX.

McGuire, W., McGuire, C., Child, P., & Fujioka, T. (1978). Salience of ethnicity in the spontaneous self-concept as a function of one's ethnic distinctiveness in the social environment. *Journal of Personality and Social Psychology, 36*, 511–520.

Mendoza-Denton, R., Downey, G., Purdie, V. J., Davis, A., & Pietrzak, J. (2002). Sensitivity to status-based rejection: Implications for African American students' college experience. *Journal of Personality and Social Psychology, 83*, 896–918.

Monteith, M. J., & Spicer, C. V. (2000). Contents and correlates of Whites' and Blacks' racial attitudes. *Journal of Experimental Social Psychology, 36*, 125–154.

National Conference for Community and Justice. (2000). *Taking America's pulse: NCCJ's survey of intergroup relations in the United States.* New York: Author.

Pettigrew, T. F. (1998). Intergroup contact theory. *Annual Review of Psychology, 49*, 65–85.

Pettigrew, T. F., & Tropp, L. R. (2000). Does intergroup contact reduce prejudice? Recent meta-analytic findings. In S. Oskamp (Ed.), *Reducing prejudice and discrimination* (pp. 93–114). Mahwah, NJ: Lawrence Erlbaum Associates.

Pettigrew, T. F., & Tropp, L. R. (in press-a). A meta-analytic test of intergroup contact theory. *Journal of Personality and Social Psychology.*

Pettigrew, T. F., & Tropp, L. R. (in press-b). Allport's intergroup contact hypothesis: Its history and influence. In J. F. Dovidio, P. Glick, & L. Rudman (Eds.), *On the nature of prejudice: Fifty years after Allport.* Malden, MA: Blackwell.

Pinel, E. C. (1999). Stigma consciousness: The psychological legacy of social stereotypes. *Journal of Personality and Social Psychology, 76*, 114–128.

Pinel, E. C. (2002). Stigma consciousness in intergroup contexts: The power of conviction. *Journal of Experimental Social Psychology, 38*, 178–185.

Plant, E. A., & Devine, P. G. (2003). The antecedents and implications of interracial anxiety. *Personality and Social Psychology Bulletin, 29*, 790–801.

Riordan, C. (1978). Equal-status interracial contact: A review and revision of the concept. *International Journal of Intercultural Relations, 2*, 161–185.

Robinson, J. W., & Preston, J. D. (1976). Equal status contact and modification of racial prejudice: A reexamination of the contact hypothesis. *Social Forces, 54*, 911–924.

Rosenthal, R. (1991). *Meta-analytic procedures for social research.* Newbury Park, CA: Sage.

Shelton, J. N. (2000). A reconceptualization of how we study issues of racial prejudice. *Personality and Social Psychology Review, 4*, 374–390.

Sigelman, L., & Tuch, S. A. (1997). Meta-stereotypes: Blacks' perceptions of Whites' stereotypes of Blacks. *Public Opinion Quarterly, 61*, 87–101.

Steele, C. M., Spencer, S. J., & Aronson, J. (2002). Contending with group image: The psychology of stereotype and social identity threat. *Advances in Experimental Social Psychology, 34*, 379–440.

Stephan, W. G., & Stephan, C. W. (1985). Intergroup anxiety. *Journal of Social Issues, 41*, 157–175.

Swim, J. K., Cohen, L. L., & Hyers, L. L. (1998). Experiencing everyday prejudice and discrimination. In J. K. Swim & C. Stangor (Eds.), *Prejudice: The target's perspective* (pp. 37–60). San Diego, CA: Academic Press.

Swim, J. K., Hyers, L. L., Cohen, L. L., Fitzgerald, D. C., & Bylsma, W. H. (2003). African American college students' experiences with everyday racism: Characteristics of and responses to these incidents. *Journal of Black Psychology, 29*, 38–67.

Tropp, L. R. (2003). The psychological impact of prejudice: Implications for intergroup contact. *Group Processes and Intergroup Relations, 6*, 131–149.

Tropp, L. R. (2004). [*Perceived norms of tolerance, perceived discrimination, and feelings toward intergroup relationships*]. Unpublished raw data, Boston College.

Tropp, L. R. (2005). *Perceived discrimination and interracial contact: Predicting interracial closeness among Black and White Americans*. Manuscript under review.

Tropp, L. R., & Pettigrew, T. F. (in press). Responses to intergroup contact among members of minority and majority status groups. *Psychological Science.*

Tropp, L. R., & Pettigrew, T. F. (2005). Differential relationships between intergroup contact and affective and cognitive indicators of prejudice. *Personality and Social Psychology Bulletin, 31*, 1145–1158.

Vorauer, J. D., Main, K. J., & O'Connell, G. B. (1998). How do individuals expect to be viewed by members of lower status groups? Content and implications of meta-stereotypes. *Journal of Personality and Social Psychology, 75*, 917–937.

Williams, R. M., Jr. (1947). *The reduction of intergroup tensions*. New York: Social Science Research Council.

Wilner, D. M., Walkley, R. P., & Cook, S. W. (1955). *Human relations in interracial housing: A study of the contact hypothesis*. Minneapolis: University of Minnesota Press.

Works, E. (1961). The prejudice-interaction hypothesis from the point of view of the Negro minority group. *American Journal of Sociology, 67*, 47–52.

Wright, S. C., Van der Zande, C., Ropp, S. A., Tropp, L. R., Young, K., Zanna, M., & Aron, A. (2004). *Cross-group friendships can reduce prejudice: Experimental evidence of a causal direction*. Manuscript in preparation.

CHAPTER

10

New Perspectives on Stigma and Psychological Well-Being

Brenda Major
University of California, Santa Barbara

What are the affective, cognitive, and behavioral implications of being stigmatized—of being socially devalued and targeted by negative stereotypes, prejudicial attitudes, and discrimination? This question is central to understanding the phenomenology and effects of stigmatization. *Stigma* is the possession of, or belief that one possesses, some attribute or characteristic that conveys a social identity that is devalued in a particular social context (Crocker, Major, & Steele, 1998). Although psychologists have long been interested in studying stereotyping, prejudice, and discrimination, only recently have they begun to examine in earnest the psychological effects of these processes on those who are their targets. As reflected in the chapters in this volume, researchers have begun to investigate a variety of cognitive, emotional, and behavioral consequences of stigmatization, including self-stereotyping, group identification, collective self-esteem, outgroup-directed hostility, task performance, social interactions, and personal self-esteem, among other outcomes.

The prevailing view among psychologists has been that stigmatization cannot help but have negative effects on the psychological well-being of its victims. As Miller (chap. 2, this volume) points out, "big" problems (such as prejudice) are assumed to have "big" effects. There is substantial evidence that negative stereotypes, prejudicial attitudes, and discriminatory treatment do have direct, harmful effects on the stigmatized (see also Crocker & Major, 1989). Prejudice and discrimination limit access to resources such as employment, occupational advancement, income, housing, education, and medical care. Inability to obtain these resources compromises the physical well-being of the stigmatized, especially if structural discrimination is repeated, pervasive, and severe (Allison, 1998; R. Clark, Anderson, V. R. Clark, & Williams, 1999). The stigmatized are also ignored, excluded, patronized, and targeted by physical violence. These interpersonal threats also have negative implications for psychological and physical well-being (Leary, Tambor, Terdal, & Downs, 1995). Stigmatization may also lead directly to stress responses such as increased anxiety (R. Clark et al., 1999) and cardiovascular reactivity (Tomaka, Blascovich, Kelsey, & Leitten, 1993).

Many classic theories of the effects of stigmatization further assumed that for many of its victims, stigma becomes internalized into chronic feelings of inferiority. Exposure to prejudice and discrimination is assumed to leave a "mark of oppression" on the personalities and self-esteem of the stigmatized (see Crocker & Major, 1989, for a discussion). Dorwin Cartwright (1950) proposed, for example, "To a considerable extent, personal feelings of worth depend on the social evaluation of the group with which a person is identified. Self-hatred and feelings of worthlessness tend to arise from membership in underprivileged or outcast groups" (p. 440). Likewise, in commenting on their observation that a large percentage of African American children in their study seemed to prefer White skin coloring to Black skin coloring, K. B. Clark and M. P. Clark (1950) wrote, "They [their data] would seem to point strongly to the need for a definite mental hygiene and educational program that would relieve children of the tremendous burden of feelings of inadequacy and inferiority which seem to become integrated into the very structure of the personality as it is developing" (p. 350). Even Allport (1954) observed, "One's reputation, whether false or true, cannot be hammered, hammered, hammered into one's head without doing something to one's character" (p. 142).

Starting in the 1980s a number of papers began to appear that challenged the view that stigma is internalized into the self-concepts of its targets and uniformly and inevitably has negative consequences for them. For example, reviews of the literature on group differences in self-esteem concluded that members of many chronically stigmatized groups, such as African Americans, have levels of self-esteem as high if not higher than nonstigmatized groups (Crocker & Major, 1989; Simpson & Yinger, 1985). Reviews of the literature on subjective well-being observed that members of many chronically stigmatized groups, such as those who are blind, quadriplegic, or developmentally disabled, report positive levels of well-being (Diener, 1984). In addition, research on ability-stigmatized groups demonstrated that test performance is remarkably sensitive to situations—although the stigmatized sometimes perform more poorly on intellectual tasks than those not so stigmatized, at other times they perform just as well (e.g., Steele & Aronson, 1995). On the basis of these accumulating findings, new theoretical perspectives on stigma emerged that challenged traditional understandings of the effects of stigma (e.g., Crocker et al., 1998; Steele, 1997). The chapters in this volume reflect and advance this new perspective on stigma. In this chapter, I summarize the core themes of this "new look" in stigma research, and provide examples of research that reflects these themes.

THE "NEW LOOK" OF STIGMA RESEARCH

The Assumption of Variability

As reflected in much of the research discussed by the authors of this book, stigma can have a variety of negative effects for the stigmatized individual. When stigma is relevant to and activated in the situation, it can negatively affect their intellectual performance, trust in outgroup members and institutions, attachment to domains in which they are negatively stereotyped, accuracy and stability of self-knowledge, and psychological well-being, among other things. Nonetheless, in contrast to traditional perspectives, contemporary perspectives on stigma assert that the effects of stigma are not uniformly and inevitably negative. Contemporary perspectives emphasize variability in targets' responses to prejudice and discrimination—variability across situations, persons, and groups (e.g., Crocker, 1999; Friedman & Brownell, 1995; Major & Schmader, 2001; see Miller, chap. 2, this volume). Research illustrates that differential responses to stigma are observed between stigmatized groups, within stigmatized groups, and even within the same individual across contexts. For example, meta-analyses reveal that African Americans, on average, have higher self-esteem than Euro-Americans (Twenge & Crocker, 2002). But on average, overweight women have lower self-esteem than nonoverweight women (Miller & Downey, 1999), and Euro-American women have lower self-esteem than Euro-American men (Major, Barr, Zubek, & Babey, 1999). Within the same stigmatized groups, some individuals appear resilient to prejudice and display positive well-being, whereas other members of the same group do not (Friedman & Brownell, 1995). In addition, the same individual may show different responses to prejudice as the context changes, as research on stereotype threat demonstrates (Steele & Aronson, 1995). Thus, contemporary scholars acknowledge both vulnerability and resilience as common responses to negative stereotypes, prejudice, and discrimination, and seek to identify factors that differentiate these responses. As chapters by Miller (chap. 2, this volume) and Swim and Thomas (chap. 6, this volume) discuss, the effects of stigma depend upon how stigma-relevant situations are appraised, and on how stigmatized individuals cope with stigma-related threat. These appraisals and coping strategies, in turn, are shaped by characteristics of the situation (e.g., Inzlicht & Good, chap. 7, this volume), the person (e.g., Mendoza-Denton, Page-Gould, & Pietrzak, chap. 8, this volume), and the type of stigma (e.g., Quinn, chap. 5, this volume).

The Importance of Construals

A central assumption of contemporary views of stigma is that the effects of stigmatization are mediated through the stigmatized person's understanding of how others view them and their interpretations of social contexts and social events (e.g., Crocker, 1999; Crocker et al., 1998; Major, McCoy, Kaiser, & Quinton, 2003; Major & O'Brien, 2005; Major, Quinton, & McCoy, 2002; Steele, 1997; Steele, Spencer, & Aronson, 2002). Although not ignoring the direct, negative effects of prejudice and discrimination, the new view of stigma is "top–down" in that it emphasizes the importance of people's construals of their environment in shaping their emotions, behavior, intergroup attitudes, and intellectual performance.

Based on their prior experiences (direct or vicarious) with being the target of negative stereotypes, prejudice, and discrimination, and on their exposure to representations of their stigma in the dominant culture, members of stigmatized groups are assumed to develop shared feelings, beliefs, and expectations about their stigma and its potential effects. These "collective representations" include: (a) awareness of the negative value that is placed on their social identity, (b) knowledge of the dominant cultural stereotypes of their stigmatized identity, and (c) uncertainty and apprehension about whether they will be a target of prejudice (Crocker et al., 1998). These collective representations may also include shared understandings of why one's group occupies the position it does in the social hierarchy. Mendoza-Denton, Page-Gould, and Pietrzak (chap. 8, this volume) refer to these "states of mind" as culturally specific cognitive–affective units (CAUs)—that is, construals, expectations/beliefs, affects, and goals that are shared as a result of having similar experiences specific to one's cultural (or stigmatized) group.

Importantly, even if they themselves do not endorse the dominant cultural representation of their stigma, it is assumed that members of stigmatized groups are aware of the dominant cultural stereotypes and evaluations of their group. These dominant stereotypes and attitudes thus constitute what Steele (1997) called a "threat in the air" (p. 613). Once the dominant cultural stereotypes and attitudes of their stigma are known to the stigmatized, this knowledge influences how they approach and interpret situations in which their stigma is relevant. These collective representations have the potential to affect their behavior in ways that do not involve obvious forms of discriminatory behavior on the part of others. In addition, they can affect the behavior of the stigmatized even when no other person is present in the immediate situation.

A TRANSACTIONAL MODEL OF RESPONSES TO STIGMA

Contemporary scholars increasingly draw on transactional stress and coping models to understand responses of the stigmatized to their predicament (e.g., Allison, 1998; R. Clark et al., 1999; Kaiser, Major, & McCoy, 2004; Major, Quinton, & McCoy, 2002; Major, McCoy, et al., 2003; Major & O'Brien, 2005; Miller & Kaiser, 2001; Miller & Major, 2000). From this perspective, possessing a consensually devalued social identity is a stressor similar to other types of chronic and acute stressors. Thus, theoretical and empirical insights gained from research on adjustment to stressful events in general can be usefully applied to advance understanding of how people respond to social devaluation and stigma.

Transactional models of stress and coping were designed to explain significant variability across individuals in adaptation and response to stressful events (Bandura, 1982; Lazarus, 1999; Lazarus & Folkman, 1984). A core premise of transactional models is that organisms do not respond in the same way to stressors; rather, responses to stressful life events vary across individuals. Responses to stressful events are assumed to be a function of two key processes: how individuals cognitively appraise the event and the coping strategies they use to deal with events that are appraised as stressful. Appraisals and coping are assumed to be shaped by characteristics of the situation and characteristics of the person. Consistent with this view, a growing amount of research demonstrates that situational and personal factors moderate how the stigmatized appraise and cope with stigma-related stressors.

Appraisal Processes

Cognitive appraisals are judgments about the relationship between an individual and his or her environment and the implications of this relationship for psychological well-being (Lazarus & Folkman, 1984). In primary appraisal, a person assesses whether an event has the potential to threaten important, self-relevant goals or values. In secondary appraisal, an individual considers whether he or she has the resources to remedy a stressful person–environment relationship. Events are appraised as *threatening* when internal or external demands are seen as taxing or exceeding the adaptive resources of the individual, and as *challenging* when resources are appraised to exceed demands. Although primary and secondary appraisals

ceptually distinguished, they are interdependent, and often em-
distinguishable (Lazarus, 1999).

Lazarus' model of appraisal processes has been criticized as being overly cognitive and overly conscious. Contemporary models of responses to stressful events observe that appraisals are not necessarily cognitive; nor are they necessarily conscious. For example, Blascovich and Mendes (2000) theorized that a person may make nonconscious demand and resource appraisals. Furthermore, appraisals may involve affective (i.e., feeling) processes as well as cognitive (i.e., semantic) processes. This view is consistent with a growing body of research demonstrating that affective processing can occur independently of cognitive processing (e.g., LeDoux, 1996; Zajonc, 2000). Affective cues are objects in the situation that elicit affective responses or meaning; they can be either innate (e.g., a snake) or learned (e.g., a swastika). Affective cues can influence demand as well as resource appraisals via affective processing and thereby lead to threat or challenge appraisals. Furthermore, just as cognitive processing can be unconscious (occurring below awareness) so too can affective processing. Stimuli presented below levels of awareness can elicit emotional reactions strong enough to drive judgment and behavior in the absence of any conscious feelings accompanying these reactions (Winkielman & Berridge, 2004).

Contemporary perspectives on stigma assume that when cues in a situation make stigma *relevant* (i.e., lead them to suspect that they could be devalued, stereotyped, or discriminated against because of a particular social identity), that situation is often appraised (consciously or nonconsciously) as containing *threats to the self* (Crocker et al., 1998; Major & O'Brien, 2005; Steele et al., 2002; Swim & Thomas, chap. 6, this volume). Crocker et al. (1998), for example, stated that stigma threatens one's sense that one has a "safe, valued, and valuable self" (p. 543). Swim and Thomas (chap. 6, this volume) posit that stigma threatens *core social motives*, such as the need to belong, to have control, and to feel good about the self. Steele (1997) theorized that awareness of negative stereotypes and the accusations contained in them creates *stereotype threat*, defined as a situational threat consisting of fear that one may be judged and treated stereotypically, and that one's behavior might confirm the stereotype in one's own or others' eyes (Steele & Aronson, 1995). More recently, Steele et al. (2002) speculated that people with a stigmatized identity experience *social identity threat* (see also Major & O'Brien, 2005). This leads them to become alert to situational cues that signify they may be devalued on the basis of their social identity. Being on guard for such cues and trying to repudiate them if necessary is an extra burden that may impair their performance. Mendoza-Denton, Page-Gould, and Pietrzak (chap. 8, this volume) observe that direct or vicarious experiences of exclusion, discrimination, and prejudice can also lead to *prejudice apprehension*—anxious anticipation that one will be a target of prejudice in new contexts where the possibility of such treatment exists. Likewise, attributional ambiguity is presumed to be identity threatening (Major, Quinton, & McCoy, 2002). The uncertainty inherent in attributionally ambiguous circumstances can make it difficult to trust others and can make it hard for the stigmatized to make accurate assessments of key aspects of self-worth (Aronson & Inzlicht, 2004; Inzlicht & Good, chap. 7, this volume).

Most contemporary models of the experience of stigma emphasize the extent to which situations in which stigma is salient are appraised as threatening. It is important to note, however, that because the experience of threat occurs when demands are perceived as taxing or exceeding resources, it is theoretically possible for people to perceive themselves as victims of negative stereotypes, prejudice, and/or discrimination and yet not experience this as a threat. This would occur if a person feels that he or she has the resources necessary to cope with the threat of being a target of prejudice. Such resources might include perceived control over important resources or the ability to limit exposure to others who are prejudiced. Such individuals might exhibit challenge, rather than threat, in the face of prejudice. More research on situational and personal factors that lead to challenge rather than threat appraisals is needed.

Situational Determinants of Threat Appraisals

Contemporary models of stigma posit that rather than being a stable feature of individuals, the effects of stigma emerge "in the situation." Specifically, whether or not a stigma-related event is appraised as threatening is assumed to be a function of affective or semantic cues in the immediate situation that make stigma relevant to that situation, and of the cultural representations of their stigma that the stigmatized bring to that situation. As a consequence, members of stigmatized groups may show threat-related responses (e.g., impaired performance) in some situations (e.g., when a test is described as diagnostic of ability) but not others (e.g., when a test is described as nondiagnostic of ability). Because the meaning of immediate situations is shaped by the collective representations that the individual brings to that situation, the same situation may also mean very different things to different individuals. Nonstigmatized and stigmatized groups in particular may react very differently to the same local situation because of their differing understandings of how their social identity is viewed in the dominant culture. For example, research by Inzlicht and Good (chap. 7, this volume) shows that being in the numerical minority activates stereotypes, increases anxiety, and decreases performance among members of stigmatized groups. However, being in the numerical minority does not have these effects on members of nonstigmatized groups. These findings suggest that stigmatized individuals appraise this situation as threatening, whereas nonstigmatized individuals do not. These differences as a function of group status illustrate how the meaning of the local situation is shaped by collective representations that individuals bring to that situation. They also illustrate the dangers of drawing conclusions about the phenomenology of stigmatization from research based on nonstigmatized populations.

A variety of cues in the environment may activate stigma-related thoughts and lead situations to be appraised as threatening to the self (see Inzlicht & Good, chap. 7, this volume, for a review). As already noted, the original work on stereotype threat demonstrated that simply describing intellectual tests as diagnostic of ability was sufficient to create stereotype threat and accompanying poorer test performance among members of ability-stigmatized groups (e.g., Spencer, Steele, & Quinn, 1999; Steele & Aronson, 1995). Heterogeneous settings—situations in which members of more than one social group are present—also are appraised as more threatening by members of stigmatized groups. As Inzlicht and Good (chap. 7, this volume) discuss, environments in which they are outnumbered by members of nonstigmatized groups increase distinctiveness and feelings of self-consciousness, activate stereotypes, and cause anxiety that is experienced as heightened physiological arousal among members of stigmatized groups. Other cues that lead environments to be appraised (consciously or nonconsciously) as threatening and impair performance include (a) being taught by an instructor who is a member of a dominant outgroup (Marx & Roman, 2002); (b) being exposed to media images that reinforce negative stereotypes of one's group (Davies, Spencer, Quinn, & Gerhardstein, 2002); (c) hearing messages that ability or intelligence is fixed rather than malleable (Good & Dweck, 2003, cited in Inzlicht & Good, chap. 7, this volume); and (d) being asked to reveal a concealable stigma (see Quinn, chap. 5, this volume). Although the threat appraisal process may at times be deliberate and conscious, self-related threat often emerges from nonconscious affective or cognitive processing of cues in the environment.

Situational cues also affect the likelihood that people will perceive themselves as a potential victim of discrimination. Research illustrates that discrimination is more likely to be perceived in intergroup rather than ingroup situations (Major, Gramzow, et al., 2002), when prejudice cues in the immediate situation are clear rather than ambiguous (Major, Quinton, & Schmader, 2003), and when information on discrimination is presented aggregated over several individuals rather than on a case-by-case basis (Crosby, Pufall, Snyder, O'Connell, & Whalen, 1989). In general, perceiving oneself (or one's group) as a victim of prejudice is associated with threat appraisals and negative affect (Major, Quinton, & McCoy, 2002).

Individual Determinants of Threat Appraisals

The extent to which environments are appraised as threatening also is affected by characteristics of the person (see Mendoza-Denton, Page-Gould, & Pietrzak, chap. 8, this volume). Personal characteristics may influence either demand or resource appraisals or both. Several measures assess individual differences in the tendency to be vigilant for stigma-related threats. The *Stigma-Consciousness Questionnaire* (SCQ) measures a tendency to expect to be stigmatized and stereotyped on the basis of one's stigma (Pinel, 1999). Scores on the SCQ correlate positively with perceptions of discrimination against the self and ingroup, with expectations that one will be treated negatively by outgroup members, with distrust of others, and with nonconscious attention toward social identity-threatening cues (Kaiser, Vick, & Major, 2004). These relationships have been observed among ethnic minorities, women, gays, and lesbians (Pinel, 1999, 2002). The *Race Rejection Sensitivity Questionnaire* (RS-race) measures the tendency to anxiously expect, readily perceive, and intensely react to rejection based on race (Mendoza-Denton, Purdie, Downey, Davis, & Pietrzak, 2002). Individual differences on the RS-race among African American students prior to entering college prospectively predicted the extent to which they reported experiencing negative race-related events during their first 3 weeks of college, the extent to which they felt negatively toward their peers and professors, and their sense of belonging at the university. Students high in RS-race also had less diverse friendships, decreased attendance at academic review sessions, and were especially likely to experience a decrease in their grades over time (see Mendoza-Denton, Page-Gould, & Pietrzak, chap. 8, this volume). Individuals who are high in stigma consciousness or expectations of status-based rejection are more likely to be vigilant to prejudice cues in their environment and sensitive to identity-related threats in their environment. Hence, threat appraisals are likely to be exacerbated for these individuals.

Several other individual characteristics moderate the extent to which people appraise situations as relevant to their stigma. One is the extent to which an individual is identified with his or her stigmatized identity. The more identified one is with a group, the greater likelihood that negative group-related events will be appraised as self-relevant. Negative events that are more self-relevant are appraised as more threatening (Lazarus & Folkman, 1984; Patterson & Neufeld, 1987). Accordingly, the more central and important a stigmatized identity is to an individual, the more threatening it should be for that individual to perceive discrimination against that social identity or to have negative stereotypes activated about that identity. Several experiments provide support for this hypothesis.

Research has shown that being able to attribute a negative outcome to discrimination based on one's social identity instead of to internal, stable aspects of one's personal identity can protect against depressed emotion and loss of self-esteem (e.g., Crocker, Voelkl, Testa, & Major, 1991; Major, Kaiser, & McCoy, 2003; Major, Quinton, et al., 2003). McCoy and Major (2003) hypothesized that this would be truer for individuals who are not highly identified with the targeted group than for individuals who are highly identified with the group. To test this hypothesis, women, all of whom had previously completed a measure of gender identification, received negative feedback on a speech from a male evaluator. The women then subsequently learned that the evaluator had sexist or nonsexist attitudes. Women low in gender identification reported less depressed emotion and higher self-esteem in the sexist than nonsexist condition, consistent with the idea that being able to attribute negative personal feedback to discrimination based on one's social identity can protect self-esteem. Among highly gender-identified women, in contrast, self-esteem and depressed emotions did not differ between the sexist and nonsexist conditions. This interaction suggests that when social identity is a core aspect of the self, perceiving prejudice against that social identity is more personally threatening, and less likely to buffer personal self-esteem from negative feedback, than when social identity is not a core aspect of the self.

In a second experiment, Latino/a American students, all of whom had previously completed a measure of ethnic group identification, read either an article describing the existence of pervasive prejudice against Latino/as or a control article (McCoy & Major, 2003). They then completed measures of threat and self-directed emotions. As expected, group identification moderated the effects of the prejudice condition on emotions. In the control condition, group identification was negatively associated with depressed emotions, such that participants who were highly identified with their ethnic group were less depressed than those low in ethnic group identification. Among participants in the prejudice condition, however, group identification was positively associated with depressed affect, such that participants high in ethnic group identification were more depressed after reading about prejudice against their group than were participants low in ethnic-group identification. Furthermore, group identification also interacted with experimental condition to predict threat appraisals. The more Latino/a American students in the prejudice condition identified with their ethnic group, the more they reported being personally threatened by racism. These primary appraisals of threat, in turn, fully mediated the positive relationship between group identification and depressed emotion. Thus, consistent with the transactional model, group identification moderated the relationship between perceived prejudice against the group and depressed emotion via its impact on cognitive appraisals of personal threat.

Other personal characteristics also moderate emotional responses to stressors through their impact on threat appraisals. Research in the health domain, for example, indicates that people with an optimistic outlook tend to appraise potentially stressful events as less harmful and taxing than people with a pessimistic outlook on life. The former's more benign appraisals, in turn, are associated with greater psychological resilience in the face of stressful life events (Major, Richards, Cooper, Cozzarelli, & Zubek, 1998). Kaiser et al. (2004) examined whether dispositional optimism influences the extent to which people appraise prejudice against their group as personally threatening, and through this mediator, their affect and self-esteem. In their first study, men and women who had previously completed a measure of dispositional optimism were randomly assigned to read an article about prejudice against their own gender group or one of two control articles (an article about prejudice against the elderly or a neutral article unrelated to prejudice). Participants then completed measures of self-esteem and depressed emotions. Among men and women who read about pervasive sexism directed toward their own gender group, an optimistic outlook on life was associated with significantly higher self-esteem and less depression. Among participants who read control information, optimism was unrelated to depressed emotions and still significantly, but more weakly, positively related to self-esteem. There was no main effect of the prejudice manipulation on self-esteem or depressed emotions, even though participants in the sexism condition perceived greater prejudice against their gender group than participants in the control conditions.

A follow-up study examined whether cognitive appraisals of personal threat mediated the relationship between optimism and self-evaluative emotions (Kaiser et al., 2004, Study 3). Women who were dispositional optimists or pessimists were recruited and asked to read an article documenting pervasive sexism against women. They then completed measures of primary and secondary appraisals, personal self-esteem, and depressed emotions. Again, optimism was positively related to self-esteem and negatively related to depressed emotions. Furthermore, as predicted, this relationship was mediated by cognitive appraisals. Compared to pessimists, optimists appraised prejudice against their group as less personally threatening and believed they were better prepared to cope with prejudice. These more benign primary and secondary appraisals, in turn, were related to higher self-esteem and less depression. In sum, individual differences in personal resources such as dispositional optimism can affect the extent to which perceived prejudice against the group is cognitively appraised as threatening to the self.

The extent to which individuals endorse or reject beliefs that legitimize status differences in society is another personal factor that may influence threat appraisals in intergroup situations (see Kaiser, chap. 3, this volume). Status-legitimizing beliefs include the belief that status systems are permeable, that hard work is rewarded, and that one's outcomes and status are under one's own control, among others (Major & Schmader, 2001). In three studies, Major, Gramzow, et al. (2002) found that the more strongly stigmatized participants (Latino/a Americans; women) endorsed the ideology of individual mobility (e.g., agreed with items such as "advancement in American society is possible for individuals of all ethnic groups"), the less likely they were to report in general that they personally (or members of their group) were a target of ethnic discrimination and the less likely they were to blame discrimination when a higher status confederate (Euro-American; man) rejected them for a desirable role. In contrast, among members of high-status groups, the more they endorsed the ideology of individual mobility, the more likely they were to blame discrimination when a member of a lower status group rejected them for a desirable role. These differences as a function of group status further demonstrate how the meaning of the local situation is shaped by collective representations, and are another illustration of the dangers of drawing conclusions about the phenomenology of stigmatization from research based on nonstigmatized populations.

Coping

The second process central to transactional models of stress is coping. *Coping* is defined as a goal-directed process aimed at regulating emotion, cognition, behavior, physiology, and the environment in response to stressful events or circumstances (Compas, Connor-Smith, Saltzman, Thomsen, & Wadsworth, 2001). Coping efforts are process-oriented, context-specific, and can be distinguished from the outcomes of coping efforts (i.e., whether or not they are successful). Coping processes, like appraisals, are theorized to differ as a function of characteristics of both the person and the situation (Lazarus & Folkman, 1984). Situational factors that affect coping include, for example, whether supportive others are present in the situation (Lazarus, 1999). Person factors include dispositional optimism, locus of control, and self-esteem, among other things (e.g., Major et al., 1998; Scheier, Carver, & Bridges, 2001; Taylor, 1989). Structural factors, such as membership in a group with high social status and ample resources, may also moderate coping processes (e.g., Adler & Ostrove, 1999).

The concept of coping is central to contemporary perspectives on stigma. In contrast to traditional perspectives, these perspectives portray the stigmatized not as passive victims, but as active agents attempting to make sense of their world, preserve their self-esteem, and achieve their goals (see Miller, chap. 2, this volume; Swim & Thomas, chap. 6, this volume). Conceptualizing the stigmatized in this way has led to a number of new insights (see Miller, chap. 2, this volume).

A number of strategies of coping with prejudice have been identified (e.g., Allport, 1954; Crocker & Major, 1989; Goffman, 1963; Jones et al., 1984).

For example, Allport described 13 different "ego-defenses" that targets of prejudice may employ in response to their situation, including obsessive concern, denial of membership, withdrawal and passivity, clowning, strengthening in-group ties, slyness and cunning, identification with the dominant group (self-hate), aggression against own group, prejudice against out-groups, sympathy with other oppressed out-groups, fighting back (militancy), enhanced striving, and symbolic status-striving.

Crocker and Major (1989) addressed three strategies by which members of stigmatized groups may cope with threats to their self-esteem posed by being a target of prejudice: (a) devaluing the importance of domains in which they or their group are disadvantaged (Major & Schmader, 1998); (b) comparing with members of their ingroup rather than with advantaged outgroup members (Major, Sciacchitano, & Crocker, 1993); and (c) attributing negative events to discrimination, instead of to internal, stable qualities of themselves (Crocker & Major, 1989; Major & Crocker, 1993). Their suggestion that attributing negative outcomes to discrimination is a coping strategy proved highly controversial. How can attributing negative events to discrimination be a coping strategy if the perception of discrimination is also a perceived demand that leads to a threat appraisal? As I discussed extensively elsewhere (Major et al., 2002), a key distinction is whether or not the person has experienced a specific negative outcome (e.g., a rejection) that threatens his or her personal self. If they have, attributing the negative event to discrimination (a more external cause) may be an effective coping strategy for protecting self-esteem because it shifts blame from stable, unique aspects of the personal self to the prejudice of others. For example, Major, Kaiser, et al. (2003) found that women blamed themselves less, and experienced less depressed affect, if they imagined being rejected from a course by a sexist professor than if they imagined being rejected by a professor who thought they were unintelligent. Furthermore, self-blame mediated the effects of the attribution condition on depressed affect. When people perceive discrimination in the absence of an immediate personal threat, however, this perception serves no such defensive purpose. Under these conditions, reports of discrimination may reflect the frequency or severity of discrimination, rather than attributional processes.

Identifying more closely with one's stigmatized group also has been identified as an effective coping strategy in response to prejudice and devaluation (Allport, 1954; Branscombe, Schmitt, & Harvey, 1999). Groups can provide emotional, informational, and instrumental support, social validation for one's perceptions, and social consensus for one's attributions. Turning to the group can facilitate attempts to directly solve the problems of prejudice and discrimination (e.g., collective action) as well as facilitate attempts to deal with the emotions resulting from perceiving prejudice. Branscombe and her colleagues propose that group identification increases in response to perceived prejudice against the group, and that this increased group identification enhances psychological well-being. They further propose that this increase in identification with the group partially offsets the negative effects of perceiving pervasive prejudice against the group on personal self-esteem and psychological well-being. Consistent with this model, several studies have shown that perceptions of prejudice and group identification are positively associated (Branscombe et al., 1999; Major, Quinton, et al., 2003; Operario & Fiske, 2001). Further, Jetten, Branscombe, Schmitt, and Spears (2001) showed experimentally that customers in a piercing salon who read that prejudice existed against body piercers subsequently identified more strongly with that group than customers who read that prejudice against body piercers was decreasing. A number of studies also report a positive association between group identification and self-esteem among stigmatized groups (e.g., Bat-Chava, 1994; Branscombe et al., 1999; Phinney, 1990; Rowley, Sellers, Chavous, & Smith, 1998). These findings are consistent with the idea that group identification can be an effective coping strategy in response to perceptions of prejudice against the group.

As Allport (1954) speculated, however, not all members of stigmatized groups may cope with prejudice by increasing their identification with the group. Some individuals and groups may cope with prejudice by decreasing their affiliation and identification with a group. Research by Ellemers and colleagues suggests that highly identified members of a group respond to threats to the group by increasing their identification with the group, whereas those members who are low in identification decrease their identification even more in response to threats to the group (see Ellemers, Spears, & Doosje, 2002, for a review). McCoy and Major (2003) observed this pattern in the second of their experiments described. Specifically, after reading about pervasive discrimination toward their ethnic group, Latino/a American students who had previously reported low levels of ethnic group identification identified even less with their ethnic group, whereas previously highly group identified Latino/a American students identified even more strongly with their ethnic group. Further research is needed to determine when group identification is a buffer against versus a source of vulnerability to prejudice against the group.

CONCLUSIONS

Research on coping strategies in response to stigmatization is burgeoning (see Miller, chap. 2, this volume). One important lesson of this research is that different types of prejudice may require different types of coping (see Miller, chap. 2, this volume). Another important lesson emerging from this research is that coping often involves *trade-offs*; that is, strategies that are engaged in to achieve one goal (such as protection of self-esteem) may inhibit attainment of other goals (such as achievement; see Swim & Thomas, chap. 6, this volume). Protecting self-esteem by disengaging from the academic domain can potentially impair performance in that domain (Crocker & Major, 1989); attributing negative outcomes to discrimination to protect self-esteem can interfere with accurate knowledge of one's strengths and weaknesses (Aronson & Inzlicht, 2004); complaining about prejudice might lead one to be socially derogated (Kaiser, chap. 3, this volume); and being vigilant for prejudice can spur one to act in ways that lead one to be treated more negatively by unsuspecting others (Pinel, 2002) and can impair intergroup relations (Tropp, chap. 9, this volume).

These trade-offs point to the importance of looking at multiple effects of stigma. Looking at only one outcome, such as self-esteem, or intergroup attitudes, or intellectual performance, cannot provide a full picture of the phenomenology of stigma. Further, these trade-offs point to the various ways in which psychological well-being can be conceptualized: Is it feeling good about the self? Doing well in school? Feeling identified with one's ingroup? Getting along well with members of outgroups? Engaging in efforts to combat prejudice? Maintaining a sense of control over one's outcomes? All of these have been discussed as valid measures of favorable outcomes (see Swim & Thomas, chap. 6, this volume). Obtaining any one of these outcomes may be achievable for those who are stigmatized, but achieving all in the face of stigma may be difficult. Researchers need to think broadly about the effects of stigma, and examine multiple outcomes simultaneously in order to fully understand the phenomenology of stigmatization.

REFERENCES

Adler, N. E., & Ostrove, J. M. (1999). Socioeconomic status and health: What we know and what we don't. In N. E. Adler & M. Marmot (Eds.), *Socioeconomic status and health in industrial nations: Social psychological and biological pathways. Annals of the New York Academy of Sciences, 896* (pp. 3–15). New York: New York Academy of Sciences.

Allison, K. W. (1998). Stress and oppressed category membership. In J. K. Swim & C. Stangor (Eds.), *Prejudice: The target's perspective* (pp. 145–170). San Diego, CA: Academic Press.

Allport, G. (1954). *The nature of prejudice.* New York: Doubleday Anchor.

Aronson, J., & Inzlicht, M. (2004). The ups and downs of attributional ambiguity: Stereotype vulnerability and the academic self-knowledge of African American college students. *Psychological Science, 15,* 829–836.

Bandura, A. (1982). Self-efficacy mechanism in human agency. *American Psychologist, 37*(2), 122–147.

Bat-Chava, Y. (1994). Group identification and self-esteem of deaf adults. *Personality and Social Psychology Bulletin, 20,* 494–502.

Blascovich, J., & Mendes, W. B. (2000). Challenge and threat appraisals: The role of affective cues. In J. P. Forgas (Ed.), *Feeling and thinking: The role of affect in social cognition* (pp. 59–82). Cambridge, England: Cambridge University Press.

Branscombe, N. R., Schmitt, M. T., & Harvey, R. D. (1999). Perceiving pervasive discrimination among African Americans: Implications for group identification and well-being. *Journal of Personality and Social Psychology, 77,* 135–149.

Cartwright, D. (1950). Emotional dimensions of group life. In M. L. Raymert (Ed.), *Feelings and emotions* (pp. 439–447). New York: McGraw Hill.

Clark, K. B., & Clark, M. P. (1950). Emotional factors in racial identification and preference in Negro children. *Journal of Negro Education, 19,* 341–350.

Clark, R., Anderson, N. B., Clark, V. R., & Williams, D. R. (1999). Racism as a stressor for African Americans: A biopsychosocial model. *American Psychologist, 54,* 805–816.

Compas, B. E., Connor-Smith, J. K., Saltzman, H., Thomsen, A. H., & Wadsworth, M. E. (2001). Coping with stress during childhood and adolescence: Problems, progress and potential in theory and research. *Psychological Bulletin, 127,* 87–127.

Crocker, J. (1999). Social stigma and self-esteem: Situational construction of self-worth. *Journal of Experimental Social Psychology, 35,* 89–107.

Crocker, J., & Major, B. (1989). Social stigma and self-esteem: The self-protective properties of stigma. *Psychological Review, 96,* 608–630.

Crocker, J., Major, B., & Steele, C. M. (1998). Social stigma. In D. Gilbert, S. T. Fiske, & G. Lindzey (Eds.), *Handbook of social psychology* (4th ed., pp. 504–553). Boston, MA: McGraw Hill.

Crocker, J., Voelkl, K., Testa, M., & Major, B. (1991). Social stigma: The affective consequences of attributional ambiguity. *Journal of Personality and Social Psychology, 60,* 218–228.

Crosby, F. J., Pufall, A., Snyder, R. C., O'Connell, M., & Whalen, P. (1989). The denial of personal disadvantage among you, me, and all the other ostriches. In M. Crawford & M. Gentry (Eds.), *Gender and thought: Psychological perspectives* (pp. 79–99). New York: Springer-Verlag.

Davies, P. G., Spencer, S. J., Quinn, D. M., & Gerhardstein, R. (2002). Consuming images: How television commercials that elicit stereotype threat can constrain women academically and professionally. *Personality and Social Psychology Bulletin, 28,* 1615–1628.

Diener, E. (1984). Subjective well-being. *Psychological Bulletin, 95,* 542–575.

Ellemers, N., Spears, R., & Doosje, B. (2002). Self and social identity. In S. T. Fiske, D. L Schacter, & C. Zahn-Waxler (Eds.), *Annual Review of Psychology, 53,* 161–186.

Friedman, M. A., & Brownell, K. D. (1995). Psychological correlates of obesity: Moving to the next research generation. *Psychological Bulletin, 117,* 3–20.

Goffman, E. (1963). *Stigma: Notes on the management of spoiled identity.* Englewood Cliffs, NJ: Prentice-Hall.

Jetten, J., Branscombe, N. R., Schmitt, M. T., & Spears, R. (2001). Rebels with a cause: Group identification as a response to perceived discrimination from the mainstream. *Personality and Social Psychology Bulletin, 27*(9), 1204–1213.

Jones, E. E., Farina, A., Hastorf, A. H., Markus, H., Miller, D. T., & Scott, R. A. (1984). *Social stigma: The psychology of marked relationships.* New York: Freeman.

Kaiser, C. R., Major, B., & McCoy, S. K. (2004). Expectations about the future and the emotional consequences of perceiving prejudice. *Personality and Social Psychology Bulletin, 30,* 173–184.

Kaiser, C. R., Vick, S. B., & Major, B. (2004). *Prejudice expectations moderate preconscious attention to social identity threatening cues.* Manuscript under review.

Lazarus, R. S. (1999). *Stress and emotion: A new synthesis.* New York: Springer.

Lazarus, R. S., & Folkman, S. (1984). *Stress, appraisal, and coping.* New York: Springer.

Leary, M. R., Tambor, E. S., Terdal, S. K., & Downs, D. L. (1995). Self-esteem as an interpersonal monitor: The sociometer hypothesis. *Journal of Personality and Social Psychology, 68,* 518–530.

LeDoux, J. E. (1996). *The emotional brain: The mysterious underpinnings of emotional life.* New York: Simon & Schuster.

Major, B., Barr, L., Zubek, J., & Babey, S. (1999). Gender and self-esteem: A meta-analysis. In W. B. Swann, J. H. Langlois, & L. A. Gilbert (Eds.), *Sexism and stereotypes in modern society.* Washington, DC: American Psychological Association.

Major, B., & Crocker, J. (1993). Social stigma: The affective consequences of attributional ambiguity. In D. M. Mackie & D. L. Hamilton (Eds.), *Affect, cognition, and stereotyping: Interactive processes in intergroup perception* (pp. 345–370). New York: Academic Press.

Major, B., Gramzow, R., McCoy, S. K., Levin, S., Schmader, T., & Sidanius, J. (2002). Perceiving personal discrimination: The role of group status and status legitimizing ideology. *Journal of Personality and Social Psychology, 82,* 269–282.

Major, B., Kaiser, C., & McCoy, S. K. (2003). It's not my fault: When and why attributions to prejudice protect self-esteem. *Personality and Social Psychology Bulletin, 29,* 772–781.

Major, B., McCoy, S. K., Kaiser, C. R., & Quinton, W. J. (2003). Prejudice and self-esteem: A transactional model. *European Review of Social Psychology, 14,* 77–104.

Major, B., & O'Brien, L. T. (2005). The social psychology of stigma. In S. Fiske (Ed.), *Annual Review of Psychology, 56,* 393–421.

Major, B., Quinton, W. J., & McCoy, S. K. (2002). Antecedents and consequences of attributions to discrimination: Theoretical and empirical advances. In M. P. Zanna (Ed.), *Advances in experimental social psychology, Vol. 34* (pp. 251–330). New York: Academic Press.

Major, B., Quinton, W. J., & Schmader, T. (2003). Attributions to discrimination and self-esteem: Impact of group identification and situational ambiguity. *Journal of Experimental Social Psychology, 39,* 220–231.

Major, B., Richards, M. C., Cooper, M. L., Cozzarelli, C., & Zubek, J. M. (1998). Personal resilience, cognitive appraisals, and coping: An integrative model of adjustment to abortion. *Journal of Personality and Social Psychology, 74,* 735–752.

Major, B., & Schmader, T. (1998). Coping with stigma through psychological disengagement. In J. K. Swim & C. Stangor (Eds.), *Prejudice: The target's perspective* (pp. 219–241). San Diego, CA: Academic Press.

Major, B., & Schmader, T. (2001). Legitimacy and the construal of social disadvantage. In J. Jost & B. Major (Eds.), *The psychology of legitimacy: Emerging perspectives on ideology, justice, and intergroup relationships* (pp. 176–204). New York: Cambridge University Press.

Major, B., Sciacchitano, A. M., & Crocker, J. (1993). In-group versus out-group comparisons and self-esteem. *Personality and Social Psychology Bulletin, 19,* 711–721.

Marx, D., & Roman, J. S. (2002). Female role-models: Protecting women's math test performance. *Personality and Social Psychology Bulletin, 28,* 1183–1193.

McCoy, S. K., & Major, B. (2003). Group identification moderates emotional responses to perceived prejudice. *Personality and Social Psychology Bulletin, 29,* 1005–1017.

Mendoza-Denton, R., Purdie, V. J., Downey, G., Davis, A., & Pietrzak, J. (2002). Sensitivity to status-based rejection: Implications for African American students' college experience. *Journal of Personality and Social Psychology, 83,* 896–918.

Miller, C. T., & Downey, K. T. (1999). A meta-analysis of heavyweight and self-esteem. *Personality and Social Psychology Review, 3,* 68–84.

Miller, C. T., & Kaiser, C. R. (2001). A theoretical perspective on coping with stigma. *Journal of Social Issues, 57,* 73–92.

Miller, C. T., & Major, B. (2000). Coping with stigma and prejudice. In T. F. Heatherton, R. E. Kleck, M. R. Hebl, & J. G. Hull (Eds.), *The social psychology of stigma* (pp. 243–272). New York: Guilford.

Operario, D., & Fiske, S. T. (2001). Ethnic identity moderates perceptions of prejudice: Judgments of personal versus group discrimination and subtle versus blatant bias. *Personality and Social Psychology Bulletin, 27,* 550–561.

Patterson, R. J., & Neufeld, W. J. (1987). Clear danger: Situational determinants of the appraisal of threat. *Psychological Bulletin, 101,* 404–416.

Phinney, J. S. (1990). Ethnic identity in adolescents and adults: Review of research. *Psychological Bulletin, 10,* 499–514.

Pinel, E. C. (1999). Stigma consciousness: The psychological legacy of social stereotypes. *Journal of Personality and Social Psychology, 76,* 114–128.

Pinel, E. C. (2002). Stigma consciousness in intergroup contexts: The power of conviction. *Journal of Experimental Social Psychology, 38,* 178–185.

Rowley, S. J., Sellers, R. M., Chavous, T. M., & Smith, M. A. (1998). The relationship between racial identity and self-esteem in African American college and high school students. *Journal of Personality and Social Psychology, 74,* 715–724.

Scheier, M. F., Carver, C. S., & Bridges, M. W. (2001). Optimism, pessimism, and psychological well-being. In E. C. Chang (Ed.), *Optimism and pessimism: Implications for theory, research, and practice* (pp. 189–216). Washington, DC: American Psychological Association.

Simpson, G. E., & Yinger, J. M. (1985). The consequences of prejudice and discrimination. In L. Susskind & L. Rodwin (Series Eds.), *Racial and cultural minorities: An analysis of prejudice and discrimination* (5th ed., pp. 111–136). New York: Plenum.

Spencer, S. J., Steele, C. M., & Quinn, D. M. (1999). Stereotype threat and women's math performance. *Journal of Experimental Social Psychology, 35,* 4–28.

Steele, C. M. (1997). A threat in the air: How stereotypes shape intellectual identity and performance. *American Psychologist, 52,* 613–629.

Steele, C. M., & Aronson, J. (1995). Stereotype threat and the intellectual test performance of African Americans. *Journal of Personality and Social Psychology, 69,* 797–811.

Steele, C. M., Spencer, S., & Aronson, J. (2002). Contending with images of one's group: The psychology of stereotype and social identity threat. In M. Zanna (Ed.), *Advances in experimental social psychology* (Vol. 34, pp. 379–440). San Diego, CA: Academic Press.

Taylor, S. E. (1989). *Positive illusions: Creative self-deception and the healthy mind.* New York: Basic Books.

Tomaka, J., Blascovich, J., Kelsey, R. M., & Leitten, C. L. (1993). Subjective, physiological, and behavioral effects of threat and challenge. *Journal of Personality and Social Psychology, 65,* 248–260.

Twenge, J. M., & Crocker, J. (2002). Race and self-esteem: Meta-analysis comparing Whites, Blacks, Hispanics, Asians, and American Indians and comment on Gray-Little and Hafdahl (2000). *Psychological Bulletin, 128,* 371–408.

Williams, K. D. (1997). Social ostracism. In R. M. Kowalski (Ed.), *Aversive interpersonal behaviors* (pp. 133–170). New York: Plenum Press.

Winkielman, P., & Berridge, K. C. (2004). Unconscious emotion. *Current Directions in Psychological Science, 13,* 120–123.

Zajonc, R. B. (2000). Feeling and thinking: Closing the debate over the independence of affect. In J. P. Forgas (Ed.), *Feeling and thinking: The role of affect in social cognition* (pp. 31–58). Cambridge University Press.

PART

III

STIGMA AND THE SOCIAL BASIS OF THE SELF

CHAPTER

11

Understanding Stigma From the Perspective of the Self-Expansion Model

Tracy McLaughlin-Volpe
University of Vermont

This chapter was inspired, in part, by a memorable colleague. He is a beloved African American professor at a predominantly White University. Having heard that he was the driving force behind a new program on his campus, the goal of which is to improve the college experience of students who belong to ethnic minority groups, I set out to get to know him and eventually had the opportunity to ask him about his own personal college experience. He vividly remembered his very first day of college and spoke to me of the excitement that preceded his arrival at college, the great expectations he had, and how in just one day—his very first day—his enthusiasm was replaced by a feeling of hopelessness and despair.

You may wonder what could have caused this dramatic change in his attitude. Did he meet a racist student or professor? Was he ignored, treated poorly, or attacked? His first experiences at college were in fact not at all negative. He was welcomed warmly by almost everyone he met, and especially by the small, cohesive group of African American students on campus. His interactions with students and staff were quite positive. But on this first day he also received an important message from his new African American friends. They took him aside and told him that in order to survive on this campus he needed to rely on the African American community because the White majority on campus did not care about students like him and did not think that he belonged there. Surprised and shocked by this information, his initial excitement about being accepted at a prestigious college was quickly replaced by a bitter sense of disillusionment. He discovered that most of the other African American students were suffering from what he now calls a case of "collective depression." Over time, he became depressed himself and thought about dropping out of college, feeling that he was wasting his time there.

What was it about the information this young man received on his first day at college that had such a powerful impact? On one level, he believed that perhaps not everyone on this campus welcomed his arrival there, that he could expect some of the White students to reject him. He also found a community of others like him who would be his friends simply because they shared a common skin color and as a result common experiences. Thus, there would be rejection but also instant friendships. He might not have the opportunity to connect with White students, but there would be plenty of support by the African American students.

A more thorough analysis, however, has to take into account the power differential between the groups involved. Not being able to connect as an equal with members of the White majority on campus would likely mean that he would not have equal access to the resources to which privileged White students have disproportionate access. For example, fearing discrimination, he might be reluctant to approach his professors or take advantage of the learning resources provided on campus (Mendoza-Denton, Downey, Purdie, Davis, & Pietrzak, 2002; Mendoza-Denton, Page-Gould, & Pietrzak, chap. 8, this volume). He may suspect that his personal achievements would not be evaluated fairly. In addition, students who learn of another group's dislike for them may be deprived of the freedom to choose their friends, their reference group, and—to an extent—their identity. While members of the dominant group are able to choose with relative freedom who to befriend and which groups to join, stigmatized students are restricted in their ability and freedom to actively construct their identity because it is at least partially defined by the dominant group. Being forced to confront the possibility that one is not valued and appreciated is thus an experience that is quite threatening to one's self-esteem and one's goals for the future. In terms of meeting important life goals, it means that, compared to a person who is not stigmatized, one will have to work harder, surmount more barriers, and likely have less help on the way. It may also mean that there are very real limits placed on how much one will be able to achieve. Because stigma may limit a person's access to those relationship partners and groups that are in control of important resources, it may hamper a person's opportunities to grow, explore freely, and thus expand the self.

The idea that people partially satisfy their basic need to acquire resources that will put them in the best possible position to achieve future life goals through close personal relationships is an idea captured in the self-expansion model (A. Aron & E. N. Aron, 1997). This chapter applies this model to an analysis of what it means to be stigmatized. The chapter describes self-expansion theory and supporting research, shows how it is relevant to understanding the experience of being a member of a stigmatized group, and discusses how the hypothesized processes play out at institutions of higher learning and what types of interventions may help members of stigmatized groups fulfill their self-expansion needs.

THE SELF-EXPANSION MODEL

The self-expansion model (A. Aron & E. N. Aron, 1986; A. Aron, E. N. Aron, & Norman, 2001) was originally developed as a framework for understanding why people are motivated to enter into and maintain close relationships. According to this model, people have a basic desire to explore, to expand the self, and to enhance potential self-efficacy by gaining or increasing their access to material and social resources, perspectives, and identities (A. Aron & McLaughlin-Volpe, 2001). In contrast to other motivational theories of the self (e.g., Bandura, 1977; Deci & Ryan, 1987; Gecas, 1989; Higgins & Sorrentino, 1990; Maslow, 1970; Taylor, Neter, & Wayment, 1995; White, 1959), the *self-expansion model* defines the desire to expand the self as the desire to enhance potential efficacy. According to this view, people are motivated to acquire resources that will make the achievement of goals possible; whether or not these goals are eventually pursued and achieved is of secondary importance (A. Aron, Norman, & E. N. Aron, 1998).

The model also provides a description of one of the hypothesized processes by which self-expansion is pursued; people form and maintain close relationships with others who provide access to desired resources, perspectives, and identities. By including another person in their self-concept, people come to perceive the other person (and with that person, his or her resources, perspectives, and identities) as part of themselves. Thus, people typically share what they and their partner bring to the relationship, they actively try to understand each other's experiences and perspectives, and they come to at least partially take on their partner's identities (A. Aron, E. N. Aron, Tudor, & Nelson, 1991; A. Aron & Fraley, 1999). Growing close to another person expands the self because the partner's attributes, perspectives, and identities are added to one's own attributes, perspectives, and identities, resulting in a more complex sense of self that contains more unique self-domains (A. Aron, Paris, & E. N. Aron, 1995). This process becomes especially salient when people grow close to another person very quickly, for example when they fall in love. However, romantic relationships are only one type of relationship that provides these benefits; friendships and group-memberships are thought to provide similar rewards and opportunities for self-expansion (see Aron & McLaughlin-Volpe, 2001; Smith, 2002; Tropp & Wright, 2001; Wright, A. Aron, & Tropp, 2002).

Research on Self-Expansion

To date, only a few studies have demonstrated the idea that relationships can expand the self. One of these studies investigated the self-concepts of people who had just fallen in love. Aron et al. (1995) followed college students for 10 weeks and tracked whether or not they had become involved in a new romantic relationship. During four separate testing sessions, participants in this study were asked to engage in a spontaneous adjective-generation task (W. J. McGuire & C. V. McGuire, 1988) in response to the question, "Who are you today?" Aron and his colleagues hypothesized that if a developing close relationship is experienced as self-expanding, participants' self-descriptions should reflect this change. In support of this idea, they found that compared to students who did not fall in love, students who had fallen in love listed a significantly greater number of distinct self-content domains, indicating a more diverse, complex, and expanded sense of self. A second study found that falling in love was also associated with significant increases in self-efficacy and self-esteem. Thus, in this model, self-expansion is operationalized as self-complexity (adding dimensions to the self), and a resulting greater sense of self-efficacy and self-esteem.

Following up on this work, McLaughlin-Volpe and Wright (2002) set out to test whether newly formed friendships would also result in self-expansion. Further, they wondered whether the potential for self-expansion may be larger to the extent that the close relationship partner is a person who belongs to an outgroup and/or is experienced as very different from the self. Using the same basic design as Aron et al. (1995), they collected descriptions of college students' self-concepts, and measures of self-efficacy and self-esteem four times during a 6-week period. The questionnaire also contained a section that asked participants to indicate whether a number of different life events had occurred since the last testing session. If participants responded that they had developed one or more close friendships, they were asked to report for each person how close they felt to this person and how satisfied they were with this relationship. At the end of the 6-week period, participants were asked to provide additional information about each of their new friends. Among other items, they were asked to report each person's gender, ethnicity/race, and religious and political party affiliations. They also listed three ways in which they felt each friend was different from them and indicated—on a 7-point scale—how meaningful they perceived each difference to be.

Analyses revealed that the extent to which a new friend was perceived as different from the self was positively related to continuous self-concept change over the 6-week period. In other words, people who developed a friendship with a person whom they perceived to be different from themselves were more likely to report unique new self-descriptions at each testing session and this recognition of new self-attributes tended to increase over time. This study thus provided initial evidence for the idea that new friendships can initiate changes in people's self-concepts. However, in this study this was only true when the relationship partner was perceived to be somewhat different or dissimilar from the self. It is possible that friends who are similar to us provide us with relatively few benefits that would result in self-expansion (McLaughlin-Volpe, A. Aron, Wright, & Lewandowsky, 2005), or perhaps these changes are more subtle and thus less easily measured. This argument leads to an intriguing hypothesis: It may be that when we are motivated to expand the self, we are more likely to select dissimilar friends whose resources, perspectives, and identities complement our own and who thereby maximize our potential for self-expansion.

However, considering the potential costs of pursuing relationships with dissimilar others, people generally balance their desire for self-expansion with their desire to build lasting relationships. Research on interpersonal attraction shows that people prefer partners who offer a number of desirable qualities (e.g., high status), but who also like and value them (A. Aron, Dutton, E. N. Aron, & Iverson, 1989; Baumeister & Wotman, 1992; Walster, Aronson, Abrahams, & Rottman, 1966). Thus, when we know that other people's interests differ from our own, we tend to pursue a relationship with them only when we have reason to think that they like us or are interested in having a relationship with us (A. Aron, Steele, & Kashdan, 2002). On balance, having a successful and stable relationship with someone who is similar to us is more rewarding than having a short-lived relationship with a highly attractive dissimilar person because only close and stable relationships with partners who like and appreciate us provide the conditions that make continued self-expansion possible.

Achieving Expansion Through the Inclusion of Others in the Self

Perhaps more intriguing than the idea that relationships provide people with opportunities to expand their self-concepts is the process by which this occurs. When a relationship develops, people tend to spend time with one another, participate in joint activities, and engage in mutual self-disclosure. Over time people start to feel close to their partner, influence each other's thinking and feeling, and adopt a communal orientation toward the other (Clark & Mills, 1993; Kelley et al., 1983; Reis & Shaver, 1988). As a result, relationship partners increasingly see themselves as interdependent and can be said to have interconnected selves.

In support of this idea, studies have demonstrated that close relationship partners act, think, and feel as if certain aspects of the other, such as his or her resources, perspectives, and characteristics are partially the individual's own (A. Aron & E. N. Aron, 1986; A. Aron et al., 1991). With increasing relationship closeness, two formerly separate selves begin to merge and may even become confused; the close other becomes included in the self (cf. A. Aron & E. N. Aron, 1986, 1996, 1997). Although a detailed description of the studies that support the idea that others become included in the self is beyond the scope of this chapter, one representative study illustrates the consequences of self–other merging. This experiment sought to establish the idea that close relationship partners, because their selves are interconnected, come to incorporate attributes of their partner into their self-concepts.

A. Aron and colleagues (1991, Experiment 3) set out to test the hypothesis that people will show a tendency to confuse traits that are true of themselves with the traits that are true of another person only when the other person is a close relationship partner. Married participants first rated a series of trait adjectives for their descriptiveness of themselves and their spouse. After a distracting intermediate task, they then responded to these same words, deciding as quickly as possible whether or not each trait was true for the self. The prediction was that if one's spouse is in fact included in the self, it should be difficult to respond to those trait words that were true of the self but not true of one's spouse and vice versa, resulting in longer response latencies. The results were as predicted: Longer response times were recorded when a trait was characteristic of oneself but not of one's spouse and vice versa. Other studies have found a similar self–other confusion effect for episodic memory (Mashek, A. Aron, & Boncimino, 2003; Omoto & Gunn, 1994), suggesting that in a personal relationship, identities are sufficiently intermixed that people even confuse biographical memories of self and other.

In sum, self-expansion is achieved when an individual enters into a close relationship with another person in which they include the other in their concept of self in the sense that they feel as if the other's perspectives, resources, and identities are to some extent their own. This model is supported by studies showing self–other merging with regard to personal characteristics and episodic memories.

Expansion of Self Through Group Membership

Recent theorizing and research has applied the self-expansion model to understanding why people seek membership in social groups. Wright and colleagues (2002) believed that people are motivated to join groups for some of the same reasons that motivate them to engage in dyadic relationships: group-membership expands the self when the group provides access to desired resources, perspectives, and identities. Group identification then can be seen as an effort to access desired benefits because having these benefits available to us increases our confidence that we can meet the demands of our world and achieve our goals. Benefits of group membership include the material and social resources a particular organization offers. For example, group membership can provide members with physical protection, connections to people with status and power, and help in emergency situations. In addition, a group can become an important source of identity and its collective perspective (e.g., its worldviews, values, norms, etc.) can provide a framework for understanding and negotiating the world.

McLaughlin-Volpe and colleagues (2005) argued that group membership may be an especially powerful avenue for achieving potential self-efficacy because it provides multiple sources of self-expansion. First, there are the benefits provided by the organization or group itself (e.g., particular resources, perspectives, and identities). Second, there are the benefits provided by individual group members. Thus, groups may be attractive because they potentially offer access to a host of desirable benefits as well as to a number of attractive relationship partners who—because they share an important group membership with us—are more likely to form relationships with us.

Whether or not membership in a given group is attractive depends in part on the benefits of group membership. When membership in a group offers access to valued social and material resources, provides its members with important perspectives, or a desired identity, people are likely to be highly motivated to join and remain in the group. This hypothesis is supported by studies showing that people tend to be more attracted to high-status groups (Ellemers, 1993; Sachdev & Bourhis, 1991). However, the attractiveness of a given group should also depend on whether or not one feels valued as a group member (Luhtanen & Crocker, 1992), because resources are typically distributed first to high-ranking and valued members of the group. Group members with low status can simply not be completely sure that they will be granted access to the group's resources. Low-ranking group members therefore tend to expend considerable effort on attempts to strengthen their position within the group (Noel, Wann, & Branscombe, 1995). Should these efforts fail, they tend to feel much less positive about the group and often actively devalue the group (Dittes & Kelly, 1956; Snoek, 1962).

Achieving Self-Expansion Through the Inclusion of Groups in the Self

The mechanism by which group membership expands a person's sense of self is thought to be analogous to how close relationships lead to self-expansion. It is hypothesized that during group identification, mental representations of self and group merge, leading to the perception of greater similarity between self and group and the inclusion of the group's attributes in one's self-concept. Existing research supports, in particular, the idea that people who identify with a group come to see themselves in terms of the characteristics that describe the group as a whole.

According to the *ingroup-homogeneity effect,* for example, the process of group formation leads to the perception of fellow ingroup members as more similar to each other. The effect has been demonstrated reliably in several studies (e.g., Brown & Wootton-Millward, 1993; Oakes, Haslam, Morrison, & Grace, 1995; Worchel, Coutant-Sassic, & Grossman, 1992), and seems to be particularly strong when the potential for the inclusion of the ingroup in the self is facilitated by considerable personal contact between group members.

The notion that characteristics of an ingroup often become accepted as self-descriptive is also illustrated by research on self-stereotyping. *Self-categorization theory* (Turner, Hogg, Oakes, Reicher, & Wetherell, 1987) postulates that self-categorization as a group member leads to self-stereotyping because it "systematically biases self-perception and behavior to render it more closely in accordance with stereotypical ingroup characteristics and norms" (Hogg & Turner, 1987, p. 326). In other words, social identification motivates people to perceive themselves as representative members of their group and thus results in self-stereotyping (Simon & Hamilton, 1994).

Similar to the ingroup homogeneity effect, self-stereotyping appears to increase with the strength of the social identification with the ingroup (Spears, Doosje, & Ellemers, 1997). Simon and his colleagues (Simon, Glaessner-Bayerl, & Stratenwerth, 1991; Simon & Hamilton, 1994), for example, found self-stereotyping to be most pronounced when the ingroup was a minority group (this was true for positively and negatively valenced attributes), and especially when it was a high status or elite minority group. These results were consistent for three different self-stereotyping measures: for self-descriptions, for similarity-ratings of self to other ingroup members, and for ratings of ingroup homogeneity. Thus, when individuals self-categorize as members of a particular group, the adoption of self-stereotypes affects not only their self-conception as group members, but also their individual self-concepts (Sinclair & Huntsinger, chap. 12, this volume).

Finally, Smith and his colleagues' program of research demonstrates that attributes belonging to the ingroup and attributes of the self can become cognitively confused for individuals who identify with a particular group (Smith, Coats, & Walling, 1999; Smith & Henry, 1996). For example, Smith and Henry argued that if the proposition is true that an ingroup can become part of the psychological self, then to the extent that one identifies with a particular group, there should be a tendency to confuse traits of the self with traits thought typical (or stereotypical) of the ingroup. In their study, participants rated each of 90 trait adjectives in terms of their descriptiveness of the self, an ingroup, and an outgroup. Subsequently, they participated in a reaction-time task that involved judging as quickly as possible whether each of the same 90 trait adjectives were descriptive of the self. Results revealed the expected effect of reaction time facilitation for traits that were perceived as typical for both the self and the ingroup, and of reaction time inhibition for traits on which the self and the ingroup mismatched. The results of this study thus demonstrate that when a person is asked to rate a particular trait as true or false of the self, confusion may occur for traits seen as typical of the self but not of the group because the group has, to an extent, become a part of the self.

To test whether the degree of confusion between the mental representations of the self and the ingroup is moderated by the strength with which individuals identify with their ingroup, Tropp and Wright (2001) adapted the same reaction-time paradigm. Extending the findings by Smith et al. (1999), they found that only those participants who strongly identified with their group showed significantly faster reaction times when asked to rate the self-descriptiveness of attributes on which the self and ingroup matched versus attributes on which the ingroup mismatched the self.

In sum, the idea that ingroups become included in people's self-concepts is supported by the ingroup-homogeneity effect, the phenomenon of self-stereotyping, and experimental evidence that shows that people who identify with a particular group have trouble distinguishing between traits that are descriptive of the self but not the ingroup and traits that are true for the ingroup but not self-descriptive. All this suggests that for people who identify with a particular group, the ingroup (and with the group its members) becomes increasingly connected with their self-concepts. To the extent that a group provides its members with important resources, perspectives, and identities, this merging with an ingroup is likely experienced as satisfying people's need for self-expansion.

STIGMA AND SELF-EXPANSION

The main argument of this chapter so far can be summarized as follows: Self-expansion is a basic human motive and is achieved by gaining access to valued resources, perspectives, and identities. Because we can access desired benefits by forming relationships with others and groups, our ability to expand the self depends in part on whether or not we form successful close relationships and become valuable group members. If this premise is correct, being stigmatized may limit one's opportunities for self-expansion in several ways. First, a member of a stigmatized group may be less attractive to potential relationship partners and may thus have fewer partners from which to choose. In addition, belonging to a stigmatized group may make one a less attractive group member or less eligible to join a desirable group. Any stigmatized person who is aware of these processes is expected to find this knowledge extremely painful. In particular, when one's stigmatized status is linked to a marker that one has no control over (e.g., skin color), feelings of anger, helplessness, and despair are likely consequences. Findings from the literature on exclusion and discrimination support this argument and illustrate how stigmatized individuals' sense of self is affected by prejudice and discrimination.

Consider the example discussed in the introduction to this chapter of the African American student who has just arrived on a predominantly White college campus to find out that he is not really welcome there. In terms of the self-expansion model, he receives several important messages. The first is that the White students on campus are unlikely to consider him a potential friend. Some will actively dislike his presence on campus and others will shy away from an interracial friendship because they may be worried about alienating their White friends or because they are concerned that they might be disliked and rejected by an African American student who believes they are prejudiced (Devine, Evett, & Vasquez-Suson, 1996; Kaiser, chap. 3, this volume; Shelton, Richeson, Salvatore, & Hill, chap. 4, this volume). Like most people, the African American student himself is unwilling to pursue relationships with others whom he perceives as disliking him, and he will therefore find that the White majority of the student body is eliminated as potential friends. The second message he receives, closely linked to the first, is that White students as a group are unlikely to treat him like a member of their group. Because he is African American (and depending on the local culture and social norms prevalent on this campus), he may not be welcome to participate in the activities of the White students. He will not be invited into their study groups, fraternities, or to their social gatherings. If, unexpectedly, he were invited to join, he suspects that it would probably be as a low-status group member. He would always feel suspect and he would likely be marginalized. Finally, he will be confronted with some of the negative stereotypes about African Americans that are the presumptive cause of his group's rejection by the dominant group on campus. Even if these stereotypes are not explicitly mentioned, the implicit message he receives is that his group is somehow not worthy of acceptance, that his social identity is spoiled. This awareness is likely to affect how he feels about himself, and may also alter how he views other African Americans and members of the White majority group.

Personal and vicarious experiences of discrimination thus communicate to members of a stigmatized group that they are not valuable relationship partners, not part of the majority group, and not valued as potential group members (Crocker, Major, & Steele, 1998; Tropp, chap. 9, this volume). To the extent that the formation of successful bonds with other individuals and groups is indeed an important avenue for self-expansion, being excluded from potential interpersonal relationships or groups may be experienced as the loss of valuable opportunities for future self-expansion. Not being eligible to join a group means that a person will be unable to access the potential psychological, social, and material benefits that group offers. To the extent that the excluding group is also a major source of future relationship partners, the loss in potential self-efficacy would be exacerbated. Thus, the self-expansion model predicts that the social exclusion that stigmatized individuals perceive and experience at the hands of nonstigmatized individuals, whether they are potential relationship partners or members of a desirable group, represents an attack on their sense of self that is experienced as a threat to desired self-expansion and that has measurable (negative) cognitive and behavioral consequences.

Consequences of Self-Expansion Threat

The cognitive consequences of forming new relationships can be measured in terms of the inclusion of the partner's or the group's attributes in the self and the resulting increase in perceived self-efficacy and self-complexity (e.g., Aron et al., 1995; Smith & Henry, 1996). A person who is stigmatized, however, is likely to become the target of social exclusion and therefore is denied the benefits of those relationships that are withheld. Consequently, social exclusion can result in self-expansion threat which, depending on the degree to which access to desired relationships and group memberships is denied, can take the form of a smaller than desired rate of self-expansion, a stagnation of perceived self-expansion, or even negative self-expansion (operationalized as the addition of negative self-attributes). The perceived threat to a person's self-concept is hypothesized to be greater to the extent that the stigmatized person was motivated to grow and expand the self and did not expect to be the target of discrimination. This threat should be particularly strong for people whose bond with members of their own (stigmatized) group is not sufficient to buffer against the rejection by an outgroup.

In an initial test of these ideas, McLaughlin-Volpe (2002) hypothesized that students who had recently experienced more rejection and social exclusion than acceptance and inclusion would provide self-descriptions that included fewer unique self-attributes and would report lower levels of self-efficacy. Participants were first-year college students who were asked to describe themselves in response to the question, "Who are you?," and then filled out a measure of recent life events, as well as a measure of self-efficacy. Results indicated that students whose recent experiences of rejection and exclusion outweighed their experiences of acceptance spontaneously listed significantly fewer unique self-descriptions and reported significantly lower levels of self-efficacy. To the extent that members of stigmatized groups are more likely to experience exclusion and rejection than members of nonstigmatized groups, they are also less likely to experience self-expansion and should as a result be less confident that they will be able to achieve their goals. Not surprisingly then, ethnic minority college students have been found to arrive at college with extremely bright and hopeful expectations for their future, but tend to feel rather pessimistic about their economic prospects during the last 2 years of college (van Laar, 2001). The study by McLaughlin-Volpe (2002), however, also suggested that experiences of acceptance by, for example, members of one's own group, can serve as a buffer against the negative consequences of rejection and exclusion, a finding that is consistent with the observation that ethnic minority students on predominately White campuses often choose to navigate college life surrounded and supported by members of their ingroup. When, however, students are unable to find acceptance in any group, the negative effects of discrimination are likely to be compounded (see also Branscombe, Schmitt, & Harvey, 1999).

Being stigmatized can lead to self-expansion threat also indirectly in situations where ingroup members behave negatively. Schmader and Lickel (chap. 13, this volume), for example, study how people respond when others in their own (stigmatized) group confirm negative stereotypes commonly held about their group. They find that people who identify with their group or—using this chapter's terminology—include the ingroup in their self-concept, report feeling shame when observing the negative behavior of ingroup members. Stereotype-confirming behavior by an ingroup member can threaten self-expansion at multiple levels. First, a person who displays negative behavior that confirms commonly held stereotypes about one's group tarnishes one's view of one's ingroup and (because the ingroup is part of the self) can also affect negatively one's own self-concept. Second, stereotype-confirming behavior by an ingroup member may lower one's group's (and by extension one's own) attractiveness in the eyes of the majority group and thereby diminish one's chances of developing potentially rewarding relationships with members of the dominant group. Not surprisingly, Schmader and Lickel find that people tend to feel angry at and even distance themselves from the offending ingroup member as a result of this threat to the self.

How does a stigmatized person respond to self-expansion threat? If self-expansion is a truly fundamental human motive, people are unlikely to simply accept the denial of desired avenues for self-expansion. Instead, stigmatized individuals are likely to actively search for strategies that maximize the achievement of potential self-efficacy. Which strategy they choose is likely to depend on personal preferences or strengths, and the extent to which personal circumstances and a given situation may make a particular strategy easy or difficult to implement (Major, chap. 10, this volume; Miller, chap. 2, this volume; Swim & Thomas, chap. 6, this volume).

Faced with discrimination and the associated threat to their sense of self, a stigmatized person is hypothesized to invest in and maintain those relationships that provide continued and stable access to desired benefits. Benefits of self-expansion (access to desired resources, perspectives, and identities, and the resulting sense of potential self-efficacy) are available from relationships with ingroup as well as certain outgroup members. Thus, stigmatized people may respond to perceived exclusion and discrimination by (a) investing in their ingroup membership as well as their personal relationships with members of the ingroup, and thereby maximizing access to the expansion opportunities the ingroup provides; (b) attempting to establish, maintain, or improve the desired but threatened relationship with the dominant group and its members when these represent important opportunities for self-expansion; or (c) using a combination of these strategies. Undoubtedly, there are large individual differences in the extent to which people are able to confront threats to their self-expansion needs, and some individuals may compensate for barriers to self-expansion by, for example, focusing on the development of personal resources (e.g., career, education) or altogether leaving the threatening situation (e.g., dropping out of school). Because of this chapter's theoretical focus on motivation in close relationships, the present discussion emphasizes social ways of responding to exclusion.

Support for the idea that stigmatized individuals often focus on existing relationships can be found in the prejudice and discrimination literature. In response to perceived prejudice and discrimination by the majority group, members of devalued groups tend to self-segregate and intensify their identification with their ingroup (e.g., Branscombe et al., 1999; Chavira & Phinney, 1991; Dion, 1975; Sidanius, van Laar, Levin, & Sinclair, 2004), which in turn is related to well-being, lower depression (Arroyo & Zigler, 1995; Munford, 1994), higher self-esteem (e.g., Bat-Chava, 1994; Phinney, 1989; Rowley, Sellers, Chavous, & Smith, 1998), and more general psychological adjustment (Arroyo & Zigler, 1995). An emphasis on existing relationships and the ingroup reassures stigmatized people of their worth, reestablishes a sense of belonging and trust, and allows targets of discrimination to come to a shared understanding of the causes and consequences of discrimination. Strengthening one's ties to an accepting ingroup also serves to make the ingroup stronger; the more members commit energy and resources to a group the more powerful it will become. A stronger ingroup in turn will provide improved access to resources and other benefits and thus aid members' self-expansion needs. In support of these ideas, a longitudinal study of minority college students found that when these students joined ethnically oriented student organizations, their ethnic identification grew stronger and they became increasingly interested in political activism on behalf of their group (Sidanius et al., 2004). This activism was also associated with improved academic outcomes. Thus, self-segregation can be understood as a creative adaptation to a hostile social environment in which targets of prejudice can "achieve their goals despite the existence of prejudice" (Miller & Kaiser, 2001, p. 83; see also Major, chap. 10, this volume; Miller, chap. 2, this volume; Swim & Thomas, chap. 6, this volume). In sum, when confronted with prejudice and discrimination, a focus on one's ingroup provides important benefits to members of minority or stigmatized groups that are quite consistent with a self-expansion perspective: A strong minority ingroup offers access to important social and material resources (such as social support, legal aid, etc.), perspectives (a shared understanding of the experience of discrimination), and identities (a sense of belonging, a set of values) that are likely to enhance a person's sense of self-efficacy.

An alternate strategy to perceived self-expansion threat in situations in which the majority group's norms are not accepting of outsiders is for stigmatized individuals to seek out relationships with individual members of the majority group who may not be identified with these norms. Through a close relationship with a member of the excluding group, a stigmatized person may be able to develop a sense of trust and belonging at the institution, and may gain access to some of the resources, perspectives, and identities that the majority group provides (McLaughlin-Volpe, Mendoza-Denton, & Shelton, in press). Potentially self-expanding benefits of engaging in such a relationship are access to social and material resources (social support), being exposed to and perhaps adopting new perspectives (regarding, e.g., the college experience or future careers), trying on new identities (e.g., as a member of the larger university community), and as a result, perhaps developing multiple social identities. Finally, the social self-efficacy that develops as the result of developing successful relationships with members of the dominant group is itself an important resource in the quest for self-expansion (McLaughlin-Volpe et al., in press). Thus, forming a close relationship with a member of the dominant group may provide members of the stigmatized group with important new knowledge and perspectives, and may increase their confidence that they will be able to successfully navigate a world where many of the best jobs and other resources are controlled by the dominant group. Although the focus of this chapter is on the stigmatized partner within such a relationship, self–other inclusion or merging in close relationships is by definition mutual—thus, both partners are expected to benefit from the relationship.

McLaughlin-Volpe (2001) examined these ideas in a field study of minority students' college adjustment on a predominately White campus. In support of the idea that having close relationships with outgroup friends may have benefits for minority students that are consistent with self-expansion, she found that minority students who had a close White friend tended to be more identified with the institution and felt less alienated from the campus community. These students were also significantly more likely to indicate that they would choose the same university if they could make this choice again. These results held even when controlling for the total number of the participants' White friends and for the quality of their relationships with their same-group friends. Thus, the extent to which a White friend was included in the self uniquely predicted minority students' sense of belonging and whether or not they felt pride in being a student at their university (see also Mendoza-Denton, Page-Gould, & Pietrzak, chap. 8, this volume).

In sum, both strategies of coping with self-expansion threat—strengthening one's identification with a stigmatized ingroup and developing close relationships with members of the outgroup—can help people cope with discrimination and achieve their desire for self-expansion. Each strategy is likely to come with important benefits and some drawbacks. Ethnic identification, especially in conjunction with political activism, is likely to create a strong sense of belonging and can strengthen the ingroup, but it is unlikely to improve intergroup attitudes (see Sidanius et al., 2004). Close relationships with members of the outgroup may provide access to the outgroup's resources and improve intergroup attitudes, but may undermine the stigmatized person's standing in their own group. Furthermore, it is important to caution that relationships with members of the dominant group may under certain conditions be hazardous to a person's sense of self. The work of Sinclair and Huntsinger (chap. 12, this volume) provides an example of how the inclusion of an outgroup member in the self may lead to negative consequences for individuals who are motivated to form a relationship with a person who holds negative stereotypes about their group. Their program of research demonstrates that stigmatized individuals sometimes incorporate negative stereotypes about their group into their self-concepts in situations in which they interact with a powerful person who they believe holds these stereotypes. Presumably, participants in this study were willing to emphasize aspects of themselves that serve to establish and maintain a desired relationship in order to access the self-expanding benefits that the partner and the relationship might offer. Relationships between people belonging to different groups can thus be problematic when the partner who belongs to the dominant group rejects aspects of the stigmatized person's personal or social identity and/or when the stigmatized person feels that they may have to suppress or give up important aspects of their identity in order to become an attractive relationship partner. It is unlikely that true self-expansion and the associated sense of self-efficacy can result from such a relationship.

In sum, work such as the research program by Sinclair and Huntsinger suggests that it is important to investigate what aspects of a cross-group relationship will help or hinder self-expansion. It may be that a relationship's self-expansion potential depends importantly on whether the relationship is close, equitable, and characterized by mutual respect and appreciation (see also Tropp, chap. 9, this volume). Professionals who are interested in developing intervention strategies designed to enhance opportunities for the growth and development of stigmatized groups will have to keep in mind how central the quality of personal relationships is for self-expansion. In the next section of the chapter, potential interventions are discussed with respect to how institutions concerned with issues of social justice and equity between groups can help to create the kind of social environments that allow members of all groups to have optimal chances for learning and growth.

SUGGESTIONS FOR INTERVENTIONS: PROVIDING A CLIMATE THAT MAKES SELF-EXPANSION POSSIBLE

Several intervention strategies build on Allport's (1954) idea of the contact hypothesis and the structural conditions that promote the development of positive intergroup relations (see also Amir, 1976). From the perspective of the self-expansion model, two of Allport's conditions are likely to be promising avenues for intervention: First, elevating and equalizing the status of minority groups and their members and second, providing opportunities for positive and meaningful intergroup interactions are two strategies that would make mutually self-expanding relationships between members of minority and majority groups more likely. A climate in which one group is given more status or power than other groups implicitly carries the message that members of the lower status group are less valuable to the institution, a message that undermines their attractiveness as potential relationship partners. Unequal status between groups is also linked to prejudice and discrimination and thereby undermines minority students' trust in the institutions and its members (Tropp, 2003; Tropp, chap. 9, this volume).

Equal status relationships can be accomplished in schools by, for example, increasing the number of student organizations, clubs, teams, and activities, and acknowledging the extent to which they are all equally valued by the institution. Institutions in which a small number of exclusive groups have access to most of the resources are more likely to have environments that create intense competition for membership in these groups. One likely consequence of such environments is that many students are excluded from membership in these groups, with members of stigmatized groups being least likely to be selected for membership. On the other hand, an environment in which a large number of groups are all equally valued by the institution can provide most students with the desired opportunities for belonging and self-expansion and create an atmosphere in which the majority of students can achieve desired levels of self-efficacy.

As part of the recommended expansion of organizations and activities, multicultural institutions might also allow and encourage avenues for within-group self-expansion by, for example, supporting the creation of ethnic minority clubs and organizations. The social networks and sense of identity that such organizations provide are especially important for students who have experienced discrimination and need an environment in which they can connect with others who have had similar experiences.

The self-expansion model also suggests that a policy that communicates an appreciation of and respect for diversity may be preferable over a colorblind approach (see Allport's [1954] idea of authority sanction). A focus on diversity can aid self-expansion needs in at least two ways: First, as already discussed, a genuine appreciation of diverse groups within an institution is likely to result in a more equitable distribution of resources to these groups and will thereby provide more opportunities for membership in groups that provide valuable benefits and identities to their members. Second, members of diverse groups are likely to become more attractive relationship partners in each other's eyes when what they have to offer (e.g., each group's unique perspectives) is valued equally by the institution. A policy of support for diversity thus is likely to increase the development of close relationships across group boundaries. Finally, institutions that openly advertise that they value diversity make members of minority groups feel comfortable and produce significant increases in institutional trust (Purdie, Steele, Davies, & Crosby, 2001). Perceptions of the dominant group in turn are likely to become more positive and intergroup relations will be seen as less competitive.

In sum, institutions can increase the well-being of minority and stigmatized groups and provide important avenues for self-expansion by publicly supporting the development and existence of diversity in all its forms. This can be achieved by (a) recruiting a more diverse student body, (b) acknowledging the importance to the institution of a variety of groups, and (c) creating norms for appropriate behavior that emphasize the acceptance and appreciation of differences. This type of strategy would communicate to stigmatized groups that there is a place for them within the institution, that they belong to and are valued by the institution as much as other groups, and that they are free and encouraged to explore the opportunities that the institution provides. Self-expansion needs are met more easily in such an environment because it provides multiple and easily accessible opportunities for group membership and identification, which in turn encourage the development of close relationships within and between groups.

In addition to these more global approaches, institutions may also want to invest in training programs that enhance intergroup competence and increase the confidence needed to build relationships with others who are perceived to be different or threatening. Research by Mendoza-Denton et al. (2002; Mendoza-Denton, Page-Gould, & Pietrzak, chap. 8, this volume), for example, shows that minority students' fear of being rejected on the basis of their race or ethnicity, and the associated mistrust of members of the dominant group, is associated with an avoidance of White students and professors on campus. As a result, students who fear being rejected due to their race or ethnicity are unlikely to experience the positive interactions with members of the dominant group that could disconfirm their negative expectations. This is problematic because stigmatized students who feel uncomfortable building relationships with members of the dominant group are less likely to develop feelings of belonging vis-à-vis the institution and are more likely to give up in the face of adversity (McLaughlin-Volpe et al., in press). Likewise, White students who hold negative attitudes toward minority students find interactions with these students stressful and even threatening (Vorauer & Kumhyr, 2001). Recent research suggests that there may be important negative consequences to this kind of anxiety when intergroup contact is not avoidable: Prejudice can impair people's functioning on tasks requiring executive control (Richeson & Shelton, 2003) and negative emotions, more generally, are not conducive to learning and self-expansion (Fredrickson, 2001; Fredrickson & Branigan, in press). Thus, opportunities to experience positive cross-group relationships will over time reduce the stress and anxiety associated with prejudice and discrimination and free up considerable cognitive and emotional resources that can now be invested in the achievement of self-expansion.

CONCLUSION

This chapter is a first attempt to apply the self-expansion model to the study of stigma. The self-expansion model locates the reasons for our actions in a basic human motive to expand the self and achieve self-efficacy. As such, the model provides a novel and useful framework for understanding how people are affected by being stigmatized.

Examining the experience of stigma from the perspective of the self-expansion model emphasizes that being stigmatized affects people's access to desired relationships and resources, and in turn determines their self-concepts, expectations for future success, and sense of preparedness for life's challenges. An analysis of the cognitive, affective, and behavioral consequences of living with stigma results in a deeper understanding of the stigmatized person's life experiences, and is a fundamental first step in the development of effective intervention programs. Ultimately, it is hoped that some of the ideas presented in this chapter will be used to change social environments in ways that allow members of stigmatized groups an equal chance to fulfill their dreams and achieve their potential.

REFERENCES

Allport, G. (1954). *The nature of prejudice*. Reading, MA: Addison-Wesley.

Amir, Y. (1976). The role of intergroup contact in change of prejudice in race relations. In P. Katz (Ed.), *Towards the elimination of racism* (pp. 245–308). New York: Pergamon.

Aron, A., & Aron, E. N. (1986). *Love as the expansion of self: Understanding attraction and satisfaction*. New York: Hemisphere.

Aron, A., & Aron, E. N. (1996). Self and self-expansion in relationships. In G. J. O. Fletcher & J. Fitness (Eds.), *Knowledge structures in close relationships: A social psychological approach* (pp. 325–344). Mahwah, NJ: Lawrence Erlbaum Associates.

Aron, A., & Aron, E. N. (1997). Self-expansion motivation and including other in the self. In W. Ickes (Section Ed.) & S. Duck (Ed.), *Handbook of personal relationships* (2nd ed., Vol. 1, pp. 251–270). London: Wiley.

Aron, A., Aron, E. N., & Norman, C. (2001). Self-expansion model of motivation and cognition in close relationships and beyond. In M. Clark & G. Fletcher (Eds.), *Blackwell's handbook of social psychology, Vol. 2: Interpersonal processes*. Oxford: Blackwell Publishers.

Aron, A., Aron, E. N., Tudor, M., & Nelson, G. (1991). Close relationships as including other in the self. *Journal of Personality and Social Psychology, 60*, 241–253.

Aron, A., Dutton, D. G., Aron, E., & Iverson, A. (1989). Experiences of falling in love. *Journal of Social and Personal Relationships, 6*, 243–257.

Aron, A., & Fraley, B. (1999). Relationship closeness as including other in the self: Cognitive underpinnings and measures. *Social Cognition, 17*, 140–160.

Aron, A., & McLaughlin-Volpe, T. (2002). Including others in the self: Extensions to own and partner's group memberships. In M. Brewer & C. Sedikides (Eds.), *Individual self, relational self, and collective self: Partners, opponents, or strangers* (pp. 89–108). New York: Psychology Press.

Aron, A., Norman, C. C., & Aron, E. N. (1998). The self-expansion model and motivation. *Representative Research in Social Psychology, 22*, 1–13.

Aron, A., Paris, M., & Aron, E. N. (1995). Falling in love: Prospective studies of self-concept change. *Journal of Personality and Social Psychology, 69*, 1102–1112.

Aron, A., Steele, J., & Kashdan, T. (2002). *When opposites attract: A test of the self-expansion model*. Manuscript in preparation.

Arroyo, C. G., & Zigler, E. (1995). Racial identity, academic achievement, and the psychological well-being of economically disadvantaged adolescents. *Journal of Personality and Social Psychology, 69*, 903–914.

Bandura, A. (1977). Self-efficacy: Toward a unifying theory of behavioral change. *Psychological Review, 84*, 191–215.

Bat-Chava, Y. (1994). Group identification and self-esteem of deaf adults. *Personality and Social Psychology Bulletin, 20*, 494–502.

Baumeister, R. F., & Wotman, S. R. (1992). *Breaking hearts: The two sides of unrequited love*. New York: Guilford Press.

Branscombe, N. R., Schmitt, M. T., & Harvey, R. D. (1999). Perceiving pervasive discrimination among African Americans: Implications for group identification and well-being. *Journal of Personality and Social Psychology, 77*, 135–149.

Brown, R. J., & Wootton-Millward, L. (1993). Perceptions of group homogeneity during group formation and change. *Social Cognition, 11*, 126–149.

Chavira, V., & Phinney, J. S. (1991). Adolescents' ethnic identity, self-esteem, and strategies for dealing with ethnicity and minority status. *Hispanic Journal of Behavioral Sciences, 13*, 226–227.

Clark, M. S., & Mills, J. (1993). The difference between communal and exchange relationships: What it is and is not. *Personality and Social Psychology Bulletin, 19*, 684–691.

Crocker, J., Major, B., & Steele, C. (1998). Social stigma. In D. T. Gilbert, S. T. Fiske, & G. Lindzey (Eds.), *The handbook of social psychology* (4th ed., Vol. 2, pp. 364–392). New York: McGraw Hill.

Deci, E. L., & Ryan, R. (1987). The support of autonomy and the control of behavior. *Journal of Personality and Social Psychology, 53*, 1024–1037.

Devine, P. G., Evett, S. R., & Vasquez-Suson, K. A. (1996). Exploring the interpersonal dynamics of intergroup contact. In R. M. Sorrentino & E. T. Higgins (Eds.), *Handbook of motivation and cognition, Vol. 3: The interpersonal context* (pp. 423–464). New York: Guilford.

Dion, K. L. (1975). Women's reactions to discrimination from members of the opposite sex. *Journal of Research in Personality, 9*, 294–306.

Dittes, J. E., & Kelley, H. H. (1956). Effects of different conditions of acceptance upon conformity to group norms. *Journal of Abnormal and Social Psychology, 53*, 100–107.

Ellemers, N. (1993). The influence of socio-structural variables on identity management strategies. *European Review of Social Psychology, 4*, 27–57.

Fredrickson, B. L. (2001). The role of positive emotions in positive psychology: The broaden-and-build theory of positive emotions. *American Psychologist, 56*, 218–226.

Fredrickson, B. L., & Branigan, C. (2005). Positive emotions broaden the scope of attention and thought-action repertoires. *Cognition and Emotion, 19*, 313–332.

Gecas, V. (1989). Social psychology of self-efficacy. *American Sociological Review, 15*, 291–316.

Higgins, E. T., & Sorrentino, R. M. (1990). *Handbook of motivation and cognition: Foundations of social behavior.* New York: Guilford.

Hogg, M. A., & Turner, J. C. (1987). Intergroup behaviour, self stereotyping and the salience of social categories. *British Journal of Social Psychology, 26*, 325–340.

Kelley, H. H., Berscheid, E., Christensen, A., Harvey, J. H., Huston, T. L., Levinger, G., McClintock, E., Peplau, L. A., & Peterson, D. R. (1983). *Analyzing close relationships* (pp. 20–67). San Francisco: Freeman.

Luhtanen, R., & Crocker, J. (1992). A collective self-esteem scale: Self-evaluation of one's social identity. *Personality & Social Psychology Bulletin, 18*, 302–318.

Mashek, D. J., Aron, A., & Boncimino, M. (2003). Confusions of self with close others. *Personality & Social Psychology Bulletin, 29*, 382–392.

Maslow, A. H. (1970). *Motivation and personality.* New York: Harper & Row.

McGuire, W. J., & McGuire, C. V. (1988). Content and process in the experience of the self. In L. Berkowitz (Ed.), *Advances in experimental social psychology, Vol. 21: Social psychological studies of the self: Perspectives and programs* (pp. 97–144). San Diego, CA: Academic Press.

McLaughlin-Volpe, T. (2001, February). The self-expansion model: Extensions to ingroup identification. In R. Mendoza-Denton & G. Downey (Chairs), *Institutional and interpersonal trust in shaping minority experience in predominantly majority institutions.* Paper presented at the Society for Personality and Social Psychology (SPSP) Conference, San Antonio, TX.

McLaughlin-Volpe, T. (2002). *Contraction of self in response to social exclusion.* Unpublished data.

McLaughlin-Volpe, T., Aron, A., Wright, S. C., & Lewandowski, G. W. (2005). Exclusion of the self by close others and by groups: Implications of the self-expansion model. In D. Abrams, M. Hogg, & J. Marques (Eds.), *The social psychology of inclusion and exclusion* (pp. 113–134). New York: Psychology Press.

McLaughlin-Volpe, T., Mendoza-Denton, R., & Shelton, J. N. (in press). The experience of minority students at predominantly White universities: The role of cross-race friendships. In G. Downey, C. S. Dweck, J. Eccles, & C. Chatman (Eds.), *Social identity, coping, and life tasks.* New York: Russell Sage.

McLaughlin-Volpe, T., & Wright, S. C. (2002, July). The hidden rewards of cross-group friendships: Self-expansion across group membership. In R. González & A. Voci (Chairs), *Intergroup contact and prejudice reduction: Current development in theory and research.* Paper presented at the 13th General Meeting of the European Association of Experimental Social Psychology, San Sebastián, Spain.

Mendoza-Denton, R., Downey, G., Purdie, V. J., Davis, A., & Pietrzak, J. (2002). Sensitivity to status-based rejection: Implications for African American students' college experience. *Journal of Personality & Social Psychology, 83,* 896–918.

Miller, C. T., & Kaiser, C. R. (2001). A theoretical perspective on coping with stigma. *Journal of Social Issues, 57,* 73–92.

Munford, M. B. (1994). Relationship of gender, self-esteem, social class, and racial identity to depression in Blacks. *Journal of Black Psychology, 20,* 157–174.

Noel, J. G., Wann, D. L., & Branscombe, N. R. (1995). Peripheral ingroup membership status and public negativity towards outgroups. *Journal of Personality and Social Psychology, 68,* 127–137.

Oakes, P. J., Haslam, A., Morrison, B., & Grace, D. (1995). Becoming an ingroup: Reexamining the impact of familiarity on perceptions of group homogeneity. *Social Psychology Quarterly, 58,* 52–61.

Omoto, A. M., & Gunn, D. O. (1994, May). *The effect of relationship closeness on encoding and recall for relationship-irrelevant information.* Paper presented at the May Meeting of the International Network on Personal Relationships, Iowa City, IA.

Phinney, J. S. (1989). Stages of ethnic identity development in minority group adolescents. *Journal of Early Adolescence, 9,* 34–49.

Purdie, V. J., Steele, C. M., Davies, P. G., & Crosby, J. R. (2001, August). *The business of diversity: Minority trust within organizational cultures.* Paper presented at the annual meeting of the American Psychological Association, San Francisco, CA.

Reis, H. T., & Shaver, P. (1988). Intimacy as interpersonal process. In S. Duck (Ed.), *Handbook of personal relationships: Theory, research and interventions* (pp. 367–389). Chichester, England: Wiley.

Richeson, J. A., & Shelton, J. N. (2003). When prejudice does not pay: Effects of interracial contact on executive functioning. *Psychological Science, 14,* 287–290.

Rowley, S. J., Sellers, R. M., Chavous, T. M., & Smith, M. A. (1998). The relationship between racial identity and self-esteem in African-American college and high school students. *Journal of Personality and Social Psychology, 74,* 715–724.

Sachdev, I., & Bourhis, R. Y. (1991). Power and status differentials in minority and majority group relations. *European Journal of Social Psychology, 21,* 1–24.

Sidanius, J., van Laar, C., Levin, S., & Sinclair, S. (2004). Ethnic enclaves and the dynamics of social identity on the college campus: The good, the bad, and the ugly. *Journal of Personality and Social Psychology, 87,* 96–110.

Simon, B., Glaessner-Bayerl, B., & Stratenwerth, I. (1991). Stereotyping and self-stereotyping in a natural intergroup context: The case of heterosexual and homosexual men. *Social Psychology Quarterly, 54,* 252–266.

Simon, B., & Hamilton, D. L. (1994). Self-stereotyping and social context: The effect of relative in-group size and in-group status. *Journal of Personality and Social Psychology, 66,* 699–711.

Smith, E. R. (2002). Overlapping mental representations of self and group: Evidence and implications. In J. P. Forgas & K. D. Williams (Eds.), *The social self: Cognitive, interpersonal and intergroup perspectives* (pp. 21–35). New York: Psychology Press.

Smith, E., Coats, S., & Walling, D. (1999). Overlapping mental representations of self, in-group, and partner: Further response time evidence and a connectionist model. *Personality and Social Psychology Bulletin, 25,* 873–882.

Smith, E., & Henry, S. (1996). An ingroup becomes part of the self: Response time evidence. *Personality and Social Psychology Bulletin, 22,* 635–642.

Snoek, J. D. (1962). Some effects or rejection upon attraction to a group. *Journal of Abnormal and Social Psychology, 64*, 175–182.

Spears, R., Doosje, B., & Ellemers, N. (1997). Self-stereotyping in the face of threats to group status and distinctiveness: The role of group identification. *Personality and Social Psychology Bulletin, 23*, 538–553.

Taylor, S. E., Neter, E., & Wayment, H. A. (1995). Self-evaluative processes. *Personality and Social Psychology Bulletin, 21*, 1278–1287.

Tropp, L. R. (2003). The psychological impact of prejudice: Implications for intergroup contact. *Group Processes and Intergroup Relations, 6*, 131–149.

Tropp, L. R., & Wright, S. C. (2001). Ingroup identification as inclusion of ingroup in the self. *Personality and Social Psychology Bulletin, 27*, 585–600.

Turner, J. C., Hogg, M. A., Oakes, P. J., Reicher, S. D., & Wetherell, M. S. (1987). *Rediscovering the social group. A self-categorization theory.* Oxford, England: Basil Blackwell.

van Laar, C. (2001). Declining optimism in ethnic minority students: The role of attributions and self-esteem. In F. Salili, C. Chiu, & Y. Hong (Eds.), *Student motivation: The culture and context of learning* (pp. 79–104). New York: Kluwer Academic/Plenum.

Vorauer, J. D., & Kumhyr, S. M. (2001). Is this about you or me? Self- versus other-directed judgments and feelings in response to intergroup interaction. *Personality and Social Psychology Bulletin, 27*, 706–709.

Walster, E., Aronson, V., Abrahams, D., & Rottman, L. (1966). Importance of physical attractiveness in dating behavior. *Journal of Personality and Social Psychology, 4*, 508–516.

White, R. W. (1959). Motivation reconsidered: The concept of confidence. *Psychological Review, 66*, 297–333.

Worchel, S., Coutant-Sassic, D., & Grossman, M. (1992). A developmental approach to group dynamics: A model and illustrative research. In S. Worchel, W. Wood, & J. Simpson (Eds.), *Group process and productivity* (pp. 181–202). Newbury Park, CA: Sage.

Wright, S. C., Aron, A., & Tropp, L. R. (2002). Including others (and groups) in the self: Self-expansion and intergroup relations. In J. P. Forgas & K. D. Williams (Eds.), *The social self: Cognitive, interpersonal, and intergroup perspectives* (pp. 343–363). New York: Psychology Press.

CHAPTER

12

The Interpersonal Basis of Self-Stereotyping

Stacey Sinclair
Jeff Huntsinger
University of Virginia

Members of stereotyped groups live in a social world in which cultural stereotypes often influence the way others see them and behave toward them (Crocker, Major, & Steele, 1998). One consequence of this state of affairs is that stereotype targets are regularly in the position of interacting with other social actors who hold, or are perceived to hold, stereotypical attitudes about their group. Classic perspectives on the social basis of self-understanding such as symbolic interactionism suggest that self-stereotyping (i.e., application of cultural stereotypes to the self) is an unavoidable consequence of these stereotype-tinged social interactions (e.g., Allport, 1954; Cartwright, 1950; Cooley, 1902; Mead, 1934). According to these approaches, the self is derived from internalization of the way peoples' social interaction partners view them. In this analysis, stereotype targets simply absorb cultural beliefs about their group into their own self-concepts whenever they interact with individuals who subscribe to these stereotypic beliefs. Because stereotypes pervade society, this analysis suggests that self-stereotyping is a highly prevalent, perhaps ubiquitous, phenomenon. Our research takes a decidedly different approach to understanding the social basis of self-stereotyping. Although we agree that self-stereotyping can be a product of one's social relationships, our research suggests that it is far from unavoidable. Rather, self-stereotyping is situation specific and contingent on the perceived views of salient social interaction partners and the desire to get along with them.

THE SOCIAL BASIS OF THE SELF

Psychologists recognized long ago that the individuals people interact with shape self-understanding. Specifically, symbolic interactionists argued that intersubjectivity with those around us was a critical element in the development and maintenance of self-understanding (see Shrauger & Schoeneman, 1979; Stryker & Statham, 1985, for reviews). For example, Mead (1934) proposed that self-concepts are formed and continually regulated by adopting the perspectives others have about the self. Similarly, Cooley (1902) contended that self-understanding is predicated on the way individuals think others understand them. In essence, these theorists argued that self-evaluations were situationally constructed such that they corresponded with the evaluations of others.

Recent research on relational schemas (Baldwin, 1992; Baldwin & Sinclair, 1996) and transference (Andersen & Chen, 2002; Chen & Andersen, 1999) renewed focus on the interpersonal basis of self-understanding. According to these approaches, self-evaluations are shaped by the perceived views of individuals with whom one has developed a long-term significant relationship. Influenced by research on social cognition, they posit that aspects of the self become associated with significant others. When reminded of a given significant other, self-evaluations corresponding to the way one typically behaves with that person come to the forefront of working memory, thus dictating how people see themselves at that moment.

Our research is motivated by shared reality theory (Hardin & Conley, 2001; Hardin & Higgins, 1996), which unites classic perspectives' focus on intersubjectivity, modern research on communication (e.g., Higgins, 1992; Krauss & Fussell, 1996), and social cognitive underpinnings. Shared reality theory suggests that all social beliefs, including beliefs about the self, are situationally derived via intersubjectivity with other social actors. Specifically, this perspective contends that social bonds and social beliefs are maintained through perceived consensus or "shared reality." The establishment of specific shared realities in particular social interactions both creates social bonds and structures understanding of the world. In other words, social beliefs are established and maintained to the degree that social interaction partners are thought to share them. In addition, social bonds are established and maintained to the degree that participants in social interactions believe they have achieved mutually shared understanding of relevant beliefs and experiences (Hardin & Conley, 2001; Hardin & Higgins, 1996).

Affiliative Social-Tuning Hypothesis

These basic assertions yield two hypotheses that guide the research discussed in this chapter. First, because achieving shared reality is thought to create social bonds, it follows that people should experience a heightened need to develop shared reality with another social actor to the extent that they are motivated to get along with this person. One way for individuals to achieve this is to "tune" their social beliefs, including beliefs about the self, toward the views of the other person when affiliative motivation is high. We refer to this as the *affiliative social-tuning hypothesis*.

Although our research on self-stereotyping is the first to expressly test the affiliative social-tuning hypothesis with respect to self-evaluations, there is evidence of affiliative social-tuning of other social beliefs (e.g., Chen, Shechter, & Chaiken, 1996; Davis & Rusbult, 2001; McCann & Hancock, 1983; McCann & Higgins, 1992). For example, Higgins & McCann (1984) found that the descriptions of an individual provided by people who valued positive interactions with superiors (i.e., "high authoritarians") corresponded with the ostensible views of a high-status audience, but not a low-status audience. In other words, these individuals experienced attitude convergence with superiors, whom they care about, but not inferiors, whom they do not care about. Sinclair and colleagues (in press-b) also found that even automatic attitudes about others were subject to affiliative social tuning. We showed that people who interacted with a likable experimenter shifted their automatic ethnic attitudes toward the experimenter's ostensible attitudes, but people who interacted with a rude experimenter did not experience commensurate attitude shift (see also Lowery, Hardin & Sinclair, 2001).

Domain Relevance Hypothesis

In every day social interaction, individuals that engender high affiliative motivation may espouse many social beliefs. Drawing on the communication literature (Higgins, 1992; Krauss & Fussell, 1996), shared reality theory also provides some guidance as to which of these beliefs is most likely to form the basis of one's attempts to create shared reality via social tuning. One source of this guidance is the *domain relevance hypothesis*. It states that a social belief that is under negotiation will respond to the other social actor's view that is most local or specific to it. For example, one could know another person's views of people in general, people from your town and you as an individual. Although each of these views is potentially relevant to the self, attempts to achieve shared reality regarding the self with that person should entail adjusting to his or her views about you as an individual, as doing so yields the best chance of creating mutual understanding. The less precise match between the self and what this person thinks of people in general or people from your town has greater potential for slippage. If this person thinks you are different from the aforementioned groups, adjusting the self to conform to his or her beliefs about these groups will actually violate the person's expectations, decrease mutual understanding, and likely make the social interaction less pleasant (Krauss & Fussell, 1996; Orive, 1988).

One can see the critical role of intersubjectivity with others that characterized classic perspectives on the social basis of the self, such as symbolic interactionism, in the notion of social tuning presented in these hypotheses. Individuals are thought to adjust beliefs that are relevant to important social interactions (including beliefs about the self) to the ostensible beliefs of other people involved in these interactions to achieve *shared reality*, the state of perceived mutual understanding (i.e., intersubjectivity). However, unlike recent perspectives on the social basis of the self that focus on the role of significant others in constructing one's self-understanding, our perspective suggests that both significant others and novel social actors who are the object of situationally derived affiliative motivation can elicit social tuning. From this perspective, the phenomenological sense of a stable self that most individuals enjoy is a product of two things: stable environmental and motivational input. People experience the self as stable because they tend to interact with similar types of people (Andersen, Reznik & Manzella, 1996), frequent similar types of environments, and hold long-term social roles (e.g. occupational, familial) that structure their interpersonal interactions.

The potential for dramatic flexibility of implicit and explicit attitudes as a function of the perceived views in one's interpersonal context and affiliative motives proposed by shared reality theory is predicated on connectionist models of mental representation (Smith, 1996). Connectionist models suggest that information is not contained in inert nodes; but rather, distributed across an array of processing units connected by unidirectional links. A given mental state is a pattern of activation across these units and links that best fit the amalgam of current input. As such, all mental representation is highly flexible and dependent on immediate experiences, motives, and so forth. Thus, classic notions of intersubjectivity dynamically structuring social beliefs feasibly combine with modern notions of cognitive representation.

THE INTERPERSONAL BASIS OF SELF-STEREOTYPING

Given that stereotypes are widely shared cultural beliefs that influence how stereotype targets are evaluated (Devine & Elliot, 1995; Stangor & Lange, 1994), and stereotype targets are well aware of that fact that stereotypes may influence how they are perceived (Crocker et al., 1998), it is likely that stereotype targets face a great many situations in which they must interact with individuals who hold, or are presumed to hold, stereotypes of their group. How does being subject to this predicament affect the way in which stereotype targets see themselves? The affiliative social-tuning hypothesis and the domain relevance hypothesis make clear predictions regarding the impact of this predicament. According to the affiliative social-tuning hypothesis, the stereotype-relevant evaluations of others will translate into self-evaluations and corresponding behavior when affiliative motivation is high as opposed to low. In other words, stereotype targets' self-evaluations will become more stereotype consistent when they possess high as opposed to low affiliative motivation toward another social actor perceived to hold stereotype consistent attitudes about their social group. In contrast, stereotype targets' self-evaluations will become less stereotype consistent when they possess high as opposed to low affiliative motivation toward another social actor believed to hold stereotype-inconsistent attitudes. The domain relevance hypothesis suggests that once individuals' stereotype-relevant self-evaluations are under negotiation, they will tune to the beliefs that are most closely related to them. In other words, if someone is privy to another social actor's views of themselves as individuals and stereotype-relevant views of members of their social group, that person's self-evaluations should tune to the social actor's views of themselves as individuals because these beliefs are more relevant to the self than are beliefs about members of the group to which one belongs, and are therefore more likely to create mutual understanding. In the remainder of this chapter, we discuss several experiments that examine the veracity of these predictions.

Affiliative Social-Tuning Experiments

To examine the affiliative social-tuning hypothesis, we manipulated whether participants believed their interaction partner held stereotype consistent or inconsistent attitudes of their social group in three experiments. We also manipulated (Experiments 1 and 3) or measured (Experiment 2) participants' affiliative motivation toward that person. In each of these experiments, we found clear and consistent support for our predictions (see Sinclair, Huntsinger, Skorinko, & Hardin, in press, for a more detailed presentation of these results).

In Experiment 1, we tested the affiliative social-tuning hypothesis with respect to self-stereotyping on gender-relevant traits. Eighty-three participants (50 women and 33 men) participated in the experiment. Participants were greeted by a female experimenter and informed that the experiment concerned the transmission of rumors. Participants then completed a brief demographics questionnaire; among the questions was an item asking the date of their birthday. At this point, participants were assigned to one of two affiliative motivation conditions. We employed a twofold manipulation of affiliative motivation based on previous work (Griffitt, 1968; Kelley & Thibaut, 1978; Miller, Downs, & Prentice, 1998). Participants were told that they were going to have a relatively long interaction with someone who happened to share their birthday (high affiliative motivation) or a short interaction with someone whose birthday differed from theirs (low affiliative motivation).

After this, participants were told they would read some information allegedly completed by the other participant in order to give participants some information about this person. This information constituted the manipulation of the ostensible group attitudes of the interaction partner (always female). Embedded within this packet of information was a questionnaire, "Attitudes About Women," that was designed to convey to participants that their imminent social interaction partner had stereotype-consistent or inconsistent attitudes about women. For example, in the stereotype-consistent condition, the questionnaire indicated that her social interaction partner strongly agreed with the statement, "Women should be cherished and protected by men." In contrast, in the stereotype-inconsistent condition, her partner purportedly agreed with the statement, "Women often miss out on good jobs due to sexual discrimination."

After being given time to peruse the questionnaire, participants were informed that they would complete several questions about themselves that their partner would also have the opportunity to view. The dependent measure in this experiment was the degree to which participants rated ten traits stereotypically associated with women (calm, caring, compassionate, faithful, attractive, sensitive, sweet, sad, shy, weak) and nine traits stereotypically associated with men (athletic, competitive, confident, outspoken, intelligent, strong, aggressive, arrogant, insensitive) as indicative of the self on this questionnaire. To create an index of stereotypicality of self-evaluation, we transformed each item into a *z* score within gender, separately averaged the female and male traits, and created a difference score by subtracting the stereotypically male traits from the stereotypically female traits. Higher numbers indicated self-evaluations that were more consistent with the cultural stereotype of females.

If the affiliative social tuning hypothesis is correct, we should have found that female participants' self-evaluations were more stereotype consistent when they had high as opposed to low affiliative motivation toward an interaction partner who was believed to hold stereotype-consistent attitudes about their group. The opposite pattern of self-evaluations should have emerged when the interaction partner was believed to hold stereotype-inconsistent attitudes: female participants' self-evaluations should have been less stereotype consistent when they had high versus low affiliative motivation toward their interaction partner. Furthermore, we did not expect male participants to evidence similar shifts in self-evaluation because their interaction partner's attitudes about women were less germane or relevant to their self-views.

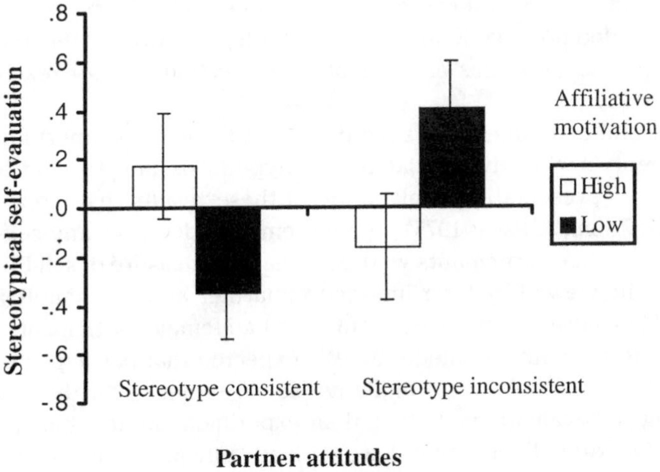

FIG. 12.1. Female participants' stereotypicality of self-evaluations as a function of affiliative motivation and the ostensible attitudes of an interaction partner in Experiment 1. Note: Higher numbers indicate more stereotype consistent self-evaluations. Adapted from Sinclair, Huntsinger, Skorinko, & Hardin, *Journal of Personality and Social Psychology*, in press. Copyright © by the American Psychological Association. Reprinted with permission.

To test these predictions, we ran a 2 (partner attitudes) × 2 (affiliative motivation) × 2 (gender) between participants ANOVA on participants' responses to the self-evaluation measure. As expected, the only reliable effect was a three-way interaction between partner attitudes, affiliative motivation, and participant gender, $F(1, 75) = 6.11$, $p = .02$, $\eta^2 = .08$. To more fully explore this three-way interaction, we conducted separate ANOVAs on female and male participants' responses to the measure of self-evaluation.

First, as predicted and consistent with the affiliative social tuning hypothesis, the only effect to emerge for female participants was a two-way interaction between partner attitudes and affiliative motivation, $F(1, 46) = 6.97$, $p = .01$, $\eta^2 = .13$ (see Fig. 12.1). As hypothesized, when the ostensible attitudes of the interaction partner were stereotype consistent, women's self-evaluations were more stereotype consistent when they possessed high affiliative motivation than low affiliative motivation toward that partner ($p = .04$, one-tailed[1]). The opposite pattern of self-evaluations was found when the ostensible attitudes of the interaction partner were stereotype inconsistent; women's self-evaluations were more stereotype inconsistent when they possessed high affiliative motivation than low affiliative motivation (p

[1]All simple effects tests were one-tailed due to strong directional hypotheses (Abelson, 1995).

= .03, one-tailed). Furthermore, investigation of male participants' responses yielded no reliable main effects (both *p's* > .13) and the interaction between partner attitudes and affiliative motivation did not reach significance, $p = .29$.

In a second experiment, we sought to provide further support for shared reality theory's affiliative social tuning hypothesis and to gain leverage against a self-presentation explanation of these results (e.g., Jones & Pittman, 1982; Zanna & Pack, 1975). In an attempt to decrease any self-presentational concerns, participants were told that the measure of self-evaluation would not be viewed by their interaction partner and was simply for "our records." Furthermore, in Experiment 2 we had female participants ($n = 75$) actually interact with a confederate. We expected that participants' behavior would also be subject to affiliative social tuning, with their behavior mimicking self-evaluations. Rather than experimentally manipulating affiliative motivation in Experiment 2, we took advantage of naturally occurring differences in the extent to which one wishes to form (or avoid) interpersonal relationships. To accomplish this, we measured participants' sense of loneliness or sense of being socially overburdened via two questionnaires. Participants were assigned to either a loneliness or socially overburdened scale. From scores on these two scales, we created high (either lonely or not socially overburdened) and low (either not lonely or socially overburdened) affiliative motivation groups. Similar to Experiment 1, participants were informed that the experiment dealt with first impressions and they would get a chance to view some information about their interaction partner (always male) and would then get a chance to interact with this person. First, participants were given the opportunity to view their interaction partner's answers to a series of questions. This constituted the ostensible group attitudes of the interaction partner and was the same as that in the first experiment. Next, participants were given the measure of affiliative motivation already discussed in text. After participants completed this measure, the experimenter claimed that she forgot to have them complete a background questionnaire earlier in the experiment. This background questionnaire was for the experimenter's files and their partner would not view their answers to these items. The measure of self-evaluation was contained within this questionnaire. By making the measure of self-evaluation not tied to the interaction with their partner in any way (i.e., this person would never view their answers), we sought to minimize participants' self-presentational concerns when completing this measure. The items that comprised this measure were similar to the series of stereotypically female and stereotypically male traits as those used in the first experiment. After completing these items, participants commenced with an unstructured interaction with their interaction partner, actually a male confederate blind to the experimental condition. Following the interaction, the confederate rated the stereotypicality of participants' behavior, with higher numbers indicating greater stereotype-consistent behavior than stereotype-inconsistent behavior enacted during the course of the interaction. Predictions for both participants' behavior and self-evaluation were the same as those in Experiment 1.

To test these predictions, we conducted a 2 (partner attitudes) × 2 (affiliative motivation) between participants ANOVA on participants' behavior as rated by the confederate. The only reliable effect to emerge from this analysis was the predicted interaction between partner attitudes and affiliative motivation, $F(1, 64) = 6.15$, $p = .02$, $\eta^2 = .09$ (see Fig. 12.2). Consistent with the affiliative social-tuning hypothesis, when the interaction partner's ostensible attitudes about women were stereotype consistent, participants' behavior was more stereotype consistent when they possessed high affiliative motivation than low affiliative motivation toward that partner ($p = .04$, one-tailed). This pattern was reversed when the ostensible attitudes of the interaction partner were stereotype inconsistent, with participants' behavior being more stereotype inconsistent in the high affiliative motivation condition than the low affiliative motivation condition ($p = .05$, one-tailed). In addition, we replicated the same pattern of self-evaluation as that found

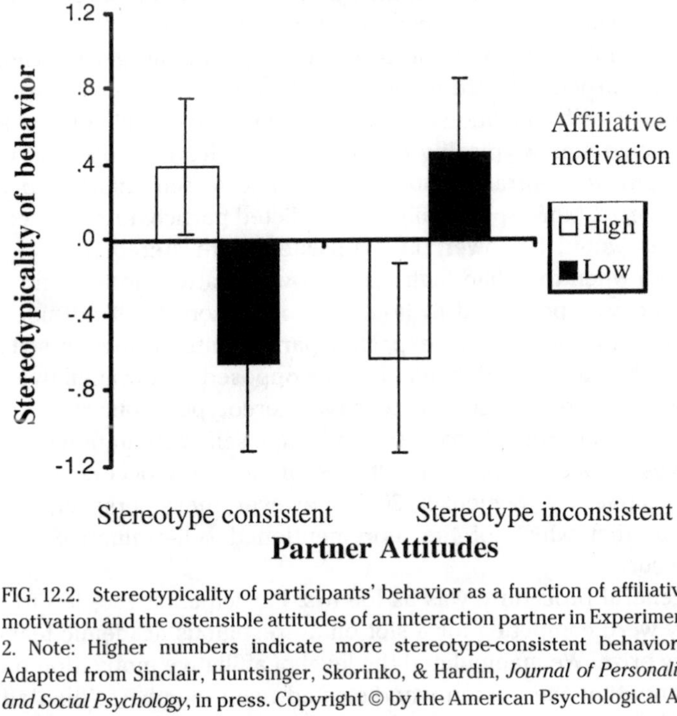

FIG. 12.2. Stereotypicality of participants' behavior as a function of affiliative motivation and the ostensible attitudes of an interaction partner in Experiment 2. Note: Higher numbers indicate more stereotype-consistent behaviors. Adapted from Sinclair, Huntsinger, Skorinko, & Hardin, *Journal of Personality and Social Psychology*, in press. Copyright © by the American Psychological Association. Reprinted with permission.

in Experiment 1 [Interaction, $F(1, 71) = 5.88$, $p = .02$, $\eta^2 = .08$]. Consistent with the affiliative social-tuning hypothesis, when the interaction partner's ostensible attitudes about women were stereotype consistent, participants' self-evaluations were more stereotype consistent when they possessed high affiliative motivation ($M = .165$) than low affiliative motivation ($M = -.244$) toward that partner ($p = .05$, one-tailed). This pattern was reversed when the ostensible attitudes of the interaction partner were stereotype inconsistent, with participants' self-evaluations being more stereotype inconsistent in the high affiliative motivation condition ($M = -.266$) than the low affiliative motivation condition ($M = .172$; $p = .04$, one-tailed).

In Experiment 3, we wanted to generalize these findings to another stereotyped group (e.g., African Americans, $n = 29$), another type of stereotype relevant self-view (i.e., academic self-evaluation), and gain further leverage against a self-presentation explanation of previous results. Because the predominant stereotype about African Americans is that they are intellectually inferior (Devine & Elliot, 1995), this allowed us to set up a situation in which we could pit two motives against one another. To do this, we created a situation in which participants competed to gain entrance into a prestigious academic team and earn a monetary prize. If strategic self-presentation is guiding participants' responses, then we should find inflated academic self-evaluations in all conditions because this situation calls out for a maximization of academic self-evaluation to make the team and get the money. In contrast, if participants are guided by affiliative social tuning, we should find academic self-evaluations varying as a function of affiliative motivation and perceived stereotypicality of partner attitudes regardless of whether this would thwart entrance into the team and lessen chances to win the monetary prize. More specifically, we predicted participants' academic self-evaluations would be lower (i.e., consistent with stereotypes of African Americans) when they had high versus low affiliative motivation toward a person who was perceived to hold stereotype-consistent attitudes about their group. In contrast, we expected participants' academic self-evaluations to be higher when they had high as opposed to low affiliative motivation toward someone believed to have stereotype-inconsistent attitudes about their group. Some broad conceptions of self-presentation do not limit themselves to postulating that self-presentation only occurs to make one appear positive (e.g., Schlenker, 2003); however, these perspectives are unable to predict which of the aforementioned self-evaluative responses would occur.

The general procedure was as follows. Participants were led to believe that they were competing for a slot on a prestigious academic team and a monetary prize. We manipulated the level of affiliative motivation by telling participants that the person who selected team members (high affiliative motivation) or another prospective member of the team (low affiliative motivation) was next door, would view their materials, and they would later interact with this person. After being told this information, participants were informed that prior to interacting with this person, they would be given some information about him. This constituted the manipulation of ostensible group attitudes. In one case, this person was described as an economics major who liked classic rock, played golf, and wanted to be a corporate lawyer (stereotype-consistent attitudes condition). In the other condition, this person was described as a sociology major that liked hip-hop music, volunteered at a local charity, and wanted to be a civil-rights attorney (stereotype-inconsistent attitudes condition). The same picture of a Euro-American male accompanied both descriptions. Other generic information common to both descriptions was used to lessen suspicion and to flesh out the descriptions. Pretesting determined that African Americans would indeed assume the former person to have more stereotype-consistent views than the latter person. After hearing the descriptions, participants were handed a questionnaire containing the main dependent measure and informed that their answers to this questionnaire would be used to determine entrance onto the academic team. The dependent measure was Steele and Aronson's (1995) three-item measure of academic investment. The items were: "How would you rate your overall academic ability?" (1 = *not good at all* to 7 = *very good*), "How much do you value academics?" (1 = *not very much* to 7 = *very much*), and "How important are academics to you?" (1 = *not very important* to 7 = *very important*), $\alpha = .77$. To be consistent with the two previous experiments, we reverse-scored participants' responses to each item and transformed participants' responses to each item into z scores, averaging all three to create an index of self-evaluation, with higher numbers representing more negative, stereotype-consistent academic self-evaluations than lower numbers.

To test these predictions, we submitted the measure of academic self-evaluation to a 2 (partner attitudes) × 2 (affiliative motivation) between participants ANOVA. As can be seen in Fig. 12.3, the predicted interaction was obtained, $F(1, 23) = 7.25$, $p = .01$, $\eta^2 = .24$, controlling for participants' math and verbal SAT scores. In support of shared reality theory's affiliative social-tuning hypothesis, we found that when participants believed their interaction partner held stereotype-consistent attitudes of African Americans, their academic self-evaluations were more negative (i.e., more stereotype consistent) when they had high as opposed to low affiliative motivation toward him ($p = .06$, one-tailed). This pattern of academic self-evaluations is striking given that participants actually rated themselves as less academically talented to the very person who would be choosing members of the academic team. In addition, the opposite pattern of academic self-evaluations emerged when the ostensible attitudes of this person were stereotype inconsistent. In this case, African Americans' academic self-evaluations

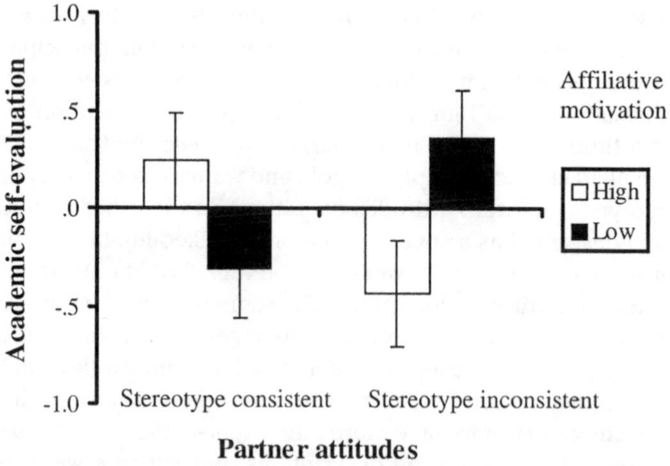

FIG. 12.3. African Americans' academic self-evaluations as a function of affiliative motivation and the ostensible attitudes of an interaction partner in Experiment 3. Note: Higher numbers indicate more stereotype consistent self-evaluations. Adapted from Sinclair, Huntsinger, Skorinko, & Hardin, *Journal of Personality and Social Psychology*, in press. Copyright © by the American Psychological Association. Reprinted with permission.

were higher (i.e., less stereotype consistent) when participants had high as opposed to low affiliative motivation toward him (p = .02, one-tailed).

Across all three experiments, two stereotype targets, two manipulations of ostensible group attitudes of another social actor, and various manipulations (and measures) of affiliative motivation we found strong and consistent evidence for the veracity of the affiliative social-tuning hypothesis. In sum, we found that stereotype targets' self-evaluations and behavior varied as a function of affiliative motivation and the perceived stereotype relevant attitudes of their interaction partner. What these experiments demonstrate is that self-stereotyping is neither unavoidable nor simply the direct result of stereotype targets internalizing the beliefs of those people with whom they interact. Social interactions can act to promote self-stereotyping or to attenuate self-stereotyping.

Furthermore, it seems that participants' self-views were genuinely changing as opposed to simply being strategically presented to make a positive impression. First, in Experiment 2, participants' responses on the self-evaluation measure were completely confidential and would not be viewed by their interaction partner, minimizing the extent to which participants would be motivated to engage in strategic self-presentation. Second, Experiment 3 directly pitted strategic self-presentational goals against affiliative social-tuning goals. In this experiment we created a situation in which participants, if guided by self-presentation, should have presented themselves in a positive light across all conditions to accomplish the goal of attaining entrance onto the academic team and the monetary reward associated with entrance on the team. However, this was not the case; participants' self-evaluations reflected processes of affiliative social tuning.

Domain Relevance Experiments: Self-Stereotyping and Exceptions to the Rule

As discussed earlier (see also Huntsinger & Sinclair, 2004), an additional unique prediction derived from shared reality theory is the *domain relevance hypothesis* (Hardin & Conley, 2001). This hypothesis suggests that when confronted with multiple applicable views on which to construct a shared understanding with another person, an individual will choose to social tune toward only those views that will lead to the development of the most precise shared understanding with this person. That is, they will choose the other social actor's belief that is most closely related to the belief under negotiation. This hypothesis can help us understand how stereotype targets contend with conflicts between how a person sees his or her group and how this person sees him or her as an individual. For example, stereotype targets may not always encounter a person who sees him or her through the lens of a group stereotype; rather, this person may see him or her as an exception to the rule, as being different from the rest of the members of a particular group (i.e., women, African Americans, etc.).

Perceivers are relatively adept at categorizing apparently stereotype-disconfirming individuals as exceptions to the rule (e.g., Allport, 1954; Hewstone, 1994). What this suggests is that stereotype targets may encounter individuals in their social environment who, for whatever reason, see them as different from other members of the group. This mismatch between group-individual attitudes could take many forms, with a person being seen as an exception to a more-or-less stereotypical image of the group. For example, someone with traditional attitudes about women could think that a woman he is interacting with is agentic, or someone with nontraditional attitudes about women could think that a woman he is interacting with is quite communal. These individual-level perceptions need not be data driven in any fashion or correspond to how a person actually sees him or herself. For example, a person may erroneously conclude that Jane is quite a good leader based on company rumor or some random first encounter he has with her at the company softball game last weekend.

How will a stereotype target (i.e., a woman) respond to this discrepancy? One possibility is that the attitudes about the group will exert more influence on a woman's self-evaluation than attitudes about her as an individual. For example, to the extent that being seen as different from her gender group makes a woman feel distinct from this valued social identity, this feeling of distinctiveness may then motivate a need to reaffirm that identity. One means of accomplishing this goal would be to see oneself as highly similar to the group (i.e., self-stereotype; Pickett, Bonner, & Coleman, 2002). In addition, self-categorization theory (Turner, 1987) implies that simply making a particular social identity and the stereotypes associated with this identity salient may induce stereotype-consistent self-evaluation (Hogg & Turner, 1987).

Although either of these alternatives is possible, shared reality theory proposes a decidedly different resolution to these group–individual mismatches. Based on the domain relevance hypothesis, it is expected that a person will seek to develop shared reality about the self based on the attitudes most closely related to the self available within a particular social interaction. In this case, although both this person's individual and group attitudes are potentially applicable to the self, the individual level attitudes about the self represent the most local or domain specific views on which to construct her self-evaluation with this person. Social tuning to the group-level attitudes would not serve her goal to develop shared reality about the self with this person, given that these are inconsistent with how this person specifically views her. Such a mismatch would not facilitate the development of shared reality or social bonds with this person (see Huntsinger & Sinclair, 2004, for a detailed discussion of the domain relevance hypothesis).

In Experiments 4 and 5, we (Huntsinger & Sinclair, 2004) tested the domain relevance hypothesis by examining the affiliative social tuning of women's self-evaluations in response to being confronted with group–individual mismatches of another social actor's attitudes and the level of affiliative motivation present within the interaction. Affiliative motivation was manipulated by varying whether the participant was in a position of low power (high affiliative motivation; they were being chosen, or not chosen, by a male confederate to become members of an interesting discussion group), or equal power (low affiliative motivation; the male confederate was simply a research assistant of no consequence to participants) in relation to another person. To manipulate the group attitudes of another social actor, we created a situation in which participants ostensibly overheard a conversation between a male confederate and a female experimenter, in which the confederate made a series of comments about women in general and a series of comments about participants in particular that either matched or mismatched his attitudes about women in general.

In Experiment 4 ($n = 65$), the confederate's attitudes toward women were stereotype consistent across all conditions and we varied whether his attitudes about participants matched or mismatched these group attitudes. In Experiment 5 ($n = 47$), the confederate's attitudes toward women were generally stereotype inconsistent and he then expressed attitudes about participants that matched or mismatched these attitudes. In both experiments, we predicted that participants' self-evaluations would social tune toward their social interaction partner's attitudes about them in particular, regardless of whether these conflicted (i.e., group–individual mismatch conditions) or corresponded (i.e., group–individual match conditions) to this person's attitudes about their gender group, when affiliative motivation was high as opposed to low toward this person.

The basic procedure across Experiments 4 and 5 was as follows: Participants were recruited under the guise that they were participating in a group discussion screening process. The discussions were described as fun, with free food and drink and a monetary prize raffled off to those who made it into the discussions. A female experimenter greeted them and informed participants that they would be completing two questionnaires. She told them that the first questionnaire would be used to determine entrance into the discussions and the second would be used to give the researchers more information about participants and would only be viewed if participants became members of the discussion.

As this was being said, participants could hear typing through a slightly ajar door directly to the right of where they were seated. Participants could hear but not see what was occurring in this adjacent room. After informing participants about what they would be doing during the experiment, the experimenter said one of two things to participants in an offhand manner. This was our manipulation of affiliative motivation. In the high affiliative motivation condition, the female experimenter informed participants that Matt, the discussion leader, was entering previous participants' responses to the first questionnaire into a computer and would be making his decisions as to who would get into the discussions later that day. In the low affiliative motivation condition, participants were told that Matt was a research assistant entering previous participants' responses to the first questionnaire into a computer for the discussion leader. The discussion leader would be in later that day to make his decisions.

After this exchange, the experimenter handed participants the first questionnaire and went into the room with the male confederate who participants thought was named Matt. In reality, this first questionnaire was bogus and the confederate's statements about participants in particular, to be discussed shortly, were supposedly based on participants' answers to this questionnaire. We were not concerned with how participants completed any of these items. After participants completed this questionnaire, the experimenter said she forgot to put together the second questionnaire and would be right back. The experimenter then went into the adjacent room with the male confederate, leaving the door ajar so participants could hear what was occurring in the room. Participants then overheard a conversation between the confederate and the experimenter in which the male confederate expressed stereotype-consistent attitudes (Experiment 4) or stereotype-inconsistent attitudes (Experiment 5) about women in general and then expressed attitudes about participants in particular that either matched or were in opposition to these group attitudes. For example, in Experiment 4, the confederate conveyed stereotype-consistent attitudes about women in general by saying that the women in the previous discussion have been great because they don't take the lead, are sensitive to other's opinions, and don't state their own opinions. He then said that, based on the bogus questionnaire the participant just completed, he expected the participant to be just like the previous female participants or just the opposite.

After participants overheard this exchange, the experimenter returned with the second questionnaire, informed participants once again that their answers to these questions would not be viewed until after the discussions had occurred, and only if they were chosen for the discussions. It should be noted that the conversation in no way suggested to participants that they were likely or unlikely to be chosen. This second questionnaire contained the measure of self-evaluation. Similar to Experiments 1 and 2, participants rated the degree to which a series of eight traits stereotypically associated with women (sympathetic, calm, caring, compassionate, feminine, verbally skilled, dependent, supportive) were indicative of the self, Experiment 4 α = .67 and Experiment 5 α = .71. As before, these items were individually z scored and averaged to form the measure of self-evaluation, with higher numbers indicating more stereotype consistent self-evaluations than lower numbers.

In both experiments, the design was a 2 (affiliative motivation: high, low) × 2 (partner attitudes: group–individual match, group–individual mismatch) between participants factorial. In Experiment 4, when the confederate's attitudes about both women in general and individual participants were consistent with prevailing stereotypes, we predicted that participants' self-evaluations would be more stereotype consistent when they had high versus low affiliative motivation toward this person, consistent with Experiments 1 through 3. In contrast, when the confederate's attitudes about women in general were consistent with prevailing stereotypes but his attitudes about individual participants were inconsistent with prevailing stereotypes, we predicted that participants' self-evaluation would be less stereotype consistent when they had high as opposed to low affiliative motivation toward this person. This finding would provide support for the domain relevance hypothesis.

In Experiment 4, the expected interaction between affiliative motivation and confederate attitudes was obtained, $F(1, 61) = 10.37$, $p = .002$, $\eta^2 = .15$ (see Fig. 12.4). Consistent with predictions, and Experiments 1 through 3, when the confederate expressed attitudes consistent with prevailing stereotypes about women in general and individual participants, participants'

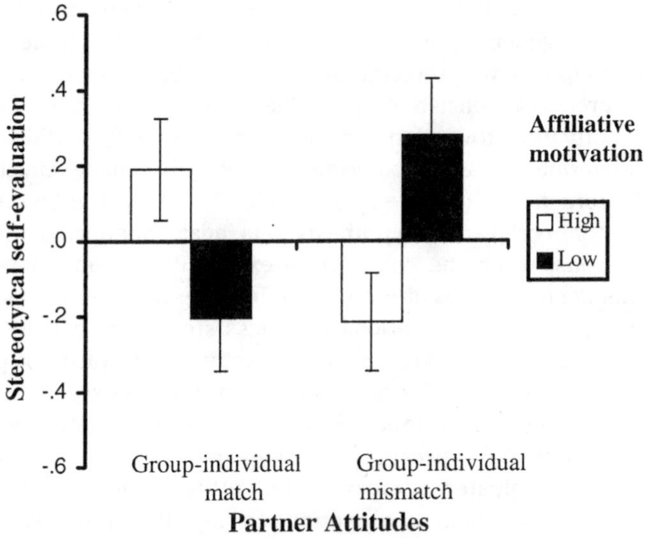

FIG. 12.4. Self-evaluation as a function of confederate attitudes (group–individual match, group–individual mismatch) and affiliative motivation (Experiment 4). Note: Higher numbers indicate more stereotype-consistent self-evaluations.

self-evaluations were more stereotype consistent when they had high affiliative motivation as opposed to low affiliative motivation toward him ($p = .03$, one-tailed). Providing evidence for the domain relevance hypothesis, the opposite pattern emerged when the confederate's attitudes about individual participants conflicted with his attitudes about their group. Specifically, when participants were seen as exceptions to the rule (i.e., the confederate had stereotype-inconsistent views of individual participants but stereotype-consistent views of women in general), we found that participants social tuned their self-evaluations toward the individual level attitudes of the confederate. Participants' self-evaluations were more stereotype inconsistent when they possessed high affiliative motivation than when they had low affiliative motivation toward the confederate ($p = .01$, one-tailed). Consistent with predictions, participants social tuned toward the most local or specific set of self-relevant attitudes of the confederate, his attitudes about them as individuals.

In Experiment 5, we predicted that when the confederate expressed stereotype-inconsistent attitudes about women in general and individual participants, participants' self-evaluations would be less stereotype consistent when they had high as opposed to low affiliative motivation toward him, consistent with Experiments 1 through 3. In contrast, based on the domain relevance hypothesis, we predicted the opposite pattern of self-evaluations when participants were seen as exceptions to the rule. Specifically, when the confederate was believed to have stereotype inconsistent attitudes about women in general, but have stereotype consistent attitudes about individual participants, we predicted that participants' self-evaluations would be more stereotype consistent when they had high as opposed to low affiliative motivation toward the confederate. This is precisely what we found. In Experiment 5, as in Experiment 4, the only reliable effect was the predicted interaction, $F(1, 43) = 5.38$, $p = .03$, $\eta^2 = .11$. As can be seen in Fig. 12.5, the domain-relevance hypothesis was again supported. Consistent with predictions, when the confederate expressed attitudes inconsistent with prevailing stereotypes about women in general and individual participants, participants' self-evaluations were less stereotype consistent when they had high as opposed to low affiliative motivation toward this person ($p = .04$, one-tailed). Providing further evidence for the veracity of the domain-relevance hypothesis, the opposite pattern of self-evaluation was found when the confederate expressed stereotype-inconsistent attitudes about women in general but stereotype-consistent attitudes about individual participants (i.e., he saw them as exceptions to the rule). In this case, participants' self-evaluations were more stereotype consistent when they had high as opposed to low affiliative motivation toward the confederate ($p = .07$, one-tailed). As in Experiment 4, participants social tuned toward those beliefs that would lead to the most local or specific shared reality, this per-

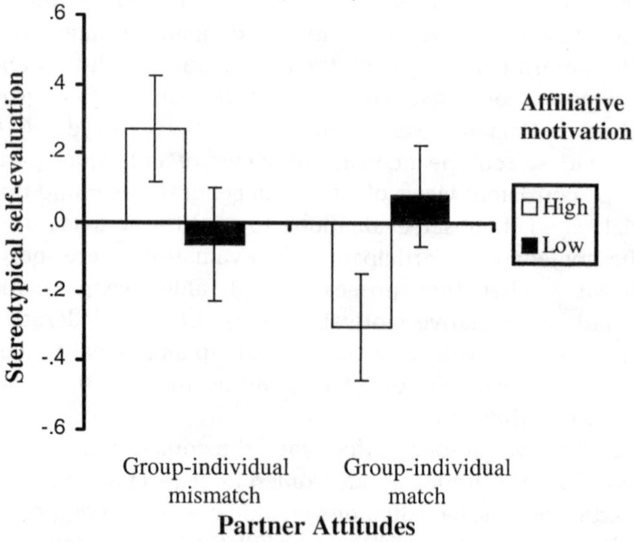

FIG. 12.5. Self-evaluation as a function of confederate attitudes (group–individual match, group–individual mismatch) and affiliative motivation (Experiment 5). Note: Higher numbers indicate more stereotype-consistent self-evaluations.

son's attitudes about them as individuals, disregarding this person's attitudes about their group.

Across both experiments, we found clear support for shared reality theory's domain relevance hypothesis. In each experiment, regardless of whether another social actor's ostensible attitudes about participants conflicted or coincided with this person's ostensible attitudes about their group, participants social tuned toward what they believed his attitudes about them were under conditions of high but not low affiliative motivation. Being seen as an exception to the rule does not motivate participants to see themselves in a manner consistent with how the group is perceived. Rather, participants' self-evaluations incorporate or social tune toward the most local or domain specific attitudes of another social actor, the person's attitudes about them as an individual, which in turn leads to the most accurate representation of the self as seen through this other person's eyes. Although being seen as an exception to the (stereotypic) rule may act to insulate one's self-evaluation from the negative effects of broader stereotypes, it could also have detrimental effects. For example, seeing certain women as exceptions to the rule may be used as a form of social control (Jackman, 1994) and allow men to maintain their general stereotypic beliefs about women. Furthermore, being seen as an exception to the rule could also thwart women's attempts at social action by decreasing their sense of group identity and shared fate (Wright, 2001).

CONCLUSIONS

Our research uses shared reality theory as a framework to examine how the fundamental need to get along with others and the ostensible views of others intersect to lead members of stereotyped groups to view themselves, and behave, in line with cultural stereotypes. This research found support for the affiliative social-tuning hypothesis, which argues that the stereotype-relevant evaluations of others will translate into self-evaluations and corresponding behavior when affiliative motivation is high as opposed to low. It also found support for the domain relevance hypothesis, which contends that a social belief under negotiation will respond to the other social actor's view that is most local or specific to it. These findings occurred across a number of operationalizations of affiliative motivation and perceived attitudes, in within-group and cross-group interactions, and for two types of stereotype targets—women and African Americans. As such, unlike perspectives highlighting the social basis of the self to suggest that the prevalence of cultural stereotypes makes self-stereotyping virtually ubiquitous and unavoidable, our research robustly demonstrates that self-stereotyping depends critically on the perceived views of one's social interaction partners and one's relationship to them.

Although research on self-presentation also finds fluctuations in self-evaluation as a function of affiliative motives (e.g., Schlenker, 2003; Zanna & Pack, 1975), we do not believe that these results can be simply attributed to self-presentation for several reasons. First, in Experiment 2, participants did not think that the other social actor would see their self-descriptions. Thus, if strategic self-presentation were driving the results, self-evaluative shift would not be warranted and should not have been found. Second, in Experiments 3 through 5 participants actually behaved in ways that likely reduced their chances of receiving social and financial rewards in order to enhance the likelihood of sharing reality with the other social actor. In Experiment 3, participants actually described themselves as less intelligent when expecting to interact with someone who seemed to have stereotypic views of African Americans when that person had the power to select them for an academic team versus did not have power over them. In Experiments 4 and 5, women tuned their self-evaluations to a high-powered person's views of them as individuals, consistent with the domain relevance hypothesis, even though this entailed saying that they were very different from women already doing well in the discussion group in which they were trying to gain entrance. Theory and research on self-presentation cannot account for the pull of affiliative motivation over the rewards; if anything, most of the self-presentation literature implies that the rewards should have dictated the manner of self-evaluative shift (Jones & Pittman, 1982).

We also believe that behavioral confirmation cannot account for our findings. According to behavioral confirmation theorists, expectancy confirming behavior is brought about by the biased behaviors of biased perceivers (for a review, see Snyder & Stukas, 1999). For example, perceivers may act less friendly toward a social actor whom they believe to be unattractive as opposed to attractive. The purportedly unattractive person then responds to this relatively sullen behavior in a commensurate way and thus fulfills the stereotype that unattractive people are not socially skilled (Snyder, Tanke, & Berscheid, 1977). However, participants only engaged in an actual social interaction in Experiment 2, and it is unlikely that the confederates in that experiment had systematic expectations because they were blind to condition. Given that participants were not subject to the biased behaviors of perceivers in the reported experiments, behavioral confirmation is unable to account for our findings.

Other research from our lab has led us to suspect that the affiliative social-tuning effects occur, at least in part, because people are not labeling the beliefs of other social actors as stereotyping and, therefore, are not bringing coping mechanisms discussed throughout this volume to bear (see Miller, chap. 2, this volume; Swim & Thomas, chap. 6, this volume). Participants do not predict that they will tune their self-evaluations to the stereotypic beliefs of another social actor when affiliative motivation is high;

rather, they predict that they will become angry and their self-views will be immobile (Huntsinger & Sinclair, 2004). We have also found tuning effects as a function of a motivational prime (Sinclair, Huntsinger, et al., in press-a) and on implicit attitudes (Sinclair, Lowery, Hardin, & Colangelo, in press-b). Future research should discern whether noting that the beliefs of others are the product of stereotypes would reduce affiliative social tuning, as well as the mechanisms by which this reduction may occur.

The interpersonal basis of self-stereotyping described in this research poses a challenge for individuals who do not want to foster self-stereotyping among stereotype targets. It suggests that individuals need not hold, or overtly express, stereotypes to elicit self-stereotyping among stereotype targets. Stereotypes may influence the self-evaluations of a stereotyped person if he or she merely believes that the other social actor holds stereotype-consistent views of their group, or of himself or herself as an individual, and high-affiliative motivation toward this social actor is warranted. For this reason, it is not sufficient for individuals who wish to avoid influencing their social interaction partners in potentially detrimental ways to simply avoid endorsing stereotypes. They must also actively seek to convey that they do not harbor stereotypical views. This task is especially difficult given that stereotyped individuals can often detect implicit stereotypes and prejudices that their social interaction partners are unaware of holding and can not consciously ameliorate (e.g. Dovidio, Kawakami, & Gaertner, 2002).

Our findings also pose a challenge for stereotype targets. It is imperative for them to be interpersonally distant from individuals that seem to hold stereotypic views of them in order to avoid self-stereotyping. This is an arduous task for several reasons. First, it is difficult to discern the views of others. This is particularly the case with respect to stereotype-relevant views because people are often motivated to appear as if they do not endorse stereotypes (or may genuinely experience themselves as not endorsing stereotypes) despite stereotypic attitudes that leak out via nonverbal channels and when the appropriate behavior is not clear (e.g., Dovidio & Gaertner, 1998). Thus, stereotype targets are faced with social interaction partners who say and believe one thing about themselves but subtly behave in a biased way. Second, although being vigilant to stereotyping is necessary to protect the self from the views of others, such vigilance has negative emotional and pragmatic costs as well (e.g. Branscombe, Schmitt, & Harvey, 1999; Pinel, 1999; see Kaiser, chap. 3, this volume). For example, Mendoza-Denton, Downey, Purdie, Davis, and Pietrzak, (2002; Mendoza-Denton, Page-Gould, & Pietrzak, chap. 8, this volume) found that African American students who are sensitive to race-based rejection were less comfortable during the transition from high school to college and experienced lower university grades. Third, many important life circumstances require successful interpersonal connections with individuals who are thought to hold stereotypic views. For example, it is hard to imagine that stereotype targets can be successful in work or educational settings without succumbing to the affiliative motivation inherent in interactions with supervisors, teachers, roommates, or teammates–some of whom may be perceived as having stereotypic views. Moreover, the fundamental human need for social connection (Baumeister & Leary, 1995) may drive stereotype targets who are solos in their environment to experience affiliative motivation toward the people around them, regardless of their apparent stereotype-relevant views.

Although this research illuminates challenges for stereotype targets and their interaction partners, it also identifies situations in which stereotype targets may be protected from self-stereotyping. For example, this research suggests that minority group members should flourish in environments in which teachers, mentors, and important others clearly express counter-stereotypic beliefs at both the group and individual level (see also Inzlicht & Good, chap. 7, this volume; Mendoza-Denton, Page-Gould, & Pietrzak, chap. 8, this volume). It also suggests a psychological mechanism by which interactions with ingroup members bolster the self-esteem, self-evaluations and performance outcomes of stereotype targets (e.g., Allen, 1992; Allen, Epps, & Haniff, 1991; Davis, 1995; Frable, Platt, & Hoey, 1998; Jackman, 1994). Because individuals are likely to experience affiliative motivation toward proximal others (Festinger, Schachter, & Back, 1950) and ingroup members are likely to have (or at least be presumed to have) less stereotypic views of their group than outgroup members (Hamilton, 1981; Linville, 1982), benefits of ingroup contact may stem from social tuning toward the presumably counterstereotypic views of ingroup members. It is interesting to note, however, that the social-tuning mechanism can account for negative effects of ingroup contact as well (Fordham & Ogbu, 1986; Ogbu, 1986). This perspective suggests that contact with ingroup members should yield stereotypic self-evaluations and behavior when ingroup members are perceived as buying into stereotypes of their own group (Fordham & Ogbu, 1986; Jackman, 1994; Ogbu, 1986).

REFERENCES

Abelson, R. P. (1995). *Statistics as principled argument.* Hillsdale, NJ: Lawrence Erlbaum Associates.

Allen, W. R. (1992). The color of success: African American college students outcomes at predominantly White and historically Black public colleges and universities. *Harvard Educational Review, 62,* 26–44.

Allen, W. R., Epps, E., & Haniff, N. Z. (Eds.). (1991). *College in Black and White: African American students in predominately White and historically Black public universities.* Albany: State University of New York Press.

Allport, G. W. (1954). *The nature of prejudice*. New York: Doubleday Anchor.

Andersen, S. M., & Chen, S. (2002). The relational self: An interpersonal social-cognitive theory. *Psychological Review, 109*, 619–645.

Andersen, S. M., Reznik, I., & Manzella, L. M. (1996). Eliciting transient affect, motivation, and expectancies in transference: Significant-other representations and the self in social relations. *Journal of Personality and Social Psychology, 71*, 1108–1129.

Baldwin, M. W. (1992). Relational schemas and the processing of information. *Psychological Bulletin, 112*, 461–484.

Baldwin, M. W., & Sinclair, L. (1996). Self-esteem and "if . . . then" contingencies of interpersonal acceptance. *Journal of Personality and Social Psychology, 71*, 1130–1141.

Baumeister, R. F., & Leary, M. R. (1995). The need to belong: Desire for interpersonal attachments as a fundamental of human motivation. *Psychological Bulletin, 117*, 497–529.

Branscombe, N. R., Schmitt, M. T., & Harvey, R. D. (1999). Perceiving pervasive discrimination among African Americans: Implications for group identification and well-being. *Journal of Personality and Social Psychology, 77*, 135–149.

Cartwright, D. (1950). Emotional dimensions of group life. In M. L. Raymert (Ed.), *Feelings and emotions* (pp. 439–477). New York: McGraw-Hill.

Chen, S., & Andersen, S. M. (1999). Relationships from the past in the present: Significant-other representations and transference in interpersonal life. In M. P. Zanna (Ed.), *Advances in experimental social psychology* (pp. 123–190). New York: Academic Press.

Chen, S., Shechter, D., & Chaiken, S. (1996). Getting at the truth or getting along: Accuracy- versus impression-motivated heuristic and systematic processing. *Journal of Personality and Social Psychology, 71*, 262–275.

Cooley, C. H. (1902). *Human nature and the social order.* New York: Harper Collins.

Crocker, J., Major, B., & Steele, C. (1998). Social stigma. In D. Gilbert, S. Fiske, & G. Lindzey (Eds.), *The handbook of social psychology, 4th ed., Vol. 2* (pp. 504–553). Boston, MA: McGraw-Hill.

Davis, J. E. (1995). College in Black and White: Campus environment and academic achievement of African American males. *Journal of Negro Education, 63,* 620–633.

Davis, J. L., & Rusbult, C. E. (2001). Attitude alignment in close relationships. *Journal of Personality and Social Psychology, 81*, 65–84.

Devine, P., & Elliot, A. (1995). Are racial stereotypes really fading? The Princeton trilogy revisited. *Personality and Social Psychology Bulletin, 21*, 1139–1150.

Dovidio, J., & Gaertner, S. (1998). On the nature of contemporary prejudice: The causes, consequences and challenges of aversive racism. In J. Eberhardt & S. Fiske (Eds.), *Confronting racism: The problem and the response* (pp. 3–32). Thousand Oaks, CA: Sage Publications.

Dovidio, J., Kawakami, K., & Gaertner, S. L. (2002). Implicit and explicit prejudice and interracial interaction. *Journal of Personality and Social Psychology, 82,* 62–68.

Festinger, L., Schachter, S., & Back, K. (1950). *Social pressures in informal groups: A study of human factors in housing.* New York: Harper Brothers.

Fordham, S., & Ogbu, J. (1986). Black students' school success: Coping with the "Burden of Acting White." *The Urban Review, 18*, 176–206.

Frable, D. E. S., Platt, L., & Hoey, S. (1998). Concealable stigmas and positive self-perceptions: Feeling better around similar others. *Journal of Personality and Social Psychology, 74*, 909–922.

Hamilton, D. (1981). Illusory correlation as a basis for stereotyping. In D. Hamilton (Ed.), *Cognitive processes in stereotyping and intergroup behavior* (pp. 125–142). Hillsdale, NJ: Lawrence Erlbaum Associates.

Hardin, C. D., & Conley, T. D. (2001). A relational approach to cognition: Shared experience and relationship affirmation in social cognition. In G. B. Moskowitz (Ed.), *Cognitive social psychology: The Princeton Symposium on the Legacy and Future of Social Cognition* (pp. 3–17). Mahwah, NJ: Lawrence Erlbaum Associates.

Hardin, C. D., & Higgins, E. T. (1996). Shared reality: How social verification makes the subjective objective. In R. Sorrentino & E. T. Higgins (Eds.), *Handbook of motivation and cognition, Vol. 3* (pp. 28–84). New York: Guilford Press.

Hewstone, M. (1994). Revision and change of stereotypic beliefs: In search of the elusive subtyping model. In W. Stroebe & M. Hewstone (Eds.), *European review of social psychology* (Vol. 5, pp. 69–109). Chichester, England: Wiley.

Higgins, E. T. (1992). Achieving 'shared reality' in the communication game: A social action that creates meaning. *Journal of Language and Social Psychology, 11*, 107–125.

Higgins, E. T., & McCann, C. D. (1984). Social encoding and subsequent attitudes, impressions and memory: "Context-driven" and motivational aspects of processing. *Journal of Personality and Social Psychology, 47*, 26–39.

Hogg, M. A., & Turner, J. C. (1987). Intergroup behavior, self-stereotyping and the salience of social categories. *British Journal of Social Psychology, 26*, 325–340.

Huntsinger, J., & Sinclair, S. (2004). *You're not like the rest: Being seen as an exception to the rule, domain relevance, and women's self-evaluation.* Manuscript submitted for publication.

Jackman, M. (1994). *The velvet glove: Paternalism and conflict in gender, class and race relations.* Berkeley, CA: University of California Press.

Jones, E. E., & Pittman, T. S. (1982). Toward a general theory of strategic self-presentation. In J. Suls (Ed.), *Psychological perspectives on the self, Vol. 1* (pp. 231–262). Hillsdale, NJ: Lawrence Erlbaum Associates.

Kelley, H. H., & Thibaut, J. W. (1978). *Interpersonal relations: A theory of interdependence.* New York: Wiley.

Krauss, R. M., & Fussell, S. R. (1996). Social psychological models of interpersonal communication. In E. T. Higgins & A. W. Kruglanski (Eds.), *Social psychology: Handbook of basic principles* (pp. 655–701). New York: Guilford Press

Linville, P. W. (1982). The complexity–extremity effect and age-based stereotyping. *Journal of Personality and Social Psychology, 42*, 367–376.

Lowery, B. S., Hardin, C. D., & Sinclair, S. (2001). Social influence effects on automatic racial prejudice. *Journal of Personality and Social Psychology, 81*, 842–855.

McCann, C. D., & Hancock, R. (1983). Self-monitoring in communicative interactions: Social cognitive consequences of goal-directed message modification. *Journal of Experimental Social Psychology, 19*, 109–121.

McCann, C. D., & Higgins, E. T. (1992). Personal and contextual factors in communication: A review of the "communication game." In G. R. Semin & K. Fiedler (Eds.), *Language, interaction, and social cognition* (pp. 144–172). London: Sage.

Mead, G. H. (1934). *Mind, self and society.* Chicago, IL: University of Chicago Press.

Mendoza-Denton, R., Downey, G., Purdie, V. J., Davis, A., & Pietrzak, J. (2002). Sensitivity to status-based rejection: Implications for African American students' college experience. *Journal of Personality and Social Psychology, 83*, 896–918.

Miller, D. T., Downs, J. S., & Prentice, D. A. (1998). Minimal conditions for the creation of a unit relationship: The social bond between birthdaymates. *European Journal of Social Psychology, 28*, 475–481.

Ogbu, J. (1986). The consequences of the American caste system. In U. Neisser (Ed.), *The school achievement of minority children: New perspectives* (pp. 19–56). Hillsdale, NJ: Lawrence Erlbaum Associates.

Orive, R. (1988). Social projection and social comparison of opinions. *Journal of Personality and Social Psychology, 54*, 953–964.

Pickett, C. L., Bonner, B. L., & Coleman, J. M. (2002). Motivated self-stereotyping: Heightened assimilation and differentiation needs result in increased levels of positive and negative self-stereotyping. *Journal of Personality and Social Psychology, 82*, 543–562.

Pinel, E. (1999). Stigma consciousness: The psychological legacy of social stereotypes. *Journal of Personality and Social Psychology, 76*, 114–128.

Schlenker, B. R. (2003). Self-presentation. In M. R. Leary & J. P. Tangney (Eds.), *Handbook of self and identity* (pp. 492–518). New York: Guilford.

Shrauger, J. S., & Schoeneman, T. J. (1979). Symbolic interactionist view of the self-concept: Through the looking glass darkly. *Psychological Bulletin, 86*, 549–573.

Sinclair, S., Huntsinger, J., Skorinko, J., & Hardin, C. D. (in press-a). Social tuning of the self: Consequences for the self-evaluations of stereotype targets. *Journal of Personality and Social Psychology.*

Sinclair, S., Lowery, B. S., Hardin, C. D., & Colangelo, A. (in press-b). Social tuning of automatic gender and ethnic attitudes: The role of relationship motivation. *Journal of Personality and Social Psychology.*

Smith, E. R. (1996). What do connectionism and psychology have to offer each other? *Journal of Personality and Social Psychology, 70*, 893–912.

Snyder, M., Tanke, E. D., & Berscheid, E. (1977). Social perception and interpersonal behavior: On the self-fulfilling nature of social stereotypes. *Journal of Personality and Social Psychology, 35*, 656–666.

Snyder, M., & Stukas, A. A. (1999). Interpersonal processes: The interplay of cognitive, motivational, and behavioral activities in social interaction. *Annual Review of Psychology, 50*, 273–303.

Steele, C., & Aronson, J. (1995). Stereotype threat and the intellectual performance of African Americans. *Journal of Personality and Social Psychology, 69*, 797–811.

Stangor, C., & Lange, J. E. (1994). Mental representations of social groups: Advances in understanding stereotypes and stereotyping. In M. P. Zanna (Ed.), *Advances in experimental social psychology* (Vol. 26, pp. 357–416). San Diego, CA: Academic Press.

Stryker, S., & Statham, A. (1985). Symbolic interaction and role theory. In G. Lindzay & E. Aronson (Eds.), *Handbook of social psychology* (pp. 311–378). New York: Random House.

Turner. J. C. (1987). A self-categorization theory. In J. C. Turner, M. A. Hogg, P. J. Oakes, S. D. Reicher, & M. S. Wetherell (Eds.), *Rediscovering the social group: A self-categorization theory* (pp. 42–67). Oxford: Blackwell.

Wright, S. C. (2001). Restricted intergroup boundaries: Tokenism, ambiguity, and the tolerance of injustice. In J. Jost & B. Major (Eds.), *The psychology of legitimacy: Emerging perspectives on ideology, justice, and intergroup relations* (pp. 223–254). New York: Cambridge University Press.

Zanna, M. P., & Pack, S. (1975). On the self-fulfilling nature of apparent sex differences in behavior. *Journal of Experimental Social Psychology, 11*, 583–591.

CHAPTER

13

Stigma and Shame: Emotional Responses to the Stereotypic Actions of One's Ethnic Ingroup

Toni Schmader
University of Arizona

Brian Lickel
University of Southern California

Classic theorists of stigma and prejudice make the assertion that under certain conditions, those who are socially stigmatized might come to feel a sense of shame for aspects of their stigmatized identity. Gordon Allport (1954) went so far as to suggest that if victims of prejudice come to identify with the dominant group, they will develop a sense of self-hate. For example, Allport stated, "... the immigrant grows *ashamed* of his faulty accent, his lack of ease and social grace, his defective education" (p. 151). In fact, it is so common to assume that stigma is associated with shame that the word processing program being used to write this chapter lists "shame" as the first suggested synonym of the word, "stigma."

In this chapter, we focus on one particular way in which stigmatization and shame are connected, namely how members of a stigmatized group are emotionally affected by acts of fellow group members that confirm the negative stereotype about the group. Whereas other chapters in this section have discussed how stigmatized individuals' self-perceptions are shaped by their interactions and associations with members of the outgroup, we turn our focus toward how those who are socially stigmatized are affected by the actions of other ingroup members. As we discuss, members of stigmatized groups are often conscious of how their own behavior could be seen as confirming negative stereotypes about their group (e.g., Pinel, 1999). However, what is less clear is the nature of their emotional response to seeing another member of their ingroup commit an act that confirms a negative stereotype about their group. Building from Allport's example, the question that we pose is whether the immigrant who has made great efforts to minimize his or her own accent and obtain an education still feels a sense of shame for the faulty accent or lack of social graces exhibited by other ingroup members.

In the first half of our chapter, we review evidence that personal confirmation of negative stereotypes is threatening to stigmatized individuals and draw on recent work on group-based emotion to articulate why a person might feel a threat to identity when someone other than the self confirms negative stereotypes about one's ingroup. In the second half, we describe work we have done examining different predictors of group-based shame (as opposed to group-based guilt) as a precursor to presenting two studies that specifically examine the degree to which Hispanic individuals feel a sense of shame when a member of their ethnic ingroup behaves in a stereotypic way. Our primary focus in this chapter is on feelings of vicarious shame for the stereotypic actions of ingroup members, but the studies we report also include measures of guilt, anger, sadness, and anxiety. By analyzing a range of negative emotional responses that individuals might have to a stereotypic group member, we are able to isolate the unique way in which feelings of shame are linked to the sense of identity threat that these situations pose.

THEORETICAL BACKGROUND: THE THREAT OF STEREOTYPE CONFIRMATION

Sinclair and Huntsinger (chap. 12, this volume) show that members of stigmatized groups sometimes behave in stereotypic ways when they are motivated to form a relationship with a prejudiced outgroup member. Although these social-tuning processes are likely to happen unconsciously, we might wonder how these individuals would feel if they were aware that their behavior confirmed negative stereotypes about their group. Many theories would lead us to predict that they should feel threatened by this possibility. For example, stereotype-threat theory (Steele & Aronson, 1995) stated it is the fear of doing something that would confirm the stereotype that leads members of negatively stereotyped groups to perform more poorly in situations where the stereotype is made salient. Not only is there evidence that stereotype threat can entail increased anxiety (Spencer, Steele, & Quinn, 1999) and threat arousal (Blascovich, Spencer, Quinn, & Steele, 2001), but research also shows that individuals are motivated to behave in a way that will disconfirm the stereotype if at all possible (e.g., Ben-Zeev, Fein, & Inzlicht, 2005; Kray, Thompson, & Galinsky, 2001; O'Brien & Crandall, 2003).

Other work suggests that members of stigmatized groups are often conscious of how others perceive them in terms of their group membership (Pinel, 1999). Pinel's work also shows that women who are particularly conscious of their stigmatized gender identity are more likely to avoid situations where they are at risk of confirming a negative stereotype about women. Similarly, research by Miller and colleagues (Miller, Rothblum, Felicio, & Brand, 1995) suggested that those who are socially stigmatized (overweight women in their studies) might personally cope with threat of negative stereotypes through compensatory behaviors designed to create a more positive impression of themselves as individuals.

Finally, at more of a group level, social-identity theory (Tajfel & Turner, 1986) stated that individuals derive a sense of self-esteem from the social groups with whom they identify. Thus, one's positive sense of self will be threatened to the extent that those groups are thought to possess negative characteristics. Tajfel and Turner discuss several options that individuals might employ to manage their tarnished group identity. One strategy is to engage in social competition where the group tries to behave in ways that increase the positive value associated with the identity. A second strategy is to physically or psychologically disassociate oneself from the negative social identity. A third strategy is to embrace the characteristics of the group that have been labeled negative by the dominant culture and to reframe them in a more positive light. Nonetheless, even given these strategies for reframing the meaning of the stereotype, it is likely that negative stereotypes will remain threatening to many members of stigmatized groups.

EMOTIONAL REACTIONS TO STEREOTYPE CONFIRMATION

This past theory and research confirms our intuitions that individuals are often loathe to do anything themselves that would confirm negative stereotypes that others hold about their racial or ethnic group. When people do see themselves as behaving in a stereotypic way, we propose that stigmatized individuals would feel a sense of shame as a result. Shame and other related emotions such as guilt and embarrassment are often labeled self-conscious or moral emotions because they are thought to regulate people's behavior with regard to moral standards and serve to maintain social relationships between individuals and in groups (Baumeister, Stillwell, & Heatherton, 1995; Eisenberg, 2000; Gilbert & Andrews, 1998; Keltner, 1995; Tangney & Fischer, 1995). People are thought to feel ashamed when they attribute a negative event to an uncontrollable and internal aspect of themselves (Weiner, 1995; Wicker, Payne, & Morgan, 1983). Shame is often characterized by feelings of self-consciousness and a fear of rejection (Lewis, 1971; Wicker et al., 1983) and is accompanied by the counterfactual thought, "If only I were a different type of person" (Niedenthal, Tangney, & Gavanski, 1994). Although shame is greater when the potential for public exposure is high (R. H. Smith, Webster, & Parrott, 2002), shame is not only experienced in truly public situations and can involve a private concern for what others would think (Tangney, Miller, Flicker, & Barlow, 1996). In other words, we feel shame when we perceive that a flaw in our character has been revealed to others and/or to ourselves.

The unique aspects of shame can be better appreciated when contrasted against the profile of a related self-conscious emotion such as guilt. Guilt is often accompanied by feeling that one had control in the situation and should have behaved in a different manner (Wicker et al., 1983). Weiner (1995) argued that people feel guilt when they attribute a negative event to a cause that is internal and controllable. Indeed, individuals who are asked to recall a guilt experience are more likely than those who recall a shame experience to have the counterfactual thought, "If only I had acted differently" (Niedenthal et al., 1994). But the primary reason we might care about distinguishing shame from guilt is that these two emotions have been shown to predict very different behavioral responses. Feelings of shame seem to evoke a desire to hide from others or distance oneself from the shame-provoking situation (Tangney, 1995; Wicker et al., 1983), whereas feelings of guilt are associated with empathy for the wronged party and a desire to confess, apologize, or in some way repair or atone for what happened (Tangney, 1995). In other words, shame elicits a very passive or withdrawing response aimed at reducing feelings of self-consciousness, whereas guilt elicits a more active or approach response aimed at repairing damage that has been done to important social relationships.

Because *stereotypes* are characterizations of the defining attributes associated with members of a particular group, the awareness that one has done something that confirms negative stereotypes about one's stigmatized group could be appraised as evidence that there is a flaw in one's identity. In this situation, people might think, "I'm one of *those* types of people?" In other words, it is particularly because people are motivated to see negative social stereotypes about their group as being inaccurate that any indication that they might possess those stereotypic traits could elicit feelings of shame. Under most circumstances, those with a desire to advance the interests of themselves and their group are likely to choose situations and behaviors that will disconfirm negative stereotypes about their social group and avoid these feelings of shame. However, it is important to realize that not all members of a racial or ethnic group will necessarily hold this same goal. For example, individuals who believe that the status hierarchy is illegitimate and their advancement is impossible might come to reject that which is valued by the dominant culture (Major & Schmader, 2001; Ogbu, 1991; Schmader, Major, Eccleston, & McCoy, 2001). To regain a sense of positive identity, these individuals might even come to value traits that are deemed part of the negative stereotype of the group and to engage in behaviors that are consistent with these stereotypes while feeling little or no threat to identity. What are the emotional consequences of witnessing other group members mismanage your identity by engaging in stereotypic behaviors that you yourself are motivated to avoid? This question is the focus of the remainder of this chapter.

AFFECTIVE CONSEQUENCES OF STIGMATIZATION AND THE LINK TO VICARIOUS SHAME

Researchers interested in the effects of stigmatization have always had an interest in the affective consequences of being targeted by negative stereotypes. In fact, there is now a large body of literature examining how perceptions of stigmatization affect global feelings of self-worth and esteem (Crocker & Major, 1989; see also Major, Quinton, & McCoy, 2002, for a review). The question that we are posing is distinct from that which has been studied in past work on the affective consequences of stigma. Whereas past research has focused on emotional reactions to being a target of prejudicial behavior enacted by the outgroup, we are interested in examining emotional reactions to stereotypic behaviors enacted by members of the ingroup. Furthermore, rather than focus on consequences for global self-worth or self-esteem, our interest is in identifying distinct emotional reactions, such as shame, that these stereotypic behaviors elicit within a given situation and linking these emotional reactions to distinct action tendencies.

Our proposition that individuals sometimes experience a sense of shame for the negative actions carried out by group members is also related to, but somewhat distinct from, work on the *black-sheep effect.* The black-sheep effect, first studied by Marques and colleagues (Marques, Yzerbyt, & Leyens, 1988) represents a polarization of people's judgments of ingroup members compared to outgroup members. Although people generally rate ingroup members more favorably than outgroup members, research on the black-sheep effect has shown that people will sometimes derogate an ingroup member more than an outgroup member when that person engages in a negative behavior, or does not have positive traits. This research has indicated a particular mechanism for this effect, namely that people hold particularly positive expectancies or stereotypes about their ingroups and also that people expect that ingroup members will uphold positive norms of expected behavior. When ingroup members do not conform to these norms or expectancies, other members of the group derogate them.

Although research on the black-sheep effect has not examined specific emotional reactions to norm violation on the part of ingroup members (but see Biernat, Vescio, & Billings, 1999, for one study that measured negative mood), we speculate that violating positive expectancies of one's group might evoke shame, and that the resulting derogation of the ingroup member is an indication of the motivation to distance oneself from shame-inducing situations. The approach that we have taken in the research we now describe extends work on the black-sheep effect. Rather than examining reactions to ingroup members who fail to live up to positive norms established by the ingroup, we explore reactions to ingroup members who specifically behave in ways that are seen as a confirmation of an existing negative stereotype applied to the identity.

We start with the question of why one should have any emotional reaction to the stereotypic behaviors of members of his or her ingroup. Categorizing oneself as belonging to the same group as the person in question is an important element in determining one's emotional reactions to that person's behavior. We know from past research that individuals tend to view their social groups as part of their self-concept (E. R. Smith & Henry, 1996; Tajfel & Turner, 1986) and work described by McLaughlin-Volpe (chap. 11, this volume) shows that the inclusion of others in the self can enable individuals to expand their self-definition. Perhaps because of these self-expansion processes, individuals take pride in their membership in positive groups and seem ready to "cut themselves off" from the failure of negative groups (Snyder, Lassegard, & Ford, 1986). Thus, our perspective is similar to that proposed by E. R. Smith (1993), who argued for the role of emotions in intergroup and intragroup behaviors. If we categorize ourselves as part of a given group and that group identity is an integral part of how we define ourselves, then it is reasonable to assume that the behaviors of other group members have the potential to affect us.

But just as this assertion seems sure to be true, it seems just as sure that the story is more complicated. Is it the case that those who belong to a stigmatized group are always affected by the behaviors of their ingroup? Are different types of groups likely to provoke different degrees and/or types of emotions? And finally, what emotions in particular should we expect to see and is there variation in the types of behaviors that these emotions provoke? We approach answering these questions in two steps. First, we discuss a general framework that we have developed to predict when people feel a sense of shame for a fellow ingroup member. Once we have placed feelings of vicarious shame in a context that is broader than the experience of stigmatized groups, we move to address feelings of shame for the actions of ethnic ingroup members and the particular role that confirmation of negative stereotypes may play in evoking vicarious shame.

VICARIOUS SHAME

Earlier, we reviewed evidence that people tend to feel shame in response to a perceived flaw in their identity and these feelings of shame elicit attempts to hide or to distance oneself from the shame-evoking event. Although this earlier work relates to how shame can be evoked by one's own actions or attributes, we argue that these same appraisal and motivational correlates that characterize personal shame are maintained when we consider shame as a group-based emotion (Lickel, Schmader, & Barquissau, 2004; Lickel, Schmader, Curtis, Ames, & Scarnier, 2005). Specifically, we assert that, like personal shame, vicarious shame is likely to be evoked by appraisals of the threat to one's personal and group identity that are caused by a group member's actions, and that vicarious shame is linked to a motivation to distance oneself from the event and the perpetrator (Johns, Schmader, & Lickel, in press). This profile of vicarious shame can be distinguished from that of other self-conscious emotions such as vicarious guilt, which is predicted by an appraisal that one should have had more control over the group member's behavior (Lickel at al., 2005) and is associated with a motivation to apologize for or repair whatever damage those actions might have caused (Doosje, Branscombe, Spears, & Manstead, 1998; Lickel at al., 2005).

Categorizing oneself as sharing a group identity with another person is one key element in experiencing shame for the other person's actions. However, beyond categorizing oneself as sharing an ingroup membership, it is possible to characterize what it is about that shared association that leads to feelings of vicarious shame. In developing our model of vicarious shame, we draw on the concept of the depth or meaningfulness of *shared identity*. One's sense of shared identity with a group can be distinguished from other elements that can define social groups such as perceptions of interpersonal interdependence with other group members (e.g., Brewer, 2000; Hamilton, Sherman & Lickel, 1998; Krech & Crutchfield, 1948; Lewin, 1948; Prentice, Miller, & Lightdale, 1994; Rabbie & Horwitz, 1988). We sometimes feel a sense of social connectedness with others whom we have never met and with whom we have no interpersonal contact if we simply feel that we share a core identity in common.

Moreover, we intuitively have a sense that some social identities are "shallow" whereas others are "deep." This intuition about the "depth" or meaningfulness of different kinds of identities was captured by Rothbart and Taylor's (1992) discussion of essentiality. According to Rothbart and Taylor, certain kinds of groups such as racial categories are viewed by perceivers as being inalterable and deeply informative aspects of identity. Likewise, Allport (1954) noted that people have an intuitive idea of race in which, "a belief in essence develops. There is an inherent 'Jewishness' in every Jew. The 'soul of the Oriental,' 'Negro blood,' 'Hiltler's Aryanism,' . . . all represent a belief in essence. A mysterious mana (for good or ill) resides in a group, all of its members partaking thereof" (p. 173). More recently, Haslam, Rothschild, and Ernst (2000) assessed the specific qualities of groups that underlie people's perceptions of essentiality. Examples of groups that perceivers are particularly likely to treat as highly essentialized include kinship, but also gender, racial, ethnic, and national identities (Gil-White, 2001; Haslam et al., 2000; Hirschfeld, 1995; Lickel et al., 2000). Still, even groups based on nominal characteristics can sometimes instill in members a sense of shared identity (Tajfel, 1970).

This feature of social association (i.e., one's feeling of shared identity with another person) is important for predicting people's shame responses to the negative actions of that individual; we might expect people to feel more ashamed for the wrongful actions of those with whom they feel a sense of shared, and even essentialized, identity. In contrast, it is one's level of interdependence (i.e., interpersonal interaction and shared communication) with the group member that seems to predict one's feeling guilty for his or her wrongdoing (Lickel et al., 2005).

What Types of Behavior Elicit Vicarious Shame Reactions?

When addressing when and why people are emotionally affected by the actions of members of their stigmatized ingroup, one important question concerns whether all negative acts committed by a fellow group member have equal potential for producing vicarious shame. From our point of view, the sense of shared identity is important, but negative actions of ingroup members should be most shame provoking when they are seen as relevant to the group identity. There are two general circumstances when this might happen. First, if the context makes group membership salient, then any negative actions carried out by group members might be taken as a reflection of the group. For example, membership in a group that is a numerical minority can lead to increased identity salience and group identification (e.g., Brewer, 1991; Ellemers, Doosje, & van Knippenberg, 1992; see also Inzlicht & Ben-Zeev, 2000; W. J. McGuire, C. V. McGuire, Child, & Fujioka, 1978). If such minority status is chronic, as is the case with most ethnic minority groups in the United States, group identity is likely to be more highly accessible across situations. However, a given context can create minority status and increase the likelihood that behaviors of ingroup members will seem to be relevant to the group. For example, if there are only a few women in a largely male corporation, the female employees are more likely to have their gender identity salient on the job, thereby increasing the degree to which any negative act committed by a fellow woman in the corporation may be likely to evoke shame in other female co-workers.

In addition to situational cues that prime group identity, high levels of group identification might make group identity chronically salient for some individuals. Moreover, those who are highly identified with their group are also likely to be more invested in maintaining a positive image of their group and thus more threatened by the negative actions of other group members. Thus, individuals who are more inclined to define themselves in terms of their group membership are likely to be more sensitive to the negative actions of other ingroup members. For example, past research shows that individuals who are highly group identified show a stronger black-sheep effect to disloyal group members (Branscombe, Wann, & Noel, 1993). We have also found evidence for this prediction in a study of Americans' reactions to Anti-Arab prejudice following the September 11th terrorist attacks on the World Trade Center and the Pentagon (Johns et al., in press). Importantly, the more highly identified Americans were with their national identity, the more ashamed they felt for very extreme acts of prejudice carried out by fellow Americans (but not for more mild forms of prejudice) and the stronger their desire to distance the offending group member from their group identity. Group identification did not significantly predict any other emotional response to these events. Thus, one's level of identification with a shared social identity can predict the intensity with which one experiences shame when a fellow ingroup member is seen as mismanaging that identity.

Beyond contextually driven salience and chronic group identification, existing social stereotypes provide an important mechanism for sorting and tagging the myriad events that occur in people's lives. Other scholars have noted how stereotypes serve as hypotheses for interpreting behavior (e.g., Darley & Gross, 1983) as well as being explanations for the outcomes that individuals receive (e.g., Fiske, Cuddy, Glick, & Xu, 2002; Kay & Jost, 2003). People may also have better memory for acts that confirm stereotypes (Rothbart, Evans, & Fulero, 1979). Thus, acts that appear to confirm negative stereotypes are likely to be noticed, interpreted, and categorized as being relevant to the group regardless of whether or not group identity was salient to begin with. Events that are not readily interpreted in light of the stereotype or social reputation of the group will be attributed to the particular characteristics of the person committing the act, unless the group membership is contextually or chronically salient.

We found initial support for the link between the relevance of the event and feelings of vicarious shame in a study in which participants were directed to recall and make ratings of three instances in which they felt ashamed or guilty for the actions of a family member, a friend, and a member of their ethnic or racial group (Lickel et al., 2005). As predicted, the perception that the person's behavior was relevant to the reputation or social stereotype of the group (i.e., friendship group, family group, or ethnic group) was associated with greater appraisals that the event was a threat to personal identity, greater feelings of shame, and a greater desire to distance oneself from the situation. Notably, this profile for vicarious shame was quite distinct from the profile of responses associated with vicarious guilt. In contrast to the relevance of the event for a shared identity, it was the perception that one shared an interdependent association with the offending group member that predicted greater appraisals of control over that person's behavior, stronger feelings of guilt, and a greater desire to apologize or make amends for his or her actions.

Thus, the relevance of the event to the shared identity of the group was significantly linked to feelings of shame and to motivations to distance oneself from the event. Although this study does not pertain directly to stigma, recall that participants in the aforementioned study were specifically instructed to recall one event that involved an ethnic ingroup member. In comparison to events involving a family member or a friend, events concerning an ethnic ingroup member received the highest ratings of relevance to a sense of shared identity. Although most participants in this study were White, these data provided us with an initial indication that members of ethnic groups might feel vicarious shame for ingroup behaviors that seem to confirm negative stereotypes about their ethnic group. We next sought to examine this possibility more directly.

AN EMPIRICAL TEST OF STIGMATIZED INDIVIDUALS' EMOTIONAL REACTIONS TO INGROUP STEREOTYPIC BEHAVIORS

In the previous sections of this chapter, we outlined our general hypothesis that members of stigmatized groups might often feel a sense of shame for the negative stereotypic behavior of other ingroup members. In the remainder of the chapter, we present the results of two studies that test this hypothesis and also examine how emotional responses to these situations of stereotype confirmation are related to group identification and certain action tendencies, like distancing from the negative event.

In Study 1, we asked Hispanic college students to recall a time when a member of their ethnic group did something that seemed to be consistent with negative stereotypes that people hold about their ethnic group. As in our previous work (Lickel et al., 2005), participants wrote about the event and made ratings of their emotional reactions and action tendencies associated with the event. In addition, we assessed their perceptions of the stereotypicality of the event and their collective self-esteem (Luhtanen & Crocker, 1992). Based on the ideas already reviewed, we tested three core hypotheses. First, we predicted that variation in the stereotypicality of the events that Hispanic students recalled would predict the intensity of their shame response to those behaviors, even after controlling for the overall severity of the event and how well they knew the group member. Second, we predicted that Hispanic students who were highly identified with their ethnic group would express higher levels of shame for the stereotypic actions of their ingroup. Finally, we predicted that shame would be the specific emotional response that would relate to a desire to distance oneself not just from the offending group member but perhaps even from the group identity more generally. We also tested whether shame would relate to a desire to repair the tarnished group image by engaging in behaviors that disconfirm the group stereotype.

STUDY 1

Participants and Procedures

Participants were 136 Hispanic college students who received credit in their introductory psychology course in exchange for their participation. Because we wanted to focus on events where participants themselves were not directly involved, 17 participants were excluded because they agreed (i.e., they had a score greater than 5 on a 9-point scale ranging from *strongly disagree* to *strongly agree*) with the statement, "I was the cause of the event" ($n = 2$), with the statement, "The event was directed at me" ($n = 11$), or with both statements ($n = 4$). Thus, our final sample included 119 participants (35 men, 84 women).

Participants were run in small groups ranging from one to seven people. They were first given an initial questionnaire to complete that included measures of collective self-esteem. After completing this measure, they were given the main survey packet. In this packet, they were asked to think about a time when they observed someone else in their ethnic group do something that seemed to them to be consistent with negative stereotypes that people have about their ethnic group. They were told that they could write about someone they know or a complete stranger and it was emphasized that we were not looking for a time when they themselves had done something stereotypic. Participants were given 5 minutes to write about the experience. After completing their narrative, participants completed a survey about the event. Upon completing the survey, all participants were thanked for their participation and were debriefed.

Measures

Unless otherwise mentioned, all of the following items were rated on 9-point scales ranging from 1 (*strongly disagree*) to 9 (*strongly agree*). Examples of items used in composites are given. A complete set of items can be obtained from the first author.

Collective self-esteem. Items from Luhtanen and Crocker's (1992) collective self-esteem scale were modified to assess participants' collective self-esteem for their ethnic group. This scale includes four subscales measuring public collective self-esteem (α = .80), private collective self-esteem (α = .83), identity importance (α = .79), and membership self-esteem (α = .82).

Stereotypicality. The stereotypicality of the event was assessed with three items (α = .65, e.g., "Regardless of what others might have thought, how stereotypical did you think the event was?": 1 = *I didn't think the event was very stereotypical,* 9 = *I thought the event was extremely stereotypical*).

Interdependence. Participants' level of interdependence with the person who they wrote about was also assessed with three items (α = .88, e.g., "How well did you know the person who caused the event?": 1 = *I didn't know the person at all,* 9 = *I know the person very well*).

Event severity. Severity of the event was assessed with two items (r = .74, p < .001; e.g., "How severe did this event seem to you?": 1 = *Not very severe at all,* 9 = *Extremely severe*).

Emotion composites. Participants were asked to rate the degree to which the event made them feel each of several emotions. Shame was assessed as the average score to four items (α = .83, *ashamed, disgraced, humiliated,* and *embarrassed*), guilt as the average of four items (α = .64, *guilty, regret, sorry,* and *remorseful*), anger as the average of four items (α = .83, *angry at the other person, offended, disgusted,* and *upset*), sadness as the average of three items (α = .74, *sad, depressed,* and *hurt*), and anxiety as the average of two items (r = .55, p < .001: *anxious* and *nervous*). Five positive emotions were added as filler items. A maximum likelihood factor analysis with oblique rotation confirmed these groupings.

Action tendencies. Distancing from the perpetrator was assessed with five items (α = .81, e.g., *At the time, I remember thinking that I didn't want to be associated in any way with the person who caused the event*). *Distancing from one's group* was assessed with three items (α = .77, e.g., *I wanted to hide my ethnicity from others). Image repair* was assessed with two items (r = .69, p < .001; e.g., *I felt like I should do something after the event that would show that people in my ethnic group are not really like that*). Finally, *event repair* was assessed with four items (α = .67, e.g., *I felt like I should do something after the event to make it better*). A maximum likelihood factor analysis with oblique rotation confirmed these groupings.

Results

Descriptive statistics. Narratives that people wrote tapped into many negative stereotypes, including those related to crime and drugs, poverty, alcoholism, sexism, lack of education or ambition, being a drain on society, illegal immigration, and general uncivilized or rude behavior. The events that people described had occurred in the past year on average, and participants witnessed the event they described first hand 82% of the time (n = 97).

In addition, there was someone else who was harmed or victimized by the event in 47% of the stories ($n = 55$) and others present to witness the event in 83% of the stories ($n = 99$). The person(s) who engaged in the stereotypic behavior were almost equally likely to be someone who the participant knew well ($n = 57$; e.g., a close friend, significant other, co-worker, or relative) or someone who they did not know well ($n = 62$; an acquaintance or a stranger). The perpetrators were male 67% of the time ($n = 80$), female 29% of the time ($n = 35$), and included both sexes in 3% of the stories ($n = 4$). Finally, a frequency analysis of perceived stereotypicality ratings revealed that, although there was considerable variance in people's ratings, 86.6% of the participants rated the event they recalled at or above the midpoint on stereotypicality ($M = 6.67$, $SD = 1.50$), suggesting that a clear majority of the participants recalled very stereotypic events.

Mean levels of emotion. A within-subjects analysis of the negative emotions revealed significant differences among the emotion clusters, $F(4, 115) = 30.00$, $p < .001$. Participants were more likely to feel angry ($M = 4.79$) and ashamed ($M = 3.82$) than they were to feel any of the other emotions (sadness $M = 2.92$; anxiety $M = 2.75$; and guilt $M = 2.41$), all $ps < .001$. Mean levels of anger and shame were significantly different from one another, $p < .001$. People also felt more sadness than guilt, $p < .01$. These data highlight that anger and shame clearly stood out as the dominant emotional responses that Hispanic students had to the stereotypic actions of their ethnic ingroup.

Predicting emotions from group variables. To assess our primary hypothesis that the stereotypicality of an ingroup member's actions is predictive of feeling shame, we conducted a series of simultaneous regression analyses in which stereotypicality and interdependence were entered as predictors of each of the emotion clusters, controlling for the perceived severity of the event. Results are summarized in Table 13.1. Consistent with our first hypothesis, the stereotypicality of the event significantly predicted shame but interdependence did not. Anger was also significantly related to perceptions of

TABLE 13.1
Standardized Coefficients from Simultaneous Regression Analyses Predicting Emotional Response from Event Severity, Stereotypicality, and Interdependence

	Outcome Variables				
	Shame	*Anger*	*Guilt*	*Sadness*	*Anxiety*
Predictors					
Severity	.31***	.54***	.43***	.56***	.18*
Stereotypicality	.26**	.21**	−.10	.09	−.10
Interdependence	.09	−.06	.19*	.22**	.10

*$p < .05$. **$p < .01$. ***$p < .001$.

stereotypicality. In contrast, interdependence and not stereotypicality was uniquely predictive of feeling guilt and sadness. Clearly, these two different aspects of the event (i.e., relevance to group stereotypes and interpersonal interdependence), predicted very distinct profiles of emotions.

Predicting emotions from collective self-esteem. To test our second hypothesis concerning the relationship between group identification and vicarious shame, we next examined the different facets of collective self-esteem as predictors of participants' emotional responses. Because collective self-esteem has to do with one's attitudes toward one's social identity, our specific prediction was that those who are more highly identified with their ethnic group (i.e., higher in importance collective self-esteem) would be most likely to feel ashamed when another group member does something to tarnish that group identity. We also thought that public and private collective self-esteem might be associated with feeling ashamed but we were less sure of the direction. On one hand, those who have a somewhat negative private or public perception of their group to begin with might be more sensitive to actions that confirm that negative perception. On the other hand, those with a positive private or public image of their group might be more shocked and appalled by behavior that is at odds with those positive perceptions. We did not have specific predictions concerning the membership subscale of the collective self-esteem scale. To assess the unique relationship of each of these four subscales in predicting emotional responses to the event, we conducted a series of simultaneous regression analyses with importance, private, public, and membership collective self-esteem entered as predictors of a given emotional response controlling for the perceived severity of the event. Results are summarized in Table 13.2.

Consistent with our hypothesis, participants were more likely to feel ashamed for the stereotypic actions of their ingroup to the degree that they

TABLE 13.2
Standardized Coefficients from Simultaneous Regression Analyses Predicting Emotional Response from Event Severity and Collective Self-Esteem (CSE)

	Outcome Variables				
	Shame	*Anger*	*Guilt*	*Sadness*	*Anxiety*
Predictors					
Severity	.22*	.50***	.39***	.55***	.17#
Importance CSE	.21*	.02	.17	.12	.12
Private CSE	−.27*	−.05	−.04	−.05	.12
Public CSE	−.20*	−.15#	−.01	.08	.01
Membership CSE	.17	.23*	−.01	.07	−.16

*$p < .05$. **$p < .01$. ***$p < .001$. #$p < .10$.

placed a great deal of importance on ethnicity as part of their self concept ($\beta = .21, p < .05$). In addition, those who had a more negative private attitude toward their ethnic group ($\beta = -.27, p < .05$) or who assumed that others had a negative perception of their ethnic group ($\beta = -.20, p < .05$) were also more likely to feel ashamed in response to their stereotypic ingroup member. These three variables (importance, private, and public collective self-esteem) were not significantly related to any of the other emotions (although public collective self-esteem was marginally related to anger, $\beta = -.15, p < .10$). The only other significant relationship for collective self-esteem in these analyses was that Hispanic participants who felt that they were good and worthy members of their ethnic group (i.e. high in membership collective self-esteem) were more likely to feel angry in response to another group member who confirms negative stereotypes about the group. Thus, even though the stereotypic actions of a group member elicited both feelings of shame and anger, these two emotions were differentiated by how they were related to aspects of collective self-esteem. As we might expect, concerns about a negative group image and the importance of ethnicity to identity was what uniquely predicted feeling ashamed. The comparison of one's own good behavior as a group member to that of the perpetrator was what uniquely predicted anger.

Emotions predicting action tendencies. In our final set of analyses, we examined what emotional reactions predict behavioral motivations. In each of these analyses, the five negative emotions were entered simultaneously as predictors of a given action tendency (i.e., (a) distancing from the group member, (b) distancing from the group identity, (c) repairing the image of the group, and (d) repairing harm caused by the event). We did not control for event severity in these analyses because initial results revealed that it was not a significant predictor of action tendencies. Results are summarized in Table 13.3. These analyses revealed that shame and anger were

TABLE 13.3
Standardized Coefficients from Simultaneous Regression Analyses Predicting Action Tendencies From Emotional Responses

	Outcome Variables			
	Distance from Group Member	*Distance from Group Identity*	*Repair Group Image*	*Repair Event*
Predictors				
Shame	.28***	.49***	.42***	.11
Anger	.54***	−.07	−.03	.06
Guilt	.16#	−.02	.08	.24*
Sadness	−.15#	.11	.10	.33**
Anxiety	−.04	.13	.00	.04

*$p < .05$. **$p < .01$. ***$p < .001$. #$p < .10$.

uniquely predictive of wanting to distance oneself from the group member. But shame was the only emotion that was uniquely predictive of wanting to distance oneself from one's ethnic group or do something to repair the tarnished image of one's group. These strategies seem to be adopted to reestablish a more positive group identity by, (a) "re-fencing" individuals who were confirming negative stereotypes about the group (i.e., distancing from the group member); (b) personally engaging in behaviors that communicate to oneself and to others that "we are not all like that" (i.e., repairing the group image); or (c) disidentifying with the group that has now been tarnished (i.e., distancing from the group identity). Finally, as we saw in our prior research (Lickel et al., 2005), direct efforts to repair whatever damage the ingroup member had caused were predicted not by shame, but by guilt as well as by sadness. Importantly, all of these relationships remained even when controlling for initial levels of collective self-esteem.

DISCUSSION

To summarize, data from this study provide evidence that shame plays a unique role in how individuals who are ethnically stigmatized react to the stereotypic behaviors of their ingroup. Although these actions elicit high levels of both shame and anger, it is shame that is predicted by the importance one places on his or her ethnic identity and it is shame that is distinctly predictive of distancing from the group or doing something to repair the image of the group in response. Although the offending actions of our ingroup might also make us very angry, shame is the reaction we seem to have in response to the feeling that an ingroup member is mismanaging the identity of our group.

This study relied on a methodology where participants recalled events from their own experiences. This event sampling technique has the advantage of allowing us to assess participants' reactions to real and sometimes fairly extreme events that would be difficult to recreate in a more controlled context. However, one limitation of this technique is that there is a great deal of variability in the type of event that participants recall. A second limitation to this first study is that there is no control group with which to make comparisons. Perhaps the events that participants recalled in the first study were the sorts of behaviors that would make anyone feel ashamed if a member of their ethnic group engaged in that behavior, even if that behavior was not consistent with negative stereotypes about one's group. We thought this was unlikely. Specifically, we predicted that given the same behavior (assuming that behavior is consistent with negative stereotypes about Hispanics), Hispanics would feel more ashamed of an ethnic ingroup member engaging in that behavior than would Whites if a member of their racial ingroup engaged in the same behavior.

To test this hypothesis, we conducted a second study in which we created scenarios describing a person (or persons) engaging in behaviors that were pretested to be consistent with negative stereotypes that people have about Hispanics (and modeled after some of the stories provided by participants in Study 1). Both White and Hispanic participants were instructed to imagine that a member of their own ethnic group had carried out the behavior that was described. Even though the events were identical, we expected that Hispanic participants would report more shame when imagining another Hispanic engaging in the behavior as compared to White participants imagining another White engaging in the same act.

STUDY 2

Participants and Procedure

Participants were 51 Hispanic and 66 White college students who participated in the study as part of a class assignment. They were given a survey that included all instructions and measures. Participants were asked to identify their racial/ethnic group and then proceeded to read and make ratings of their reactions to 12 different scenarios. For each scenario, participants were asked to imagine that the person carrying out the behavior in the scenario was of the same race or ethnicity as themselves. Each of the 12 scenarios described a situation in which an individual (or individuals) of the same racial/ethnic group as the participant engaged in either a negative (6 scenarios) or positive (6 scenarios) behavior. Their responses to three of the negative scenarios were of primary interest. The remaining scenarios were included as filler stimuli to distract participants from our focus on negative behaviors stereotypic of Hispanics.

The scenarios were developed and pretested on a different sample of Hispanic and White participants to select negative scenarios that were rated by members of both groups as being significantly more stereotypic of Hispanics than of Whites. Specifically, these scenarios described three young men being arrested for drug charges, a teenage mother who intentionally failed her last year in high school so that she could continue to receive state childcare benefits, and a group of men who yell obscene sexual remarks to a passing woman. After reading each scenario, participants made ratings of the emotional reactions they would have if they observed this event and what behaviors they would be motivated to do in response.

Participants were debriefed at the conclusion of the study and thanked for their participation.

Measures

All items were rated on 9-point scales ranging from 1 (*strongly disagree*) to 9 (*strongly agree*). Additional filler items were included that pertained to the positive scenarios.

Group identification. Prior to reading the scenarios, participants completed the identity importance subscale of the collective self-esteem scale (Luhtanen & Crocker, 1992) as a measure of group identification.

Emotions. After reading each scenario, participants made ratings of how much that scenario made them feel: *sad*, *ashamed*, *angry*, *anxious*, and *guilty* on a scale ranging from 1 (*not at all*) to 9 (*very intensely*).

Action tendencies. Distancing from the perpetrator was assessed with one item (*I would wish that this person or persons was not of my same race or ethnic group*). *Distancing from one's group* was assessed with one item (*I would wish that there was someway that I could change my ethnicity*). *Image repair* was assessed with the item (*I would want to do something to show that people in my ethnic group are not really like that*). Finally, *event repair* was assessed with one item (*I would feel like I should do something after the event to make it better*).

Results

Participants' shame ratings to each of the target scenarios were averaged together to form a composite rating of shame. This procedure was used to create indices for each variable that was measured. Responses of Hispanic and White participants were compared using a series of independent t tests.

Emotion. A 2(Race) × 5(Emotion) mixed model ANOVA yielded a significant interaction, $F(4, 111) = 2.74$, $p < .05$. Consistent with our hypothesis, Hispanic participants reported feeling significantly more shame ($M = 5.49$) than did Whites ($M = 4.40$), $t(115) = 2.84$, $p < .01$, when imagining an ingroup member engaging in these negative behaviors. Importantly, the two groups did not differ in their ratings of any of the other emotions, all ts < 1.

Action tendencies. A 2(Race) × 4(action tendency) mixed model ANOVA also yielded a significant interaction, $F(3, 113) = 6.20$, $p < .001$. Analysis of the action tendency variables revealed group differences only on the measure of image repair, $t(115) = 4.20$, $p < .001$; Hispanic participants reported that they would feel more motivated to do something to repair the image of their ethnic group ($M = 6.53$) than did White participants ($M = 4.71$). Contrary to predictions, there were no significant group differences in the tendency to distance from the perpetrator or from one's ethnic group, both *t*s < 1. There was also no difference in the desire to repair the event directly, $t < 1.30$.

Correlations with group identification. In our last set of analyses, we examined the degree to which the importance of ethnic identity was associated with Hispanic and White participants' responses to the scenarios. Within-group correlations revealed that, among Hispanic students, the more importance they placed on their ethnicity, the more they responded to an ingroup member engaging in stereotypic behaviors by feeling ashamed, $r = .39$, $p < .01$, and by wanting to repair the image of their group, $r = .39$, $p < .01$, and repair the event directly, $r = .48$, $p < .001$. Identification was not significantly related to any other emotion or action tendency among Hispanic participants, all *p*s $< .05$. Among White participants, identification was not significantly related to any of the emotion or action tendency variables, all *p*s $< .05$.

Discussion

Results of the second study extend those of the first by providing additional evidence that individuals feel a sense of shame for the stereotypic actions of their ethnic group. The same negative behaviors carried out by an ingroup member elicited equivalent levels of anger, sadness, guilt, and anxiety among Hispanic and White participants. However, Hispanic participants reported feeling significantly more ashamed for these behaviors than did Whites and reported being more motivated to do something to repair the image of their ethnic group. These results highlight that shame is a unique emotional response that individuals might have when they witness another member of their group engage in negative stereotypic behaviors. The relatively low levels of shame reported by White participants suggest that the same behaviors might not have the same implication for identity if they are not consistent with stereotypes about one's group. Likewise, group identification only predicted greater shame and a strong motive to repair the group image among Hispanic students, and not among Whites, further supporting our assertion that these behaviors should be particularly threatening to those most likely to include the stereotyped group identity as part of their self-concept.

CONCLUSIONS

Our goal in this chapter has been to develop a framework for understanding the emotional reactions that people may have when they witness another member of their ethnic group confirm negative social stereotypes about the group. Our evidence indicates that these events can have strong emotional consequences, particularly evoking feelings of shame, but also anger, for the event. These reactions of group-based shame are linked to how strongly identified individuals are with their stigmatized ingroup and shame uniquely predicts engaging in a variety of behaviors including repairing the tarnished group identity or distancing oneself from the group member or the group as a whole. In sum, these feelings of vicarious shame are so powerful, even in response to the actions of a complete stranger, because they signal to people that a core aspect of identity has been tainted and that steps must be taken to repair the group image or disidentify from the group.

The results of this research are important for both theoretical and practical reasons. By integrating elements of intergroup relations (e.g., the concept of *social identity*) with work on emotion (e.g., the unique aspects of shame), both of these literatures are extended in novel ways. Although previous research has highlighted that individuals construct a sense of identity around the social groups they belong to, the present work highlights that those social identities can sometimes come at an emotional cost. By including group members in our self-concept, we can expand our sense of who we are (McLaughlin-Volpe, chap. 11, this volume), but this also means that when those individuals engage in behaviors that are at odds with our own standards and values, we can experience the same sense of shame that we might feel in response to our own questionable acts. This is not only a novel finding for intergroup research, but it also extends past work on shame that has traditionally only examined this emotion in response to one's own actions or moral failures. It is interesting to learn that emotions like shame are so frequently experienced in response to the behavior of other people with whom one has a fairly minimal association.

At a more practical level, the present work highlights that an understanding of the distinct emotional response that people have in given situations can help us to identify who will feel the strongest negative reaction and to predict how they will be likely to behave. Results of research presented here suggest a person who feels especially guilty for an ingroup member's behavior will be motivated to be proactive and step in to repair whatever damage the ingroup member might have caused. In sharp contrast, someone whose dominant emotional response is to feel ashamed will be primarily motivated to take action designed to erase the blight on their identity. This might include disowning the perpetrator as a member of one's group, reducing one's own sense of group attachment, or counteracting the stereotypic behavior with actions designed to disconfirm the validity of the stereotype. In situations where an ingroup member has done real harm, the extent to which shame prompts behaviors in the service of identity management might preclude other actions of a more prosocial nature. For example, a Mexican American man who feels shamed by other Hispanic men who yell sexist remarks to a woman might feel more motivated to physically leave the situation that is eliciting this emotional response, than to step in and apologize or assist the woman who is being harassed. Such a response should be strongest for those individuals for whom group identity is particularly important and those behaviors that are especially relevant to one's group identity.

FUTURE RESEARCH

We believe that further research that examines specific emotional reactions to threats to people's social identities and the way in which people cope with those threats will be valuable. For example, we have found that there are a variety of responses that people may make to cope with the threat of a group member who has done something that appears to confirm the negative stereotype of the group. However, additional research is needed to understand when individuals choose one of these action tendencies over others. When does one respond to a stereotypic ingroup member by acting to repair the threatened group identity versus ousting the offending individual from the group or disidentifying from the group themselves? At present, we do not yet know all of the moderating variables that determine when each of these responses is selected. Uncovering these moderators will be essential to understanding the role that shame plays in intragroup dynamics.

In addition, although we have examined these feelings of vicarious shame in response to discrete events, one might wonder whether some stigmatized individuals feel a chronic sense of shame for the actions of other group members and, if so, what psychological impact this response might have for them. Although group identification often provides a resource that helps stigmatized individuals cope with stigma-related threat (Branscombe, Schmitt, & Harvey, 1999), this resource might not be available in circumstances where a group member behaves stereotypically and elicits in others a knee-jerk response to disidentify from the ingroup rather than turn to it for a sense of solidarity. Future research into the prevalence of chronic feelings of vicarious shame among stigmatized individuals could shed light on these questions.

Another issue that we believe is important is to understand how vicarious shame may operate within identities that are not classically considered "stigmatized." Thus, for example, Euro-Americans are not typically considered a stigmatized group. However, there is a negative stereotype of Whites as racist and many Whites are concerned about appearing racist. For example, Whites spontaneously attempt to control the use of social stereotypes in situations in which racist responses would be noticeable (Wyer, Sherman, & Stroessner, 1998) and demonstrate an activation of executive control processes in an attempt to control prejudicial responding (Richeson & Shelton, 2003). Interestingly, there is also evidence that Whites feel emotionally threatened by the suggestion that they personally are racist. For example, work by Zuwerink, Devine, Monteith, and Cook (1996) and Son Hing, Li, and Zanna (2002) showed that Whites who consider themselves to be nonprejudiced feel a combined sense of guilt and shame when they are reminded of ways in which they might stereotype members of ethnic minority groups. Thus, although in many respects Whites in North America have privileged status and a correspondingly positive stereotype that justifies their position in the status hierarchy, racism is one stigmatizing mark to which they are vulnerable. Correspondingly, Whites make efforts to not confirm the negative stereotype of their ethnic group as racist and may experience shame when they do so. By extension, we expect that at least some Whites may feel a sense of shame if they observe or learn of another White person who commits a racist act or statement. Thus, whereas members of traditionally stigmatized groups might have an increased vulnerability to feeling a sense of vicarious shame simply because negative stereotypes are more commonly associated with their group, almost every social category has some negative stereotype associated with it that leaves its members susceptible to feelings of shame when individuals act in ways that confirm that unwanted characterization.

In closing, we return again to our opening statements linking stigma and shame. Certainly the association between stigma and shame is intuitive and has been noted by others such as Allport (1954). However, beyond being merely an intuitive link, we believe that efforts to link specific emotional reactions such as shame, anger, and guilt is crucial to understanding the specific behavioral responses that people may have in social situations involving other ingroup members. Although past work on stigma has focused on global affective reactions to stigma (such as a sense of self-esteem), we advocate more work that also examines how specific emotional responses may play a role in determining people's responses to bearing a stigmatized identity.

ACKNOWLEDGMENT

Writing of this chapter was supported by collaborative grants BCS-0112473 and BCS-0112427 from the National Science Foundation to the authors. Correspondence should be sent to: Toni Schmader, PhD, Department of Psychology, University of Arizona, Tucson, AZ 85721, schmader@u.arizona.edu

REFERENCES

Allport, G. W. (1954). *The nature of prejudice*. Cambridge, MA: Addison-Wesley.

Baumeister, R. F., Stillwell, A. M., & Heatherton, T. F. (1995). Personal narratives about guilt: Role in action control and interpersonal relationships. *Basic and Applied Social Psychology, 17,* 173–198.

Ben-Zeev, T., Fein, S., & Inzlicht, M. (2005). Arousal and stereotype threat. *Journal of Experimental Social Psychology, 41,* 174–181.

Biernat, M., Vescio, T. K., & Billings, L. S. (1999). Black sheep and expectancy violation: Integrating two models of social judgment. *European Journal of Social Psychology, 29,* 523–542.

Blascovich, J., Spencer, S. J., Quinn, D., & Steele, C. (2001). African Americans and high blood pressure: The role of stereotype threat. *Psychological Science, 12,* 225–229.

Branscombe, N. R., Schmitt, M. T., & Harvey, R. D. (1999). Perceiving pervasive discrimination among African-Americans: Implications for group identification and well-being. *Journal of Personality and Social Psychology, 77,* 135–149.

Branscombe, N. R., Wann, D. L., & Noel, J. G. (1993). In-group or out-group extremity: Importance of the threatened social identity. *Personality and Social Psychology Bulletin, 19,* 381–388.

Brewer, M. B. (1991). The social self: On being the same and different at the same time. *Personality and Social Psychology Bulletin, 17,* 475–482.

Brewer, M. B. (2000). Superordinate goals versus superordinate identity as bases of intergroup cooperation. In D. Capozza & R. Brown (Eds.), *Social identity processes: Trends in theory and research* (pp. 117–132). London: Sage.

Crocker, J., & Major, B. (1989). Social stigma and self-esteem: The self-protective properties of stigma. *Psychological Review, 96,* 608–630.

Darley, J. M., & Gross, P. H. (1983). A hypothesis-confirming bias in labeling effects. *Journal of Personality and Social Psychology, 44,* 20–33.

Doosje, B., Branscombe, N. R., Spears, R., & Manstead, A. S. R. (1998). Guilty by association: When one's group has a negative history. *Journal of Personality and Social Psychology, 75,* 872–886.

Eisenberg, N. (2000). Emotion, regulation, and moral development. *Annual Review of Psychology, 51,* 665–697.

Ellemers, N., Doosje, B. J., & van Knippenberg, A. (1992). Status protection in high status minority groups. *European Journal of Social Psychology, 22,* 123–140.

Fiske, S. T., Cuddy, A., Glick, P., & Xu, J. (2002). A model of (often mixed) stereotype content: Competence and warmth respectively follow from perceived status and competition. *Journal of Personality and Social Psychology, 82,* 878–902.

Gilbert, P., & Andrews, B. (1998). *Shame: Interpersonal behavior, psychopathology, and culture.* New York: Oxford University Press.

Gil-White, F. J. (2001) Are ethnic groups biological 'species' to the human brain?: Essentialism in our cognition of some social categories. *Current Anthropology, 42,* 515–554.

Hamilton, D. L., Sherman, S. J., & Lickel, B. (1998). Perceiving social groups: The importance of the entitativity continuum. In C. Sedikides, J. Schopler, & C. A. Insko (Eds.), *Intergroup cognition and intergroup behavior* (pp. 47–74). Mahwah, NJ: Lawrence Erlbaum Associates.

Haslam, N., Rothschild, L., & Ernst, D. (2000). Essentialist beliefs about social categories. *British Journal of Social Psychology, 39,* 113–127.

Hirschfeld, L. A. (1995). Do children have a theory of race? *Cognition, 54,* 209–252.

Inzlicht, M., & Ben-Zeev, T. (2000). A threatening intellectual environment: Why females are susceptible to experiencing problem-solving deficits in the presence of males. *Psychological Science, 11,* 365–371.

Johns, M., Schmader, T., & Lickel, B. (in press). Ashamed to be an American?: The role of identification in predicting vicarious shame for Anti-Arab prejudice after 9-11. *Self and Identity.*

Kay, A. C., & Jost, J. T. (2003). Complementary justice: Effects of "poor but happy" and "poor but honest" stereotype exemplars on system justification and implicit activation of the justice motive. *Journal of Personality and Social Psychology, 85*, 823–837.

Keltner, D. (1995). The signs of appeasement: Evidence for the distinct displays of embarrassment, amusement, and shame. *Journal of Personality and Social Psychology, 68,* 441–454.

Kray, L. J., Thompson, L., & Galinsky, A. (2001). Battle of the sexes: Gender stereotype confirmation and reactance in negotiations. *Journal of Personality and Social Psychology, 80,* 942–958.

Krech, D., & Crutchfield, R. S. (1948). *Theory and problems of social psychology.* New York: McGraw-Hill.

Lewin, K. (1948). *Resolving social conflicts.* New York: Harper.

Lewis, H. B. (1971). *Shame and guilt in neurosis.* New York: International Universities Press.

Lickel, B., Hamilton, D. L., Wieczorkowska, G., Lewis, A., Sherman, S. J., & Uhles, A. N. (2000). Varieties of groups and the perception of group entitativity. *Journal of Personality and Social Psychology, 78,* 223–246.

Lickel, B., Schmader, T., & Barquissau, M. (2004). The evocation of moral emotions in intergroup contexts: The distinction between collective guilt and collective shame. In N. R. Branscombe & B. Doosje (Eds.), *Collective guilt: International perspectives* (pp. 35–55). New York: Cambridge University Press.

Lickel, B., Schmader, T., Curtis, M., Ames, D. R., & Scarnier, M. (2005). Vicarious shame and guilt. *Group Processes and Intergroup Relations.*

Luhtanen, R. & Crocker, J. (1992). A collective self-esteem scale: Self-evaluation of one's social identity. *Journal of Personality and Social Psychology, 18*, 302–318.

Major, B., Quinton, W. J., McCoy, S. K. (2002). Antecedents and consequences of attributions to discrimination: Theoretical and empirical advances. In M. P. Zanna (Ed.), *Advances in experimental social psychology* (Vol. 34, pp. 251–330). San Diego, CA: Academic Press.

Major, B., & Schmader, T. (2001). Legitimacy and the construal of social disadvantage. In B. Major & J. Jost (Eds.), *The psychology of legitimacy: Emerging perspectives on ideology, justice, and intergroup relations* (pp. 176–204). New York: Cambridge University Press.

Marques, J. M., Yzerbyt, V. Y., & Leyens, J. P. (1988). The "black sheep effect": Extremity of judgments towards ingroup members as a function of group identification. *European Journal of Social Psychology, 18*, 1–16.

McGuire, W. J., McGuire, C. V., Child, P., & Fujioka, T. (1978). Salience of ethnicity in the spontaneous self-concept as a function of one's ethnic distinctiveness in the social environment. *Journal of Personality and Social Psychology, 36,* 511–520.

Miller, C. T., Rothblum, E. D., Felicio, D., & Brand, P. (1995). Compensating for stigma: Obese and non obese women's reactions to being visible. *Personality and Social Psychology Bulletin, 21,* 1093–1106.

Niedenthal, P. M., Tangney, J. P. & Gavanski, I. (1994). "If only I weren't" versus "If only I hadn't": Distinguishing shame and guilt in counterfactual thinking. *Journal of Personality and Social Psychology, 67,* 585–595.

O'Brien, L. T., & Crandall, C. S. (2003). Stereotype threat and arousal: Effects on women's math performance. *Personality and Social Psychology Bulletin, 29*, 782–789.

Ogbu, J. U. (1991). Minority coping responses and school experience. *Journal of Psychohistory, 18,* 433–456.

Pinel, E. C. (1999). Stigma consciousness: The psychological legacy of social stereotypes. *Journal of Personality and Social Psychology, 76*, 114–128.

Prentice, D. A., Miller, D. T., & Lightdale, J. R. (1994). Asymmetries in attachments to groups and to their members: Distinguishing between common-identity and common-bond groups. *Personality and Social Psychology Bulletin, 20*, 484–493.

Rabbie. J. M., & Horwitz, M. (1988). Categories versus groups as explanatory concepts in intergroup relations. *European Journal of Social Psychology, 18*, 117–123.

Richeson, J. A., & Shelton, J. N. (2003). When prejudice does not pay: Effects of interracial contact on executive function. *Psychological Science, 14,* 287–290.

Rothbart, M., Evans, M., & Fulero, S. (1979). Recall for confirming events: Memory processes and the maintenance of social stereotypes. *Journal of Experimental Social Psychology, 15,* 343–355.

Rothbart, M., & Taylor, M. (1992). Category labels and social reality: Do we view social categories as natural kinds? In K. Fiedler & G. R. Semin (Eds.), *Language, interaction and social cognition* (pp. 11–36). Newbury Park, CA: Sage.

Schmader, T., Major, B., Eccleston, C. P., & McCoy, S. K. (2001). Devaluing domains in response to threatening intergroup comparisons: Perceived legitimacy and the status value asymmetry. *Journal of Personality and Social Psychology, 80,* 782–796.

Smith, E. R. (1993). Social identity and social emotions: Toward new conceptualizations of prejudice. In D. M. Mackie & D. L. Hamilton (Eds.), *Affect, cognition, and stereotyping: Interactive processes in group perception* (pp. 297–315). San Diego, CA: Academic Press.

Smith, E. R., & Henry, S. (1996) An in-group becomes part of the self: Response time evidence. *Personality and Social Psychology Bulletin, 22,* 635–642.

Smith, R. H., Webster, J. M., & Parrott, W. G. (2002). The role of public exposure in moral and nonmoral shame and guilt. *Journal of Personality and Social Psychology, 83,* 138–159.

Snyder, C. R., Lassegard, M. A., & Ford, C. E. (1986). Distancing after group success and failure: Basking in reflected glory and cutting off reflected failure. *Journal of Personality and Social Psychology, 51,* 382–388.

Son Hing, L. S., Li, W., & Zanna, M. P. (2002). Inducing hypocrisy to reduce prejudicial responses among aversive racists. *Journal of Experimental Social Psychology, 38,* 71–78.

Spencer, S. J., Steele, C. M., & Quinn, D. M. (1999). Stereotype threat and women's math performance. *Journal of Experimental Social Psychology, 35,* 4–28.

Steele, C. M., & Aronson, J. (1995). Contending with a stereotype: African-American intellectual test performance and stereotype threat. *Journal of Personality and Social Psychology, 69,* 797–811.

Tajfel, H. (1970). Experiments in intergroup discrimination. *Scientific American, 223,* 96–102.

Tajfel, H., & Turner, J. C. (1986). Social identity theory of intergroup behavior. In W. Austin & S. Worchel (Eds.), *Psychology of intergroup relations* (2nd ed., pp. 7–24). Chicago: Nelson-Hall.

Tangney, J. P. (1995). Shame and guilt in interpersonal relationships. In K. W. Fischer & J. P. Tangney (Eds.), *Self-conscious emotions* (pp. 64–113). New York: Guilford.

Tangney, J. P., & Fischer, K. W. (1995). *Self-conscious emotions.* New York: Guilford.

Tangney, J. P., Miller, R. S., Flicker, L., & Barlow, D. B. (1996). Are shame, guilt, and embarrassment distinct emotions? *Journal of Personality and Social Psychology, 70,* 1256–1269.

Weiner, B. (1995). *Judgments of responsibility: A foundation for a theory of social conduct.* New York: Guilford.

Wicker, F. W., Payne, G. C., & Morgan, R. D. (1983). Participant descriptions of guilt and shame. *Motivation and Emotion, 7,* 25–39.

Wyer, N. A., Sherman, J. W., & Stroessner, S. J. (1998). The spontaneous suppression of racial stereotypes. *Social Cognition, 16,* 340–352.

Zuwerink, J. R., Devine, P. G., Monteith, M. J., & Cook, D. A. (1996). Prejudice toward Blacks: With and without compunction? *Basic and Applied Social Psychology, 18,* 131–150.

CHAPTER

14

Stigma and the Social Basis of the Self: A Synthesis

Jennifer Crocker
Julie A. Garcia
University of Michigan

Intergroup relations are notoriously problematic. When individuals or groups of individuals with different social identities interact, tension and negative emotion often abound (W. G. Stephan & C. W. Stephan, 1985). People sometimes cope with these tensions by simply withdrawing from intergroup contact (Tatum, 1997). Too often, however, tension escalates into seemingly intractable conflict, with destructive consequences (Prentice & Miller, 1999).

The chapters in this volume illustrate a dramatic shift in research and theory on intergroup relations over the past 30 years. In 1963, sociologist Erving Goffman published a monograph titled, "Stigma: Notes on the Management of Spoiled Identity," an exploration of how people cope with identities that are devalued, stigmatized, or stereotyped. Goffman's analysis inspired researchers to investigate the experiences of people with stigmatized identities. Unfortunately, it was published just as the cognitive revolution transformed psychology. Since the 1960s, social psychological research on intergroup relations has been dominated by the cognitive perspective, examining the role that stereotypes and categorization processes play in creating and exacerbating intergroup tensions. Although much was learned about those processes, this research largely neglected the experiences of people who are targets of those stereotypes. Furthermore, research emphasized the cooler side of intergroup relations, focusing on beliefs and cognitions while neglecting emotional experiences and motivations.

Eventually, a strictly cognitive perspective on intergroup relations seemed too limited, and in the 1990s, a few researchers began to revive the

… s of people who are the targets of stereotypes and … to shift from a focus on categorization of people … members and the beliefs and stereotypes held … rd outgroups members, to a focus on the emo- … ping strategies of people who are stigmatized. … e illustrate just how much this perspective has … in the past 15 years.

One of the main difficulties of people with stigmatized identities concerns how to respond to prejudice and discrimination they perceive. When the stigmatized confront others about their prejudiced attitudes or discriminatory behavior, other people may derogate the stigmatized person, as Kaiser's chapter 3 documents. On the other hand, to ignore or overlook prejudice and discrimination is, in a sense, to collude in it, leading to guilt, regret, and disappointment for the stigmatized person (Shelton, Richeson, Salvatore, & Hill, chap. 4, this volume). In sum, the stigmatized often feel caught between two alternatives—confront or overlook prejudice—each of which has undesirable consequences. It is no wonder then that people who can conceal their stigmatized identity often choose to do so, as Quinn (chap. 5, this volume) notes. The predicaments the stigmatized experience regarding disclosing or concealing a stigma and confronting or overlooking prejudice can be conceptualized in the framework of the coping literature, as Miller (chap. 2, this volume) notes, or alternatively, it can be conceptualized as a self-regulation process in which the stigmatized regulate their behavior in the face of obstacles to their goals, as Swim and Thomas (chap. 6, this volume) point out. Bringing the existing literatures on coping and self-regulation to bear on the experience of stigmatized people provides new insights and raises a number of intriguing hypotheses.

As Goffman suggested and other researchers have reiterated, the predicaments of the stigmatized are mainly situational or context dependent. In other words, stigmatized people feel devalued or threatened in some contexts more than others. For example, subtle features of the situation may raise the specter of being devalued or stereotyped, affecting performance on intellectual tasks, a phenomenon explored by Inzlicht and Good (chap. 7, this volume). Mendoza-Denton, Page-Gould, and Pietrzak (chap. 8, this volume), in their research on prejudice apprehension, show that some stigmatized individuals are particularly vigilant for prejudice and discrimination, with potentially negative consequences. Perceptions of prejudice and discrimination adversely affect the intergroup contact experience for members of minority ethnic groups (Tropp, chap. 9, this volume). Yet, reactions to the experience of stigma are by no means uniform; as Major (chap. 10, this volume) notes, there is variability in responses to stigma across individuals, situations, and dependent variables, and these responses are transactional in nature.

At its core, the experience of stigma is fundamentally a threat to the self. Although all of the chapters in this volume implicate the self indirectly, in this third section of the volume, the self becomes the focus of research and theory. Sinclair and Huntsinger (chap. 12, this volume) build on shared-reality theory to understand how the self-concepts of the stigmatized are subtly shaped in their interactions with nonstigmatized individuals. Specifically, shared-reality theory contends that social relationships and social beliefs are developed and maintained through perceived consensus or "shared reality" established in particular social relationships. Shared-reality theory describes a subtle but profound aspect of social relationships; smooth social interactions require that people share common assumptions and beliefs about the nature of reality, including assumptions about who each of the interaction partners is as a person. People are particularly likely to tune their beliefs to those of relationship partners when their motivation to establish and maintain relationships is high, and when the belief is relevant to the relationship. By incorporating the views that relationship partners hold of the self, shared realities are established and relationships are maintained. This process is problematic for people who are stigmatized because establishing a shared reality may require incorporating negative stereotypes of the self that the other holds into one's own self-views, especially if the relationship is important and the stereotype is relevant to the relationship. Thus, whereas developing a shared reality can be self-expanding when others hold positive views of the self, it can be self-limiting when it involves incorporating negative stereotypes held by interaction partners into self-views.

From a very different theoretical perspective, McLaughlin-Volpe (chap. 11, this volume) takes as her starting point research on the inclusion of others in the self by Aron and his colleagues (A. Aron, E. N. Aron, Tudor, & Nelson, 1991). According to this perspective, people have the motive to grow and expand the self by acquiring new interests, skills, and knowledge. Close relationships can be self-expanding, because when the other is seen as part of the self, the interests, skills, and knowledge of the relationship partner become a part of the self. Thus, close relationships are an important source of personal growth and self-expansion. This can be particularly true for close relationships between stigmatized and nonstigmatized people, whose interests, skills, and knowledge may differ because of their different life experiences. That's the good news. The bad news is that because of stereotypes and prejudice, nonstigmatized people may be reluctant to form close relationships with stigmatized people, who in turn may have limited opportunities to form close relationships with nonstigmatized people. Thus, stigma can limit opportunities for personal growth and self-expansion for stigmatized and nonstigmatized people alike.

In their chapter, Schmader and Lickel (chap. 13, this volume) explore another version of including others in the self. As noted by Tesser (1988) and others, when people feel close to others, they may bask in the reflected glory of the others' success. For example, parents bask in their children's athletic accomplishments, professors bask in their students' professional success, and many of us bask in the fame or fortune of our friends and relatives. In yet another way, then, inclusion of others in the self can be self-expanding. However, as Schmader and Lickel note, the same process of including others in the self can lead to a sense of shame or guilt for people who are stigmatized. Stigmatized people may include others who share their identity in the self, and consequently may experience a sense of shame or guilt when members of their group act in ways that confirm negative stereotypes.

We applaud these authors for focusing on how the experience of social stigma can be problematic for the self and for the self-relevant emotions that are elicited in intergroup contexts. In the remainder of this chapter, we propose a framework that places the self at the center of the dynamics of intergroup relations, linking our own perspective to the research and theory presented in the rest of this volume.

THE PURSUIT OF SELF-ESTEEM

We begin with the observation people are motivated by the desire to sustain a view of the self as valuable and worthy (Pyszczynski, Greenberg, Solomon, Arndt, & Schimel, 2004; Steele, 1988). The pursuit of self-esteem is so pervasive that many psychologists have assumed it is a universal and fundamental human need (Allport, 1955; Baumeister, Heatherton, & Tice, 1993; Maslow, 1968; Rogers, 1961; Rosenberg, 1979; Solomon, Greenberg, & Pyszczynski, 1991; Taylor & Brown, 1988); some have even argued that humans evolved as a species to pursue self-esteem (Leary & Baumeister, 2000; Leary & Downs, 1995). Although we question whether people truly need self-esteem (Crocker & Nuer, 2004), it seems clear that at least in Western societies, people want self-esteem (Heine, Lehman, Markus, & Kitayama, 1999).

People have beliefs about what they need to be or do to have worth and value as a person (Crocker & Wolfe, 2001). These beliefs, or *contingencies of self-worth*, are shaped by individual and collective experiences across the life span, from early attachment relationships with caregivers, to interactions within the family, neighborhood, school, community, and culture, that convey what makes a person valuable and worthwhile (Crocker & Park, 2004). In addition, the immediate context may suggest what one needs to be or do to have value and worth in that context (Garcia & Crocker, 2003). In the classroom, intelligence is valued; in the ballroom, physical grace is valued; and in the boardroom, business acumen is valued.

Regardless of their source, contingencies of self-worth shape people's goals. In these domains, people have *self-validation goals*; that is, they want to prove that they satisfy their contingencies of self-worth, and therefore demonstrate that they are valuable and worthy (Crocker & Park, 2004; Wolfe & Crocker, 2003). For example, students who base their self-esteem on doing well in school have the goal of demonstrating their intelligence through their schoolwork (Crocker, 2003). Because it is difficult, if not impossible, to sustain a view of the self if others with whom one interacts do not share that view, people want others to see themselves as succeeding in the domains in which their self-esteem is based. A person could simply decide that he is brilliant, beautiful, or has a lovely voice, but if at least some other people do not concur with this opinion, self-doubts will quickly develop, and interactions will be strained because the interactants are operating from different views of reality. Reaching agreement on a shared reality regarding the qualities and attributes of the self is particularly urgent when a relationship is important, and when self-attributes are relevant to the interaction (Sinclair & Huntsinger, chap. 12, this volume).

One way to achieve shared reality in interactions is by adapting or adjusting one's self-views in the direction of one's interaction partner's beliefs about the self (Sinclair & Huntsinger, chap. 12, this volume). This adjustment of the self to others' views eases and smoothes interactions because both parties are operating on the same assumptions. Yet, when people need others to recognize and validate particular qualities in the self in order to sustain self-esteem, adjusting the self to others' views that threaten self-esteem creates difficulties for the self even though it smoothes interactions. Consequently, when self-attributes are relevant to their contingencies of self-worth, people act in ways that ensure that others will adjust their views of the self to be consistent with these desired, ego-relevant self-views. In other words, people act in ways that create and sustain what we call a "desired image." The desired image goes beyond simply being what one's self-esteem depends on, to acting in ways that ensure that others will see and acknowledge that one has that quality, with the goal of creating a shared reality that sustains one's self-esteem. For example, a student with the desired image of "intelligent" may deliberately try to say something clever in each class meeting, while avoiding asking questions that could reveal confusion or failure to understand a point. As this example illustrates, some of the things people do to sustain their desired image are self-defeating; a student who will not ask questions when he does not understand what is being taught undermines accomplishment of his long-term goals.

Success at achieving self-validation and sustaining the desired image leads to positive self-relevant emotions such as pride; threats or obstacles to these self-validation goals trigger negative self-relevant emotions such as shame, guilt, or humiliation. Although success at any goal elicits positive emotions and failure elicits negative emotions (Carver & Scheier, 1998), the emotions connected to self-validation goals include self-relevant emotions such as shame and guilt, which have particularly potency (Tangney, 1999). When people are driven by self-validation goals, they are prone to act and think in ways that maintain, protect, and enhance self-esteem, and engage in "defensive routines" (Argyris, 1990) that can be destructive, costly, and even self-defeating (Crocker & Park, 2004). For example, when people are uncertain of success, they will often self-handicap, or act in ways that create a good excuse or explanation for failure, such as procrastinating (Tice, 1991). These self-handicapping strategies are clearly defensive because, although they protect one's desired image and self-esteem by providing an explanation for failure, they undermine the likelihood of success.

Although our perspective is different in focus from shared-reality theory as described by Sinclair and Huntsinger (chap. 12, this volume), our view is not contradictory to theirs. Whereas, Sinclair and Huntsinger emphasize how people adjust their self-views toward the views that their interaction partners hold of them, we suggest that for some self-views, people will be highly motivated to create a shared reality by getting others to see them in ways that sustain self-esteem. Thus, it is not necessarily the case that stigmatized people will adjust their self views to those of their interaction partners by evaluating themselves and behaving in stereotype-consistent ways. On the other hand, a shared reality can be developed by stigmatized people striving to get their interaction partners to see them in positive ways that counter negative stereotypes. The latter alternative ensures that self-esteem is maintained for the stigmatized person, while the nonstigmatized person's self-esteem is likely to be diminished. The desire to create a shared reality will be greatest when relationship motivation is high and when the self-view in question is relevant to contingencies of self-worth.

STIGMA AND THE PURSUIT OF SELF-ESTEEM

In our view, sustaining the belief that the self is worthy and valuable is fundamentally difficult in interactions between the stigmatized and the nonstigmatized, and goes to the heart of why these interactions are often problematic. In intergroup interactions, people bring with them their usual desired images that they are likely to have in any interaction (e.g., competent, virtuous, kind), but most salient to them will be those aspects that are specifically relevant to their identity or identities as a member of a valued or devalued group (e.g., fair, unprejudiced, deserving of respect, intelligent). For the stigmatized, interactions with nonstigmatized people raise the specters of devaluation, negative stereotypes, and discrimination, which threaten desired images that the stigmatized person needs to sustain to maintain self-esteem. Likewise, contexts in which one's identity is valued or idealized may activate the goal to demonstrate that one possesses in sufficient measure the positive traits the identity is supposed to bestow; that one is fair and unprejudiced, or that one has not benefited unfairly from one's privileged status. Thus, whether stigmatized or idealized, social identities can trigger self-validation goals linked to desired images in intergroup interactions.

Stigma: The Target's Perspective

Goffman (1963) used the term, *stigma*, to refer to an attribute of a person that is deeply discrediting, and reduces the person "in our minds from a whole and usual person to a tainted, discounted one" (p. 3). People who are stigmatized have some characteristic that raises doubts about their full humanity–the person is devalued, spoiled, or flawed in the eyes of others (Jones et al., 1984). The experience of having a stigmatized attribute, condition, or diagnosis raises the possibility that in social interactions one will be devalued, stereotyped, discriminated against, rejected, or dehumanized by others (Crocker, Major, & Steele, 1998). Consequently, stigma fundamentally poses a threat to the desired image and, hence, self-esteem of the stigmatized person (Crocker et al., 1998).

When other people are included in the self, because they share a social identity with the self, people may have identity validation goals, in addition to self-validation goals. In particular, as Schmader and Lickel (chap. 13, this volume) note, members of stereotyped groups may be highly motivated to prove wrong negative stereotypes of their groups. For example, a woman might want to validate that women are competent and tough-minded, or an African American student might want to validate that African Americans are intelligent. When people believe that they or members of their group have been or could be perceived stereotypically, they may adopt goals to validate the positive qualities of the self or the group (Steele, Spencer, & Aronson, 2002). Avoiding confirming negative stereotypes allows the stigmatized person to protect the group's desired image.

When social interactions require negotiating a shared reality, how does the stigmatized person respond to this devaluation? As Sinclair and Huntsinger (chap. 12, this volume) show, if the relationship is important and the perceiver's beliefs about the self are relevant to the interaction, the stigmatized person may adjust his or her self-concept to be aligned with the perceiver's stereotypic beliefs. However, achieving shared reality in this way may come at a price to the stigmatized person's desired image and self-esteem because it may require agreeing that one has negative qualities stereotypically associated with one's stigmatized identity. Alternatively, the stigmatized person can actively assert a desired image and contest the stereotypic belief, attempting to demonstrate that the negative stereotype does not apply to the self. As Schmader and Lickel (chap. 13, this volume) note, contexts in which one's identity is stigmatized or devalued may activate the goal to prove that negative stereotypes about one's identity group do not apply to the self. For example, African American students about to take a test of their intellectual ability describe themselves in counter-stereotypic ways (Steele & Aronson, 1995). One interpretation of this finding is that African American students who feel at risk of being judged in the context of negative stereotypes are motivated to distance themselves in the eyes of others from the stereotypic characterizations of their group.

In addition to the desired image threat inherent in others holding negative beliefs or stereotypes about the stigmatized person, the desired image of a stigmatized person can also come from how other group members are perceived. As Schmader and Lickel (chap. 13, this volume) note, sharing a social identity with other stigmatized people means that their behavior in some ways reflects on the self. Similarly, how other group members are viewed by others reflects on the desired image of the group, and therefore on the self. Consequently, when ingroup members act in ways that confirm negative stereotypes, stigmatized individuals feel many of the same negative emotions—shame and anger—that they feel when their own desired image is threatened (Schmader & Lickel, chap. 13, this volume).

How do stigmatized people deal with this threat to their personal or collective desired image? The usual responses involve either creating conflict or avoiding conflict. As the chapters by Shelton, Richeson, Salvatore, and Hill (chap. 4, this volume) and Kaiser (chap. 3, this volume) note, the stigmatized person may actively cope with this situation by complaining about being stereotyped or discriminated against, a choice that is likely to create a conflict with the other. The costs associated with complaining about prejudice and discrimination can be great. Such complaints bring into sharp relief the fact that there is no shared reality, making interactions difficult. Furthermore, complaining about prejudice and discrimination can threaten other cherished desired images, such as the image of being nice, easygoing, cooperative, nondefensive, and so on, and can threaten the motive to be accepted and included by others (Swim & Thomas, chap. 6, this volume). Complaints about prejudice can lead to arguments about who is right and who is wrong that can damage relationships. Alternatively, the stigmatized person can avoid conflict by concealing the stigma, being vigilant for cues of stigma-based rejection, stifling complaints, or withdrawing.

Concealment. Stigmatized people whose stigmas are concealable might avoid conflict by choosing to "pass" as nonstigmatized (see Quinn, chap. 5, this volume). In their analysis of social stigma, Jones et al. (1984) suggested that "individuals who can conceal their affliction will do just that" (p. 29). When cultural stereotypes are inconsistent with the desired image the stigmatized person wishes to project, concealing the stigma may seem like a good idea. However, concealing a stigma does not decrease psychological distress (Link, Mirotznik, & Cullen, 1991), and "passing" as nonstigmatized can actually create distress for the concealer (Goffman, 1963). From the perspective of shared-reality theory, concealing a stigma creates difficulties for interactions when the stigma is relevant and the relationship is important because the concealer knows that interaction partners do not share crucial knowledge about the self. People who conceal a stigma constantly worry about revealing information about the stigma; if they do, their desired image is challenged both because the stigma becomes known, and because the concealer may be considered deceitful for having concealed it, potentially threatening the desired image of "honest" or "trustworthy." Thus, concealing a stigma is a risky strategy both because of the danger to one's desired image if the stigma becomes known, and because of the psychological distress and other health consequences concealment creates in the long-term (Cole, Kemeny, & Taylor, 1997; Cole, Kemeny, Taylor, & Visscher, 1996).

Vigilance. Vigilance for early cues of prejudice and devaluation might help the stigmatized person avoid conflict by taking defensive measures to avoid experiences with prejudice. However, when people are vigilant for signs of devaluation, they tend to see it everywhere, because they interpret the intentions of their interaction partner as hostile (Kramer, 1988). African Americans who are high in prejudice apprehension, or the anxious expectation of race-based rejection, perceive rejection more often and react to it more strongly (Mendoza-Denton, Downey, Purdie, Davis, & Pietrzak, 2002; Mendoza-Denton, Page-Gould, & Pietrzak, chap. 8, this volume). People who anxiously expect rejection actually can behave in ways that increase their likelihood of experiencing rejection (Downey, Freitas, Michaelis, & Khouri, 1998), again creating a downward spiral.

Stifling Complaints. Another strategy for avoiding conflict about prejudice is stifling one's complaints. However, as Shelton, Richeson, Salvatore, and Hill (chap. 4, this volume) note, the cost of not confronting another person about prejudice may be negative feelings about the self. In addition, stifling complaints builds obstacles to creating a shared reality with the other. Exiting from the situation or relationship eliminates the need to negotiate a shared reality with the potential to threaten self-esteem, but has its own costs.

Withdrawal. Withdrawal is another strategy to avoid conflict about prejudice and discrimination. However, withdrawal can result in greater experiences of rejection, which can, in turn, result in increased withdrawal, creating a downward spiral (Wright, Gronfien, & Owens, 2000). Moreover, withdrawing limits opportunities to form relationships with outgroup members, with costs for self-expansion and self-efficacy (McLaughlin-Volpe, chap. 11, this volume).

In sum, from the perspective of the stigmatized person, stigma poses a threat to cherished desired images, and hence self-esteem, and raises questions about one's worth and value as a person. Stigmatized people may adjust their self-images to be consistent with stereotypes others hold of them, fostering a sense of shared reality. However, this strategy for creating shared reality is costly, in that it may diminish self-esteem. Alternatively, the stigmatized person can try to induce the interaction partner to shift his or her beliefs in line with the self-concept of the stigmatized person. Specifically, the stigmatized person may confront the other, pointing out evidence of prejudice and discrimination. Although this may bolster the desired image by refuting negative stereotypes and devaluation, it can threaten desired images of being good-natured, easygoing, or likeable. In addition, confronting has costs for relationships (Kaiser, chap. 3, this volume). Alternatively, the stigmatized person may conceal the stigma from others, become especially vigilant for signs of devaluation, stifle complaints about prejudice, or withdraw from the relationship. Each of these solutions has potential long-term costs. Thus, as Shelton, Richeson, Salvatore, and Hill (chap. 4, this volume) suggest, the stigmatized person may be caught between "a rock and a hard place," with the choice of confronting the other and creating conflict, or withdrawing, concealing, being vigilant, or stifling, and avoiding conflict. As the authors of *Difficult Conversations* note, delivering a difficult message, such as confronting someone about their prejudice, is like throwing a hand grenade; choosing not to deliver a difficult message, for example by avoiding confronting someone about their prejudice, is "like hanging onto a hand grenade once you've pulled the pin" (Stone, Patton, & Heen, 1999, p. xviii). There are costs associated with either option.

Stigma: The Perceiver's Perspective

Stigma can pose a threat to the desired image of the nonstigmatized, as well. Although having the valued identity in an interaction with a stigmatized person might seem to bolster the desired image and self-esteem of the nonstigmatized person, in actuality there are perils for the nonstigmatized person's desired image in this situation. First, just as having a devalued identity is linked to stereotypes about negative qualities that presumably go with that identity, having a valued identity is linked to stereotypes about positive qualities that presumably go with that identity. Men are supposed to be masculine, strong, and tough; professors are supposed to be intellectual and well-read, and so on. Thus, having a valued social identity raises the possibility that one will be judged as not measuring up to the positive qualities that are presumed to go with the identity. In addition, even valued identities often have negative stereotypes associated with them; Boston Brahmins are presumed to be well-educated but cold; men are strong but emotionally distant; professors are intellectual but out of touch with real life. Second, people with valued identities run the risk of being accused of benefiting from their privileged identity, and lacking the merit other people must have to achieve the same status. For example, many White students feel very uncomfortable with exercises designed to help them see how they benefit from whiteness. Such exercises threaten the desired image that their accomplishments are based on merit, rather than favoritism or privilege. Third, most people include in their desired image attributes like fair, thoughtful, just, unbiased, nice, likable, and so on. Interacting with a stigmatized person can threaten these desired images by raising the possibility that one will be "caught" expressing prejudice. Being caught in prejudice threatens the desired image and the self-esteem of people who cling to the idea that they are unprejudiced (Monteith, 1996; Monteith, Devine, & Zuwerink, 1993). Fourth, just as being stigmatized broadly threatens desired image and self-esteem because one is devalued, being nonstigmatized puts one at risk of being seen by others as the oppressor or the beneficiary of prejudice and discrimination. Whereas the stigmatized are easily seen as the victims of prejudice, the nonstigmatized are easily seen as the perpetrators of prejudice. Simply having a valued identity can place one at risk of being seen as the perpetrator of injustice in certain situations.

When social interactions require negotiating a shared reality, how does the nonstigmatized person respond to this desired image threat? One strategy is to adjust one's self-image in a negative direction, to bring it into alignment with the stigmatized person's (real or imagined) views of the self, acknowledging that one is the beneficiary of privilege and a perpetrator of prejudice and discrimination. Although little studied, we think this strategy is used, albeit rarely, when interactions are important and the attribute is relevant. For example, in our experience, White men who work in social-justice programs linked to race and gender often freely acknowledge their privileged status and their role as oppressors. Although adjusting one's self-concept to the stereotype that one is the oppressor threatens desired images of fairness, we suspect that this strategy can also bolster cherished desired images that are most closely linked to self-esteem, such as the image of being a "good guy" who acknowledges his advantaged status and is on the side of creating social justice. And for White men who work in social-justice programs, reaching shared reality regarding whether one is the oppressor or not is both important and relevant.

For the vast majority of nonstigmatized individuals, however, social norms against being prejudiced mean that being nonprejudiced is an important part of their desired image, and they try to behave in ways that ensure that others will see them as nonprejudiced. When students were asked to rate a variety of groups both in terms of how acceptable it would be to have negative feelings toward the group and their own feelings toward the group, participants reported their own prejudices only when they perceived prejudice against a group to be socially acceptable (Crandall, Eshleman, & O'Brien, 2002). Furthermore, when a social norm against prejudice is salient, people are less inclined to display prejudicial responses (Monteith, Deneen, & Tooman, 1996). Thus, egalitarian social norms lead people to suppress expressions of prejudice, which may then "leak" out in covert or subtle prejudice (Beal, O'Neal, Ong, & Ruscher, 2000; McConahay, 1981, 1986).

Some people act in a discriminatory manner despite egalitarian norms, suggesting that being nonprejudiced is not part of their desired image. Discrepancies between how people believe they should act (i.e., their desired image) and how they would act with stigmatized others have emotional consequences (Devine, Monteith, Zuwerink, & Elliot, 1991; Zuwerink, Devine, Monteith, & Cook, 1996). Specifically, when low-prejudiced people act more prejudiced than their personal values dictate, they feel guilty and criticize themselves.

To summarize, for nonstigmatized people, interacting with stigmatized others can threaten cherished desired images, and hence, self-esteem. Most nonstigmatized people believe that good, fair, likable people are not prejudiced; when confronted with evidence of their prejudice, their nonprejudiced desired image is threatened, and they feel guilt and discomfort.

Thus, interactions can pose a predicament for both stigmatized and nonstigmatized individuals; the stigmatized person faces potential devaluation because of his or her stigmatizing attribute, whereas the nonstigmatized person faces the possibility of being judged as prejudiced, bigoted, or a perpetrator of injustice. In the context of social interactions, these potential self-threats can lead to mistrust, discomfort, anxiety, and even avoidance and withdrawal (Monteith et al., 1993; W. G. Stephan & C. W. Stephan, 1985). Social interactions between the stigmatized and nonstigmatized can be more than uncomfortable; they can reinforce the negative views that each person in the interaction holds of the other. It is in these mixed interactions that "the causes and effects of stigma must be directly confronted by both sides" (Goffman, 1963, p. 13). For a variety of reasons, interactions between stigmatized and nonstigmatized others can be uncomfortable for both parties and even positive conditions of contact may not be sufficient to lead to positive effects of contact for members of nonstigmatized groups (Tropp, chap. 9, this volume).

THE STIGMA CYCLE

In interactions, two (or more) people's efforts to sustain their desired images can become intertwined and mutually reinforcing, creating a downward spiral that is difficult to break. In interactions between stigmatized and nonstigmatized people, the ego issues at stake loom large, including who is the "good guy" and who is the "bad guy," who is the victim, and who is the perpetrator in the interaction. Both people in the interaction tend to view their behavior as a reaction to the other's behavior, and do not see their behavior as the cause of the other's response. Thus, each party tends to see themselves as the victim, and the other person as the perpetrator, regardless of whether they have a stigmatized or valued social identity. Admitting that one has made a mistake, apologizing for harm caused to another, or acknowledging that one is in some respects a perpetrator, can deescalate conflict, but threaten one's desired image of being competent, right, or morally just. For ego-defensive reasons, then, people resist taking actions that could reduce the level of tension in interactions between stigmatized and nonstigmatized people.

The resulting dynamic can be painful for both parties. Each person in the interaction, driven by his or her own desired image, tends to behave in ways that trigger the desired image concerns of the other person. Of course, there are many versions of this, depending on whether the stigmatized person withdraws, conceals, or accuses, and on whether the nonstigmatized person reacts to this behavior with guilt or anger. The general rule, in our experience, is that each person acts in ways that make it more, rather than less, likely that his or her worst fears will come true.

Consider the dynamic depicted in Fig. 14.1, a typical dynamic between the stigmatized and nonstigmatized, in our experience. To help the discussion, we refer to the stigmatized person as "she" and the nonstigmatized person as "he." The stigmatized person in this dynamic begins with anxiety about being devalued, related to the belief or concern that the other may be prejudiced. Her belief might be accurate, based in past experience or knowledge gleaned from others' experiences. She is likely to be vigilant for signs of prejudice in him, whether it is justified by past experience or not. And that vigilance will result in a level of scrutiny that few could pass. Sensing that he is under scrutiny, the nonstigmatized person might become nervous, distracted, or focused on suppressing inappropriate thoughts, which paradoxically can lead to a slip of the tongue (or a slip of the mind), and the unwanted expression of prejudice. The stigmatized person may respond with complicated emotions—on one hand, her worst fears have come true. On the other hand, she knows that she was right to be vigilant and mistrusting, and there is something satisfying in being right. She may confront him about his behavior. He, thinking of himself as a good, fair, and

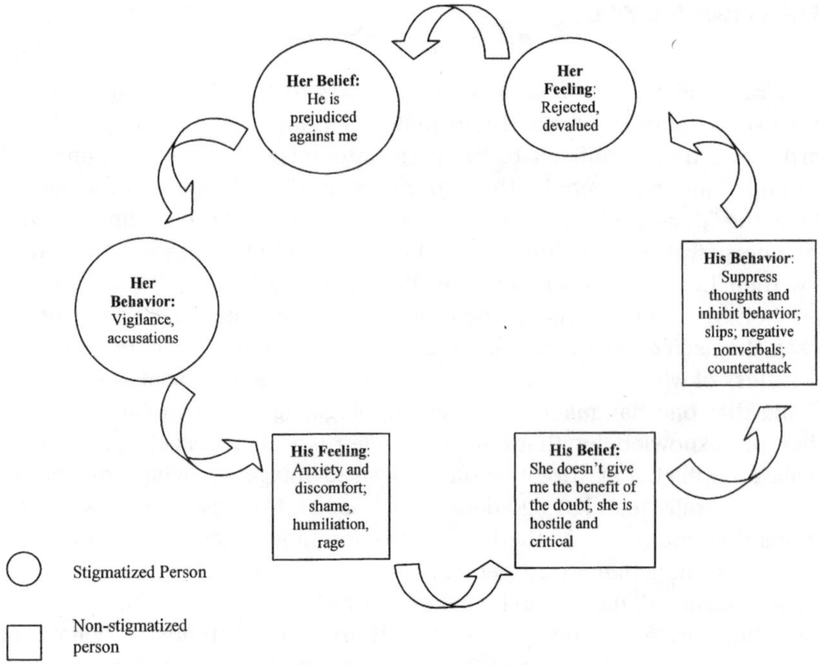

FIG. 14.1. Diagram of the cycle that might occur when the stigmatized and the nonstigmatized blame one another.

nonprejudiced person, may react to this accusation either with rage, or with shame and humiliation, or both. He may become angry, defensive, and feel that his good intentions are unappreciated. He may conclude that she always sees herself as a victim, is critical and judgmental, and never gives him the benefit of the doubt. He may respond with greater anxiety about being accused of prejudice, defending himself, counterattacking, withdrawing, or resisting. She, in turn, will feel misunderstood, judged, and disrespected, and this will reinforce her conclusion that he is prejudiced.

We began describing the cycle with her, the stigmatized person's, belief that she might be devalued, because the authors have both observed how we can begin our interactions with this belief. But the starting point of the cycle could just as easily have been the nonstigmatized person, and his anxiety about being accused of prejudice. We have both been in this situation, too. There is no single person who started this cycle–both people in this dynamic bring with them their beliefs and assumptions about the other, desired images and ego dynamics; both contribute to the cycle.

In this cycle, the worst fears of both the stigmatized and the nonstigmatized person are confirmed. He was right to be worried about being accused of prejudice, and she was right to worry that he is prejudiced. What is difficult for either of them to see is how they are each responsible for this reality. In fact, having a conversation about who is right and who is wrong in this dynamic is not a way out of the cycle; instead, it is counterproductive. Both are right, and both are wrongly accused. Both are innocent victims in their own minds, and both are perpetrators in the other person's mind. In reality, each person in this interaction is both a victim and a perpetrator. After this interaction, each will approach the next interaction with more negative beliefs about the other, anxiety, mistrust, and suspicion, and create a new destructive cycle.

What Initiates the Cycle?

How does a destructive cycle like this get started? In our experience, the precursor to this cycle is a threat to desired image or a "pinch" to the ego, which may be quite subtle. For example, momentary feelings of incompetence, powerlessness, or guilt can subtly threaten self-esteem, creating the context for a destructive cycle. Alternatively, realizing that another person's views of the self are inconsistent with one's desired image can set the stage for the cycle. At these moments, the person feels a deep, if unidentified, discomfort with the self. Reflecting on the reasons for the discomfort may require facing unpleasant realities about the self—"I'm sometimes selfish," or "I'm not as smart as I'd like to think," or "My students see me as someone who isn't open-minded," for example. Unconsciously, to avoid facing unpleasant realities about the self, the person focuses on the weaknesses or shortcomings of others. Negative beliefs about others become salient, triggering negative interaction cycles. In our experience, for example, there are times when the foibles of others do not faze us as all, and times when the same foibles drive us to distraction. The main difference in these situations, we suspect, is that when our egos have been pinched by something perhaps completely unrelated (e.g., an e-mail message that is unsettling, feeling stuck on a writing project), we focus on and cannot bear the foibles of the other. We communicate our dissatisfaction, creating a conflict that confirms our worst views of the other. Similarly, we suspect that moments when negative beliefs about outgroup members are salient have been preceded by some type of pinch to the ego, which leads us to focus on what is wrong with the other.

What Sustains the Cycle?

In light of how painful it is, and how inevitable the downward spiral, we might expect that people would quickly learn that they need more effective methods to deal with the downward spiral of intergroup relations. But there are at least four powerful forces sustaining the cycle. First, and most obviously, the desire to maintain and protect self-esteem sustains the downward spiral. The behaviors that can stop the cycle are things like admitting mistakes, acknowledging one's responsibility, apologizing, and making reparations. Yet, each of these behaviors threaten the desired image because they require acknowledging that one is not always good, right, competent, fair, and just.

Second, the cycle is difficult to break because there are some subtle additional advantages that people get from being in the cycle. For example, both participants in these cycles tend to see themselves as the victim, which in their view absolves them of responsibility for any damage that is done to the other, and excuses them from responsibility for change.

Third, these cycles can consume time, energy, and emotional resources, making it possible to avoid thinking about or addressing other, real difficulties facing the participants, such as unpleasant realities about the self. Being caught in an argument about who is the victim and who is the perpetrator in these interactions can provide a great excuse not to look at one's weaknesses and areas for improvement, such as whether one has a difficulty with trust or with considering the needs of the other. For the stigmatized person, focusing on how one is (or might be) a victim of discrimination can be a welcome distraction from addressing the areas where one needs to improve. For the nonstigmatized person, focusing on how others are untrusting and unfairly accusing can be a welcome distraction from addressing the real issues in one's behavior and relationships and examining one's beliefs and assumptions about outgroup members. For both, the cycle can provide a distraction from the possibility that one has issues to address with the other and one does not know how to address them constructively, without either creating or avoiding conflict.

Fourth, these cycles can be difficult to break because they are self-reinforcing. The stigmatized person who assumes that others will devalue or reject him may act in ways that increase the likelihood of those events, increasing the stigmatized person's conviction that others cannot be trusted and vigilance is required. The nonstigmatized person's belief that she will be unfairly accused of prejudice increases the likelihood that she will behave in cool or distant ways that others interpret as prejudice, reinforcing her concern that she will be unfairly accused. Each pass through the cycle reinforces the conception of reality that creates the cycle.

The Way Out

How can we break this cycle of suspicion, mistrust, and anxiety between stigmatized and nonstigmatized people? Trying to sort out misconceptions from accurate perceptions of reality is not an effective way to break the cycle because both people are convinced that their beliefs and assumptions about the other are right, and behave in ways that induce the other to confirm the belief, so both participants' *are* right, based on their own experience.

The cycle can be broken if each person identifies and takes responsibility for his or her part of the cycle. The typical view in these situations is that one person is to blame and the other is the innocent victim—of course, we all tend to think that we are the innocent victim. Yet, it is very rare that difficult interactions are completely due to the actions of one person, with the other person making no contribution at all. Breaking the cycle requires shifting from blame and judgment to understanding joint responsibility (Stone et al., 1999). Only when people begin to see that they are not only a victim in this cycle, but also a perpetrator, do they see where they have the possibility of altering the cycle. It is precisely where one has responsibility for what went wrong that one has the possibility to create something different. The motivation to take responsibility for breaking the cycle can come from a clear-eyed view of its costs and benefits. Of course, that requires risking threat to one's desired image and self-esteem.

Framing the problematic nature of intergroup relations in terms of self-validation goals and defensive routines leads one to question what alternative goals people might have in intergroup contexts that could improve the dynamics of these interactions.

Learning Goals. Social psychological research has shown that one way to reduce ego threat in difficult situations is to adopt a learning orientation (Dweck, 2000). For example, students who failed a verbal test and whose self-esteem was staked on their academic competence showed a large drop in self-esteem; this loss of self-esteem was entirely eliminated when students were given a learning orientation by priming the belief that intelligence can improve (Niiya, Crocker, & Bartmess, 2004).

These insights dovetail nicely with organizational research on diversity, which suggests that when culturally diverse work groups treat their diversity as a resource for learning how best to do the group's core work, group members actively explore diverse views, deal more constructively with intergroup conflict, and feel more valued and respected, which enhances the group's performance (Ely & Thomas, 2001). In groups that are motivated to learn from members' cultural differences, discussions about cultural identity are legitimate and tend to be more constructive because they are seen as task- rather than ego-related. In addition, openness to learning from cultural differences fosters a safe environment in which members of different cultural identity groups can provide and solicit feedback, air conflicts, and learn from their mistakes (Ely & Thomas, 2003). By identifying some of the individual and interpersonal dynamics that hinder—and enhance—people's capacity to learn, we hope to identify and elaborate a framework for understanding how to reap the performance benefits of diversity while avoiding many of the costs.

Learning goals can be a very powerful way to break many negative cycles. Asking "What can I learn from this situation or experience?" can be helpful. When a stigmatized person feels stuck between two bad options—confronting another person about his prejudice and creating conflict, or stifling complaints and avoiding conflict—it is possible to find a third alternative by having what Stone et al. (1999) called a "learning conversation." Instead of assuming that one's interpretation of the other's behavior is right, one might try to learn what the other person's interpretation is. A nonstigmatized person who believes another person is being vigilant for prejudice could check that out, again in a way that acknowledges that the perception might be wrong. A person accused of prejudice, or accused of being vigilant for prejudice, can ask, "What am I doing that might lead the other to see me as prejudiced?" This open-minded learning orientation can go a long way toward breaking destructive cycles in intergroup interactions, for both the stigmatized and the nonstigmatized person.

Relationship Goals. Another helpful goal is a goal that includes the other person, such as a goal to create trust in the relationship, or to build effective communication. This might be how self-expansion can be beneficial for interactions between the stigmatized and nonstigmatized. To the degree that the other is included in the self, and one has a goal that is good for the other as well as the self, then there is a strong motivation to break the cycle, which is costly for both the self and the other (McLaughlin-Volpe, chap. 11, this volume).

Goals That Are Larger Than the Self. Goals that are larger than the self can help break these cycles. Asking, "What do I want to create, contribute, or build that is larger than me, about more than just me?" can take the focus off of what the interaction means about *me*.

Entering interactions with any or all of these goals—learning goals, relationship goals that include the other, and goals to create something larger than the self—can break destructive cycles in several ways. They reduce anxiety and fear, because mistakes, failures, and criticism are great learning opportunities. With a learning goal, people should be less afraid of being accused or devalued, and more interested in understanding the other's perspective and discovering what is useful for them in the exchange. Relationship goals can serve as a compass for how to behave, no matter what the other person says or does. For example, the goal of creating trust suggests that one should listen to what the other person says, try to understand, and not judge or criticize the other. The goal of creating something larger than the self can inspire the other person with that goal, leading to alignment rather than competition. Each of these goals creates safety for the other person, which in turn creates safety for the self.

CONCLUSION

The great discomfort that stigmatized and nonstigmatized people feel when interacting is, in the final analysis, largely about ego. Each is afraid of being devalued, being wrong, being accused, being the perpetrator, or being inferior. It is easy to see how these ego concerns can be costly in intergroup conflicts, when actions that could resolve a conflict such as making a concession or admitting past mistakes are resisted because of the desire to validate that one (or one's group) is competent, right, virtuous, or just. These experiences are painful for self-esteem, but they do not represent real dangers to well-being. People want to see themselves as the victim, and the other person as the perpetrator. But everyone is both a victim and a perpetrator when they are driven by their egos.

The solution, we have argued, lies in finding goals that are not driven by the ego. Goals about what one can learn, what relationship one wants to create, or what one wants to build or contribute that is larger than the self can provide the way out of the destructive cycles of interaction between the stigmatized and nonstigmatized. They can help create trust, find common ground, and make a difference in the world.

As a final note, we want to be clear about what we are not arguing in this chapter. We are not arguing that there is no reality to the prejudice, discrimination, and stereotyping that people with stigmatized identities experience. The evidence that prejudice, discrimination, and stereotyping are real is overwhelming. In fact, having a spoiled identity, and hence being devalued, is a defining characteristic of stigma. Rather, we suggest that when people get ego-involved in that devaluation, when they focus on the threat to their self-esteem implicit in that devaluation, they act in ways that create the opposite of what they really want, which is to be treated fairly, with respect, and as fully human. The feelings of shame and humiliation that accompany ego threats do not usually help people address the threat effectively; they are counterproductive (Tangney, 1999). Similarly, we do not mean to suggest that concerns that others are vigilant for signs of prejudice, or that they could accuse one of being a perpetrator, are disconnected from reality. Some stigmatized people are, indeed, very concerned about the possibilities of rejection, prejudice, discrimination, and being stereotyped, as the chapter by Mendoza-Denton, Page-Gould, & Pietrzak (chap. 8, this volume) demonstrates. We do suggest, however, that when nonstigmatized people take these concerns as a personal affront to their self-esteem, and respond with attempts to validate their desired image, their responses are counterproductive. When people disconnect their own ego from the experience of being stigmatized and stigmatizer, and are guided instead by learning goals and goals that are larger than the self, they are more likely to create the experiences they want in their own lives and in others' lives. To be sure, there are real issues to address; being caught in maintaining the desired image and pursuing self-esteem does not help people to address those issues.

ACKNOWLEDGMENT

Julie A. Garcia was supported by a National Science Foundation graduate fellowship, and Jennifer Crocker was supported by National Institute of Mental Health grants R01 MH58869 and K02 MH01747 during the preparation of this chapter.

REFERENCES

Allport, G. W. (1955). *Becoming*. New Haven, CT: Yale University Press.

Aron, A., Aron, E. N., Tudor, M., & Nelson, G. (1991). Close relationships as including other in the self. *Journal of Personality and Social Psychology, 60*, 241–253.

Argyris, C. (1990). *Overcoming organizational defenses: Facilitating organizational learning*. Needham Heights, MA: Allyn & Bacon.

Baumeister, R. F., Heatherton, T. F., & Tice, D. M. (1993). When ego threats lead to self-regulation failure: Negative consequences of high self-esteem. *Journal of Personality and Social Psychology, 64*, 141–156.

Beal, D. J., O'Neal, E. C., Ong, J., & Ruscher, J. B. (2000). The ways and means of interracial aggression: Modern racists' use of covert retaliation. *Personality & Social Psychology Bulletin, 26*(10), 1225–1238.

Carver, C. S., & Scheier, M. F. (1998). *On the self-regulation of behavior*. New York: Cambridge University Press.

Cole, S. W., Kemeny, M. E., & Taylor, S. E. (1997). Social identity and physical health: Accelerated HIV progression in rejection-sensitive gay men. *Journal of Personality & Social Psychology, 72*(2), 320–335.

Cole, S. W., Kemeny, M. E., Taylor, S. E., & Visscher, B. R. (1996). Elevated physical health risk among gay men who conceal their homosexual identity. *Health Psychology, 15*(4), 243–251.

Crandall, C. S., Eshleman, A., & O'Brien, L. (2002). Social norms and the expression and suppression of prejudice: The struggle for internalization. *Journal of Personality & Social Psychology, 82*(3), 359–378.

Crocker, J. (2003). *Contingencies of self-worth and self-validation goals in achievement domains*. Ann Arbor, MI: University of Michigan.

Crocker, J., Major, B., & Steele, C. M. (1998). Social stigma. In D. Gilbert, S. T. Fiske, & G. Lindzey (Eds.), *Handbook of social psychology, 4th ed.* (Vol. 2, pp. 504–553). New York: McGraw-Hill.

Crocker, J., & Nuer, N. (2004). Do people need self-esteem? A comment on Pyszczynski, Greenberg, Solomon, & Schimel (2004). *Psychological Bulletin, 130*, 469–472.

Crocker, J., & Park, L. E. (2004). The costly pursuit of self-esteem. *Psychological Bulletin, 130*, 392–414.

Crocker, J., & Wolfe, C. T. (2001). Contingencies of self-worth. *Psychological Review, 108*, 593–623.

Devine, P. G., Monteith, M. J., Zuwerink, J. R., & Elliot, A. J. (1991). Prejudice with and without compunction. *Journal of Personality and Social Psychology, 60*, 817–830.

Downey, G., Freitas, A. L., Michaelis, B., & Khouri, H. (1998). The self-fulfilling prophecy in close relationships: Rejection sensitivity and rejection by romantic partners. *Journal of Personality and Social Psychology, 75*, 545–560.

Dweck, C. S. (2000). *Self-theories: Their role in motivation, personality, and development*. Philadelphia: Psychology Press.

Ely, R. J., & Thomas, D. A. (2001). Cultural diversity at work: The effects of diversity perspectives on work group processes and outcomes. *Administrative Science Quarterly, 46*, 229–273.

Ely, R. J., & Thomas, D. A. (2003). *Learning from diversity: The effects of learning on performance in racially diverse teams*. Unpublished manuscript.

Garcia, J. A., & Crocker, J. (2003). *Women of color in the academy: Effects of context and identity on contingent self-worth*. Unpublished manuscript.

Goffman, E. (1963). *Stigma: Notes on the management of spoiled identity*. Englewood Cliffs, NJ: Prentice-Hall.

Heine, S. J., Lehman, D. R., Markus, H. R., & Kitayama, S. (1999). Is there a universal need for positive self-regard? *Psychological Review, 106*, 766–795.

Jones, E. E., Farina, A., Hastorf, A. H., Markus, H., Miller, D. T., & Scott, R. A. (1984). *Social stigma: The psychology of marked relationships*. New York: Freeman.

Kramer, R. M. (1998). Paranoid cognition in social systems: Thinking and acting in the shadow of doubt. *Personality and Social Psychology Review, 2*, 251–175.

Leary, M. R., & Baumeister, R. F. (2000). The nature and function of self-esteem: Sociometer theory. In M. Zanna (Ed.), *Advances in experimental social psychology* (Vol. 32, pp. 1–62). San Diego, CA: Academic Press.

Leary, M. R., & Downs, D. L. (1995). Interpersonal functions of the self-esteem motive: The self-esteem system as sociometer. In M. H. Kernis (Ed.), *Efficacy, agency, and self-esteem* (pp. 123–144). New York: Plenum.

Link, B. G., Mirotznik, J., & Cullen, F. T. (1991). The effectiveness of stigma coping orientations: Can negative consequences of mental illness stigma be avoided? *Journal of Health and Social Behavior, 32*, 302–320.

Maslow, A. H. (1968). *Motivation and personality*. New York: Harper & Row.

McConahay, J. B. (1981). Has racism declined in America? It depends on who is asking and what is asked. *Journal of Conflict Resolution, 25*, 563–579.

McConahay, J. B. (1986). Modern racism, ambivalence, and the modern racism scale. In J. F. Dovidio & S. L. Gaertner (Eds.), *Prejudice, discrimination, and racism* (pp. 91–125). San Diego, CA: Academic Press.

Mendoza-Denton, R., Downey, G., Purdie, V. J., Davis, A., & Pietrzak, J. (2002). Sensitivity to race-based rejection: Implications for African-American students' college experience. *Journal of Personality and Social Psychology, 83*, 896–918.

Monteith, M. J. (1996). Affective reactions to prejudice-related discrepant responses: The impact of standard salience. *Personality and Social Psychology Bulletin, 22*, 48–59.

Monteith, M. J., Deneen, N. E., & Tooman, G. D. (1996). The effect of social norm activation on the expression of opinions concerning gay men and Blacks. *Basic & Applied Social Psychology, 18*(3), 267–288.

Monteith, M. J., Devine, P. G., & Zuwerink, J. R. (1993). Self-directed vs. other-directed affect as a consequence of prejudice-related discrepancies. *Journal of Personality and Social Psychology, 64*, 198–210.

Niiya, Y., Crocker, J., & Bartmess, E. (2004). From vulnerability to resilience: Learning orientations buffer contingent self-esteem from failure. *Psychological Science, 15*, 801–805.

Prentice, D. A., & Miller, D. T. (Eds.). (1999). *Cultural divides: Understanding and overcoming group conflict*. New York: Russell Sage Foundation.

Pyszczynski, T., Greenberg, J., Solomon, S., Arndt, J., & Schimel, J. (2004). Why do people need self-esteem? A theoretical and empirical review. *Psychological Bulletin, 130*, 435–468.

Rogers, C. R. (1961). *On becoming a person*. Boston: Houghton Mifflin.

Rosenberg, M. (1979). *Conceiving the self*. New York: Basic Books.

Solomon, S., Greenberg, J., & Pyszczynski, T. (1991). A terror-management theory of social behavior: The psychological functions of self-esteem and cultural worldviews. In M. P. Zanna (Ed.), *Advances in experimental social psychology* (Vol. 24, pp. 91–159). San Diego, CA: Academic Press.

Steele, C. M. (1988). The psychology of self-affirmation: Sustaining the integrity of the self. In L. Berkowitz (Ed.), *Advances in experimental social psychology* (Vol. 21, pp. 261–302). New York: Academic Press.

Steele, C. M., & Aronson, J. (1995). Stereotype threat and the intellectual test performance of African Americans. *Journal of Personality and Social Psychology, 69*, 797–811.

Steele, C. M., Spencer, S. J., & Aronson, J. (2002). Contending with group image: The psychology of stereotype and social identity threat. In M. P. Zanna (Ed.), *Advances in experimental social psychology* (Vol. 34, pp. 379–440). San Diego, CA: Academic Press.

Stephan, W. G., & Stephan, C. W. (1985). Intergroup anxiety. *Journal of Social Issues, 41*, 157–175.

Stone, D., Patton, B., & Heen, S. (1999). *Difficult conversations: How to discuss what matters most*. New York: Penguin.

Tangney, J. P. (1999). The self-conscious emotions: Shame, guilt, embarrassment and pride. In T. Dalgleish & M. J. Power (Eds.), *Handbook of cognition and emotion* (pp. 541–568). Chichester, England: Wiley.

Tatum, B. D. (1997). *Why are all the Black kids sitting together in the cafeteria?* New York: Basic.

Taylor, S. E., & Brown, J. D. (1988). Illusion and well-being: A social-psychological perspective on mental health. *Psychological Bulletin, 103*, 193–210.

Tesser, A. (1988). Toward a self-evaluation maintenance model of social behavior. In L. Berkowitz (Ed.), *Advances in experimental social psychology* (Vol. 21, pp. 181–227). San Diego, CA: Academic Press.

Tice, D. M. (1991). Esteem protection or enhancement? Self-handicapping motives and attributions differ by trait self-esteem. *Journal of Personality and Social Psychology, 60*, 711–725.

Wolfe, C., & Crocker, J. (2003). What does the self want? Contingencies of self-worth and goals. In S. Spencer, S. Fein, M. P. Zanna, & J. M. Olson (Eds.), *The Ontario Symposium: Motivated social perception* (Vol. 9, pp. 147–170). Hillsdale, NJ: Lawrence Erlbaum Associates.

Wright, E. R., Gronfien, W. P., & Owens, T. J. (2000). Deinstitutionalization, social rejection, and the self-esteem of former mental patients. *Journal of Health and Social Behavior, 41*, 68–90.

Zuwerink, J. R., Devine, P. G., Monteith, M. J., & Cook, D. A. (1996). Prejudice toward Blacks: With and without compunction? *Basic & Applied Social Psychology, 18*(2), 131–150.

About the Authors

Jennifer Crocker is Professor of Psychology at the University of Michigan and Research Professor at the Research Center for Group Dynamics, Institute for Social Research. Her research focuses on two motivational systems, the ego system (the goal to prove or demonstrate one's worth or value) and the alternative ecosystem (the goal to create or contribute to something larger than the self). In the context of social stigma, she is interested in how having a valued or devalued identity raises concerns about self-worth (Do I deserve my privileged position? Am I prejudiced or will I be accused of prejudice? Am I at risk of being rejected or devalued?), how those concerns shape intergroup interactions, and whether ecosystem goals for these interactions yield more satisfying outcomes.

Julie A. Garcia is a National Science Foundation postdoctoral fellow at Stanford University. Her research interests include the contextual and individual difference factors that influence decisions to conceal or disclose a concealable stigma and the implications of social stigma for self-esteem in different settings.

Catherine Good is a postdoctoral research fellow in the Department of Psychology at Columbia University in New York. She completed her B.A. and M.A. in Mathematics at the University of Kansas, and her PhD in Mathematics Education and Social Psychology at The University of Texas. Her work focuses on the ways that stereotypes, achievement-related beliefs, and the environment influence stigmatized individuals' intellectual performance, sense of belonging, and persistence in the stereotyped domain, as well as the processes through which they do so. In addition to her behavior research, Catherine uses a neurophysiological approach to study how these psychological forces affect stigmatized individuals' allocation of attention and depth of processing on a stereotyped task.

Diana M. Hill earned her B.A. from Washington University in St. Louis and is now a graduate student in social psychology at Princeton University. Her research interests include cognitive dissonance, social comparison, and self-discrepancy theory.

Jeff Huntsinger is currently an advanced graduate student in the social psychology program at the University of Virginia. He received a B.A. in psychology from the Pennsylvania State University and an M.A. in social psychology from the University of Virginia. Currently, his research focuses on how affiliative motives within interpersonal interactions structure self-understanding and behavior, especially among members of stereotyped social groups. More recently, he has examined how affective experience is structured by affiliative motives within interpersonal interactions.

Michael Inzlicht is an assistant professor of psychology in the Department of Life Sciences at the University of Toronto at Scarborough. He completed his B.Sc. in anatomical sciences at McGill University, his PhD in experimental psychology at Brown University, and his postdoctoral fellowship in applied psychology at New York University. His work focuses on the psychology of stigmatization and explores how the environment can affect the intellectual performance, self-control capabilities, and self-knowledge of those belonging to socially devalued groups. His research on stigma was honored by him being named a 2004 fellow of the National Academy of Education. In addition to his main pursuits, Michael is interested in the automaticity of behavior, psychophysiology, and his glorious Montreal Canadiens.

Cheryl R. Kaiser is an assistant professor of psychology at Michigan State University. She earned her PhD in psychology from the University of Vermont in 2001. She then spent 2 years as a National Institute of Mental Health sponsored postdoctoral fellow at the University of California, Santa Barbara. Much of her research addresses how individuals construe and cope with threats against their personal and social identities as well as threats against their worldviews. She investigates these topics within the realm of prejudice, intergroup relations, and social justice.

Shana Levin is an associate professor of psychology at Claremont McKenna College. She received her PhD in social psychology from the University of

California, Los Angeles. She has been a visiting scholar at the Russell Sage Foundation and a member of the governing council of the Society for the Psychological Study of Social Issues and the governing council of the International Society of Political Psychology. Her research examines ethnic identification, group dominance motives, ideologies of group inequality, perceived discrimination, diversity in higher education, and intergroup attitudes in the United States, Israel, Northern Ireland, and Lebanon.

Brian Lickel is an assistant professor of psychology at the University of Southern California. He conducts research on social cognition, emotion, and intergroup relations. He has particularly focused on lay people's intuitive understanding of social groups and is currently investigating people's beliefs about when and why groups should be held collectively responsible for the actions of individual group members.

Brenda Major is a professor of psychology at the University of California, Santa Barbara. She received her PhD in social psychology from Purdue University in 1978. She was awarded the Gordon Allport Intergroup Relations Prize from the Society for the Psychological Study of Social Issues in 1986, in 1988, and received honorable mention in 2002. She has been associate editor of *Personality and Social Psychology Bulletin* and is currently president-elect of the Society of Personality and Social Psychology. Her research centers on psychological resilience—how people cope with, adapt to, and overcome adverse life circumstances. Current research interests include the psychology of stigma, self- and social identity, and the psychology of legitimacy. Her work has been supported by grants from the National Science Foundation and the National Institute of Mental Health.

Tracy McLaughlin-Volpe is an assistant professor of social psychology at the University of Vermont. She earned her PhD at the State University of New York at Stony Brook and was a postdoctoral research fellow for the Social Identity Consortium at the Graduate School and University Center of the City University of New York. Her primary research interests are in group processes, especially intergroup relations and prejudice.

Rodolfo Mendoza-Denton is an assistant professor of psychology at the University of California, Berkeley. A native of Mexico, he lived in West Africa and Thailand before completing his undergraduate studies at Yale University. He then completed his graduate and postdoctoral studies at Columbia University. His intercultural experiences led to, and shaped, a professional interest in culture, prejudice, and intergroup relations. His current research focuses on how experiences of discrimination and prejudice affect adjustment and relationship development among students at historically homogenous universities.

Carol T. Miller received her PhD from Purdue University. Since 1979, she has been a faculty member at the University of Vermont, where she is now a professor of psychology. Her editorial experiences include a term as associate editor of *Personality and Social Psychology Bulletin*. Her research examines how stigmatized people cope with prejudice, with particular attention to the ways in which stigmatized people achieve their goals despite the obstacles created by prejudice. Her research also investigates the reactions that other people have to stigmatize people's efforts to cope with prejudice.

Elizabeth Page-Gould is a doctoral student in the social psychology graduate program at the University of California, Berkeley. She received her B.S. in psychology and statistics from Carnegie Mellon University. Her research interests include stereotyping, prejudice, and physiological correlates of intergroup interaction. Her recent research has focused on the influence of close intergroup relationships on prejudice reduction and academic outcomes among college students. Her work is supported by fellowships from the National Science Foundation and the Center for Peace and Well-Being.

Janina Pietrzak is currently in the department of psychology at the University of Warsaw. She received her PhD in psychology from Columbia University in 2004. Her research interests span issues of minority identity and the role of expectations in interpersonal and intergroup contact.

Diane M. Quinn is an associate professor of psychology at the University of Connecticut. She received her PhD in social psychology in 1999 from the University of Michigan. Her research focuses on the experiences of members of stigmatized or stereotyped groups, including research on the effects of gender stereotypes on women's math achievement; the effects of different cultural ideologies on the psychological well-being and behavior of overweight women; experiences and consequences of self-objectification; and the negotiation of concealed stigmatized identities.

Jennifer A. Richeson is an assistant professor of psychology at Dartmouth College. She earned her B.A. in psychology from Brown University in 1994 and her PhD in psychology from Harvard University in 2000. Her research interests include: intergroup contact, including how situational status cues impact the interaction; how individuals control the expression of prejudice; detecting and confronting prejudice and discrimination; and racial categorization.

Jessica Salvatore earned her B.A. from Swarthmore College and is now a graduate student in social psychology at Princeton University. Her research interests include the psychology of stigma, identity and self processes, and norms.

Toni Schmader is an associate professor of psychology at the University of Arizona. Her research, which has received funding from the National Science Foundation and the National Institute of Mental Health, investigates how individuals are affected by their social groups, particularly when those groups are socially stigmatized. One line of work, conducted in collaboration with Brian Lickel, examines processes by which individuals come to feel a sense of shame or guilt for the negative actions of other group members. In other work, Dr. Schmader investigates how social stereotypes affect the performance and psychological engagement of stigmatized individuals in stereotyped domains.

J. Nicole Shelton is an assistant professor of Psychology at Princeton University. She earned her B.A. in psychology from the College of William and Mary in 1993 and her PhD in psychology from the University of Virginia in 1998. She was a postdoctoral fellow at the University of Michigan from 1998 to 2000. Her research interests include intergroup contact, the psychology of stigma, and social identity.

Stacey Sinclair is an assistant professor of psychology at University of Virginia. She earned her B.A. from Stanford University and her PhD from University of California, Los Angeles. Her research focuses on how individuals' motivational states and the perceived views of their social interaction partners work in concert to shape their implicit and explicit attitudes, self-views, and behaviors. She also examines the impact of intergroup contact and implicit self-stereotyping.

Janet K. Swim obtained her PhD in social psychology at the University of Minnesota and is now a professor of psychology at the Pennsylvania State University. Her research concerns how people come to decide when they or others have been targets of prejudice or discrimination; the consequences of being a target of discrimination or recognizing others' experiences with discrimination; and how people cope with experiencing or recognizing prejudice and discrimination. Her work primarily addresses everyday forms of sexism, racism, and heterosexism. Her current work includes identity formation and coping with discrimination among Asian children adopted in to White/European American homes and how goals influence how people choose to cope with discrimination.

Margaret A. Thomas is a graduate student at The Pennsylvania State University. Her research interests include issues of identity, core social goals, stereotyping and self-stereotyping, discrimination from the target's perspective, gender roles and transgression, sexism, feminism, and lesbian, gay, bisexual, and transgender issues.

Linda R. Tropp received her B.A. from Wellesley College and her PhD in social psychology from the University of California, Santa Cruz. She is currently an assistant professor of psychology at Boston College and a member of the governing council of the Society for the Psychological Study of Social Issues. Her main research programs concern expectations for and outcomes of intergroup contact among members of minority and majority status groups, group membership and identification with social groups, and responses to prejudice and disadvantage among members of socially devalued groups. In 2003, she received the Gordon W. Allport Intergroup Relations Award from the Society for the Psychological Study of Social Issues for her paper, *A Meta-Analytic Test and Reformulation of Intergroup Contact Theory* (co-authored with Thomas F. Pettigrew).

Colette van Laar is a faculty member in social and organizational psychology at Leiden University in the Netherlands. She received her PhD in social psychology from the University of California, Los Angeles. Her research addresses the consequences of stigma for cognition, affect, and motivation in members of low-status groups. Her current work includes social identity and stereotype threat; the function of positive ingroup domains for maintaining motivation and performance of low-status groups; and the social psychological aspects of the battle over the (Islamic) veil in Europe. She has also been engaged for some time in a longitudinal study funded by the Russell Sage Foundation and the National Science Foundation on the development of intergroup attitudes and behaviors.

Author Index

C

D

E

F

G

H

I

J

K

L

N

O

P

Q

R

S

W

X–Z

Subject Index

A

B

C

D

E

J

L

M

N

O

P

T

U–V

W